THE M. & E. CASEBOOK SERIES

CASES IN COMPANY LAW

M. C. OLIVER, M.A.

Barrister
Head of the Department of Law
City of London Polytechnic

SECOND EDITION

MACDONALD AND EVANS

MACDONALD AND EVANS LTD.
Estover, Plymouth PL6 7PZ

First published 1972
Reprinted 1974
Second edition 1976
Reprinted in this format 1978
©
MACDONALD AND EVANS LIMITED
1976

ISBN: 0 7121 0365 1

*Printed in Great Britain by Richard Clay (The Chaucer Press), Ltd.,
Bungay, Suffolk*

P.W.Gillam
29 Gray St.
Locmett, Dundee

M & E Casebooks are recommended reading for examination syllabuses all over the world.

Each book contains a series of cases which illustrate the important legal principles and doctrines relevant to the area of law which they cover, its scope and its development. The facts of each case are clearly set out together with a commentary and the judge's summing-up.

The handy pocket-book size and competitive price make Casebooks the perfect companion to M & E law Handbooks and a useful pre-examination revision aid in their own right. Casebooks are also invaluable to anyone who wants to grasp quickly and easily the essential principles of a particular area of law.

PREFACE TO THE FIRST EDITION

This CASEBOOK could be called a collection of short stories. The stories are not entirely true ones, for proof is not truth, but they concern real people who became involved in real difficulties and who produced enough evidence of the relevant facts for the court to accept them as true.

I have chosen to occupy the permitted space with selected cases of importance presented as fully as possible, rather than with several hundred in an abbreviated form. This is partly because a case may be useful not so much for what it decides as for what it contains. Primarily, however, it is because this is a book for students, and students, like Dickens' hungry orphan, always want more. They like to know about the characters in the stories, and they often have strong, if misconceived, views about them. I hope that they will now be convinced that Mr. Aron Salomon was a sad man, and not a bad one.

The book is designed either to accompany the HANDBOOK on Company Law and, it is hoped, to illustrate and enliven it, or to be used on its own. For all student readers, however, a copy of the *Companies Act*, 1948, ought to be at hand, since the problems of space have prevented me from setting out statutory provisions or the clauses of Table A. Many of the cases concern the interpretation or the application of these provisions or clauses, and their exact wording is therefore important.

In the HANDBOOK on Company Law my main aim is simplicity. I accordingly often give a possible viewpoint where the law is doubtful, although I hope that I do so with suitable qualifications. In this book I have presented the cases as they are, without comment, and left it to the student to draw from them his own deductions. For this purpose, I have throughout arranged the cases on each topic chronologically so that the developments can be easily traced. This leaves the problems as one finds them, especially where there are conflicting decisions on the same point, but it at least demonstrates that the law is a living creature made for society by those whom society appoints to make it, and that it is therefore as much a social study as a scientific one.

My thanks are due in the first place to the Incorporated Society of Law Reporting for England and Wales and to Butterworth & Co. (Publishers) Ltd. who have kindly given me permission to reproduce such extracts from their reports as I wished. I must again thank my students for their vociferous expression of their needs with their questions, answers, vitality and humour. Finally, I owe to my husband an apology for my repeated raids on his set of reports and profound appreciation of his unfailing forgiveness when the particular volume he needed—as well as his wife—was missing.

February 1972   M. C. Oliver

PREFACE TO THE SECOND EDITION

In this edition it has been possible to make a considerable number of changes both in content and in arrangement. It seemed that the Section on Pre-incorporation Contracts was no longer justified since classroom discussions now normally centre on S.9 (2) European Communities Act. 1972. This Section has accordingly been removed, enabling me both to expand the Section on Directors and to add a new Section—Fraud on the Minority—in the hope that these alterations will be useful.

April 1976   M. C. Oliver

AUTHOR'S NOTE

Students should remember to take into account S.9 European Communities Act, 1972 when reading the cases relating to the doctrine of *ultra vires* in Section III and the authority of the directors as the company's agents in Section XII.

CONTENTS

		Page
Preface		v
Author's Note		vii

I. THE LEGAL PERSONALITY OF CORPORATIONS

Foss v. Harbottle	1
Salomon v. Salomon and Company, Ltd.	8

II. THE NAME OF THE COMPANY

Aerators, Ltd. v. Tollitt	27
Ewing v. Buttercup Margarine Company, Ltd.	30
Durham Fancy Goods, Ltd. v. Michael Jackson (Fancy Goods), Ltd.	32

III. THE DOCTRINE OF *ULTRA VIRES*

1. *The Construction of the Objects Clause of the Memorandum of Association*

Ashbury Railway Carriage and Iron Company, Ltd. v. Riche	37
Re German Date Coffee Company, Ltd.	45
Cotman v. Brougham	49
Bell Houses, Ltd. v. City Wall Properties, Ltd.	56

2. *The Doctrine of* Ultra Vires *Applied to Borrowing Powers*

Re David Payne & Co., Ltd.	65
Sinclair v. Brougham	68
Introductions, Ltd. v. National Provincial Bank, Ltd.	83

3. *Gratuitous Acts and Payments*

Hutton v. West Cork Railway Company	86
Evans v. Brunner, Mond and Company, Ltd.	95
Re Lee, Behrens and Company, Ltd.	98
Parke v. Daily News, Ltd.	100
Re W. and M. Roith, Ltd.	103
Charterbridge Corporation, Ltd. v. Lloyds Bank, Ltd.	106

                                                        Page
IV.   THE ARTICLES OF ASSOCIATION
      1. *The Company's Power to Alter its Articles*
          Allen *v.* Gold Reefs of West Africa, Ltd.   110
          Sidebottom *v.* Kershaw, Leese and Company,
              Ltd.   120
          Shuttleworth *v.* Cox Brothers and Company
              (Maidenhead), Ltd.   125
      2. *The Legal Effect of the Articles*
          Eley *v.* Positive, etc., Life Assurance Com-
              pany, Ltd.   132
          Rayfield *v.* Hands   137
          Re Richmond Gate Property Company, Ltd.   139

V.   THE PROMOTERS OF A COMPANY
          Emile Erlanger *v.* The New Sombrero Phosphate
              Company   142
          The Emma Silver Mining Company, Ltd. *v.* Lewis
              and Son.   153
          Whaley Bridge Calico Printing Company, Ltd. *v.*
              Green and Smith   158
          Gluckstein *v.* Barnes   162
          Re Leeds and Hanley Theatres of Varieties, Ltd. 168

VI.   THE PROSPECTUS
          Re South of England Natural Gas and Petroleum
              Company, Ltd.   175
          Governments Stock Investment Company, Ltd. *v.*
              Christopher   177

VII. PAYMENT FOR SHARES
          Spargo's Case   180
          Ooregum Gold Mining Company of India *v.* Roper 183
          Mosely *v.* Koffyfontein Mines, Ltd.   191

VIII. THE PRESERVATION OF THE COMPANY'S
      SHARE CAPITAL
          Trevor *v.* Whitworth   195
          Bellerby *v.* Rowland and Marwood's Steamship
              Company, Ltd.   204
          Rowell *v.* John Rowell and Sons, Ltd.   209
          Victor Battery Company, Ltd. *v.* Curry's, Ltd. 212
          Heald *v.* O'Connor   215

Page

IX. **DIVIDENDS**

Verner *v.* General and Commercial Investment Trust   218

Foster *v.* New Trinidad Lake Asphalt Company, Ltd.   222

Dimbula Valley (Ceylon) Tea Company, Ltd. *v.* Laurie   224

X. **THE AUDITORS OF A COMPANY**

Re Kingston Cotton Mill Company (No. 2)   228

Dean *v.* Prince   232

XI. **SHARES**

The Bradford Banking Company, Ltd. *v.* Henry Briggs, Son and Company, Ltd.   235

Simpson *v.* Molsons' Bank   237

Bloomenthal *v.* Ford   241

Galloway *v.* Hallé Concerts Society   247

Re Copal Varnish Company, Ltd.   249

XII. **THE DIRECTORS OF A COMPANY**

1. *Directors as Agents of the Company*

The Royal British Bank *v.* Turquand   253

Mahony *v.* East Holyford Mining Company   255

Craven-Ellis *v.* Canons, Ltd.   262

Rama Corporation, Ltd. *v.* Proved Tin and General Investments, Ltd.   267

Freeman and Lockyer *v.* Buckhurst Park Properties (Mangal), Ltd.   269

2. *The Fiduciary Duty of Directors*

Re Forest of Dean Coal Mining Company   278

Re Cape Breton Company   285

Percival *v.* Wright   291

Regal (Hastings), Ltd. *v.* Gulliver   294

Bamford *v.* Bamford   299

Industrial Development Consultants, Ltd. *v.* Cooley   303

Smith (Howard), Ltd. *v.* Ampol Petroleum, Ltd.   306

3. *The Directors' Duty of Care*

Re City Equitable Fire Insurance Company, Ltd.   311

Page

4. *Directors' Qualification Shares*
Sutton *v.* English and Colonial Produce Company   318

XIII. THE SECRETARY OF A COMPANY
Panorama Developments (Guildford), Ltd. *v.* Fidelis Furnishing Fabrics, Ltd.   321

XIV. COMPANY MEETINGS
East *v.* Bennett Brothers, Ltd.   326
Morgan *v.* Gray   329
Re West Canadian Collieries, Ltd.   332
Musselwhite *v.* C. H. Musselwhite and Son, Ltd.   333
Re London Flats, Ltd.   337
Re Duomatic, Ltd.   338
Bushell *v.* Faith   346

XV. FRAUD ON THE MINORITY
North-West Transportation Company, Ltd. *v.* Beatty   353
Burland *v.* Earle   362
Cook *v.* G. S. Deeks   368
Phillips *v.* Manufacturers' Securities, Ltd.   374
Greenhalgh *v.* Arderne Cinemas, Ltd.   380
Edwards *v.* Halliwell   383

XVI. THE REMEDY UNDER S.210 AGAINST OPPRESSION
Scottish Co-operative Wholesale Society, Ltd. *v.* Meyer   388
Re H. R. Harmer, Ltd.   397

XVII. WINDING UP UNDER S.222 (f)
Ebrahimi (A. P.) *v.* Westbourne Galleries, Ltd.   407

XVIII. SCHEMES OF ARRANGEMENT AND TAKE-OVER BIDS
Re Sussex Brick Company, Ltd.   415
Re Bugle Press, Ltd.   417
Re Hellenic and General Trust, Ltd.   421

Table of Cases   428

Index   431

I. THE LEGAL PERSONALITY OF CORPORATIONS

Foss *v*. Harbottle. (1843) 2 Ha. 461

Where a wrong is done to a company, the proper plaintiff is the company and not its individual members; for as long as the company is in existence, it is bound by the decisions of the majority in general meeting, who may well ratify or confirm the very act of which those individuals are complaining.

The Victoria Park Company was incorporated by an Act of Parliament which received the Royal assent on the 5th May 1837, and which was entitled "An Act for Establishing a Company for the Purpose of Laying Out and Maintaining an Ornamental Park within the Townships of Rusholme, Charlton-upon-Medlock and Moss Side, in the County of Lancaster.'

The Act declared, *inter alia*, that the capital of the company was to be £500,000, divided into 5,000 shares of £100 each; that the business affairs of the company were to be exclusively under the control of five shareholders, to be appointed directors; and that the first directors were to be Thomas Harbottle, Joseph Adshead, Henry Byrom, John Westhead and Richard Bealey. It further provided that three directors should constitute a board, and that the acts of three or more should be as effectual as if done by the five.

In October 1842 an action was brought by two shareholders in the company, Richard Foss and Edward Turton, on behalf of themselves and all the other shareholders in the company except the defendants. The defendants were the five directors, three of whom by this time had become bankrupt, the respective assignees in bankruptcy, a shareholder, Joseph Denison, who was not a director, the company's solicitor Thomas Bunting and its architect Richard Lane.

The plaintiffs alleged that the defendants had effected

various fraudulent and illegal transactions whereby the property of the company was misapplied, aliened and wasted; that owing to the three bankruptcies there had ceased to be a sufficient number of qualified directors to constitute a board; that the company had no clerk or office, but its affairs had been principally conducted at the office of Bunting, to whom its title-deeds, books and papers had been transferred; and that in such circumstances the shareholders had no power to take the property out of the hands of the defendants, or satisfy the liabilities or wind up the affairs of the company. Accordingly they sought that the defendants might be decreed to make good to the company the losses and expenses occasioned by the acts complained of, and the appointment of a receiver to take and apply the property of the company in discharge of its liabilities, and secure the surplus.

The defendants contended that an action complaining of injuries to the corporation could not be brought by some of its individual members, but only by the corporation itself. The plaintiffs, they argued, were not entitled to represent the corporate body.

THE VICE-CHANCELLOR (SIR JAMES WIGRAM): . . . The Victoria Park Company is an incorporated body, and the conduct with which the Defendants are charged in this suit is an injury not to the Plaintiffs exclusively; it is an injury to the whole corporation by individuals whom the corporation entrusted with powers to be exercised only for the good of the corporation. . . . [I]t may be stated as undoubted law that a bill or information by a corporation will lie to be relieved in respect of injuries which the corporation has suffered at the hands of persons standing in the situation of the directors upon this record. . . . [H]owever, . . . instead of the corporation being formally represented as Plaintiffs, the bill in this case is brought by two individual corporators, professedly on behalf of themselves and all the other members of the corporation, except those who committed the injuries complained of —the Plaintiffs assuming to themselves the right and power in that manner to sue on behalf of and represent the corporation itself.

It was not, nor could it successfully be, argued that it was a matter of course for any individual members of a corporation thus to assume to themselves the right of suing in the name of the corporation. In law the corporation and the aggregate members of the corporation are not the same thing for purposes like this; and the only question can be whether the facts alleged in this case justify a departure from the rule which, prima facie, would require that the corporation should sue in its own name and in its corporate character, or in the name of someone whom the law has appointed to be its representative. . . . The first objection taken in the argument for the Defendants was that the individual members of the corporation cannot in any case sue in the form in which this bill is framed . . . [T]he rule was much too broadly stated on the part of the Defendants. I think there are cases in which a suit might properly be so framed. Corporations like this, of a private nature, are in truth little more than private partnerships; and in cases which may easily be suggested it would be too much to hold that a society of private persons associated together in undertakings, which, though certainly beneficial to the public, are nevertheless matters of private property, are to be deprived of their civil rights, *inter se*, because, in order to make their common objects more attainable, the Crown or the Legislature may have conferred upon them the benefit of a corporate character. If a case should arise of injury to a corporation by some of its members, for which no adequate remedy remained, except that of a suit by individual corporators in their private characters, and asking in such character the protection of those rights to which in their corporate character they were entitled, I cannot but think that . . . the claims of justice would be found superior to any difficulties arising out of technical rules respecting the mode in which corporations are required to sue.

But, on the other hand, it must not be without reasons of a very urgent character that established rules of law and practice are to be departed from, rules which, though in a sense technical, are founded on general principles of justice and convenience; and the question is whether a case is stated in this bill entitling the Plaintiffs to sue in their private characters. The result of these clauses [*in the Act of Incorporation*] is that the directors are made the governing body, subject to the superior control of the proprietors assembled in general meetings; and, as I understand the Act, the proprietors so assembled have power, due notice being given of the purposes of the meeting, to originate proceedings for any purpose within the scope of the company's powers, as well as to control the directors in any acts which they may have originated.

. . . [I]t is only necessary to refer to the clauses of the Act to show that, whilst the supreme governing body, the proprietors at a special general meeting assembled, retain the power of exercising the functions conferred upon them by the Act of Incorporation, it cannot be competent to individual corporators to sue in the manner proposed by the Plaintiffs on the present record. This in effect purports to be a suit by cestui que trusts complaining of a fraud committed or alleged to have been committed by persons in a fiduciary character. . . . The proposition I have advanced is that, although the act should prove to be voidable, the cestui que trusts may elect to confirm it. Now, who are the cestui que trusts in this case? The corporation, in a sense, is undoubtedly the cestui que trust; but the majority of the proprietors at a special general meeting assembled . . . has power to bind the whole body, and every individual corporator must be taken to have come into the corporation upon the terms of being liable to be so bound. How then can this Court act in a suit constituted as this is, if it is to be assumed, for the purposes of the argument, that the powers of the body of the proprietors are still in existence, and may lawfully be exercised for a purpose like that I have suggested? Whilst the Court may be declaring the acts complained of to be void at the suit of the present Plaintiffs, who in fact may be the only proprietors who disapprove of them, the governing body of proprietors may defeat the decree by lawfully resolving upon the confirmation of the very acts which are the subject of the suit. The very fact that the governing body of proprietors assembled at the special general meeting may so bind even a reluctant minority is decisive to show that the frame of this suit cannot be sustained whilst that body retains its functions. In order then that this suit may be sustained it must be shown either that there is no such power as I have supposed remaining in the proprietors, or, at least, that all means have been resorted to and found ineffectual to set that body in motion: this latter point is nowhere suggested in the bill: there is no suggestion that an attempt has been made by any proprietor to set the body of proprietors in motion, or to procure a meeting to be convened for the purpose of revoking the acts complained of. The question then is whether this bill is so framed as of necessity to exclude the supposition that the supreme body of proprietors is now in a condition to confirm the transactions in question; or, if those transactions are to be impeached in a Court of Justice, whether the proprietors have not power to set the corporation in motion for the purpose of vindicating its own rights.

I pause here to examine the difficulty which is supposed by the bill to oppose itself to the body of proprietors assembling and acting at an extraordinary general meeting. The 48th section of the Act says that a certain number of proprietors may call such a meeting by means of a notice to be addressed to the board of directors, and left with the clerk or secretary, at the principal office of the company, one month before the time of meeting, or the board is not bound to notice it. The bill says that there is no board of directors properly constituted, no clerk, no principal office of the company, no power of electing more directors, and that, the appointment of the clerk being in the board of directors, no clerk can in fact now be appointed. I am certainly not prepared to go the whole length of the Plaintiff's argument founded upon the 48th section. . . . I attribute to the proprietors no power which the Act does not give them: they have the power, without the consent and against the will of the directors, of calling a meeting, and of controlling their acts; and if by any inevitable accident the prescribed form of calling a meeting should become impracticable, there is still a mode of calling it, which, upon the general principles that govern the powers of corporations, I think would be held to be sufficient for the purpose.

It is not, however, upon such considerations that I shall decide this case. The view of the case which has appeared to me conclusive is that the existence of a board of directors *de facto* is sufficiently apparent upon the statements in the bill. The bankruptcy of Westhead, the last of the three directors who became bankrupt, took place on the 2nd of January 1840: the bill alleges that he thereupon ceased to be *qualified* to act as director, and his office became vacated; but it does not say that he ceased to *act* as a director; nor, although it is said that thenceforward there was no board "properly constituted," is it alleged that there was no board *de facto* exercising the functions of directors. These, and several other statements of the bill, are pregnant with the admission of the existence of a board *de facto*. . . . Whatever the bill may say of the *illegal* constitution of the board of directors, because the individual directors are not duly qualified, it does not anywhere suggest that there has not been during the whole period, and that there was not when the bill was filed, a board of directors *de facto*, acting in and carrying on the affairs of the corporation, and whose acting must have been acquiesced in by the body of proprietors; at least, ever since the illegal constitution of the board of directors became known, and the acts in question were discovered. But if there has been or is a board *de facto*, their acts may be valid, although the persons so acting may not have been duly qualified. [*The 114th section of the Act of Incorporation was similar to S.180, Companies Act, 1948*]. . . . The foundation upon which I consider the Plaintiffs can alone have a right to sue in the form of this bill must wholly fail, if there has been a governing body of directors *de facto*. There is no longer the impediment to convening a meeting of proprietors, who by their vote might direct proceedings like the present to be taken in the name of the corporation; . . . or who, by rejecting such a proposal, would, in effect, decide that the corporation was not aggrieved by the transactions in question. . . . In the absence of any special allegation to the contrary I am bound to assume that the affairs of the company have been carried on by the body in whom alone the powers for that purpose were vested by the Act, namely, a board of directors.

. . . Assuming then, as I am bound to do, the existence, for some time at least, of a state of things in which the company was governed by a board of directors *de facto*, some of the members of which were individually disqualified, and in which, notwithstanding the want of a clerk, treasurer or office, the powers of the proprietors were called into exercise at general meetings, the question is, when did that state of things cease to exist, so as to justify the extraordinary proceeding of the Plaintiffs by this suit? The Plaintiffs have not stated by their bill any facts to show that such was not the actual state of things at the time their bill was filed, and, in the absence of any statement to the contrary, I must intend that it was so.

. . . The bill, I cannot but observe, is framed with great care, and with more than ordinary professional skill and knowledge; but the averments do not exclude that which, *prima facie*, must be taken to have been the case, that during the years 1840, 1841 and 1842 there was a governing body, that by such body the business of the company was carried on, that there was no insurmountable impediment to the exercise of the powers of the proprietors assembled in general meetings to control the affairs of the company, and that such general meetings were actually held. The continued existence of a board *de facto* is not merely not excluded by the averments, but the statements in the bill of the acts which have been done suppose, and even require, the existence of such a board.

. . .[I]f a transaction be void, and not merely voidable, the corporation cannot confirm it, so as to bind a dissenting minority of its members. But that will not dispose of this question. . . . The object of this bill against the Defendants is to make them individually and personally responsible to the extent of the injury alleged to have been received by the corporation. . . . [V]ery different considerations arise in a case like the present, in which the consequences only of the alleged illegal acts are sought to be visited personally upon the directors. . . . [O]ne question appears to me to be, whether the company could confirm the former transactions, . . . and yet, as against the directors personally, complain of the acts which they have done, by means whereof the company obtains that benefit which I suppose to have been admitted and adopted by such confirmation. I think it would not be open to the company to do this. . . . I am of opinion that this question—the question of confirmation or avoidance—cannot properly be litigated upon this record, regard being had to the existing state and powers of the corporation. . . .

Salomon v. Salomon and Company, Limited. [1897] A.C. 22

A company which has been validly constituted under the Companies Acts is a legal person distinct from its members, and for this purpose it is immaterial whether any member has a large or small proportion of the shares, and whether he holds those shares beneficially or as a bare trustee.

The appellant, Aron Salomon, for many years carried on business on his own account as a leather merchant and wholesale boot manufacturer. With the design of transferring his business to a joint stock company which was to consist exclusively of himself and members of his own family, he on 20th July 1892 entered into a preliminary agreement with one Adolph Anholt, as trustee for the future company, settling the terms upon which the transfer was to be made by him, one of its conditions being that part payment might be made to him in debentures of the company. A memorandum of association was then executed by the appellant, his wife, a daughter and four sons, each of them subscribing for one share, in which the leading object for which the company was formed was stated to be the adoption and carrying into effect of the provisional agreement of 20th July. The memorandum was registered on 28th July 1892; and the effect of registration, if otherwise valid, was to incorporate the company under the name of "Aron Salomon and Company, Limited" with liability limited by shares, and having a nominal capital of £40,000 divided into 40,000 shares of £1 each.

The company adopted the agreement of 20th July, and an agreement to that effect was executed between them and the appellant on 2nd August 1892. Within a month or two after that date the whole stipulations of the agreement were fulfilled by both parties. In terms thereof, 100 debentures for £100 each were issued to the appellant who, upon the security of these documents, obtained an advance of £5,000 from Edmund Broderip. In February 1893 the original debentures were returned to the company and cancelled; and in lieu thereof, with the consent of the appellant as beneficial owner, fresh debentures to the same amount were issued to Mr. Broderip, in order to secure the repayment of his loan, with interest at 8 per cent.

In September 1892 the appellant applied for and obtained an allotment of 20,000 shares; for these he paid £1 per share out of the purchase-money which by agreement he was to receive for the transfer of his business to the company, and from that date until an order was made for its compulsory liquidation, the share register of the company remained unaltered, 20,001 shares being held by the appellant, and six shares by his wife and family. It was all along the intention of these persons to retain the business in their own hands, and not to permit any outsider to acquire an interest in it.

Default having been made in the payment of interest upon his debentures, Mr. Broderip in September 1893 instituted an action on behalf of himself and all the other debenture-holders, including the appellant, in order to enforce his security against the assets of the company. Thereafter a liquidation order was made, and a liquidator appointed, at the instance of unsecured creditors of the company. If the amount realised from the assets of the company had been applied in the first place in extinction of Mr. Broderip's debt and interest there would have remained a balance of about £1,055, which was claimed by the appellant as beneficial owner of the debentures. In the event of his claim being sustained there would have been no funds left for payment of the unsecured creditors, whose debts amounted to £7,733 8s. 3d.

The liquidator lodged a defence, in the name of the company, to the debenture suit, in which he counter-claimed against the appellant to have the agreements of 20th July and 2nd August 1892 rescinded, to have the debentures delivered up and cancelled, judgment against the appellant for all sums paid by the company to the appellant under these agreements, and a lien for these sums upon the business and assets. The averments made in support of these claims were to the effect that the price paid by the company exceeded the real value of the business and assets by upwards of £8,200; that the arrangements made by the appellant for the formation of the company were a fraud upon the creditors of the company; that no board of directors of the company was ever appointed and that in any case such board consisted entirely of the appellant, and there never was an independent board.

The evidence showed that before its transfer to the new company the business had been prosperous, and had yielded to the appellant annual profits sufficient to maintain himself and his family and to add to his capital. It also showed that at the date of transfer the business was perfectly solvent. The ultimate insolvency of the business after it came into the hands of the company was attributed by the witness Emanuel Salomon, the appellant's son, to a succession of strikes in the boot trade. There was no evidence to modify or contradict his statement. It also appeared from the evidence that all the members of the company were fully cognisant of the terms of the agreements of 20th July and 2nd August 1892, and that they were willing to accept and did accept these terms.

Vaughan Williams J., before whom the action came, was not prepared to grant the relief craved by the company. He suggested that a different remedy might be open to the company and allowed the counter-claim to be amended. In conformity with his suggestion, a new and alternative claim was added for a declaration that the company or the liquidator was entitled to be indemnified by the appellant against the whole of the company's unsecured debts, namely, £7,733 8s. 3d.; to judgment against the appellant for that sum; and to a lien for that amount upon all sums which might be payable to the appellant by the company in respect of his debentures or otherwise until the judgment was satisfied. There were also added averments to the effect that the company was formed by the appellant, and that the debentures for £10,000 were issued in order that he might carry on the business, and take all the profits without risk to himself; and also that the company was the "mere nominee and agent" of the appellant.

VAUGHAN WILLIAMS J. made an order for a declaration in the terms of the new and alternative counter-claim above stated, without making any order on the original counter-claim.

Both parties appealed. The Court of Appeal, being of opinion that the formation of the company, the agreement of August 1892, and the issue of debentures to the appellant pursuant to such agreement, were a mere scheme to enable him to carry on business in the name of the company with limited liability contrary to the true intent and meaning of the *Companies Act*, 1862, and further to enable him to obtain a preference over other creditors of the company by procuring a first charge on the assets of the company by means of such debentures, dismissed the appeal and declined to make any order on the original counter-claim.

Against this order the appellant appealed to the House of Lords, and the company brought a cross-appeal against so much of it as declined to make any order upon the original counter-claim.

LORD HALSBURY L.C.: My Lords, the important question in this case, I am not certain it is not the only question, is whether the respondent company was a company at all—whether in truth that artificial creation of the Legislature had been validly constituted in this instance; and in order to determine that question it is necessary to look at what the statute itself has determined in that respect. I have no right to add to the requirements of the statute, nor to take from the requirements thus enacted. The sole guide must be the statute itself.

Now, that there were seven actual living persons who held shares in the company has not been doubted. As to the proportionate amounts held by each I will deal presently; but it is important to observe that this first condition of the statute is satisfied, and it follows as a consequence that it would not be competent to anyone—and certainly not to these persons themselves—to deny that they were shareholders.

I must pause here to point out that the statute enacts nothing as to the extent or degree of interest which may be held by each of the seven, or as to the proportion of interest or influence possessed by one or the majority of the share-holders over the others. One share is enough. Still less is it possible to contend that the motive of becoming shareholders or of making them shareholders is a field of inquiry which the statute itself recognises as legitimate. If they are share-holders, they are shareholders for all purposes; and even if the statute was silent as to the recognition of trusts, I should be prepared to hold that if six of them were the cestuis que trust of the seventh, whatever might be their rights *inter se*, the statute would have made them shareholders to all intents and purposes with their respective rights and liabilities, and, dealing with them in their relation to the company, the only relations which I believe the law would sanction would be that they were corporators of the corporate body.

I am simply here dealing with the provisions of the statute, and it seems to me to be essential to the artificial creation that the law should recognise only that artificial existence—quite apart from the motives or conduct of individual corporators. In saying this, I do not at all mean to suggest that if it could be established that this provision of the statute to which I am adverting had not been complied with, you could not go behind the certificate of incorporation to show that a fraud had been committed upon the officer entrusted with the duty of giving the certificate, and that by some proceeding in the nature of *scire facias* you could not prove the fact that the company had no real legal existence. But short of such proof it seems to me impossible to dispute that once the company is legally incorporated it must be treated like any other independent person with its rights and liabilities appropriate to itself, and that the motives of those who took part in the promotion of the company are absolutely irrelevant in discussing what those rights and liabilities are.

I will for the sake of argument assume the proposition that the Court of Appeal lays down—that the formation of the company was a mere scheme to enable Aron Salomon to carry on business in the name of the company. I am wholly unable to follow the proposition that this was contrary to the true intent and meaning of the *Companies Act*. I can only find the true intent and meaning of the Act from the Act itself; and the Act appears to me to give a company a legal existence with, as I have said, rights and liabilities of its own, whatever may have been the ideas or schemes of those who brought it into existence.

I observe that the learned judge [VAUGHAN WILLIAMS J.] held that the business was Mr. Salomon's business, and no one else's, and that he chose to employ as agent a limited company; and he proceeded to argue that he was employing that limited company as agent, and that he was bound to indemnify that agent (the company). I confess it seems to me that that very learned judge becomes involved by this argument in a very singular contradiction. Either the limited company was a legal entity or it was not. If it was, the business belonged to it and not to Mr. Salomon. If it was not, there was no person and no thing to be an agent at all; and it is impossible to say at the same time that there is a company and there is not.

LINDLEY L.J., on the other hand, affirms that there were seven members of the company; but he says it is manifest that six of them were members simply in order to enable the seventh himself to carry on business with limited liability. The object of the whole arrangement is to do the very thing which the Legislature intended not to be done.

It is obvious to inquire where is that intention of the Legislature manifested in the statute. Even if we were at liberty to insert words to manifest that intention, I should have great difficulty in ascertaining what the exact intention thus imputed to the Legislature is, or was. In this particular case it is the members of one family that represent all the shares; but if the supposed intention is not limited to so narrow a proposition as this, that the seven shareholders must not be members of one family, to what extent may influence or authority or intentional purchase of a majority among the shareholders be carried so as to bring it within the supposed prohibition? It is, of course, easy to say that it was contrary to the intention of the Legislature—a proposition which, by reason of its generality, it is difficult to bring to the test; but when one seeks to put as an affirmative proposition what the thing is which the Legislature has prohibited, there is, as it appears to me, an insuperable difficulty in the way of those who seek to insert by construction such a prohibition into the statute.

As one mode of testing the proposition, it would be pertinent to ask whether two or three, or indeed all seven, may constitute the whole of the shareholders? Whether they must be all independent of each other in the sense of each having an independent beneficial interest? And this is a question that cannot be answered by the reply that it is a matter of degree. If the Legislature intended to prohibit something, you ought to know what that something is. All it has said is that one share is sufficient to constitute a shareholder, though the shares may be 100,000 in number. Where am I to get from the statute itself a limitation of that provision that that shareholder must be an independent and beneficially interested person?

My Lords, the learned judges appear to me not to have been absolutely certain in their own minds whether to treat the company as a real thing or not. If it was a real thing; if it had a legal existence, and if consequently the law attributed to it certain rights and liabilities in its constitution as a company, it appears to me to follow as a consequence that it is impossible to deny the validity of the transactions into which it has entered.

Vaughan Williams J. appears to me to have disposed of the argument that the company (which for this purpose he assumed to be a legal entity) was defrauded into the purchase of Aron Salomon's business because, assuming that the price paid for the business was an exorbitant one, as to which I am myself not satisfied, but assuming that it was, the learned judge most cogently observes that when all the shareholders are perfectly cognisant of the conditions under which the company is formed and the conditions of the purchase, it is impossible to contend that the company is being defrauded. . . . [I]f every member of the company—every shareholder— knows exactly what is the true state of the facts (which for this purpose must be assumed to be the case here), Vaughan Williams J.'s conclusion seems to me to be inevitable that no case of fraud upon the company could here be established.

If there was no fraud and no agency, and if the company was a real one and not a fiction or a myth, every one of the grounds upon which it is sought to support the judgment is disposed of.

My Lords, the truth is that the learned judges have never allowed in their own minds the proposition that the company has a real existence. They have been struck by what they have considered the inexpediency of permitting one man to be in influence and authority over the whole company; and, assuming that such a thing could not have been intended by the Legislature, they have sought various grounds upon which they might insert into the Act some prohibition of such a result. Whether such a result be right or wrong, politic or impolitic, I say, with the utmost deference to the learned judges, that we have nothing to do with that question if this company has been duly constituted by law; and, whatever may be the motives of those who constitute it, I must decline to insert into that Act of Parliament limitations which are not to be found there.

I have dealt with this matter upon the narrow hypothesis propounded by the learned judges below; but it is, I think, only justice to the appellant to say that I see nothing whatever to justify the imputations which are implied in some of the observations made by more than one of the learned judges. The appellant, in my opinion, is not shown to have done or to have intended to do anything dishonest or unworthy, but to have suffered a great misfortune without any fault of his own.

The result is that I move your Lordships that the judgment appealed from be reversed. . . .

LORD WATSON: . . . I have come to the conclusion that the orders appealed from ought to be reversed. . . .

LORD HERSCHELL: . . . The learned judges in the Court of Appeal dissented from the view taken by VAUGHAN WILLIAMS J. that the company was to be regarded as the agent of the appellant. They considered the relation between them to be that of trustee and cestui que trust; but this difference of view, of course, did not affect the conclusion that the right to the indemnity claimed had been established.

It is to be observed that both Courts treated the company as a legal entity distinct from Salomon and the then members who composed it, and therefore as a validly constituted corporation. This is, indeed, necessarily involved in the judgment which declared that the company was entitled to certain rights as against Salomon. Under these circumstances, I am at a loss to understand what is meant by saying that A. Salomon & Co., Limited, is but an "alias" for A. Salomon. It is not another name for the same person; the company is *ex hypothesi* a distinct legal persona. As little am I able to adopt the view that the company was the agent of Salomon to carry on his business for him. In a popular sense, a company may in every case be said to carry on business for and on behalf of its shareholders; but this certainly does not in point of law constitute the relation of principal and agent between them or render the shareholders liable to indemnify the company against the debts which it incurs. Here, it is true, Salomon owned all the shares except six, so that if the business were profitable he would be entitled, substantially, to the whole of the profits. The other shareholders, too, are said to have been "dummies," the nominees of Salomon. But when once it is conceded that they were individual members of the company distinct from Salomon, and sufficiently so to bring into existence in conjunction with him a validly constituted corporation, I am unable to see how the facts to which I have just referred can affect the legal position of the company, or give it rights as against its members which it would not otherwise possess.

The Court of Appeal based their judgment on the proposition that the formation of the company and all that followed on it were a mere scheme to enable the appellant to carry on business in the name of the company, with limited liability, contrary to the true intent and meaning of the *Companies Act*, 1862. The conclusion which they drew from this premise was, that the company was a trustee and Salomon their cestui que trust. I cannot think that the conclusion follows even if the premise be sound. It seems to me that the logical result would be that the company had not been validly constituted, and therefore had no legal existence. But, apart from this, it is necessary to examine the proposition. . . . Many industrial and banking concerns of the highest standing and credit have, in recent years, been . . . converted into joint stock companies, . . . where the whole of the shares are held by the former partners. It appears to me that all these might be pronounced "schemes to enable" them "to carry on business in the name of the company, with limited liability," in the very sense in which those words are used in the judgment of the Court of Appeal. The profits of the concern carried on by the company will go to the persons whose business it was before the transfer, and in the same proportions as before, the only difference being that the liability of those who take the profits will no longer be unlimited. The very object of the creation of the company and the transfer to it of the business is, that whereas the liability of the partners for debts incurred was without limit, the liability of the members for the debts incurred by the company shall be limited. In no other respect is it intended that there shall be any difference: the conduct of the business and the division of the profits are intended to be the same as before. If the judgment of the Court of Appeal be pushed to its logical conclusion, all these companies must, I think, be held to be trustees for the partners who transferred the business to them, and those partners must be declared liable without limit to discharge the debts of the company. For this is the effect of the judgment as regards the respondent company. The position of the members of the company is just the same whether they are declared liable to pay the debts incurred by the company, or by way of indemnity to furnish the company with the means of paying them. I do not think the learned judges in the Court below have contemplated the application of their judgment to such cases as I have been considering; but I can see no solid distinction between those cases and the present one.

It is said that the respondent company is a "one man" company, and that in this respect it differs from such companies as those to which I have alluded. But it has often happened that a business transferred to a joint stock company has been the property of three or four persons only, and that the other subscribers of the memorandum have been clerks or other persons who possessed little or no interest in the concern. I am unable to see how it can be lawful for three or four or six persons to form a company for the purpose of employing their capital in trading, with the benefit of limited liability, and not for one person to do so, provided, in each case, the requirements of the statute have been complied with and the company has been validly constituted. How does it concern the creditor whether the capital of the company is owned by seven persons in equal shares, with the rights to an equal share of the profits, or whether it is almost entirely owned by one person, who practically takes the whole of the profits? The creditor has notice that he is dealing with a company the liability of the members of which is limited, and the register of shareholders informs him how the shares are held, and that they are substantially in the hands of one person, if this be the fact. The creditors in the present case gave credit to and contracted with a limited company; the effect of the decision is to give them the benefit, as regards one of the shareholders, of unlimited liability. . . .

The Court of Appeal has declared that the formation of the respondent company and the agreement to take over the business of the appellant were a scheme "contrary to the true intent and meaning of the Companies Act." I know of no means of ascertaining what is the intent and meaning of the Companies Act except by examining its provisions and finding what regulations it has imposed as a condition of trading with limited liability. The memorandum must state the amount of the capital of the company and the number of shares into which it is divided, and no subscriber is to take less than one share. The shares may, however, be of as small a nominal value as those who form the company please: the statute prescribes no minimum; and though there must be seven shareholders, it is enough if each of them holds one share, however small its denomination. The Legislature, therefore, clearly sanctions a scheme by which all the shares except six are owned by a single individual, and these six are of a value little more than nominal.

It was said that in the present case the six shareholders other than the appellant were mere dummies, his nominees, and held their shares in trust for him. I will assume that this was so. In my opinion, it makes no difference. The statute forbids the entry in the register of any trust; and it certainly contains no enactment that each of the seven persons subscribing the memorandum must be beneficially entitled to the share or shares for which he subscribes. The persons who subscribe the memorandum, or who have agreed to become members of the company and whose names are on the register, are alone regarded as, and in fact are, the shareholders. They are subject to all the liability which attaches to the holding of the share. They can be compelled to make any payment which the ownership of a share involves. Whether they are beneficial owners or bare trustees is a matter with which neither the company nor creditors have anything to do: it concerns only them and their cestuis que trust if they have any. If, then, in the present case all the requirements of the statute were complied with, and a company was effectually constituted, and this is the hypothesis of the judgment appealed from, what warrant is there for saying that what was done was contrary to the true intent and meaning of the Companies Act?

It may be that a company constituted like that under consideration was not in the contemplation of the Legislature at the time when the Act authorising limited liability was passed; that if what is possible under the enactments as they stand had been foreseen a minimum sum would have been fixed as the least denomination of share permissible; and that it would have been made a condition that each of the seven persons should have a substantial interest in the company. But we have to interpret the law, not to make it; and it must be remembered that no one need trust a limited liability company unless he so please, and that before he does so he can ascertain, if he so please, what is the capital of the company and how it is held.

I have hitherto made no reference to the debentures which

the appellant received in part-payment of the purchase-money
of the business which he transferred to the company. . . . The
issue of debentures to the vendor of a business as part of the
price is certainly open to great abuse, and has often worked
grave mischief. . . . But as the law at present stands, there is
certainly nothing unlawful in the creation of such debentures.
For these reasons I have come to the conclusion that the appeal
should be allowed.

LORD MACNAGHTEN: My Lords, I cannot help thinking that
the appellant, Aron Salomon, has been dealt with somewhat
hardly in this case.

Mr. Salomon, who is now suing as a pauper, was a wealthy
man in July 1892. He was a boot and shoe manufacturer
trading on his own sole account under the firm of "A. Salomon
& Co.," in High Street, Whitechapel, where he had extensive
warehouses and a large establishment. He had been in the trade
over thirty years. He had lived in the same neighbourhood
all along, and for many years past he had occupied the same
premises. So far things had gone very well with him. Beginning with little or no capital, he had gradually built up a
thriving business, and he was undoubtedly in good credit
and repute.

It is impossible to say exactly what the value of the business
was. But there was a substantial surplus of assets over liabilities. And it seems to me to be pretty clear that if Mr. Salomon
had been minded to dispose of his business in the market as
a going concern he might fairly have counted upon retiring
with at least £10,000 in his pocket.

Mr. Salomon, however, did not want to part with the business. He had a wife and family consisting of five sons and a
daughter. Four of the sons were working with their father.
The eldest, who was about thirty years of age, was practically
the manager. But the sons were not partners: they were only
servants. Not unnaturally, perhaps, they were dissatisfied with
their position. They kept pressing their father to give them a
share in the concern. "They troubled me," says Mr. Salomon,
"all the while." So at length Mr. Salomon did what hundreds

of others have done under similar circumstances. He turned his business into a limited company. He wanted, he says, to extend the business and make provision for his family. In those words, I think, he fairly describes the principal motives which influenced his action.

All the usual formalities were gone through; all the requirements of the *Companies Act*, 1862, were duly observed. . . .

The subscribers to the memorandum were Mr. Salomon, his wife, and five of his children who were grown up. The subscribers met and appointed Mr. Salomon and his two elder sons directors. The directors then proceeded to carry out the proposed transfer. By an agreement dated August 2nd, 1892, the company adopted the preliminary contract, and in accordance with it the business was taken over by the company as from June 1st, 1892. The price fixed by the contract was duly paid. The price on paper was extravagant. It amounted to over £39,000—a sum which represented the sanguine expectations of a fond owner rather than anything that can be called a businesslike or reasonable estimate of value. . . . In the result, therefore, Mr. Salomon received for his business about £1,000 in cash, £10,000 in debentures, and half the nominal capital of the company in fully paid shares for what they were worth. No other shares were issued except the seven shares taken by the subscribers to the memorandum, who, of course, knew all the circumstances, and had therefore no ground for complaint on the score of overvaluation.

The company had a brief career: it fell upon evil days. Shortly after it was started there seems to have come a period of great depression in the boot and shoe trade. There were strikes of workmen too; and in view of that danger contracts with public bodies, which were the principal source of Mr. Salomon's profit, were split up and divided between different firms. The attempts made to push the business on behalf of the new company crammed its warehouses with unsaleable stock. Mr. Salomon seems to have done what he could: both he and his wife lent the company money; and then he got his debentures cancelled and reissued to a Mr. Broderip, who advanced him £5,000 which he immediately handed over

to the company on loan. The temporary relief only hastened
ruin. Mr. Broderip's interest was not paid when it became due.
He took proceedings at once and got a receiver appointed.
Then, of course, came liquidation and a forced sale of the
company's assets. They realised enough to pay Mr. Broderip,
but not enough to pay the debentures in full; and the unsecured
creditors were consequently left out in the cold.

. . . The order of the learned judge [VAUGHAN WILLIAMS J.]
appears to me to be founded on a misconception of the scope
and effect of the *Companies Act*, 1862. In order to form a
company limited by shares, the Act requires that a memorandum of association should be signed by seven persons,
who are each to take one share at least. If these conditions
are complied with, what can it matter whether the signatories
are relations or strangers? There is nothing in the Act requiring that the subscribers to the memorandum should be
independent or unconnected, or that they or any one of them
should take a substantial interest in the undertaking, or that
they should have a mind and will of their own, . . . or that there
should be anything like a balance of power in the constitution
of the company. In almost every company that is formed
the statutory number is eked out by clerks or friends, who sign
their names at the request of the promoter or promoters
without intending to take any further part or interest in the
matter.

When the memorandum is duly signed and registered,
though there be only seven shares taken, the subscribers
are a body corporate "capable forthwith," to use the words
of the enactment, "of exercising all the functions of an incorporated company." Those are strong words. The company
attains maturity on its birth. There is no period of minority
—no interval of incapacity. I cannot understand how a body
corporate thus made "capable" by statute can lose its in-
dividuality by issuing the bulk of its capital to one person,
whether he be a subscriber to the memorandum or not. The
company is at law a different person altogether from the
subscribers to the memorandum; and, though it may be that
after incorporation the business is precisely the same as it

was before, and the same persons are managers, and the same hands receive the profits, the company is not in law the agent of the subscribers or trustee for them. Nor are the subscribers as members liable, in any shape or form, except to the extent and in the manner provided by the Act. That is, I think, the declared intention of the enactment. If the view of the learned judge were sound, it would follow that no common law partnership could register as a company limited by shares without remaining subject to unlimited liability.

. . . Among the principal reasons which induce persons to form . . . companies, . . . are the desire to avoid the risk of bankruptcy, and the increased facility afforded for borrowing money. By means of a . . . company, . . . a trade can be carried on with limited liability, and without exposing the persons interested in it in the event of failure to the harsh provisions of the bankruptcy law. A company, too, can raise money on debentures, which an ordinary trader cannot do. Any member of a company, acting in good faith, is as much entitled to take and hold the company's debentures as any outside creditor. Every creditor is entitled to get and to hold the best security the law allows him to take.

. . . The unsecured creditors of A. Salomon and Company, Limited, may be entitled to sympathy, but they have only themselves to blame for their misfortunes. They trusted the company, I suppose, because they had long dealt with Mr. Salomon, and he had always paid his way; but they had full notice that they were no longer dealing with an individual, and they must be taken to have been cognisant of the memorandum and of the articles of association. For such a catastrophe as has occurred in this case some would blame the law that allows the creation of a floating charge. But a floating charge is too convenient a form of security to be lightly abolished. I have long thought, and I believe some of your Lordships also think, that the ordinary trade creditors of a trading company ought to have a preferential claim on the assets in liquidation in respect of debts incurred within a certain limited time before the winding-up. But that is not the law at present. Everybody knows that when there is a winding-up debenture-holders generally step in and sweep off everything; and a great scandal it is.

It has become the fashion to call companies of this class "one man companies." That is a taking nickname, but it does not help one much in the way of argument. If it is intended to convey the meaning that a company which is under the absolute control of one person is not a company legally incorporated, although the requirements of the Act of 1862 may have been complied with, it is inaccurate and misleading: if it merely means that there is a predominant partner possessing an overwhelming influence and entitled practically to the whole of the profits, there is nothing in that that I can see contrary to the true intention of the Act of 1862, or against public policy, or detrimental to the interests of creditors. If the shares are fully paid up, it cannot matter whether they are in the hands of one or many. If the shares are not fully paid, it is as easy to gauge the solvency of an individual as to estimate the financial ability of a crowd. . . . I am of opinion that the appeal ought to be allowed, and the counter-claim of the company dismissed.

LORD MORRIS: My Lords, I quite concur in the judgment which has been announced, and in the reasons which have been so fully given for it.

LORD DAVEY: . . . It was not argued in this case that there was no association of seven persons to be registered, and the registration therefore operated nothing, or that the so-called company was a sham and might be disregarded; and, indeed, it would have been difficult for the learned counsel for the respondents . . . to contend that their clients were non-existent. . . .

We start, then, with the assumption that the respondents have a corporate existence with power to sue and be sued, to incur debts and be wound up, and to act as agents or trustees, and I suppose, therefore, to hold property. Both the Courts below have, however, held that the appellant is liable to indemnify the company against all its debts and liabilities.

VAUGHAN WILLIAMS J. held that the company was an

"alias" for the appellant, who carried on his business through the company as his agent, and that he was bound to indemnify his own agent; and he arrived at this conclusion on the ground that the other members of the company had no substantial interest in it, and the business in substance was the appellant's. The Court of Appeal thought the relation of the company to the appellant was that of trustee to cestui que trust.

The ground on which the learned judges seem to have chiefly relied was that it was an attempt by an individual to carry on his business with limited liability, which was forbidden by the Act and unlawful. I observe, in passing, that nothing turns upon there being only one person interested. The argument would have been just as good if there had been six members holding the bulk of the shares and one member with a very small interest, say, one share. I am at a loss to see how in either view taken in the Courts below the conclusion follows from the premises, or in what way the company became an agent or trustee for the appellant, except in the sense in which every company may loosely and inaccurately be said to be an agent for earning profits for its members, or a trustee of its profits for the members amongst whom they are to be divided. There was certainly no express trust for the appellant; and an implied or constructive trust can only be raised by virtue of some equity. I took the liberty of asking the learned counsel what the equity was, but got no answer. By an "alias" is usually understood a second name for one individual; but here . . . we have, *ex hypothesi*, a duly formed legal persona, with corporate attributes and capable of incurring legal liabilities. Nor do I think it legitimate to inquire whether the interest of any member is substantial when the Act has declared that no member need hold more than one share, and has not prescribed any minimum amount of a share. If, as was said in the Court of Appeal, the company was formed for an unlawful purpose, or in order to achieve an object not permitted by the provisions of the Act, the appropriate remedy (if any) would seem to be to set aside the certificate of incorporation, or to treat the company as a nullity, or, if the appellant had committed a fraud or misdemeanour (which I do not think he has), he may be proceeded against civilly or criminally; but how either of those states of circumstances creates the relation of cestui que trust and trustee, or principal and agent, between the appellant and respondents, is not apparent to my understanding.

I am, therefore, of opinion that the order appealed from cannot be supported on the grounds stated by the learned judges.

But Mr. Farwell [*leading counsel for the respondents*] also relied on the alternative relief claimed by his pleadings, . . . namely, that the contract for purchase of the appellant's business ought to be set aside for fraud. The fraud seems to consist in the alleged exorbitance of the price and the fact that there was no independent board of directors with whom the appellant could contract. I am of opinion that the fraud was not made out. I do not think the price of the appellant's business . . . was so excessive as to afford grounds for rescission; and as regards the cash portion of the price, it must be observed that, as the appellant held the bulk of the shares, or (the respondents say) was the only shareholder, the money required for the payment of it came from himself in the form either of calls on his shares or profits which would otherwise be divisible. Nor was the absence of any independent board material in a case like the present. I think it an inevitable inference from the circumstances of the case that every member of the company assented to the purchase, and the company is bound in a matter *intra vires* by the unanimous agreement of its members.

. . . That a company may contract with the holder of the bulk of its shares, and such contract will be binding though carried by the votes of that shareholder, was decided in *North-West Transportation Co.* v. *Beatty.*

For these reasons, I am of opinion that the appellant's appeal should be allowed and the cross-appeal should be dismissed.

II. THE NAME OF THE COMPANY

Aerators, Limited *v*. Tollitt. [1902] 2 Ch. 319

In considering whether the names of two companies are so similar as to induce the belief that the companies are identical, it is material to ascertain (1) whether the objects of the second company are similar to those of the first, and (2) what sort of name has been adopted by the first company. If its name is a word in common use representing an article of commerce, there is less likelihood of deception than in the case of a fancy word.

The plaintiff company Aerators, Limited was incorporated in February 1900 for the purpose of working a certain patent for the instantaneous automatic aeration of liquids. They had a large and increasing business in England and the Colonies. The apparatus which they sold was portable, had become known in the trade and to the public under the name of "Sparklets" and was very suitable for private use. The defendants were the seven signatories to the memorandum and articles of association of a new company to be called "Automatic Aerators Patents, Limited." Its object also was to work certain patents for the instantaneous automatic aeration of liquids; but its patents and apparatus were quite different from those of the plaintiff company, and were more suitable for hotels, public-houses and refreshment bars. The defendants lodged the necessary papers for registration on 14th May 1902. Early in May the directors of the plaintiff company heard that a new company to be called "Automatic Aerators, Limited" was about to be formed. Accordingly, with the view of protecting the name of their company, they prepared a memorandum and articles of association of a new company under the title of "Automatic Aerators, Limited," which they tendered for registration; but the registrar declined to accept them because the defendants' papers had already been lodged.

The plaintiffs thereupon issued a writ claiming an injunction to restrain the defendants from registering a company under the title of "Automatic Aerators Patents, Limited," or in any other name so nearly resembling the name of the plaintiff company as to be calculated to deceive within the meaning of S.20, *Companies Act*, 1862 [*the forerunner of S.18, Companies Act, 1948*].

FARWELL J.: It will be observed that a company has . . . a greater right than an individual in respect of names that are identical. For John Smith cannot prevent other persons of the same name from using their own name; but John Smith, Limited can prevent the registration of any other company as John Smith, Limited. I do not, however, consider that it follows that the Legislature has intended to give companies any greater rights than individuals possess in respect of names which are not identical, but only similar, and it has been held that "calculated to deceive" does not point to intentional fraud; but it is a question of fact in each case whether the name of the new company is so similar to that of the old company as to induce the belief that the two companies are identical. In considering this question it is material to ascertain —(1) what business has been or is intended to be carried on by the old company, and what is intended to be carried on by the new one; (2) what sort of name has been adopted by the old company. As to the first point, I do not think that it is sufficient for an existing company to point to clauses in its memorandum which will enable it to extend its operations to numerous classes of trade, unless it can satisfy the Court that it either has carried on or really proposes within a limited time to carry on such particular business. It cannot, I think, be enough in these days, when the objects of a company are usually limited only by the number of letters in the alphabet and extend to every form of business, whether connected or not with the principal object, to show that the intended new company includes some similar objects. It is necessary to see whether the real objects of the second company are similar. As to the second point, I think that it is necessary to consider the nature of the title registered by the old company. . . .

[I]t appears to me impossible to say, as a general proposition, that a company can, by registering a single word, whatever its nature, remove that word from the English language so far as regards its use in the title of subsequent companies. In the present case the plaintiffs have taken a word which, and which only, aptly and rightly describes a machine for producing a particular result. The word has been in common use in the English language for at least thirty years. . . . It would obviously lead to the greatest inconvenience if any company could prevent all other companies from using as part of their title the one word in the English language which aptly describes the articles they manufacture or deal in, or the name of the individual associated for years with a particular firm. . . . In considering whether a name is calculated to deceive it is, as I have said, material to see what that name is; and if the name is simply a word in ordinary use representing a machine or an article of commerce, the probability of deception is out of all proportion less than it would be in the case of an invented or fancy word, or even of the name of a place. The latter may well point to a particular company; the former certainly points prima facie to the machine or article, and can only under very exceptional circumstances and by a long course of usage point to the company, rather than the thing itself.

. . . [The plaintiffs] can no more acquire a monopoly in the use of the word "Aerators," by adopting that as their title, than an individual can acquire a monopoly in his own name or the name of the article he manufactures; as in the latter case it is necessary for the individual to show, not merely that the defendant is trading under his name or is making the article the name of which he has adopted, but also that the name or article is exclusively identified with his own manufacture so as to have acquired a secondary meaning; so a company must also show that the name which prima facie refers to a number of persons or articles is in fact identified solely with the plaintiffs before they can satisfy the Court that its use as part of another company's name is calculated to deceive. A name is not necessarily calculated to deceive because it is similar; it must depend in great measure upon what the nature of the name is; and if it merely represents the name of the article supplied by the company, it would require very strong evidence to show that such name had lost its primary meaning, and had become identified with the plaintiff company.

In the case before me, . . . there is in fact no evidence, to my mind, of any probability of deception. . . . In my opinion, the plaintiffs' action is an attempt to monopolise for the purpose of nomenclature a word in ordinary use in the English language, and fails. . . .

Ewing *v.* Buttercup Margarine Company, Ltd. [1917] 2 Ch. 1

Where a company's name is so similar to that of another company that it is likely to cause confusion between the two businesses, an injunction will be granted to restrain its use.

The plaintiff Andrew Ewing was a wholesale and retail provision merchant of Leith, Scotland. In 1904 he commenced opening retail shops for the sale of butter, margarine, eggs, tea, cream and condensed milk, and carried on this retail business under the trade name of the Buttercup Dairy Company. He had at the time of the action 150 shops in Scotland and seven in the North of England, and he intended to come farther south after the war.

The business was well known to the public, the wholesale merchants, and the manufacturers and producers of the goods, and was popularly called the Buttercup Company or the Buttercup. The total turnover was half a million pounds a year, and the sale of margarine was fifty tons a week. Goods were always bought in the name of the Buttercup Dairy Company, by which name the business was known in the markets.

On 15th November 1916 the defendant company—the Buttercup Margarine Company, Limited—was incorporated as a private company. Its office was in Westminster, and although the memorandum authorised both wholesale and retail trade in milk, cream, butter, margarine, etc., its main object and intention was to manufacture margarine by means of a secret process and to trade wholesale in it. The three directors, two of whom were the signatories, had never heard of the plaintiff or his trade name, and adopted the name "Buttercup Margarine Company, Limited" quite innocently after ascertaining that there was no similar name on the Company Register.

On 23rd November 1916 the plaintiff complained of the name, and on 31st January 1917 after some preliminary correspondence, he commenced proceedings to restrain the company and the directors from carrying on business under the name of the Buttercup Margarine Company, Limited, or any name resembling the plaintiff's trade name, or from carrying on business under any description calculated to produce the belief that the defendant company's business was that of the plaintiff.

ASTBURY J.: . . . The present case is very near the line. The ground of interference by the Court in these name cases is that the use of the defendant company's name, or intended name, is calculated to deceive. . . .

If the name, although not actually used by the plaintiff for the particular kind of goods to which the defendant has applied, or is proposing to apply it, is so identified with the name that the defendant uses that it may induce the belief that his goods are those of the plaintiff, or secondly that his business is an extension of, or otherwise connected with, the plaintiff's business, then the Court can grant relief. . . .

Now in the present case I have to decide, as a fact, whether on the evidence before me the use of the name "Buttercup Margarine Company, Limited" is calculated to deceive by diverting customers or potential customers from the plaintiff; or to occasion . . . confusion between the two businesses.

. . . I think the plaintiff has made out a prima facie case that he will be, or may be, damaged . . . if the defendant company is allowed to commence trading and to continue trading in its present name. . . .

On the whole, having regard to the evidence, the plaintiff has made out his right to the injunction he asks.

From this decision of ASTBURY J. the defendants appealed to the Court of Appeal.

LORD COZENS-HARDY M.R.: This is an appeal from a decision of ASTBURY J. I agree with his judgment, and I think with every passage in it, with only one exception. He says that this is a case very near the line. In my opinion it is a perfectly plain and clear case, not very near the line, but well over the line.

. . . I cannot bring myself to doubt that serious damage to the credit and prosperity of the plaintiff's business would arise from the confusion caused by the defendant company deliberately and wilfully continuing to carry on business in a name so nearly resembling that under which the plaintiff is trading as to be calculated to deceive.

. . . I think the judgment of ASTBURY J. was perfectly right, and that the appeal must be dismissed.

BANKES L.J.: I agree. . . .

WARRINGTON L.J.: I am of the same opinion. . . . [I]t seems to me that the plaintiff has proved enough. He has proved that the defendants have adopted such a name as may lead people who have dealings with the plaintiff to believe that the defendant's business is a branch of or associated with the plaintiff's business. To induce the belief that my business is a branch of another man's business may do that other man damage in various ways. The quality of goods I sell, the kind of business I do, the credit or otherwise which I enjoy are all things which may injure the other man who is assumed wrongly to be associated with me. And it is just that kind of injury that what the defendants have done here is likely to occasion. I think, therefore, the learned judge was perfectly right.

Durham Fancy Goods, Ltd. *v.* Michael Jackson (Fancy Goods) Ltd. and Another. [1968] 2 Q.B. 839

The holder of a bill of exchange on which the company's name has been incorrectly stated will not be able to enforce the personal liability under S.108 (4), Companies Act 1948, against the officer concerned if the error was due to the holder's own act. The principle of equitable estoppel will preclude him from doing so.

The facts sufficiently appear from the judgment.

DONALDSON J.: This is a cautionary tale which should, perhaps, be required reading for all directors of companies.

Michael Jackson and Florence Jackson were the sole directors and shareholders of a Manchester company, Michael Jackson (Fancy Goods) Ltd., to which I will refer as "Jacksons." Mr. Jackson was also the company secretary. Durham Fancy Goods Ltd., the plaintiffs, a London company, had business dealings with Jacksons which, in the course of those dealings, was variously referred to as "Michael Jackson (Fancy Goods) Ltd." its proper name, and as "M. Jackson (Fancy Goods) Ltd." The nomenclature adopted at any particular point of time was fortuitous and devoid of significance to anyone concerned.

On September 18, 1967, the plaintiffs drew a 90-day bill of exchange on Jacksons, no doubt in settlement of a business transaction. It was drawn on the printed letter paper of the plaintiffs and the following words were typed on the right-hand side of the paper:

"£740 17*s.* 6*d.* 18.9.67. At 90 (Ninety) Days after date pay to our order the sum of Seven hundred and Forty pounds seventeen shillings and sixpence only for value received. For and on behalf of DURHAM FANCY GOODS LTD."

Then there was a sixpenny stamp cancelled with an illegible signature, and the bill continued: "To: M. Jackson (Fancy Goods) Ltd., 263 Bury New Road, Manchester." On the left-hand side of the paper the following words were typed: "Accepted payable: Westminster Bank Ltd., 110 Regent Road, Salford 5. For and on behalf of M. JACKSON (FANCY GOODS) LTD., Manchester."

This was the form of the draft when it left the plaintiffs and when it was received by Jacksons. Upon receiving it, Mr. Jackson added his signature in the appropriate place, namely below the words "For and on behalf of M. Jackson (Fancy

Goods) Ltd., Manchester" and returned the bill to the plaintiffs.

The bill should have been honoured not later than December 20th, 1967, but before that date both Michael Jackson and Florence Jackson sold all their shares in Jacksons and re-signed from their respective positions as director/secretary and director. The bill was dishonoured upon maturity and Jacksons are now in liquidation.

Thus far, I am confident, neither the plaintiffs, Jacksons nor Mr. Michael Jackson had ever given a thought to section 108 of the Companies Act, 1948, if indeed any of them had ever heard of it. In this they were surely not alone. However, that happy state did not continue and the plaintiffs, in reliance upon the section, now contend that when Mr. Michael Jackson signed the form of acceptance prepared by them he committed a criminal offence punishable with a fine of up to £50 and, more important, he made himself personally liable on the bill. Exercising their new-found knowledge of the law, they say that he should either have returned the bill to them with a request that they re-address it to Michael Jackson (Fancy Goods) Ltd., and amend the form of acceptance or he should have accepted it "M. Jackson (Fancy Goods) Ltd., p.p. Michael Jackson (Fancy Goods) Ltd., Michael Jackson."

Section 108 of the Companies Act, 1948, has a respectable pedigree which can be traced back at least as far as the Joint Stock Companies Act, 1856, but there has been no reported case on the topic for over half a century. . . .

Mr. Rokison [*counsel for Mr. Jackson*] submitted that just as "Ltd." was an acceptable abbreviation for "Limited", so "M" was an acceptable abbreviation for "Michael." This I do not accept. The word "Limited" is included in a company's name by way of description and not identification. Accordingly a generally accepted abbreviation will serve this purpose as well as the word in full. The rest of the name, by contrast, serves as a means of identification and may be compounded of or include initials or abbreviations. The use of any abbreviation of the registered name is calculated to create problems of identification which are not created by an abbreviation of "Limited." I should therefore be prepared to hold that no abbreviation was permissible of any part of a company's name other than "Ltd." for "Limited" and, possibly, the ampersand for "and." However, it is not necessary to go as far as this. Any abbreviation must convey the full word unambiguously and the initial "M" neither shows that it is an abbreviation nor does it convey "Michael."

I have therefore no doubt that Mr. Jackson committed an offence under section 108 of the Act of 1948, although a court might well decide to impose no penalty. I have also no doubt that he is liable to the plaintiffs who are admitted to be the holders of the bill of exchange since this is what the statute says. But can the plaintiffs enforce that liability? That is a different question.

This case is distinguished from all previous cases under the earlier statutory versions of the section in that here it was the holders of the bill of exchange who inscribed the words of acceptance, who chose the wrong words and who now seek to rely upon their own error, coupled it is true with the defendant's failure to detect and remedy it, as entitling them to relief. Common sense and justice seem to me to dictate that they shall fail. If I am right thus far, I should be surprised if the law compelled me to find in the plaintiffs' favour because, contrary to popular belief, the law, justice and common sense are not unrelated concepts.

In my judgment the principle of equity upon which the promissory estoppel cases are based is applicable to and bars the plaintiffs' claim. . . . [T]he plaintiffs did not, as one would have expected, send the bill to Jacksons without words of acceptance, but instead inscribed words of acceptance including a name which was deceptively similar to, but not the same as, that of Jacksons. In saying that the name was deceptively similar, I intend only to state what is an obvious fact and wish to emphasise that no deception was intended by the plaintiffs. The plaintiffs thereby implied that acceptance of the bill in that form would be, or would be accepted by them as, a regular acceptance of the bill. Such an acceptance would not, of course, have involved Mr. Jackson in personal liability. In these circumstances it would be inequitable that the plaintiffs should be allowed to enforce the statutory liability of Mr. Jackson without first giving him an opportunity of regularising the acceptance by inscribing the correct name of Jacksons on the bill and that it is now too late to do. Accordingly the plaintiffs are unable to enforce the statutory liability, although it continues to exist and would have been available to other holders, who were unaffected by the equitable defence. . . .

For the reasons given, I consider that the plaintiffs' claim fails.

III. THE DOCTRINE OF *ULTRA VIRES*

1. The Construction of the Objects Clause of the Memorandum of Association

Ashbury Railway Carriage and Iron Company, Limited *v.* Riche. (1875) L.R. 7 H.L. 653

An ultra vires *contract is void and cannot be ratified even by the unanimous consent of the shareholders.*

At two places in Lancashire Mr. John Ashbury had carried on a very extensive business in making railway carriages and waggons, turn-tables, points, crossings and roofs, and other things of a similar kind needed by a railway company, but he had not been concerned in the construction of railways themselves.

A company called "The Ashbury Railway Carriage and Iron Company," incorporated under the *Companies Act*, 1862, was started for the purpose of buying Mr. John Ashbury's business. A memorandum of association dated 12th September 1862 was drawn up. By the third clause the objects of the company were thus defined: "The objects for which the company is established are to make and sell, or lend on hire, railway-carriages and waggons, and all kinds of railway plant, fittings, machinery, and rolling-stock; to carry on the business of *mechanical engineers and general contractors*; to purchase and sell, as merchants, timber, coal, metals, or other materials; and to buy and sell any such materials on commission, or as agents.

In 1864 Mr. Hector Riche, the defendant, was carrying on business in Belgium in partnership with his brother (since deceased) as a railway contractor. On 14th March 1864 the Belgian Government granted to persons named Gillon and Bertsoen a provisional concession for making a line of railway from Antwerp to Tournay. These two persons desired a company to be formed to carry this concession into effect. It was agreed that Messrs. Riche were to have the construction of the line; and in the early part of 1865 Gillon and Bertsoen and Messrs. Riche and the directors of the Ashbury Company met together and agreed to form a company (*société anonyme*) to work the concession. The arrangement was for the Ashbury Company to purchase the concession from Messrs. Gillon for £70,000, and to give the contract for its construction to Messrs. Riche, the company becoming in fact the contractor for the construction of the line. In this way the duty imposed by the Belgian Government on rails imported from England would, it was thought, be avoided.

Messrs. Riche began and for some time continued the works for the construction of the line; and for some time the Ashbury directors paid, in the name of their company, money to the *société anonyme* to which Messrs. Riche had become entitled. Difficulties about payment arose as the work went on, the English shareholders not adopting the views of their directors as to the speculation. Finally the company, dealing with the brothers Riche, repudiated the contract for constructing the line as one *ultra vires*. Messrs. Riche brought an action for damages for breach of contract. The case was heard on 25th November 1872 before the Court of Exchequer, when the judges differed in opinion, BARON BRAMWELL thinking that the verdict ought to be entered for the defendants and the other two learned BARONS MARTIN and CHANNELL being in favour of entering the verdict for the plaintiffs, the Messrs. Riche. It was so entered, and the judgment was accordingly taken to the Exchequer Chamber. Here there was again a difference of opinion, the six judges being equally divided, so that the judgment stood affirmed.

The case then came before the House of Lords.

THE LORD CHANCELLOR (LORD CAIRNS): . . . The purposes for which a company, established under the Act of 1862, is formed, are always to be looked for in the memorandum of association of the company. . . . Part of the argument at your Lordships' Bar was as to the meaning of two of the words used in this part of the memorandum—the words "general contractors." My Lords, as it appears to me, upon all ordinary principles of construction those words must be referred to the part of the sentence which immediately precedes them . . . and would indicate the making generally of contracts connected with the business of mechanical engineers—such contracts as mechanical engineers are in the habit of making, and are in their business required, or find it convenient, to make for the purpose of carrying on their business. . . .

My Lords, if the term "general contractors" were not to be interpreted as I have suggested, the consequence would be that it would stand absolutely without any limit of any kind. It would authorise the making, therefore, of contracts of any and every description, and the memorandum in place of specifying a particular kind of business would virtually point to the carrying on of business of any kind whatever, and would therefore be altogether unmeaning. . . .

My Lords, I agree entirely . . . with the conclusion at which [BARON BRAMWELL] arrived, that a contract of this kind was not within the words of the memorandum of association.

. . . I will ask your Lordships now to consider the effect of the Act of Parliament—the *Joint Stock Companies Act* of 1862—on this state of things . . . Your Lordships are well aware that this is the Act which put upon its present permanent footing the regulation of joint stock companies, and more especially of those joint stock companies which were to be authorised to trade with a limit to their liability.

The provisions under which that system of limiting liability was inaugurated, were provisions not merely, perhaps I might say not mainly, for the benefit of the shareholders for the time being in the company, but were enactments intended also to provide for the interests of two other very important bodies; in the first place, those who might become shareholders in succession to the persons who were shareholders for the time being; and secondly, the outside public, and more particularly those who might be creditors of companies of this kind. And I will ask your Lordships to observe . . . the marked and entire difference there is between the two documents which form the title deeds of companies of this description— I mean the memorandum of association on the one hand, and

the articles of association on the other hand. With regard to
the memorandum of association, your Lordships will find . . .
that that is, as it were, the charter, and defines the limitation
of the powers of a company to be established under the Act.
With regard to the articles of association, those articles play
a part subsidiary to the memorandum of association. They
accept the memorandum of association as the charter of incorporation of the company, and so accepting it, the articles
proceed to define the duties, the rights and the powers of the
governing body as between themselves and the company at
large, and the mode and form in which the business of the
company is to be carried on, and the mode and form in which
changes in the internal regulations of the company may from
time to time be made. With regard, therefore, to the memorandum of association, if you find anything which goes beyond
that memorandum, or is not warranted by it, the question will
arise whether that which is so done is *ultra vires*, not only of
the directors of the company, but of the company itself. With
regard to the articles of association, if you find anything which,
still keeping within the memorandum of association, is a
violation of the articles of association, or in excess of them,
the question will arise whether that is anything more than an
act *extra vires* the directors, but *intra vires* the company.

. . . [I]t is a mode of incorporation which contains in it
both that which is affirmative and that which is negative. It
states affirmatively the ambit and extent of vitality and power
which by law are given to the corporation, and it states, if it
is necessary so to state, negatively, that nothing shall be done
beyond that ambit, and that no attempt shall be made to use
the corporate life for any other purpose than that which is so
specified.

. . . Of the internal regulations of the company the members
of it are the absolute masters, and, provided they pursue the
course marked out in the Act, that is to say, holding a general
meeting and obtaining the consent of the shareholders, they
may alter those regulations from time to time; but all must be
done in the way of alteration subject to the conditions contained in the memorandum of association. That is to override

and overrule any provisions of the articles which may be at variance with it. The memorandum of association is, as it were, the area beyond which the action of the company cannot go; inside that area the shareholders may make such regulations for their own government as they think fit. . . .

In a case such as that which your Lordships have now to deal with, . . . [t]he question is not as to the legality of the contract; the question is as to the competency and power of the company to make the contract. Now, I am clearly of opinion that this contract was entirely, as I have said, beyond the objects in the memorandum of association. If so, it was thereby placed beyond the powers of the company to make the contract. If so, my Lords, it is not a question whether the contract ever was ratified or was not ratified. If it was a contract void at its beginning, it was void because the company could not make the contract. If every shareholder of the company had been in the room, and every shareholder of the company had said, "That is a contract which we desire to make, which we authorise the directors to make, to which we sanction the placing the seal of the company," the case would not have stood in any different position from that in which it stands now. The shareholders would thereby, by unanimous consent, have been attempting to do the very thing which, by the Act of Parliament, they were prohibited from doing.

But, my Lords, if the shareholders of this company could not *ab ante* have authorised a contract of this kind to be made, how could they subsequently sanction the contract after it had, in point of fact, been made. Mr. Benjamin [*leading counsel for Riche*] endeavoured to contend that when the shareholders had found that something had been done by the directors which ought not to have been done, they might be authorised to make the best they could of a difficulty into which they had thus been thrown, and therefrom might be deemed to possess power to sanction the contract being proceeded with. My Lords, I am unable to adopt that suggestion. It appears to me that it would be perfectly fatal to the whole scheme of legislation to which I have referred, if you were to hold that, in the first place, directors might do that which even the whole company could not do, and that then, the shareholders finding out what had been done, could sanction, subsequently, what they could not antecedently have authorised. ... This contract, in my judgment, could not have been ratified by the unanimous assent of the whole corporation. ...

My Lords, for the reasons which I have thus endeavoured to express, I submit to your Lordships and move your Lordships that the judgment in the present case should be reversed.

LORD CHELMSFORD: ... [T]he contract was *ultra vires*, and therefore not voidable merely, but absolutely void. ... It is exactly in the same condition as if no contract at all had been made, and therefore a ratification of it is not possible. If there had been an actual ratification, it could not have given life to a contract which had no existence in itself; but at the utmost it would have amounted to a sanction by the shareholders to the act of the directors, which, if given before the contract was entered into, would not have made it valid, as it does not relate to an object within the scope of the memorandum of association.

... If the contract entered into by the directors in the present case had been beyond the powers given to them by the articles of association, not being contrary to the objects contained in the memorandum of association, it might have been previously authorised or subsequently ratified by the whole body of shareholders. ...

I agree that the judgment of the Exchequer Chamber ought to be reversed.

LORD HATHERLEY: My Lords, I am of the same opinion. ...

LORD O'HAGAN: My Lords, I am clearly of the same opinion. The case ... depends for its result on the answers to three questions. First, were the contracts we have to deal with *ultra vires* of the directors? Secondly, if they were, was it possible to ratify them through the action of the shareholders? Thirdly, were they, in fact, so ratified? ...

On the first question, I think ... that the contracts in controversy were clearly *ultra vires* of the directors of the company. ... I cannot agree with the contention that the memorandum of association is not be be interpreted according to the ordinary rules of construction; and, so construed, it seems to me quite plain that the words "general contractors" cannot be held to indicate the possession, by the persons so described, of unlimited authority to enter into any sort of contract. . . .

The rule "*noscitur a sociis*" was never more clearly applicable, and its reasonable application was never more clearly necessary if we would give any practical effect to the memorandum in connection with the Act under which it was framed. That Act gave certain privileges and imposed certain conditions, and one of them was, that the memorandum of association should specify the objects of men seeking to trade with limited liability, for the manifest purpose that those objects should be clear and definite, and known precisely to all who might have dealings with the company. But if, in a case like this, it were competent for persons making and registering such a memorandum to segregate particular words, as "contractor" and "merchant," and insist that their generality should be confined not by the declared purposes of the formation of the company, not by the conterminous phraseology, nor even by the manifest reason of the thing, the purpose of the Act would be defeated, and the favour given by it would be enjoyed without fulfilment of the condition properly imposed for the public benefit. To hold that in such a case, and with such a memorandum, a company describing itself as the Railway Carriage and Iron Company should be at liberty to contract for the clothing of the army, or to trade in diamonds from Natal, would seem to me to nullify the statute alike in its policy and in its terms.

Having therefore no doubt that the action of this company was *ultra vires*, I confess I have as little that there was no valid ratification of the impeached contracts. Again, we must keep in mind the purpose of the legislation with which we are dealing. It was, as I have said, to give a privilege upon a condition; and the privilege was to be enjoyed upon the terms and with the limitations indicated in the memorandum of association. That memorandum, when put on record, was to be, for contractors, for creditors, and for all the world, a reliable description of the exact character, purposes, and powers of the company described in it. And the admission of an authority in shareholders to warrant anything inconsistent with that character, antagonistic to those purposes, and beyond those powers (and in this case it was so undoubtedly), would seem to encourage evasion of the statute to abrogate the condition, whilst continuing the privilege, and so to give the benefit without the burthen. . . . It is plain that if the ratification for which the defendant . . . contends, could validly affirm the contracts on which he relies, there is no amount of divergence from the original object of the company which might not have been approved. . . . And if this be so, I cannot think that a conclusion pregnant with consequences so very serious, can properly be sustained. It is not warranted by the statute, . . . and any such ratification if relied on, being in clear contravention of the purpose and the letter of the law, should in my opinion be held void and illegal.

This disposes of the second question and concludes the case, but it is right to say on the third point that, whatever may be the possibility or impossibility of legal ratification, I do not think any ratification was in fact accomplished by the shareholders. . . .

I am therefore, my Lords, clearly of opinion . . . that the plaintiffs . . . are right, and that the appeal should be allowed.

LORD SELBORNE: . . . [A] statutory corporation, created by Act of Parliament for a particular purpose, is limited, as to all its powers, by the purposes of its incorporation as defined in that Act. The present and all other companies incorporated by virtue of the *Companies Act* of 1862 appear to me to be statutory corporations within this principle. The memorandum of association is under that Act their fundamental . . . law; and they are incorporated only for the objects and purposes expressed in that memorandum. . . . I am unable to see any distinction for this purpose between statutory corporations under Railway Acts, and statutory corporations under the *Joint Stock Companies Act* of 1862. . . . I think that contracts for objects and purposes foreign to, or inconsistent with, the memorandum of association are *ultra vires* of the corporation itself. . . . This being so, it necessarily follows . . . that, where there could be no mandate, there cannot be any ratification; and that the assent of all the shareholders can make no difference when a stranger to the corporation is suing the company itself in its corporate name, upon a contract under the common seal. No agreement of shareholders can make that a contract of the corporation which the law says cannot and shall not be so. . . .

Re German Date Coffee Company, Ltd. (1882) 20 Ch. D. 169

When the main object or substratum of the company fails, it is just and equitable that the company should be wound up.

The company was registered on 16th February 1881 with a capital of £100,000 in shares of £1 each. By the memorandum of association the objects of the company were stated to be:

"1. To acquire and purchase, and to use, exercise, and vend certain inventions for manufacturing from dates a substitute for coffee, for which a patent has or will be granted by the Empire of Germany to Thomas Frederick Henley; and also to acquire and purchase any other patents or privileges which may be granted to the said Thomas Frederick Henley . . . by the said Empire of Germany.

7. To acquire by purchase or otherwise, and to use, exercise, and vend any other inventions for the above-mentioned or cognate purposes.

8. To import all descriptions of produce for the purposes of food, and the exporting of the same, and the selling and disposing thereof respectively; and to acquire by purchase, or to lease or hire any land and buildings, steam engines, etc., either in connection with the above-mentioned purposes or otherwise, for the purposes of the company. . . ."

The company issued a prospectus in which it was stated that the company was formed for the purpose of purchasing and working Henley's German patent at Frankfort, to manufacture a partial substitute for coffee from the date fruit. On the prospectus was printed what professed to be a copy of the articles of association, in which the first object of the company was stated to be "to acquire and purchase, and to use, exercise, and vend certain inventions for manufacturing from dates a substitute for coffee, for which a patent has been granted by the Empire of Germany to T. F. Henley."

At the time when the company was formed Henley had applied for a patent in the Empire of Germany for his inventions, but such patent was never granted. In consequence of this misrepresentation some of the shareholders surrendered their shares, amounting in number to about 27,000, and withdrew from the company.

On 12th October 1881 the company entered into an agreement with another company for the purchase of a Swedish patent in the same inventions. It had also expended £3,000 on a manufactory at Hamburg, where it was carrying on a very profitable business in making coffee from dates, though without any German patent.

On 30th January 1882 a petition was presented by two shareholders, one of whom was the holder of 100 shares and the other of ten shares, praying for the winding-up of the company on the ground that its objects had entirely failed.

KAY J.: In this case the petition is presented by two shareholders of the company, one of whom holds 100 shares and the other ten, for a winding-up of the company, and it is supported by a sufficient number of shareholders to make me quite sure that the application is a thoroughly bona fide one. On the other hand, it is opposed by the company and by a considerable body of shareholders. It does not appear that the company had passed any special resolution to wind up, but the clause upon which the application is made is the 5th sub-section of S.79 [*now S.222 (f) Companies Act, 1948*]. . . .

About the law which I have to apply to this case there really can now be no kind of doubt. . . . [I]f the whole substratum of the company is gone, it is within S.79 [*now S.222 (f)*] "just and equitable" that the company should be wound up. . . .

[W]here on the face of the memorandum you see there is a distinct purpose which is the foundation of the company, then, although the memorandum may contain other general words which include the doing of other objects, those general words must be read as being ancillary to that which the memorandum shows to be the main purpose, and if the main purpose fails and fails altogether, then . . . the substratum of the association fails.

. . . In this case the name of the company is the German Date Coffee Company, Limited, and the name seems to me to be rather material in determining what the real object and purpose of the company was. I cannot really doubt that the meaning of this memorandum is that the first purpose, the main object of the company, is to acquire an invention patented in Germany, and to work that invention.

. . . It is said the company have works in Hamburg, which they acquired when they hoped to obtain the German patent, and that they are carrying on some manufacture of date coffee, but of course not under a German patent, because they have not got the German patent. . . . Certainly, according to the memorandum of association of this company, the acquisition of a German patent and working under it was the main and principal object of the existence of this German Date Coffee Company. Any other thing in the memorandum, if there be any, seems to be subsidiary and auxiliary only to that object of working a German patent. Therefore it seems to me . . . that this is a case in which that which is, or rather was to be, the substratum, the main object of the company, to which all other objects are merely subsidiary or auxiliary, namely, the obtaining of a German patent for a particular invention, has completely failed. Therefore it seems to me that it is a case in which it would be beyond the purposes of this company to carry on the business which they now propose to carry on, and that I ought to regard the wish of the minority, who say we decline to be involved in the carrying on of a business which was really not contemplated by the memorandum of association at all.

But then it is said another patent has been obtained, namely, the Swedish patent. It seems almost ludicrous to imagine that the German Company, a company formed for the purpose of carrying on business in Germany, can say that it has taken any steps towards the accomplishment of that object by obtaining a Swedish patent for the same invention. I look to the memorandum of association again, and the only clause under which it is pretended to justify that acquisition of the Swedish patent . . . is the 7th clause. . . . The Swedish patent is not another invention but it is another patent for the same invention in another country, and I think it would be entirely *ultra vires* to acquire the Swedish patent. . . .

I therefore think the whole substratum of the company has failed . . . I therefore make the usual winding-up order. . . .

From this judgment the company appealed and the case accordingly came before the Court of Appeal.

JESSEL M.R.: . . . It appears to me the learned Judge in the Court below has arrived at the right conclusion, and that this appeal ought to be dismissed. . . .

BAGGALLAY L.J.: I am of the same opinion. . . .

It appears to me beyond all question that there is an impossibility of carrying on the business of the company, and I think that the order Mr. Justice KAY made is quite correct. . . .

LINDLEY L.J.: I am of the same opinion. . . . In construing this memorandum of association, and any other memorandum of association in which there are general words, care must be taken to construe those general words so as not to make them a trap for unwary people. General words construed literally may mean anything; but they must be taken in connection with what are shown by the context to be the dominant or main objects. It will not do under general words to turn a company for manufacturing one thing into a company for importing something else, however general the words are. Taking that as the governing principle, it appears to me plain beyond all reasonable dispute that the real object of this company . . . was to manufacture a substitute for coffee in Germany under a patent, valid according to German law. It is what the company was formed for, and all the rest is subordinate to that. The words are general, but that is the thing for which the people subscribe their money. . . .

It appears to me, therefore, that the judgment of Mr. Justice KAY was perfectly correct, and that the facts warrant the judgment he pronounced, and the application ought to be dismissed.

Cotman v. Brougham. [1918] A.C. 514

A company can do everything which it is expressly authorised to do by the objects clause of its memorandum of association. On the issue of whether a particular act is ultra vires, *it is not necessary to distinguish between powers and objects, though this may be necessary for the purpose of determining whether the company should be wound up for failure of its main object or substratum.*

In November 1910 the Essequibo Rubber and Tobacco Estates, Limited, which was incorporated under the *Companies* (*Consolidation*) *Act*, 1908, agreed to sub-underwrite 20,000 shares of 10s. each in the Anglo-Cuban Oil, Bitumen, and Asphalt Company, Limited (which was being promoted by the London and Mexican Exploitation Company, Limited), and received an allotment of 17,200 shares in the Anglo-Cuban Company. There remained due and owing from the Essequibo Company to the Anglo-Cuban Company the sum of £14,456 odd for unpaid calls in respect of these shares.

On 25th June 1912 an order was made for the winding up of the Essequibo Company, and the appellant Cotman was appointed liquidator thereof.

On 6th September 1912 the Essequibo Company transferred the 17,200 shares in the Anglo-Cuban Company to the London and Mexican Company, who failed to pay the amount remaining due thereon.

On 12th November 1912 an order was made for the winding up of the Anglo-Cuban Company.

The respondent Brougham, the official receiver, as liquidator of the Anglo-Cuban Company, settled the London and Mexican Company on the A list and the Essequibo Company on the B list of contributories in respect of the sum due on the 17,200 shares.

The appellant applied to vary the B list by excluding therefrom the Essequibo Company, upon the ground that upon the true construction of its memorandum of association the application for the shares was *ultra vires*.

In the High Court NEVILLE J. dismissed the application, and his order was affirmed by the Court of Appeal. Cotman then appealed to the House of Lords.

The facts and the material provisions of the memorandum of association sufficiently appear from the judgment of the Lord Chancellor.

LORD FINLAY L.C.: My Lords, the Essequibo Rubber and Tobacco Estates, Limited, is a company which was registered on April 6, 1910. The memorandum of association is one of a type which unfortunately has become common. . . . [I]n clause 3 [it] set out a vast variety of objects, and wound up with the following extraordinary provision:

> "The objects set forth in any sub-clause of this clause shall not, except when the context expressly so requires, be in any wise limited or restricted by reference to or inference from the terms of any other sub-clause, or by the name of the company. None of such sub-clauses or the objects therein specified or the powers thereby conferred shall be deemed subsidiary or auxiliary merely to the objects mentioned in the first sub-clause of this clause, but the company shall have full power to exercise all or any of the powers conferred by any part of this clause in any part of the world, and notwithstanding that the business, undertaking, property or acts proposed to be transacted, acquired, dealt with or performed do not fall within the objects of the first sub-clause."

WARRINGTON L.J. [*in the Court of Appeal*] expressed some doubt in his judgment in this case whether a memorandum setting out such a profusion of objects was a compliance with the Act, and it is possible that in some future case the question may arise on application for a mandamus if the registrar should refuse registration, taking the ground that the Act requires that the memorandum should be in such a form that the real objects of the company are made intelligible to the public.

In the present case no such question arises. The registrar accepted the memorandum of association and gave a certificate of incorporation, and that certificate is conclusive [*see now S.15, Companies Act, 1948*]. . . . All that the Courts can do is to construe the memorandum as it stands.

In the present case the question is whether it was *intra vires* of the Essequibo Rubber Company to enter into the transaction which has ended in the company's being put upon the B list of contributories to another company, the Anglo-Cuban Oil, Bitumen, and Asphalt Company, Limited. . . .

The question depends upon the interpretation to be put upon the 3rd clause of the memorandum of association. This clause has 30 heads dealing with a multitude of objects and powers. It is only necessary to refer to the 8th and 12th heads of that clause, in addition to the general provision at the end of the clause which I have already quoted:

"8. To promote, form, issue and be interested in any company or companies, either in Great Britain, British Guiana or elsewhere, and take, acquire, hold, transfer, sell, surrender or otherwise dispose of and deal in shares, stocks, bonds, obligations, debentures, debenture stock, scrip or securities in or of any such company, and to transfer to any such company any property of this company, and to subsidise or otherwise assist any such company; and in the event of any property sold to such company proving unsatisfactory, to make over to it, gratuitously or otherwise, any other property or rights, either in lieu of the property sold or transferred or otherwise."

"12. To buy or otherwise acquire in any way, and hold, sell or deal with or in any stocks, shares, securities or obligations of any Government, authority, corporation or company which may be considered capable of being profitably held or dealt in or with by the company."

I agree with both Courts below in thinking that it is impossible to say that the acquisition of these powers was *ultra vires* of the Essequibo Company.

It is well worthy of consideration whether, if it should appear that the law as it stands is not sufficient to cope with such abuses as are exemplified in the memorandum now in consideration, the *Companies Act* should not be amended so as to bring the practice into conformity with what must have been the intention of the framers of the Act. But the only question before us now is the construction of the memorandum as it stands, and in my opinion this appeal must be dismissed.

LORD ATKINSON: My Lords, I concur.

LORD PARKER OF WADDINGTON: My Lords, I agree. It may well be that the memorandum of association in the present case is not framed on the lines contemplated by the *Companies (Consolidation) Act*, 1908. This point would no doubt have been open to argument on proceedings for a mandamus had the registrar refused to accept it. Possibly, also, it might have been raised in proceedings on behalf of the Crown to cancel the company's certificate of incorporation. . . . It cannot, however, be raised in these proceedings, because the 17th section [*now S.15*] of the Act makes the certificate of incorporation conclusive evidence that *inter alia* the provisions of S.3 [*now S.2*] as to stating the objects of the company in its memorandum of association have been duly complied with. The only point, therefore, open to your Lordship's House is the true construction of such memorandum, and on this point I find myself in such complete agreement with the Lord Chancellor that I have little to add. Clause 3, sub-clauses 8 and 12, of the memorandum are in their terms amply wide enough to cover the transaction in question, and the concluding words of sub-clause 30 were clearly introduced to preclude the operation of these (among other) sub-clauses being cut down. . . .

My Lords, Mr. Whinney [*counsel for the appellant*] in his able argument suggested that, in considering whether a particular transaction was or was not *ultra vires* a company, regard ought to be had to the question whether at the date of the transaction the company could have been wound up on the ground that its substratum had failed. Upon consideration I cannot accept this suggestion. The question whether or not a company can be wound up for failure of substratum is a question of equity between a company and its shareholders. The question whether or not a transaction is *ultra vires* is a question of law between the company and a third party. The truth is that the statement of a company's objects in its memorandum is intended to serve a double purpose. In the first place it gives protection to subscribers, who learn from it the purposes to which their money can be applied. In the second place it gives protection to persons who deal with the company, and who can infer from it the extent of the company's powers. The narrower the objects expressed in the memorandum the less is the subscribers' risk, but the wider such objects the greater is the security of those who transact business with the company. Moreover, experience soon showed that persons who transact business with companies do not like having to depend on inference when the validity of a proposed transaction is in question. Even a power to borrow money could not always be safely inferred, much less such a power as that of underwriting shares in another company. Thus arose the practice of specifying powers as objects, a practice rendered possible by the fact that there is no statutory limit on the number of objects which may be specified. But even thus, a person proposing to deal with a company could not be absolutely safe, for powers specified as objects might be read as ancillary to and exercisable only for the purpose of attaining what might be held to be the company's main or paramount object, and on this construction no one could be quite certain whether the Court would not hold any proposed transaction to be *ultra vires*. At any rate, all the surrounding circumstances would require investigation. Fresh clauses were framed to meet this difficulty, and the result is the modern memorandum of association with its multifarious list of objects and powers specified as objects and its clauses designed to prevent any specified object being read as ancillary to some other object. For the purpose of determining whether a company's substratum be gone, it may be necessary to distinguish between power and object and to determine what is the main or paramount object of the company, but I do not think this is necessary where a transaction is impeached as *ultra vires*. A person who deals with a company is entitled to assume that a company can do everything which it is expressly authorised to do by its memorandum of association, and need not investigate the equities between the company and its shareholders.

The only other point which I need mention is the company's name. In construing a memorandum of association the name of the company, being part of the memorandum, can, of course, be considered. But where the operative part of the memorandum is clear and unambiguous, I do not think its obvious meaning ought to be cut down or enlarged by reference to the name of the company. It should be remembered that the name is susceptible of alteration, and it would be impossible to hold that such alteration could diminish or enlarge a company's powers. On the other hand, the name may be very material if it be necessary to consider what is the company's main or paramount object in order to see whether its substratum is gone.

I think the appeal should be dismissed. . . .

Lord Wrenbury: . . . One ground for winding up is that the Court is of opinion that it is just and equitable that the company should be wound up. *In re German Date Coffee Co.* is the leading authority for the proposition that when that which is called the substratum is gone a winding up order may be made. . . . The substratum is gone when the "main purpose" has become impossible. This class of cases recognises the existence of a "main purpose" in a memorandum which names a host of acts in the clause which has to state the objects.

My Lords, I cannot doubt that when the Act says that the memorandum must "state the objects" the meaning is that it must specify the objects, that it must delimit and identify the objects in such plain unambiguous manner as that the reader can identify the field of industry within which the corporate activities are to be confined.

The purpose, I apprehend, is twofold. The first is that the intending corporator who contemplates the investment of his capital shall know within what field it is to be put at risk. The second is that any one who shall deal with the company shall know without reasonable doubt whether the contractual relation into which he contemplates entering with the company is one relating to a matter within its corporate objects.

The objects of the company and the powers of the company to be exercised in effecting the objects are different things. Powers are not required to be, and ought not to be, specified in the memorandum. The Act intended that the company, if it be a trading company, should by its memorandum define the trade, not that it should specify the various acts which it should be within the power of the company to do in carrying on the trade. . . .

There has grown up a pernicious practice of registering memoranda of association which, under the clause relating to objects, contain paragraph after paragraph not specifying or delimiting the proposed trade or purpose, but confusing power with purpose and indicating every class of act which the corporation is to have power to do. . . . It has arrived now at a point at which the fact is that the function of the memorandum is taken to be, not to specify, not to disclose, but to bury beneath a mass of words the real object or objects of the company with the intent that every conceivable form of activity shall be found included somewhere within its terms. The present is the very worst case of the kind that I have seen. Such a memorandum is not, I think, a compliance with the Act. The Act throws upon the registrar a great responsibility when it provides, as it does, that his certificate of incorporation "shall be conclusive evidence that all the requirements of this Act in respect of registration and of matters precedent and incidental thereto have been complied with." Before registering a memorandum of association the registrar ought to consider whether the requirements of the Act have been complied with and to refuse registration if he conceives that they have not, bearing in mind that if he does not take that course he may put the Court in the position in which your Lordships find yourselves in the present case—a position in which you must assume that all requirements in respect of matters precedent and incidental to registration have been complied with and confine yourselves to the construction of the document. . . .

My Lords, I turn to consider the transaction in question in this case, and to see whether it falls within the company's objects upon a true construction of the memorandum of association, assuming, as I am bound to do, that that is a valid instrument. . . .

The construction of the instrument does not admit of reasonable doubt. Clause 3, sub-clauses 8 and 12, are in terms so wide that an obligation in a contingent event to take up shares falls within them. The language of clause 3, sub-clause 30, is such that I cannot say that such a transaction was *ultra vires*, because it was not ancillary to or connected with or in furtherance of something which I find elsewhere in the company's memorandum to have been "its business." Upon the narrow question, upon which alone it is unfortunately within the competence of this House to determine, I think the decision below was right. It follows that this appeal must be dismissed. . . .

Bell Houses Ltd. *v.* City Wall Properties Ltd. [1966] 1 Q.B. 207; 2 Q.B. 656

Where the objects clause of a company's memorandum of association provides that the company may carry on such business as, in the opinion of the board of directors, can be advantageously carried on in connection with its general business, then the bona fide *belief of the directors that an activity is advantageous is sufficient to render it* intra vires.

The plaintiff company, Bell Houses, Ltd., and the defendant company, City Wall Properties, Ltd., were both property developers. The plaintiffs' principal business was that of developing housing estates. The relevant sub-clauses of the objects clause of their memorandum of association were as follows:

"(*a*) To carry on the trade or business of general, civil and engineering contractors and in particular but with-

out prejudice to the generality of the foregoing to construct, alter, enlarge, erect and maintain either by the
company or other parties, sewers, roads, streets, railways, sidings, tramways, electricity works, bridges,
shops, reservoirs, factories . . . and all other works,
erections, plant, machinery and things of any description whatsoever either upon land acquired by the company or upon other land and generally.

(*b*) To acquire by purchase, exchange or otherwise . . .
any lands, tenements and premises . . .

(*c*) To carry on any other trade or business whatsoever which can, in the opinion of the board of directors,
be advantageously carried on by the company in connection with or as ancillary to any of the above businesses or the general business of the company.

(*q*) To . . . turn to account, deal with or dispose of
. . . any of the property and assets . . . of the company.

(*u*) To do all such other things as are incidental or
conducive to the above objects or any of them."

The plaintiffs brought an action claiming £20,000 as a
procuration fee due from the defendants pursuant to an
alleged contract made between the parties between 5th
February and 13th March 1962. Under the contract the
plaintiffs claimed to be entitled to such fee upon the introduction by them to the defendants of a financier with whom
the defendants should be able to enter into an agreement
for the provision to them of credit for property development in the sum of £1,000,000. They claimed that they had
introduced such a financier, the Nestlé's Pension Trust,
Ltd., that the defendants were able to enter into such an
agreement and that the procuration fee was therefore due.
They claimed, in the alternative, that if they were not entitled to the fee until the defendants actually entered into
an agreement with the Trust, then the defendants were in
breach of an implied term of the contract that they would
do nothing to prevent the plaintiffs from becoming entitled
to the fee; and they claimed damages of £20,000 under
this head. The defendants admitted that the plaintiffs
introduced the Trust to them but denied that the parties
ever made the contract sued upon; alternatively, they
pleaded that if there was such a contract, they had never

been able to enter into an agreement with the Trust upon the terms set out in the contract.

At the hearing of the action the defendants applied for leave to amend their defence to plead that the agreement alleged by the plaintiffs was *ultra vires* the plaintiffs and void, in that the plaintiffs, under their memorandum of association, had no power to enter into such an agreement. The amendment having been allowed, the question was tried, by consent, as a preliminary issue.

MOCATTA J.: . . . Finally, three separate points arose for decision. First, can a defendant when sued upon a contract by a company, take the point that that contract is *ultra vires* the company; secondly, if he can do so when the contract is executory, can he do so or is the point relevant when the contract has been executed so far as the company's obligations are concerned; thirdly, assuming that the answers to the first two questions are in the affirmative, was this contract *ultra vires* the plaintiffs?

. . . I can find no reason in principle to support the proposition that a defendant, when sued upon a contract, is debarred from pleading that that contract is and always was void and a nullity in the eyes of the law. . . .

The law as to the enforceability by an infant of contracts not for necessaries is notoriously uncertain, and arguments by analogy from one uncertain branch of the law are of little assistance in dealing with another. Moreover, there may be good but special reasons for reading "absolutely void" in the Infants Relief Act as meaning "void at the option of the infant" by reason of the context in which those words are used— namely, an Act for the relief of infants and not for the relief of traders, and in the previous common law on the subject. I do not consider the law in relation to contracts by infants of any assistance . . . .

In my judgment, a defendant, when sued on a contract by a company, is entitled to take the point by way of defence that the contract was *ultra vires* the company. In short, my reasons are that any other conclusion would be inconsistent with the reasoning in the *Ashbury Railway* case in that the contract is void and in the eyes of the law non-existent, that to hold a defendant liable under a non-existent contract would be to act contrary to all principle. . . . and that the authorities . . . point strongly the other way.

As to the second point . . . [i]n my judgment, there is no ground in principle for distinguishing between executory and executed contracts. . . . If the plaintiff company that has made an *ultra vires* contract has to rely upon the terms of that contract in order to succeed in its action, it must in my judgment fail, since the contract was void *ab initio* and the defendant is entitled to raise the point. . . .

That, however, does not necessarily in every case exhaust such a company's remedies. In an appropriate case that company may be able to obtain relief *quasi-ex contractu* in an action for money had and received. . . . In other cases relief may be obtained on a *quantum meruit* basis: see the decision of the Court of Appeal in *Craven Ellis v. Canons Ltd.* . . .

There is, however, no claim put forward on a quasi-contractual basis in the present action, nor must anything I say in this judgment be taken as indicating any view on the question whether any such claim could in the circumstances of this case succeed. On this preliminary issue I can deal only with the claims raised on the pleadings before me. On those pleadings, which are based exclusively on the alleged contract between the parties, the defendants are in my judgment entitled to take the point that the contract sued upon, whether executory or executed, was *ultra vires* the plaintiffs, and, if that be right, the claims must fail.

I now, therefore, turn to the third point. Was the contract sued upon *ultra vires* the plaintiffs? Mr. Wilmers [*leading counsel for the defendants*] submitted that the plaintiffs could derive little, if any, more assistance from sub-clause (*c*) than from sub-clause (*u*). Certainly he is right that the mere fact that the board of directors of a company may be of the opinion that an activity can be advantageously carried on by the company, even if the opinion be well founded, will not *per se* make that activity *intra vires*. . . .

It is clear law that even without express words in the mem-

orandum of association, charter or statute, a company . . . has
certain rights in law to exceed its express objects. . . . It is not
easy to see, therefore, how the words in sub-clauses (c) or (u)
add anything to what the law would imply without them. . . .

In my judgment, the mere fact that a contract is entered into
to make money out of knowledge acquired in the course of
carrying on an authorised business does not constitute such a
contract one made in connection with such business. The
carrying on of any business is bound to bring some other
knowledge to a company in the persons of its directors and
staff who carry it on. As time goes on the field of such knowledge may and often does become progressively wider. If it were
held that a company could exploit such knowledge to its
profit, notwithstanding that such exploitation did not come
within its express objects, merely on the ground that it was "in
connection with" such objects, the *ultra vires* doctrine as laid
down in the *Ashbury Railway* case would be rendered nugatory.
In such a case the right course for a company to pursue is to
incorporate a subsidiary company with objects stated in its
memorandum of association expressly authorising the exploitation—a course very frequently taken—or alter, if it can,
its own memorandum of association as provided by the
Companies Act.

I am satisfied that the contract sued upon cannot be brought
within either sub-clause (c) or sub-clause (u). . . . I decide the
preliminary issue in favour of the defendants and hold that
the contract sued upon was *ultra vires* the plaintiffs.

> From this decision the plaintiffs appealed on the grounds
> that the alleged contract was not *ultra vires* their company;
> alternatively that the defence of *ultra vires* was not available
> to the defendants.

In the Court of Appeal:

SELLERS L.J.: . . . I had the opportunity and the advantage of
reading the judgment of DANCKWERTS L.J. . . . I agree with
his judgment entirely. . . .

DANCKWERTS L.J.: . . . The plaintiff company is a private
company limited by shares and its principal business in fact is

the development of housing estates. The chairman of the directors, Randal Mulcaster Bell, controls the company and its administration. The other directors were his wife and a brother of his, but the brother has left the company now. All effective dealings of the company were really done by Bell, and that was officially authorised by a resolution passed on June 10, 1955, at a meeting of the board of directors, whereby it was resolved that the administration of the company generally and with regard to sales be left for the chairman to deal with together with his principal sales agent. The directors had power to delegate in this way by virtue of article 102 of Table A in Schedule I to the *Companies Act*, 1948, which was incorporated in the company's articles. . . . It was argued on behalf of the defendants that the dealings with them were conducted by the chairman of the plaintiff company on his own behalf and not on behalf of the plaintiff company, so that the company had no interest in the matter. This argument seems to me to be completely untenable. There is no evidence that the chairman ever claimed the benefit of the £20,000 for himself. He controlled the plaintiff company and administered it completely, and it is evident that he used the company for the purposes of the business. He was authorised by the resolution of the board of directors to conduct the administration of the company's business on behalf of the board, and it is impossible to suppose that he was distinguishing business negotiations carried out by him from the business of the company. Letters written by him in the course of this transaction were always written on the company's notepaper, and though most of his letters were signed by his Christian name, that was in accordance with the terms on which these business men were, and some of the letters . . . were signed by him as "chairman." Finally, the action has been brought in the name of the plaintiff company. There is no doubt that if there was a contract to pay commission, the contract was made with the plaintiff company, through the chairman.

. . . In order to give a more convincing air to their arguments, counsel for the defendants have treated the transaction which is under discussion as though it was a deliberate embarking by the plaintiff company on a serious new business of what counsel called "mortgage broking." In my opinion this is a false approach. From the company's point of view it was not the opening of a new class of business intended to be carried on by it on any serious scale. It was simply an isolated transaction which was intended to assist the defendants, . . . and to gain goodwill with not only the defendants but also with the trust, who were thereby to be enabled to carry out a profitable financial transaction. . . . The transaction between the plaintiff company and the defendants is, of course, none the less a business transaction, even though larded with lunches and Christian names.

Clause 3 of the plaintiff company's memorandum of association contains the usual large number of paragraphs, identified by the letters (a) to (u). It does not contain the provision sometimes inserted that all the paragraphs are independent objects. . . . By clause 5 the share capital of the company is £2,100, of which £2,000 consists of preference shares, which makes it obvious that the operations of the company must be financed by borrowing. . . .

In my view, this piece of business arose "in connection with" the general business of the company and "as ancillary" to the general business of the company, which appears to be described in paragraphs (a) and (b) of clause 3 of the memorandum. In the course of his administration of the company and its business or businesses, the chairman had to find suitable sites for the development of housing estates and sources from which advances could be obtained for the purpose of financing the plaintiff company's operations. The knowledge thus acquired by him was a valuable asset and was not his personal property but was the property of the company.

In my opinion, the provisions of clause 3 (q) are also applicable. . . . It seems to me that in communicating to the defendants information as to sources of finance, the chairman, in the administration of the company, was turning to account, dealing with and disposing of an asset of the company as authorised by this sub-clause.

Finally, there is the general provision in clause 3 (u) of the company's memorandum, but it does not seem to be necessary for the company to rely upon this sub-clause in the present case. . . .

It is also necessary to consider the effect of the words in clause 3 (c) of the memorandum, "in the opinion of the board of directors." I think it is plain that these words qualify the whole of that sub-clause. . . . MOCATTA J. . . . went so far as to say that the mere fact that the board of directors of a company may be of opinion that an activity can be advantageously carried on by the company, even if the opinion be well founded, will not *per se* make that activity *intra vires*. With all respect to the judge, if he is meaning to refer to the opinion required by the sub-clause, he is not quoting it correctly. The requirement of the sub-clause is that in the opinion of the board of directors the other trade or business can be advantageously carried on by the company in connection with or as ancillary to any of the above businesses or the general business of the company. If the judge means that the opinion of the directors has no effect at all, I am afraid that I cannot agree with him. On the balance of the authorities it would appear that the opinion of the directors, if *bona fide*, can dispose of the matter. And why should it not decide the matter? The shareholders subscribe their money on the basis of the memorandum of association and if that confers the power on directors to decide whether in their opinion it is proper to undertake particular business in the circumstances specified, why should not their decision be binding? The shareholders by taking shares on the terms of the memorandum have agreed to it.

. . . [I]n my opinion, . . . a clause on the lines of sub-clause 3 (c) in the present case is able to make the *bona fida* opinion of the directors sufficient to decide whether an activity of the company is *intra vires*. There was, in the present case, no resolution of the board of directors expressing the opinion of the board. But I do not think that such a resolution was necessary and I do not understand that it was contended that a resolution was necessary. In fact, the chairman managed the operation of the company and exercised by delegation the functions of the board of directors, as he was entitled to do, by virtue of the resolution of the board of directors of June 10, 1955. It was his opinion which decided whether certain business activities should be carried out on behalf of the plaintiff company.

His opinion is evident from what he did and from his evidence. Further, the facts support his opinion. For the reasons which I have mentioned earlier in this judgment, this transaction was justified and was within the powers of the company under the terms of clause 3 (*c*). The position is also assisted by the terms of sub-clauses (*q*) and (*u*). I feel no doubt that the transaction with the defendants was within the powers of the company and was not *ultra vires*.

The result is that the question whether a defence of *ultra vires* could be raised by the defendants does not arise and we have not thought it necessary to have it argued.

In my opinion, the appeal should be allowed, and the preliminary point decided in the plaintiff company's favour.

SALMON L.J.: . . . Sub-clause (*c*) is of great importance. . . . As a matter of pure construction, the meaning of these words seems to me to be obvious. An object of the plaintiff company is to carry on any business which the directors genuinely believe can be carried on advantageously in connection with or as ancillary to the general business of the company. It may be that the directors take the wrong view and in fact the business in question cannot be carried on as the directors believe. But it matters not how mistaken the directors may be. Providing they form their view honestly, the business is within the plaintiff company's objects and powers. . . .

Accordingly, I come to the conclusion . . . that under clause 3 (*c*) of the plaintiff company's memorandum of association the contract here sued upon was *intra vires* if it constituted carrying on business which in the opinion of the plaintiffs' board of directors could be advantageously carried on by the plaintiffs in connection with or as ancillary to their general business. . . . It follows that, in my view, the contract was clearly *intra vires* subclause (*c*).

Moreover, in my judgment, the plaintiff company is also entitled to succeed under sub-clause (*u*) of clause 3, for the making of the contract was in fact as well as in the chairman's opinion "incidental and conducive" to the plaintiffs' objects of carrying-on the business of building and land development. . . .

I think that the contract was also *intra vires* sub-clause (*q*) of clause 3 of the memorandum of association. . . . For these reasons, I have come to the conclusion that the contract is clearly covered by sub-clauses (*c*), (*q*) and (*u*) of clause 3 of the memorandum and is, accordingly, *intra vires*.

Having regard to the view I have formed on this part of the case, it is unnecessary to consider the interesting, important and difficult question which would arise were the contract *ultra vires*, namely, whether, the plaintiff company having fully performed its part under the contract and the defendants having obtained all the benefits under the contract, the defendants could successfully take the point that the contract was *ultra vires* the plaintiff company and so avoid payment. It seems strange that third parties could take advantage of a doctrine, manifestly for the protection of the shareholders, in order to deprive the company of money which in justice should be paid to it by the third parties. . . . The judge in effect came to the conclusion that the reasoning in *Ashbury Railway Carriage & Iron Co. Ltd.* v. *Riche* led to this strange result. I express no opinion on this point and leave it to be decided when it arises, for we have heard no argument upon it. I agree that this appeal should be allowed.

2. The Doctrine of *Ultra Vires* Applied to Borrowing Powers

Re David Payne & Co., Ltd. [1904] 2 Ch. 608

Where a company has a general power to borrow money for the purposes of its business, a lender is not bound to inquire into the purposes for which the money is intended to be applied, and the misapplication of the money by the company does not avoid the loan unless the lender knows of the intention to misapply it.

Mr. Kolckmann, who was a director of the Exploring

Land and Minerals Co., Ltd. and was also interested in David Payne & Co., Ltd., had ascertained in his private capacity that David Payne & Co., Ltd. proposed to borrow a sum of money for a purpose outside the scope of its business. He induced the Exploring Land and Minerals Co. Ltd. to advance the money on the security of a debenture of David Payne & Co., Ltd. who applied the money in the manner proposed. David Payne & Co., Ltd. had a general power of borrowing under its memorandum and articles of association for the purposes of its business. No other director of the Exploring Land and Minerals Co., Ltd. knew how the money was intended to be applied.

In the winding up of David Payne & Co., Ltd. the liquidator made an application for a declaration that the debenture in question issued to the Exploring Land and Minerals Co., Ltd. was *ultra vires* and void.

BUCKLEY J.: In my view, the introduction into any memorandum of association of a power to borrow is, generally speaking, unnecessary. Every trading company has power to borrow for the purposes of its business, and the introduction of this clause is only to express in words what would otherwise be the law. A limitation of the borrowing to borrowing for the purposes of the company's business is necessary, of course. A corporation cannot do anything except for the purposes of its business, borrowing or anything else; everything else is beyond its power, and is *ultra vires*. So that the words "for the purposes of the company's business" are a mere expression of that which would be involved if there were no such words. If you found a power to borrow which would arise only on the happening of a particular event, then I think it would lie upon the lender to say, "I cannot lend to you until you can satisfy me that the condition has been complied with;" but where the power is merely a general power to borrow, limited only, as it must be, for the purposes of the company's business, I think the matter is to be treated in this way—that the lender cannot investigate what the borrower is going to do with the money. . . . If this borrowing was made, as it appears to me at present it was made, for a purpose illegitimate so far as the borrowing company was concerned, that may very well be a matter on which rights may arise as between the shareholders and the directors of that company. It may have been a wrongful act on the part of the directors. But I do not think that a person who lends to the company is by any words such as these required to investigate whether the money borrowed is borrowed for a proper purpose or an improper purpose. The borrowing being effected, and the money passing to the company, the subsequent application of the money is a matter in which the directors may have acted wrongly; but that does not affect the principal act, which is the borrowing of the money.

For these reasons it seems to me the Exploring Land and Minerals Company, who have paid this money and taken this debenture without notice that the money was going to be applied as it was, are not affected by anything arising in regard to that. I therefore think that they are entitled to hold the debenture. . . .

From this decision of BUCKLEY J. the liquidator appealed, and the case accordingly came before the Court of Appeal.

VAUGHAN WILLIAMS L.J.: I think that the decision of BUCKLEY J. in this case was quite right, and that this appeal must be dismissed. . . .

ROMER L.J.: . . . The only other question is as to imputed notice. I take it that there was a transaction between the Exploring Land and Minerals Company and David Payne & Company of this kind. The first company lent £6,000 secured by a debenture of the second company. Now that transaction was *intra vires* the second company. But there was some evidence to show that it was intended by some of the directors of the second company to apply the money for purposes not authorised and altogether improper *qua* the second company. Now, one director of the first company knew how that money was going to be applied. He acquired that knowledge through some conversation which he had with some people in his private capacity before that transaction was carried out by the lending company. The question is whether, inasmuch as that director took part on behalf of his company in authorising the lending of the money and the acquisition of the debenture and assisted in carrying out that transaction, the knowledge of that director so acquired is to be considered the knowledge of the lending company. Is that knowledge as a matter of law to be imputed to the lending company? In my opinion no such notice can be imputed at law. I take it that in such a transaction the lending company was not bound to inquire as to the application of the money at all by the borrowing company. That being so, it appears to me that knowledge independently acquired by a director in his personal capacity in respect to a matter which was irrelevant so far as concerned the lending company is knowledge which cannot be imputed to the company, for it was knowledge of something which really did not concern the lending company as a matter of law. Therefore, you cannot imply a duty on the part of the director to have told these facts to the lending company, or a duty on the part of the lending company to have inquired into that question. The lending company not having any reason to know how the money was to be applied apart from the knowledge of the director, it would have been wholly improper for the agent of that company to have inquired into the question of the application of the money. That being so, there was no legal duty on the director to impart his knowledge, nor any duty on the part of the company to have acquired the knowledge. Apart from the knowledge of the director, no knowledge in fact was proved against the lending company. I therefore think that the appeal fails.

COZENS HARDY L.J.: I am of the same opinion. . . .

Sinclair v. Brougham. [1914] A.C. 398

A power to borrow must be limited to borrowing for the proper objects of the company, and the lenders are not entitled to recover moneys paid by them on an ultra vires *contract of loan on the footing of money had and received by the company to their use. Their sole remedy is a claim to follow and recover the moneys lent where these are still identifiable. Where specific tracing is no longer possible, assets remaining after payment of*

*the outside creditors must be taken to represent in part moneys
which the lenders can follow, as having been invalidly borrowed,
and in part moneys which the company can follow, as having
been wrongfully employed by its agents, and ought to be distributed* pari passu *between the lenders and the shareholders
according to the amounts respectively credited to them in the
books of the company at the commencement of the winding up.*

The Birkbeck Permanent Benefit Building Society was
formed in 1851 under the *Building Societies Act*, 1836, its
object being to enable the members to raise a fund out of
which they might individually be enabled to buy or build
houses. There were two classes of shareholders: those to
whom loans were granted (advanced shareholders), and
those who were mere investors (unadvanced shareholders).

The society was empowered by its rules to borrow to an
unlimited extent, and it started and developed a banking
business. In 1911 it was ordered to be wound up and questions of priority arose between the outside creditors, the
unadvanced shareholders, and the bank customers on
current and deposit account (for convenience called the
depositors).

The assets were insufficient for payment of all the claimants in full, but were more than sufficient for payment of
the outside creditors (who were subsequently paid by
arrangement) and the shareholders. The liquidator took
out a summons for directions against representatives of
the several classes of claimants in order to determine the
validity of the claim of the depositors against the assets.

VISCOUNT HALDANE L.C. [LORD ATKINSON *concurring*]: . . .
I suppose to consider in the first place the question whether
an action for money had and received would have lain against
the society on the footing that although its conduct in receiving the depositors' money was *ultra vires*, it had become
improperly . . . enriched thereby, so that the amount received was money held to the depositors' use and recoverable as
a debt, independently of any right to trace and follow.

. . . If it be outside the power of a statutory society to enter
into the relation of debtor and creditor in a particular transaction, the only possible remedy for the person who has paid

the money would on principle appear to be one *in rem* and not *in personam*, a claim to follow and recover specifically any money which could be earmarked as never having ceased to be his property. To hold that a remedy will lie *in personam* against a statutory society, which . . . cannot in the case in question have become a debtor or entered into any contract for repayment, is to strike at the root of the doctrine of *ultra vires* as established in the jurisprudence of this country. That doctrine belongs to substantive law, and cannot be made different by any choice of form of procedure.

It is, therefore, binding both at law and in equity. In the jurisprudence of England the doctrine of *ultra vires* must now be treated as established in a stringent form. . . . This is a principle which it appears to me must today be taken as a governing one, not only at law but in equity. I think it excludes from the law of England any claim *in personam* based even on the circumstance that the defendant has been improperly enriched at the expense of the plaintiff by a transaction which is *ultra vires*. . . . Notwithstanding the wide scope of the remedy, . . . I think that it must be taken to have been given only . . . where the law could consistently impute to the defendant at least the fiction of a promise. And it appears to me that as matter of principle the law of England cannot now . . . impute the fiction of such a promise where it would have been *ultra vires* to give it. The fiction becomes . . . inapplicable where substantive law, as distinguished from that of procedure, makes the defendant incapable of undertaking contractual liability. For to impute a fictitious promise is simply to presume the existence of a state of facts, and the presumption can give rise to no higher right than would result if the facts were actual.

. . . It follows that the depositors in the present case will not succeed unless they are able to trace their money into the hands of the society or its agents as actually existing assets. . . . Their claim cannot be *in personam* and must be *in rem*, a claim to follow and recover property with which, in equity at all events, they had never really parted.

. . . The difficulty of establishing a title *in rem* in this case arises from the apparent difficulty of following money. In most cases money cannot be followed. When sovereigns or banknotes are paid over as currency, so far as the payer is concerned, they cease *ipso facto* to be the subjects of specific title as chattels. If a sovereign or banknote be offered in payment it is, under ordinary circumstances, no part of the duty of the person receiving it to inquire into title. The reason of this is that chattels of such a kind form part of what the law recognises as currency, and treats as passing from hand to hand in point, not merely of possession, but of property. It would cause great inconvenience to commerce if in this class of chattel an exception were not made to the general requirement of the law as to title.

But the exception is not extended beyond the limits which necessity imposes. If money in a bag is stolen, and can be identified in the form in which it was stolen, it can be recovered *in specie*. Even if it has been expended by the person who has wrongfully taken it in purchasing some particular asset, that asset, if capable of being earmarked as purchased with the money, can be claimed by the true owner of the money. This is a principle not merely of equity, but of the common law. It is explained in the judgment of LORD ELLENBOROUGH in *Taylor* v. *Plumer*, who pointed out that there was no reason why the doctrine that money could not be followed should apply to circumstances in which a broker had wrongfully invested money of his principal in purchasing securities into which it could be traced. The reason of this is plain. The broker could not in these circumstances set up as against his principal the rule which applies to what has been paid over as currency, that ordinarily transfer of possession is transfer of property. So long as the money which the principal has handed to his agent to be applied specifically, and not on a debtor and creditor account, can be traced into what has been procured with it, the principal can, . . . affirming the proceeding of the broker, claim that his money is invested in a specific thing, which is his. But Lord Ellenborough laid down, as a limit to this proposition, that if the money had become incapable of being traced, as, for instance, when it had been paid into the broker's general account with his banker, the principal had no remedy excepting to prove as a creditor for money had and received. The explanation was, of course, that a relation of debtor and creditor had arisen between the banker and his client, the broker, which precluded the notion of following the money.

That seems to be, so far as the doctrine of the common law is concerned, the limit to which the exception to the rule about currency was carried; whether the case be that of a thief or of a fraudulent broker, or of money paid under mistake of fact, you can, even at law, follow, but only so long as the relation of debtor and creditor has not superseded the right *in rem*. . . .

My Lords, it is, in my opinion, impossible to confine the right at law to follow to cases where there was a fiduciary relationship. The principle appears to me to cover all cases where the property in the money has not passed, and the money itself can be earmarked in the hands of the person who has wrongfully obtained it. A person standing in a fiduciary relation may be in this position, but it is not because of his trust or fiduciary duty. The common law . . . did not take cognisance of such duties. It looked simply to the question whether the property had passed, and if it had not, for instance, where no relationship of debtor and creditor had intervened, the money could be followed, notwithstanding its normal character of currency, provided it could be earmarked or traced into assets acquired with it. And this appears to me to be . . . as true of money paid under mistake of fact or on an *ultra vires* contract, under which no property could pass or relation of debtor be constituted, as it is true in the case of a broker or bailee.

But while the common law gave the remedy I have stated, it gave no remedy when the money had been paid by the wrongdoer into his account with his banker, who simply owed him a debt, so that no money was or could be . . . earmarked. Here equity, which had so far exercised a concurrent jurisdiction based upon trust, gave a further remedy. The Court of Chancery could and would declare, even as against the general creditors of the wrongdoer, that there was what it called a charge on the banker's debt to the person whose money had been paid into the latter's bank account in favour of the person whose money it really was. . . . This equity was not confined to cases of trust in the strict sense, but applied at all events to every case where there was a fiduciary relationship. It was, as I think, merely an additional right, which could be enforced by the Court of Chancery in the exercise of its auxiliary jurisdiction, wherever money was held to belong in equity to the plaintiff. If so, . . . I see no reason why the remedy . . . of declaring a charge on the investment in a debt due from bankers on balance, or on any mass of money or securities with which the plaintiff's money had been mixed, should not apply in the case of a transaction that is *ultra vires*. The property was never converted into a debt, in equity at all events, and there has been throughout a resulting trust, not of an active character, but sufficient, in my opinion, to bring the transaction within the general principle.

. . . As to the part of the assets which was acquired with money paid by the shareholders, the case appears to me to be free from difficulty. The money paid to the society by the shareholders was paid as the consideration for the shares which were issued to them. That money, therefore, beyond question become the money of the society. A large part of it has probably been applied *ultra vires* in the acquisition of the assets of the banking business. These assets can accordingly be claimed only by the society itself as belonging to it, and the shareholders have no direct title to them.

The total mass of assets which the liquidator has to distribute thus represents in part money which the depositors are entitled to follow and in part money which the society is entitled to follow. . . . The depositors can, in my opinion, only claim the depreciated assets which represent their money, and nothing more. It follows that the principle to be adopted in the distribution must be apportionment on the footing that depreciation and loss are to be borne *pro rata*. I am, of course, assuming in saying this that specific tracing is not now possible.

What is there must be apportioned accordingly among those whose money it represents, and the question of how the apportionment should be made is one of fact. . . . I think that this direction should be that . . . he [*the liquidator*] should apportion the entirety of the remaining assets between the depositors and the shareholders in proportion to the amounts paid by the depositors and the shareholders respectively. In this way I am of opinion that the nearest approach practicable to substantial justice will be done.

LORD DUNEDIN: . . . It is the case that the common law . . . works by means of a fiction which becomes inapplicable when the money has been received under an *ultra vires* contract. All, therefore, that is left to it is to vindicate in *forma specifica*, and its forms of action fail when the thing can no longer be identified. . . . I think [equity] can always . . . help the common law by tracing, and can say that if the proceeds of property can be shown to be . . . a superfluity in the person of the recipient, then it will hold that that property is traced just as surely as if it was still in the original form. To do this is to give full effect to the doctrine of *ultra vires*—for the party receiving is not ordered to pay as a debt the equivalent of what he originally got, but ordered merely to surrender what he still has as a superfluity, an enrichment which, but for the original reception of the money, he would have been without. . . . Now that the society, in the present case, has got a superfluity is obvious. The assets, shrunk as they are owing to the fall in the value of investments, are still far beyond all moneys contributed by the shareholders. But what is the measure of the superfluity? The outside creditors here were actually paid, because their claims were inconsiderable. In my judgment, they were rightly paid, . . . and had they not been, they would stand, after expenses of the liquidation, as first in the ranking. . . . Now, what is the position of the shareholders? I take it to be clear that the shareholders are not creditors of the society, but are merely the persons who are entitled on a winding up to share the assets of the society among them . . .

The position, therefore, comes to this. The shareholders are entitled to share among them the proper assets of the society.

But they are not entitled to be made rich at the expense of the depositors, by swelling the assets of the society by means of the proceeds of moneys which they themselves never contributed. There is a mixed mass of assets as to the precise composition of which as to source it is impossible to pronounce. Had the assets never shrunk there would be enough to pay both in full. But they have shrunk, and someone must bear the loss. . . . What has happened is truly this. The directors of the society have taken the moneys of the shareholders which they had a right to receive, and the moneys of the depositors which they had not, and mixed them so that they cannot be discriminated from each other, and have put them, so to speak, in the society's strong-box, where the mixed mass is found by the liquidator. . . . There being no direct evidence, the only equitable means is to let each party bear the shrinkage proportionately to the amount originally contributed, and this is the judgment of my noble and learned friend on the woolsack, in which I concur.

I wish to remark, in conclusion, that it seems to me that this line of reasoning gives full effect to the doctrine of *ultra vires*. . . . To go further . . . is, I think, to run the doctrine mad. It was a doctrine which was introduced in order to let societies keep their own money, not to appropriate other people's.

LORD PARKER OF WADDINGTON: . . . [A]lthough the society had under its rules power to borrow for the purposes of its legitimate business, it, of course, had no power to borrow for purposes which were *ultra vires*. It is reasonably clear . . . that all those persons from whom the directors and agents of the society received money on deposit or current account must have been aware that the borrowing thus constituted was borrowing in the normal course and for the purposes of a banking business and not for the legitimate purposes of the society. None of such persons, therefore, can rely on the borrowing powers conferred by the society's rules.

. . . It has been settled . . . that an *ultra vires* borrowing by persons affecting to act on behalf of a company or other

statutory association does not give rise to any indebtedness
either at law or in equity on the part of such company or
association. It is not, therefore, open to the House to hold that
in such a case the lender had an action against the company
or association for money had and received. To do so would in
effect validate the transaction so far as it embodied a contract
to repay the money lent. The implied promise on which the
action for money had and received is based would be precisely
that promise which the company or association could not
lawfully make. At the same time there seems to be nothing
in those decisions which would bind the House, if they were
considering whether an action would lie in law or in equity
to recover money paid under any *ultra vires* contract which
was not a contract of borrowing; for example, money paid to
a company or association for the purchase of land which the
company had no power to sell and the sale of which was
therefore void, or money paid to the company or association
by way of subscription for shares which it had no power
to issue. In such cases the implied promise on which the
action for money had and received depends would form no
part of, but would be merely collateral to, the *ultra vires*
contract.

Accepting the principle that no action or suit lies at law or
in equity to recover money lent to a company or association
which has no power to borrow, the question remains whether
the lender has any other remedies. . . . First, it appears to be
well settled that if the borrowed money be applied in paying
off legitimate indebtedness of the company or association
(whether the indebtedness be incurred before or after the money
was borrowed), the lenders are entitled to rank as creditors
of the company or association to the extent to which the money
has been so applied. There appears to be some doubt as to
whether this result is arrived at by treating the contract of
loan as validated to the extent to which the borrowed money
is so applied, on the ground that to this extent there is no
increase in the indebtedness of the company or association, in
which case, if the contract of loan involves a security for the
money borrowed, the security would be validated to a like

extent; or whether the better view is that the lenders are subrogated to the rights of the legitimate creditors who have been paid off. . . .

Secondly, it appears to be also well settled that the lender in an *ultra vires* loan transaction has a right to what is known as a tracing order. A company or other statutory association cannot by itself or through an agent be party to an *ultra vires* act. If its directors or agents affecting to act on its behalf borrow money which it has no power to borrow, the money borrowed is in their hands the property of the lender.

At law, therefore, the lender can recover the money, so long as he can identify it, and even if it has been employed in purchasing property, there may be cases in which, by ratifying the action of those who have so employed it, he may recover the property purchased. Equity, however, treated the matter from a different standpoint. It considered that the relationship between the directors or agents and the lender was a fiduciary relationship, and that the money in their hands was for all practical purposes trust money. Starting from a personal equity, based on the consideration that it would be unconscionable for anyone who could not plead purchase for value without notice to retain an advantage derived from the misapplication of trust money, it ended, as was so often the case, in creating what were in effect rights of property, though not recognised as such by the common law.

The principle on which, and the extent to which, trust money can be followed in equity is discussed at length in *In re Hallett's Estate* by SIR GEORGE JESSEL. He gives two instances. First, he supposes the case of property being purchased by means of the trust money alone. In such a case the beneficiary may either take the property itself or claim a lien on it for the amount of the money expended in the purchase. Secondly, he supposes the case of the purchase having been made partly with the trust money and partly with money of the trustee. In such a case the beneficiary can only claim a charge on the property for the amount of the trust money expended in the purchase. The trustee is precluded by his own misconduct from asserting any interest in the property until such amount has been refunded. By the actual decision in the case, this principle was held applicable when the trust money had been paid into the trustee's banking account. I will add two further illustrations which have some bearing on the present case. Suppose the property is acquired by means of money, part of which belongs to one owner and part to another, the purchaser being in a fiduciary relationship to both. Clearly each owner has an equal equity. Each is entitled to a charge on the property for his own money, and neither can claim priority over the other. It follows that their charges must rank *pari passu* according to their respective amounts. Further, I think that as against the fiduciary agent they could by agreement claim to take the property itself, in which case they would become tenants in common in shares proportioned to amounts for which either could claim a charge. Suppose, again, that the fiduciary agent parts with the money to a third party who cannot plead purchase for value without notice, and that the third party invests it with money of his own in the purchase of property. If the third party had notice that the money was held in a fiduciary capacity, he would be in exactly the same position as the fiduciary agent, and could not, therefore, assert any interest in the property until the money misapplied had been refunded. But if he had no such notice this would not be the case. There would on his part be no misconduct at all. On the other hand, I cannot at present see why he should have any priority as against the property over the owner of the money which had, in fact, been misapplied. . . .

My Lords, it is important to observe that in the *Crace-Calvert Case* the money was borrowed for and applied to the legitimate purposes of the society, the loan being *ultra vires* because the society, according to the Court of Appeal, had no power to borrow at all even for its legitimate purposes. In the present case the society had power to borrow for its legitimate purposes, and the borrowing in question is *ultra vires* only because, to the knowledge of the lenders, it was for a purpose not authorised by the society's constitution. This distinction is, I think, of considerable importance. In the first place, if the agents of a society, having power to borrow,

borrow money intending, to the knowledge of the lenders, to apply it for an illegitimate purpose, but in fact apply it for the legitimate purposes of the society, there seems no reason, either in law or in equity, why the loan to the extent to which it is so utilised should not be treated as valid. In the next place, if the money be in fact utilised for the illegitimate purpose for which it is borrowed, say the carrying on of an *ultra vires* banking business, to whom does this business belong? Whose are the assets and whose are the liabilities? The society cannot be a party to any transaction not within its powers. The society, therefore, is neither entitled to the assets nor subject to the liabilities acquired or incurred in the business. No doubt, if the business is a financial success, the directors or agents who carried it on would have to account to the society for the profits or surplus assets, for equity will not allow a director or other agent to make a profit out of his directorship or agency. It is quite clear, however, that the society could not be entitled to anything except the profits or surplus. It could not claim to be entitled to the assets of the business, and exempt from its liabilities on any plea of *ultra vires*, and for this purpose the borrowed moneys would be a liability of the business.

But suppose that the illegitimate business is carried on in part only with the borrowed money and in part with money belonging to the society. Even in this case the business will not belong to the society, nor will the society be entitled to its assets or subject to its liabilities. . . . Further, the society's right in equity to take the assets subject to the liabilities if the business were successful would be similarly unaffected. But the fact that the society's own money had been employed by its directors or agents in an *ultra vires* business would entitle the society to an additional equity. It would be entitled, on the principles of *In re Hallett's Estate*, to follow the money as long as it or any property acquired by its means could be identified. In other words it would have exactly the same equities in this respect as the *ultra vires* lender. . . . It follows from this that it would be entitled to take or claim a lien on any assets of the business acquired exclusively with its money, and to a lien or charge on any asset or mass of assets acquired partly only with its money, subject nevertheless to this, that if the *ultra vires* lender could establish a similar lien or charge, the two liens or charges would rank *pari passu*. . . .

The case, therefore, presents itself in this way. Here is a mass of assets arising in the course of an *ultra vires* business carried on by the directors and agents of the society. There are, on the other hand, liabilities. . . . No one claims any interest in the assets except the *ultra vires* lenders, the members of the society and the creditors, in respect of the liabilities to which I have referred. The *ultra vires* lenders and the members are willing that these liabilities and the costs of the liquidation . . . shall be first paid. If this is done, what is left may be taken to represent in part the moneys of the *ultra vires* lenders and in part the moneys of the society wrongfully employed in the business. The equities of the *ultra vires* lenders and of the society are equal, and it follows that the remainder of the assets ought to be divided between the *ultra vires* lenders and the society rateably, according to the capital amount contributed by such lenders and the society respectively. This mode of distribution gives effect to all the equities of the parties. . . . It depends solely on the fact that the assets for distribution being assets not of a legitimate but an *ultra vires* business are not the assets of the society, except in so far as they can substantiate some equity to them, and that such equity as they have can arise only from an application of the same principles to which the *ultra vires* lenders are themselves entitled to have recourse.

Lord Sumner: . . . The depositors' case has been put, first of all, as consisting in a right enforceable in a common law action. It is said that they paid their money under a mistake of fact, or for a consideration that has wholly failed, or that it has been had and received by the society to their use. My Lords, in my opinion no such actions could succeed. To hold otherwise would be indirectly to sanction an *ultra vires* borrowing. All these causes of action are common species of the *genus assumpsit*. All now rest, and long have rested, upon a notional or imputed promise to repay. The law cannot *de jure* impute promises to repay, whether for money had and received or otherwise, which, if made *de facto*, it would inexorably avoid. . . . My Lords, I think the present case must be decided upon equitable principles upon which there is no direct authority. . . . The question is one of administration. The liquidator, an officer of the Court, who has to discharge himself of the assets that come to his hands, asks for directions, and, after hearing all parties concerned, the Court has the right and the duty to direct him how to distribute all the assets. No part of them can remain undistributed as *res nullius*. No one has ventured to argue before your Lordships that the shareholders take everything, to the exclusion of the depositors, and so make a huge windfall. In my opinion, if precedent fails, the most just distribution of the whole must be directed, so only that no recognised rule of law or equity be disregarded. In this case neither the shareholders nor the depositors have the better equity; the money of each has, with the consent of all, been indiscriminately applied in acquiring assets beyond as well as within the society's powers, the former in much the larger measure. The claims of each class are equal, and, I think, for the present purpose identical.

Analogous cases have been decided with regard to chattels. They differ, no doubt, because of the fact that the property in the chattels remained unchanged, though identification and even identity of the subject-matter of the property failed, whereas here, except as to currency, and even there only in a restricted sense, the term property, as we use that term of chattels, does not apply, and, at least as far as intention could do it, both depositors and shareholders had given up the right to call the money or its proceeds their own, and had taken instead personal claims on the society. In *Buckley* v. *Gross*, where tallow in burning warehouses melted and ran down a sewer, and a stranger collected it, BLACKBURN J. says: "The tallow of the different owners was indeed mixed up into a molten mass, so that it might be difficult to apportion it among them; but I dissent from the doctrine that, because the property of different persons is confused together, that entitles a third party to steal it with impunity. Probably the legal effect of such a mixture would be to make the owners tenants in common in equal portions of the mass." Again, *Spence* v. *Union Marine Insurance Co.* is a case where cotton in bales belonging to different consignees was so damaged by sea perils that it arrived with marks obliterated and otherwise injured, and after delivery to the respective consignees of all that could be specifically identified as theirs, a mass of unidentifiable damaged cotton remained. There, as here, no doubt one bale, in fact, represented A's money and another B's; there, as here, all were depreciated, but probably not each in the same degree, but no one could say which bale was any particular person's property, or who, therefore, should bear the greater and who the less depreciation. The goods could not be treated as *bona vacantia*, they could not fall into the hands of the first person who reduced them into possession and on principles and analogies derived from Roman law the Court treated the consignees as tenants in common of the unidentifiable cotton, in the proportion borne by the numbers originally shipped by them to the number remaining. This decision has never been questioned for nearly fifty years.

My Lords, I agree, without recapitulating reasons, that the principle on which *Hallett's Case* is founded justifies an order allowing the appellants to follow the assets, not merely to the verge of actual identification, but even somewhat further in a case like the present, where after a process of exclusion only two classes or groups of persons, having equal claims, are left in and all superior claims have been eliminated. Tracing in a sense it is not, for we know that the money coming from A went into one security and that coming from B into another, and that the two securities did not probably depreciate exactly in the same percentage, and we know further that no one will ever know any more. Still I think this well within the "tracing" equity, and that among persons making up these two groups the principle of rateable division of the assets is sound. I agree in the decision proposed.

Introductions, Ltd. *v.* National Provincial Bank Ltd. [1970] Ch. 199

An "independent objects" clause does not convert a power into an object, and all powers must be exercised for an intra vires *purpose.*

The plaintiff company, Introductions, Ltd., was formed in 1951 with an issued capital of £400 in £1 shares in connection with the Festival of Britain. The relevant sub-clauses of its objects clause provided as follows:

"A. To promote, organise and provide entertainments and services for overseas and other visitors; to act as secretary to, and to render or supply any services, assistance or accommodation to travellers, merchants, manufacturers, professional men, and others. . . .

D. To carry on any other trade or business whatsoever which can in the opinion of the board of directors be advantageously carried on by the company in connection with or as ancillary to any of the above businesses or the general business of the company.

I. To promote any other company for the purpose of acquiring any property or rights or converting any of the liabilities of this company or of its undertaking.

N. To borrow or raise money in such manner as the company shall think fit and in particular by the issue of debentures or debenture stock perpetual or otherwise and to secure the repayment of any money borrowed or raised by mortgage charge or lien upon the undertaking and the whole or any part of the company's property or assets. . . .

Y. It is hereby expressly declared that each of the preceding sub-clauses shall be construed independently of and shall be in no way limited by reference to any other sub-clause and that the objects set out in each sub-clause are independent objects of the company."

For two years the company provided services for visitors from abroad. From 1953 to 1958 it merely provided deck-chairs and coin-operated amusement machines at a south coast resort. Between 1958 and 1960 it carried on no business. In 1958, 398 of the 400 shares were transferred to new shareholders and there was a complete change in

the composition of the board of directors. In 1960 it embarked on a new business, namely pig breeding, which
was its sole activity. Members of the public were invited
to contribute moneys, which were invested by the company
on their behalf in the purchase, for the contributor, of one
of the company's sows. In due course the company bought
back from the contributor the progeny of the sow in question.

In the same year the managing director approached the
defendant bank, the National Provincial Bank, Ltd., with
a view to opening an account, and in 1961 the company
duly opened an account with that bank. When this account
became overdrawn the bank required security for the overdraft, and the company offered the bank two debentures
secured on its assets. These the bank accepted. The bank
had in its possession a copy of the company's memorandum and articles and was fully aware that the company's
sole activity was pig breeding.

The pig-breeding business was not financially successful. Despite the system of marking it was impossible to
identify the pigs, some of which did not belong to the company, as belonging to any particular individual. The
company was wound up by the court in 1965 with assets
of about £100,000 and liabilities of about £2,000,000. It
owed the bank £29,571. The bank sought to enforce the
debentures, but the liquidator contended that they were
invalid as having been granted for an *ultra vires* purpose.
He took out a summons asking the court to determine
whether, on the true constructon of the memorandum
and articles, (1) pig breeding, and (2) the borrowing from
the bank, were *intra vires* the company.

In the High Court BUCKLEY J. held that the business of
pig breeding was *ultra vires*, and from this decision there
was no appeal. On the second question he held that the
loan by the bank, having knowingly been made for an
ultra vires purpose, was invalid. The bank appealed against
his decision on this point, on the ground that the borrowing was *intra vires* the company under sub-clause N and
that therefore the debentures were valid.

The case accordingly came before the Court of Appeal.

HARMAN L.J.: . . . It has always been the ambition . . . of

the commercial community to stretch the objects clause of a memorandum of association, thus obtaining the advantage of limited liability with as little fetter on the activities of the company as possible. But still you cannot have an object to do every mortal thing you want, because that is to have no object at all. There was one thing that the plaintiff company could not do and that was to breed pigs. The venture of pig breeding is the type of adventure which has always drawn money from the pockets of the British public, who apparently much prefer to regard themselves as owners of an apple or an apple tree or a pig rather than a mere share in a company.

. . . It was argued . . . that the only obligation of the bank was to satisfy itself that there was an express power to borrow money, and that this power was converted into an object by the concluding words of the objects clause. . . . It was said that, if this was so, not only need the bank inquire no further but also that it was unaffected by the knowledge which it had that the activity on which the money was to be spent was one beyond the company's powers.

The judge rejected this view, and I agree with him. He based his judgment, I think, on the view that a power or an object conferred on a company to borrow cannot mean something in the air: borrowing is not an end in itself and must be for some purpose of the company; and since this borrowing was for an *ultra vires* purpose, that is an end of the matter.

Mr. Walton [*leading counsel for the defendant bank*], I think, agreed that if sub-clause N must in truth be construed as a power, such a power must be for a purpose within the company's memorandum. He says that it is "elevated into an object" . . . by the concluding words of the objects clause in the memorandum, and this object, being an independent object of the company, will protect the lender and that that is its purpose. I answer that by saying that you cannot convert a power into an object merely by saying so. Sub-clause N cannot in truth stand by itself any more than certain other of the sub-clauses of the objects clause of the memorandum, for instance, sub-clause D.

. . . Then there is sub-clause I. . . . And there are other

similar sub-clauses which are clearly ancillary powers, although under the concluding words they are stated to be independent objects.

Mr. Walton relied on the well-known case of *Cotman* v. *Brougham*. . . . I would agree that, if the bank did not know what the purpose of the borrowing was, it need not inquire, but it did know, and I can find nothing in *Cotman* v. *Brougham* to protect it notwithstanding that knowledge.

An earlier case of *In re David Payne & Co. Ltd.* shows the limit to which this particular doctrine can go. . . . I agree with the judge [*in that case*] that it is a necessarily implied addition to a power to borrow, whether express or implied, that you should add "for the purposes of the company." This borrowing was not for a legitimate purpose of the company: the bank knew it, and, therefore, cannot rely on its debentures.

RUSSELL L.J.: I agree. . . . I too would dismiss the appeal.

KARMINSKI L.J.: I agree that this appeal must be dismissed.

3. Gratuitous Acts and Payments

Hutton v. West Cork Railway Company. (1883) 23 Ch.D. 654

Gratuitous payments made by a company are ultra vires *unless made for purposes which are reasonably incidental to the carrying on of the company's business for the company's benefit. Where a company is in liquidation and no longer a going concern, gratuitous payments to its directors or servants cannot be incidental to its business.*

The appellant was a holder of debenture stock of the West Cork Railway Company. The other facts sufficiently appear from the judgments in the Court of Appeal.

COTTON L.J.: This is an application by way of appeal from Lord Justice FRY for an injunction to restrain the Defendant company from dealing with a sum of £4,000 in accordance with a certain resolution that was passed at a general meeting of the company on the 19th of April last. Lord Justice FRY had in the then state of things granted an injunction because no meeting had been called at which a resolution could be passed in accordance with what he thought were the powers of the company in general meeting assembled; but he intimated an opinion, adversely to the present Appellant, that if a meeting were duly called and a resolution duly passed that meeting would have power to deal with the £4,000 in the way in which it has been proposed by the resolution to deal with it. The Plaintiff now applies by way of appeal for an extended injunction, the injunction of Lord Justice FRY being only until a resolution was passed by a general meeting authorising the application of the money.

The case is this, the West Cork Railway Company, who are the Defendants, are a company who under an Act of Parliament have sold their undertakings to the Bandon Railway Company and received as the purchase-money a sum settled by arbitration at £141,934. One of the sections of the Act of Parliament, S.12, upon which the question mainly turns, was a section which provided how that sum of money was to be dealt with when it was paid by the Bandon Railway Company, and the real question is—whether, having regard to that section, it was in the power of a general meeting to direct that the £4,000 should be applied in the way proposed.

. . . What has been proposed to be done is this: There was a sum of £4,000 which was set apart, and it was proposed that out of that certain costs should be paid, and then out of the balance it was estimated that there would be enough to give £1,050 as compensation to the managing director and other officials, and then that there should be a sum paid to the directors which was estimated to amount to about £1,500. The question is whether that can or ought to be done under this resolution.

As I understand, the state of things has been this: The officials for whom the £1,050 is proposed to provide were paid as long as they continued in the service of the company, and there is no evidence at all that they made any claim for a discharge without due notice, or that they have any legal claim against the company for not being continued in receipt of their salaries. It must be dealt with upon that footing. Therefore, as regards them, this sum of £1,050 must, in my opinion, be considered not as a payment made to them in respect of any legal claim which they have as against the West Cork Company, but simply as a gratuity to them for their not being continued in the receipt of that remuneration which, had the company lasted, and had they continued in its service, they would have received.

Then, as regards the directors, the matter stands on a somewhat different footing. The present directors apparently have never received any remuneration at all for their services whilst the company was carrying on the undertaking, and before the Bandon Company took possession of the railway. The evidence, I think, is that neither the present nor any other directors of the company ever did receive anything, and there is no evidence that there was any resolution in any way fixing the remuneration to be paid to the directors.

Under those circumstances there are two matters to be considered. Of course there can be no objection at all to so much of the resolution as provides for payment of the costs and expenses which are to be provided for out of the £4,000. But can the resolution be considered as *intra vires* as regards the two other matters? I will take first that which provides for compensation to the managing director and other officials. It was said that it is within the powers of the directors of a trading or business company to grant gratuities to its servants, and that this case comes within that principle, as the directors of this company retained such powers as were incident to a company of this kind, notwithstanding that its railway had been handed over to the purchasing company—the Bandon Company. I think that the directors did continue to have powers, so far as they were necessary for or incidental to the winding-up of the company. But, in my opinion, they had not such powers as only are impliedly given to general meetings or to directors because they are carrying on a business for the purpose of carrying on its business, and for the purpose of making a profit from it. . . . [H]ere the company was gone as a company carrying on business for the purpose of making profit, and the sums paid, therefore, to its officials and managing directors, could not be looked upon as an inducement to them to exert themselves in future, or as an act done reasonably for the purpose of getting the greatest profit from the business of the company, but must be looked upon simply as a gratuity, perhaps reasonable in itself, but without any prospect of its in any way reasonably conducing to the benefit of the company. In my opinion, therefore, under these circumstances, neither the directors nor the general meeting had any power in the circumstances which are before us, as I understand the facts of the case, of granting that compensation to the officials and other servants.

Then comes the question as to the directors. . . . [H]ere what we have is this—that for all the duration of this company the directors have never received any remuneration at all, and there has been no resolution saying that they shall have any. . . . [W]hen directors have for many years gone on without it even being suggested that they should have any remuneration, and we have this Act of Parliament which contains this clause S.12, . . . in my opinion it was not competent to a general meeting to deal with this fund when it came to distribute it in providing for any remuneration to the directors for those services which they had been giving during the time the company was a going concern without any remuneration, and without any resolution of a general meeting or other stipulation which entitled them to remuneration.

I do not however mean to decide . . . that a general meeting of this company could not in the winding-up . . . give to the directors what may be considered a fair remuneration for their services to the company after the railway and the undertaking had been taken over by the Bandon Company, and all that was being done was being done for the purpose not of carrying on the railway as a going concern but for the purpose of doing that which was incidental to and connected with the winding-up of the company. If it had been shown that this sum was given to the directors really as a payment to them of a proper sum for their services during the winding-up in the interval from the 1st of January, 1880, to the present time, my opinion would have been that that could not have been attacked. But I think on the evidence the necessary inference is that this sum of £1,500 was agreed to or voted to be paid to them not as a reasonable sum for remuneration for their services during that term, but as a sum which might with reasonable generosity be paid to them taking into consideration the fact that they never received anything during the years when they carried on the railway. That, I think, . . . would be *ultra vires*.

In my opinion, therefore, though the two cases are different, yet neither as regards the compensation to the officials nor as regards the vote of £1,500 put in that way for the directors, can this resolution be considered as one within the powers of a general meeting. . . . I have dealt with the case upon the footing that the Plaintiff here stands in no better position than the shareholders would, that is to say, he is a person, who by the vote of a general meeting of the company, acting within its powers, would be bound, and could not object simply because he thought the resolution unreasonable, or that it was too large a sum to vote.

Therefore the injunction, which I think ought to be granted, will be confined to this, to restrain the company from applying any part of the £4,000 in accordance with the resolution of the 19th of April otherwise than in payment of the costs and expenses which are resolved to be paid thereout.

BOWEN L.J.: I am of the same opinion. . . .

Now the directors in this case have done, it seems to me, nothing at all wrong. Let us clear the ground, because my sympathies are rather with the judgment of Lord Justice FRY, if one could really exercise sympathy in a case where questions of law have to be decided. Not only have they done nothing wrong, but I confess I think the company have done what nine companies out of ten would do, and do without the least objection being made. They have paid, perhaps liberally, perhaps not at all too liberally, persons who have served them faithfully. But that, of course, does not get rid of the difficulty. As soon as a question is raised by a dissentient shareholder, or by a person standing in the position of a dissentient shareholder, sympathy must be cut adrift, and we have simply to consider what the law is. In this particular case the Plaintiff is a person who stands *prima facie* in the condition of those who are bound by the vote of a general meeting acting within the powers of a general meeting, but he complains that the majority propose to expend certain purchase-money which the company are receiving from the Bandon Company in two ways which he thinks are beyond their powers. In the first place he says that the majority are going to spend money in compensating the managing director and other officials, who are being extinguished by this transfer to the Bandon Company, for the loss of their places. Now the compensation which is to be awarded is not compensation for any legal loss they have sustained: because I understand that these gentlemen could always have been discharged, and have received notice amply sufficient to prevent them from having any cause of legal grievance, and they simply have been asked in the usual way to cease to serve the masters who have no further cause for their services. In the second place, the Plaintiff complains that money is sought to be paid for remuneration of the directors. The facts there, again, deserve to be shortly summarised. They are directors who for many years have served the company for nothing, and I cannot help thinking that down to the time this purchase-money was to be received it was always understood that they were going to serve the company for nothing. I see no reason to think, at all events, that they ever meant to put forward any claim. But, after this arrangement of transfer to the Bandon Company, and after the company is wound up, or towards the close of its winding-up, it is proposed to pay them a lump sum, the measure taken not being the measure of service they have rendered in the winding-up, but a general view which the company entertains of their past merits. Now can a majority compel a dissentient unit in the company to give way and to submit to these payments? We must go back to the root of things. The money which is going to be spent is not the money of the majority. That is clear. It is the money of the company, and the majority want to spend it. What would be the natural limit of their power to

do so? They can only spend money which is not theirs but
the company's, if they are spending it for the purposes which
are reasonably incidental to the carrying on of the business of
the company. That is the general doctrine. *Bona fides* cannot
be the sole test, otherwise you might have a lunatic conducting
the affairs of the company, and paying away its money with
both hands in a manner perfectly *bona fide* yet perfectly
irrational. The test must be what is reasonably incidental to,
and within the reasonable scope of carrying on, the business of
the company. Applying that kind of view, what is the character
of these payments? First of all, I ask myself what is the kind
of touchstone or test to apply if the company was an ordinary
going concern; and, secondly, whether this company is still in
the same position as an ordinary railway, or whether it has
not become a railway company of a very limited kind, a business adventure of a very exceptional sort, and its business contracted accordingly within very narrow and easily defined limits.

But, first of all, let us consider in what kind of way one
would deal with the case of an ordinary railway. . . . [W]hat
is the remuneration of directors? I think it is pretty clear that,
like the compensation for loss of the services of the managing
director, it is a gratuity. A director is not a servant. He is a
person who is doing business for the company, but not upon
ordinary terms. It is not implied from the mere fact that he is a
director, that he is to have a right to be paid for it. In some
companies . . . there is a special provision for the way in which
the directors should be paid; in others there is not. If there is
a special provision for the way in which they are to be paid,
you must look to the special provision to see how to deal with
it. But if there is no special provision their payment is in the
nature of a gratuity. . . . That does not get rid of the difficulty, because one must still ask oneself what is the general
law about gratuitous payments which are made by the directors
or by a company so as to bind dissentients. It seems to me
you cannot say the company has only got power to spend
the money which it is bound to pay according to law, otherwise the wheels of business would stop. . . . They are not to
keep their pockets buttoned up and defy the world unless they

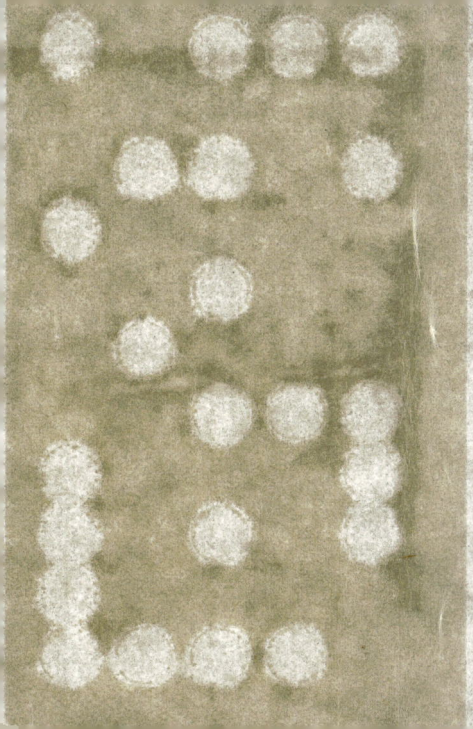

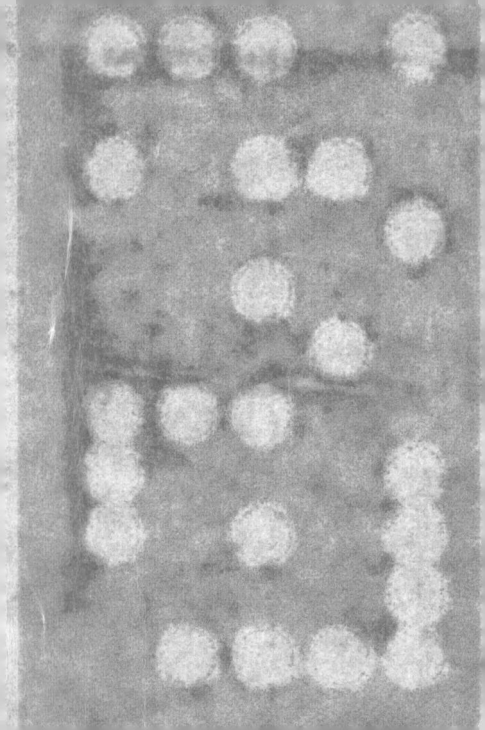

are liable in a way which could be enforced at law or in equity.
Most businesses require liberal dealings. The test there again
is not whether it is *bona fide*, but whether, as well as being
done *bona fide*, it is done within the ordinary scope of the
company's business, and whether it is reasonably incidental
to the carrying on of the company's business for the company's
benefit. Take this sort of instance. A railway company, or
the directors of the company, might send down all the porters
at a railway station to have tea in the country at the expense of
the company. Why should they not? It is for the directors
to judge, provided it is a matter which is reasonably incidental
to the carrying on of the business of the company, and a
company which always treated its employees with Draconian
severity, and never allowed them a single inch more than the
strict letter of the bond, would soon find itself deserted—at
all events, unless labour was very much more easy to obtain
in the market than it often is. The law does not say that there
are to be no cakes and ale, but there are to be no cakes and
ale except such as are required for the benefit of the company.

Now that I think is the principle to be found in the case of
Hampson v. *Price's Patent Candle Company*. The Master of the
Rolls there held that the company might lawfully expend
a week's wages as gratuities for their servants; because that
sort of liberal dealing with servants eases the friction between
masters and servants, and is, in the end, a benefit to the company. It is not charity sitting at the board of directors, because as it seems to me charity has no business to sit at boards
of directors *qua* charity. There is, however, a kind of charitable
dealing which is for the interest of those who practise it, and to
that extent and in that garb (I admit not a very philanthropic
garb) charity may sit at the board, but for no other purpose. . . .
The past remuneration of directors seems to me like the gratuitous wages in *Hampson* v. *Price's Patent Candle Company*,
to be justifiable, provided it is within the scope of the business
and secured advantage to the company.

I add one word more about compensation for dismissal of
employees. I am by no means prepared to say that directors
might not, when a meritorious servant is leaving their service,

present him with a £5 note, I should be very sorry to decide anything of the kind; but I say that there must be a limit, and the limit is what is necessary in the reasonable management of the affairs of the company. . . . [T]he ultimate test is not *bona fides*, but what is necessary for carrying on business. . . .

Such is the general view of the law I should take about a company which was a going concern. Now let us see whether this company is a going concern in the same sense, and whether we have the same limit with regard to the payment of money. This particular company had been sold to the Bandon Company. . . . [I]t remained alive only for certain purposes. It was not a going concern in the full sense of the term, nor was the venture any longer the ordinary venture of a railway company. It had a special and limited business, and that business was to preside at its own funeral, to wind itself up and carry on its own internal affairs until it had distributed the purchase-money in the way the Act of Parliament prescribed. If that be so, when one is applying the general test whether what has been done is incident to the business of the company, we have this further matter to recollect—what the business of this company is—and we have to ask ourselves whether these payments were necessary for that kind of limited business or could reasonably be said to be part of the business. . . . Compensation, and gratuity for past services generally, without references to such services as were rendered during the winding-up, can no longer be charges or expenditure reasonably incident to the carrying on—not the business of the old company—but what the business of the company would be for the purposes of its continued existence. It was moribund, and would only want to die in peace and distribute its assets, and it would not, as it seems to me, be proper to carry to the revenue account of such a company the money it voted to directors in a liberal spirit for what they had done in past years, or to a managing director for the disappointment and vexation of being deprived of an office for which he had been amply paid. The revenue debts and charges of the company must be viewed with reference to the qualified nature of its existence still left.

That being so, I think the resolution as to compensation is clearly wrong. The directors have no right to give it. It might in some instances be worth the while of a company to compensate a meritorious, but dismissed officer, but that kind of justification cannot exist in the case of a dying company. I think that makes the resolution bad. . . . I think a willing majority has no right to bind a dissentient minority by any resolution so conceived.

BAGGALLAY L.J., dissented.

Evans v. Brunner, Mond and Company, Ltd. [1921] 1 Ch. 359

For an act to be intra vires, *it must be incidental or conducive to the attainment of the main object of the company. It is not enough to prove that it is beneficial to the company.*

The memorandum of association of a limited company, whose primary object was to purchase and carry on the business of chemical manufacturers, contained in clause 3 the various objects and powers ancillary to this main object. It concluded with a provision whereby the company was enabled to do "all such business and things as may be incidental or conducive to the attainment of the above objects, or any of them." At an extraordinary general meeting the company passed a resolution authorising the directors "to distribute to such universities, or other scientific institutions in the United Kingdom as they may select for the furtherance of scientific education and research the sum of £100,000 out of invested surplus reserve account."

A shareholder of the company, Mr. William Wynn Evans, suing on behalf of himself and the other shareholders, claimed a declaration that this resolution was *ultra vires* and moved for an injunction to restrain the company from acting on it.

There was an affidavit by Roscoe Brunner, the chairman of the directors, stating that the company occupied a leading position in the chemical manufacturing industry throughout the world, and that the development of that industry depended increasingly upon the advance of pure science. The company's greatest difficulty was to find men sufficiently equipped by their previous studies to undertake research work. Hence a larger reservoir of men highly trained in the universities and scientific schools was imperative to enable the company to recruit its staff. In his judgment the proposed application of £100,000 was eminently desirable in furtherance of the company's business, and he was of opinion that the outlay was essential. There were eleven other affidavits by directors of the company in support.

An affidavit by the plaintiff stated formal matter and what happened at the meeting, but there was no contradiction of the evidence on behalf of the company.

EVE J.: . . . The first thing to ascertain is the construction of this resolution; what is the nature and extent of the authority thereby conferred on the directors? I think one might paraphrase it in this way: it is an authority to the directors to expend that £100,000 for the furtherance of scientific education and research, and for that purpose they may select, as participants therein, such universities or other scientific institutions in the United Kingdom as they think fit. It is an authority which is therefore limited in express terms, in that the money must be applied for the furtherance of scientific education and research; its destination is to a certain extent indicated, but not very strictly limited, and the authority is certainly impressed with this implied obligation on those to whom it is given, that they shall exercise the discretion vested in them *bona fide* in the interests of the company whose agents they are. The question is whether such an application of the company's funds is within or without the power of the company. The defendants say that it is within an express power to be found in the company's memorandum of association. It has been argued that the clause . . . is not really an object of the company properly stated in its memorandum but is only a power. No doubt for many years past a practice has obtained of mixing up objects and powers and inserting both in the memorandum, but for the purposes of today it is not necessary for me to distinguish between the two. . . . The wide and general objects are to be construed as ancillary to the company's main purpose, and I apprehend that the act to be *intra vires* must be one which can fairly be regarded as incidental or conducive to the main or paramount purpose for which the company was formed. . . . It is beyond dispute that the paramount object for which this company was incorporated was the carrying on in all its branches of the trade or business of chemical manufacturers, and in order that any particular application of its funds can be justified . . . it is essential that it should be established that it is an application incidental or conducive to the business of chemical manufacturers.

. . . For present purposes I think I must rest on the evidence of those responsible for the conduct of the company's affairs and accept as conclusive their unanimous opinion that this is probably the most advantageous and profitable way to the company in which this sum of money could be expended.

. . . A number of cases have been cited, and a number of instances have been suggested, in the course of argument, where particular transactions, although they might be for the benefit of the company, have nevertheless been or could be held to be *ultra vires* of the company. No doubt that is so. When an act of the company is challenged on the ground that it is beyond the powers of the company the challenge is not disposed of by proving that the act is beneficial to the company: it must be established that it is an act the doing of which is authorised by the company's constitution.

On the present occasion, assuming the plaintiff has made out a prima facie case, what the company has to establish to the satisfaction of the court, is that the proposals embodied in this resolution are incidental or conducive to the attainment of the main object of the company. On the evidence I think that the company has discharged this burden and has proved that the proposed expenditure will not only be to the direct advantage of the company, but is also conducive to, and indeed necessary for, its continued progress as chemical manufacturers.

In these circumstances, although I think the case is one which has been very properly raised, it is not one in which I ought to interfere, and accordingly I make no order on the motion.

Re Lee, Behrens and Company, Ltd. [1932] 2 Ch. 46

*Gratuitous payments may be made only for purposes reason-
ably incidental to the carrying on of the company's business,
and their validity may be tested by three questions: (1) Is the
transaction reasonably incidental to the carrying on of the
company's business? (2) Is it a* bona fide *transaction? (3) Is it
done for the benefit and to promote the prosperity of the company?*

A private company, Lee, Behrens & Co., Ltd., whose
memorandum and articles authorised the directors to
provide for the welfare of employees and their widows
and children, entered into a deed of covenant by which it
granted a pension of £500 a year to Mrs. Gertrude Eliza-
beth Southerden, the widow of a former managing director,
J. R. Southerden, five years after his death. Some three
years later the company passed a resolution for voluntary
winding-up.

Mrs. Southerden lodged a proof in the winding-up for
£8,000, the capitalised value of the annuity, but the liquidator rejected it on the grounds (1) that it was *ultra vires*
and void; (2) alternatively that it could only be authorised
by the company in general meeting and that no such meeting was summoned; (3) that it was a mere gratuity which
could only be paid out of profits, and that there were no
profits out of which to pay it.

Mrs. Southerden took out a summons to have the decision of the liquidator reviewed.

Eve J.: . . . It is not contended, nor in the face of a number of
authorities to the contrary effect could it be, that an arrangement of this nature for rewarding long and faithful service on
the part of persons employed by the company is not within
the power of an ordinary trading company such as this company
was, and indeed in the company's memorandum of association is contained an express power to provide for the welfare
of persons in the employment of the company or formerly
in its employment, and the widows and children of such
persons and others dependent upon them by granting money
or pensions, providing schools, reading rooms or places of

recreation, subscribing to sick or benefit clubs or societies or otherwise as the company may think fit.

But whether they be made under an express or implied power, all such grants involve an expenditure of the company's money, and that money can only be spent for purposes reasonably incidental to the carrying on of the company's business, and the validity of such grants is to be tested, as is shown in all the authorities, by the answers to three pertinent questions: (*i*) Is the transaction reasonably incidental to the carrying on of the company's business? (*ii*) Is it a *bona fide* transaction? and (*iii*) Is it done for the benefit and to promote the prosperity of the company? Authority for each of the foregoing propositions is to be found in the following cases: *Hampson* v. *Price's Patent Candle Co.*; *Hutton* v. *West Cork Railway Co.*; and *Henderson* v. *Bank of Australasia.*

In the present case the court is left entirely without any material for determining whether the transaction was characterised by any of these several attributes. Assuming, as I am quite prepared to do, that there are no grounds for impugning the *bona fides* of the board or applicant, no one of them has given evidence to suggest that the course adopted was taken for the benefit or to promote the prosperity of the company or that the execution of the deed of covenant and the assumption of so burdensome a liability was reasonably incidental to the carrying on of the company's business. . . .

The conclusion to which in my opinion such evidence as is available irresistibly points is that the predominant, if not the only, considerations operating in the minds of the directors, was a desire to provide for the applicant, and that the question what, if any, benefit would accrue to the company never presented itself to their minds.

If there were nothing more in the case than what I have just indicated, I should feel myself bound in the circumstances to support the liquidator's rejection of this lady's proof.

But there is another and perhaps more insurmountable difficulty with which she is faced, and it is this, that this annuity is a gift or reward given out of the company's assets by the directors to one of their own body, and this is something they cannot do unless authorised by the instrument which regulates the company or by the shareholders at a properly convened meeting—that is, a meeting convened by a notice disclosing the intention to make the proposal. . . .

The paragraph I read earlier in this judgment from the company's memorandum does not assist the plaintiff, for "a director is not a servant of the company": per BOWEN L.J. in *Hutton* v. *West Cork Ry. Co.*; nor is any managing or other director a person in the employment of the company. . . .

The alternative of getting authority from the shareholders at a meeting duly convened for the purpose was never thought of, or, if thought of, was dismissed as superfluous. . . . In my opinion, the rejection of this proof by the liquidator was quite right, and I must therefore dismiss this summons.

Parke *v.* Daily News, Ltd. [1962] Ch. 927

Gratuitous payments are prima facie ultra vires. The court will inquire into the motive behind them, and will uphold them only if the tests laid down by Eve J. in Re Lee, Behrens and Co., Ltd., are satisfied. The burden of proving this is on those asserting that the payments are valid.

The defendant company, the Daily News, Ltd., controlled two newspapers, the *News Chronicle* and the *Star*, as the major part of its business. The copyright in these newspapers was owned by two of its wholly-owned subsidiaries, the News Chronicle Ltd. and the Star Newspaper Co. Ltd. In October 1960 the three companies employed nearly 2,800 persons, of whom 2,000 were employed by Daily News Ltd. The subsidiaries ceased trading in October 1960 and all except some 100 of the 2,800 employees were dismissed.

In July 1958 the Board of Daily News Ltd., which was composed chiefly of members of the Cadbury family, had decided, owing to losses incurred in the two previous years, to sell the copyright of the newspapers together with the newspapers' plant and premises to prevent any further possible loss. Thereupon, secret negotiations began with

Associated Newspapers Ltd., who eventually agreed to take over the two newspapers in order to merge them with two of its own, and to buy the plant and premises in question. During the subsequent negotiations it emerged that Daily News Ltd. intended to distribute the balance of the purchase money, after meeting the costs of the transaction, by giving compensation to the staff in addition to making payments of not less than two weeks' wages in lieu of notice, in respect of holiday money and in respect of accrued pension rights. The contract of sale specifically provided that Associated Newspapers Ltd. was to have no responsibility for the payment of compensation by Daily News Ltd. to those of its staff who were likely to be dismissed, without imposing liability on the Daily News Ltd. to make those payments. The obligation to make the payments was purely a moral one.

On 17th October 1960 the shareholders of Daily News Ltd. were informed of the deal by a circular letter. On 20th January 1961 a further circular was sent to the shareholders giving notice of a general meeting to be held on 8th February 1961 to authorise the directors to distribute the balance of the purchase price among the former members of the staff by way of compensation.

On 3rd February 1961 the plaintiff, Mr. Hall Parke, a minority shareholder of Daily News Ltd., issued a writ on behalf of himself and all other shareholders of the defendant company except those who, being members of the board, were personal defendants. He claimed that the proposed payment of compensation was *ultra vires* and illegal, and sought an injunction to restrain the company from making it.

The defendants, it was found, were under no contractual obligation either to their employees or to Associated Newspapers Ltd. to pay the compensation in question.

PLOWMAN J.: . . . The conclusions which, I think, follow from these cases [*Hutton* v. *West Cork Railway Co.* and *Re Lee, Behrens & Co. Ltd.*] are: first, that a company's funds cannot be applied in making *ex gratia* payments as such; secondly, that the court will inquire into the motives actuating any gratuitous payment, and the objectives which it is intended to achieve; thirdly, that the court will uphold the validity of gratuitous payments if, but only if, after such inquiry, it appears that the tests enumerated by EVE J., are satisfied; fourthly, that the onus of upholding the validity of such payments lies on those who assert it.

. . . I want to make it quite clear that the integrity of the defendants is unchallenged, and I am satisfied that their motives have been honourable throughout. But at the end of the day I am not satisfied that the decision to distribute this enormous sum of money was taken simply in the interests of the company. . . . [It] was, in my judgment, motivated by other considerations. Predominant among such other considerations was, I think, the desire to treat the employees generously, beyond all entitlement, and to appear to have done so.

. . . The view that directors, in having regard to the question what is in the best interests of their company, are entitled to take into account the interests of the employees, irrespective of any consequential benefit to the company, is one which may be widely held. . . . But no authority to support that proposition as a proposition of law was cited to me; I know of none, and in my judgment such is not the law.

In *Greenhalgh* v. *Arderne Cinemas Ltd.* LORD EVERSHED, M.R., said, in a different context, that the benefit of the company meant the benefit of the shareholders as a general body, and in my opinion that is equally true in a case such as the present.

In my judgment, therefore, the defendants were prompted by motives which, however laudable, and however enlightened from the point of view of industrial relations, were such as the law does not recognise as a sufficient justification. Stripped of all its side issues, the essence of the matter is this, that the directors of the defendant company are proposing that a very large part of its funds should be given to its former employees in order to benefit those employees rather than the company, and that is an application of the company's funds which the law, as I understand it, will not allow.

If this is right, then it appears to me to follow from the *Hut-*

ton case that the proposal to pay compensation is one which a majority of shareholders is not entitled to ratify. . . .

Re W. and M. Roith Ltd. [1967] 1 W.L.R. 432

Where the motive behind the gratuitous payment is not to benefit the company, but to benefit some other person, this is sufficient to invalidate it.

W. and M. Roith Ltd. was incorporated in 1934, its business being the manufacture of ladies' clothing. In 1958, at which time the company was prospering, its paid-up capital was £13,505 divided into £1 shares of which Mr. Maurice Mancini Roith held 9,240, his wife Mrs. Rosie Roith held 326, Leah Roith held 3,124 and Mrs. Lily Lawrence held 815. Mr Roith, Mrs. Roith and Mrs. Lawrence were the three directors of the company. Mr. Roith also controlled another company, Michael Wayne Ltd., which sold by mail order the products of W. and M. Roith Ltd., and which was also prospering. Mr. Roith had been a director of W. and M. Roith Ltd. since its incorporation and had always received remuneration from the company, but had never entered into any contract of service with either company.

In 1957 Mr. Roith was fifty-seven and his health was not good. Mrs. Roith was about two years older. In that year he consulted his solicitor with regard to his will and the continuity of the businesses after his death, and said that he wished to make provision for his wife and dependants without dividing the control of either company between them.

His solicitor advised him to enter into a contract of service with one or other of the companies, whereby he undertook to serve it for the rest of his life without any specific provision for remuneration, but on terms that if he died during such service leaving his wife surviving, the company would be under a liability to pay her a pension, thus leaving him free to dispose of all his shares in both companies by his will in favour of his other dependants.

Mr. Roith accepted this advice, and in 1958 the company,

at an extraordinary general meeting, passed a special
resolution amending the objects clause of the memorandum of association by giving the company power "to
support or subscribe to any charitable or public object . . .
to give pensions, gratuities, or charitable aid to any person
who may have served the company . . . or to the wives,
children or other relatives or dependants of such persons."
The articles were also amended by adding an article similar in terms.

The service agreement recommended by Mr. Roith's
solicitor was entered into in December 1958. In this
agreement Mr. Roith undertook to serve the company,
W. and M. Roith Ltd., as general manager and director
for the rest of his life at such salary as should be agreed
between them from time to time, to devote the whole of
his time and abilities to the company's business, and to use
his best endeavours to promote its interests. The company
covenanted that in the event of his death during his re-
tention of office it would pay to his widow, if she should
survive him, a pension of £1,040 per annum during the
rest of her life.

In January 1959 Mr. Roith died of cancer in the service
of the company, leaving his widow surviving him. He had
not known, in 1958 at least, that he was suffering from this
disease. In 1963 W. and M. Roith Ltd. went into voluntary liquidation and in 1964 Mr. Roith's executors claimed
the sum of £10,400 against the liquidator in respect of the
pension, *i.e.* its capitalised value. The liquidator rejected
this claim on the grounds, *inter alia*, that the service agreement was not reasonably incidental to the carrying on of
the company's business and was not entered into for its
benefit or to promote its prosperity.

In 1965 the executors took out an originating summons
asking that the liquidator's decision be reversed, though
it was agreed by both parties that the proper figure to be
claimed was £9,270.

PLOWMAN J.: . . . It is, I think, common ground in this case
that the principle there enunciated [*in Re Lee, Behrens and Co.
Ltd.*] is applicable here. . . . Mr. Instone's submissions on behalf of the applicants were these. First, he said that a widow's

pension is a normal and customary mode of remunerating
a director and, therefore, the provision of a widow's pension
is reasonably incidental to carrying on a company's business,
and I am disposed to agree that that is so. Then he said the
provision of a pension for Mrs. Roith must have been for
the benefit of the company because it was for the benefit of
the company that the architect of its prosperity should be tied
to the company in the way in which he was tied by the service
agreement, and he pointed out that the only *quid pro quo* for
that tie was the provision of a pension for Mr. Roith's widow.
Mr. Instone pointed out, quite truly, that the capacity of
the company to pay a pension of £1,040 a year . . . was one
of the matters taken into account in coming to the arrangements that were made, and he submitted that there is no
evidence of a lack of *bona fides* on the part of anybody involved
in the transaction on the company's part, and he relied on
the fact that the liquidator has not filed evidence by either of
the other directors to say otherwise.

On the other hand, Mr. Smith, on behalf of the liquidator,
accepted that . . . the onus is on the liquidator to show that
this service agreement was not entered into *bona fide* in the
interests of the company, but . . . he submitted that he has
discharged it, and he relied on the following matters. First,
he said that Mr. Roith . . . had been a director of the company
since the year 1934, when it was incorporated, and that,
throughout that period, he had been in receipt of remuneration from the company, and he submitted that there was no
conceivable reason for altering the situation in the year 1958
except in order to provide for Mr. Roith's widow without
leaving her his shares in the company by his will.

Secondly, Mr. Smith pointed out that so long as Mr. Roith
retained control the company in fact got no benefit at all from
the service agreement, and he submitted that the facts show
that Mr. Roith intended to retain control of the company, the
relevant facts being those relating to his intended testamentary
disposition.

Thirdly, Mr. Smith pointed out—and this is, I think, a
significant fact—that it was regarded as immaterial which

company should provide the pension. . . . It seems to me that the proper inference from the facts is that [Mr. Roith] was working to a material extent for Michael Wayne Ltd., because both Mr. Roith and his solicitor quite clearly thought that he could justifiably call on either of those companies for a pension to his widow. Mr. Smith submitted that, in the light of those facts, the inference was that the real object of this scheme was not to benefit the company but was simply to provide for Mr. Roith's widow without leaving her his shares in the company and, accordingly, Mr. Smith submitted that the liquidator had discharged the onus of proof which was upon him.

. . . I feel that I am bound to accept the argument of Mr. Smith. It seems to me that the liquidator was well justified . . . in drawing the inference which he has drawn and which is stated in . . . his affidavit in this way: "as is to be inferred from the circumstances the entering into of the said agreement by the company was not reasonably incidental to the carrying on of the company's business and was not *bona fide* for the benefit and to promote the prosperity of the company."

I myself draw the same inference from the facts and I have come to the conclusion that really the whole object of the plan of campaign was to benefit, not the company, but Mrs. Roith and, in the circumstances, I must dismiss the application.

Charterbridge Corporation Ltd. *v.* Lloyds Bank Ltd. and Another. [1970] Ch. 62

Where a company is carrying out the purposes expressed in its memorandum, and does an act within the scope of a power expressed in its memorandum, that act is intra vires; *and on that issue the state of mind of the officers of the company concerned and the other party to the transaction is quite irrelevant.*

Pomeroy Developments (Castleford) Ltd., referred to as Castleford, a private company, was incorporated in 1956. Its objects were, *inter alia*, to acquire lands for investment and "to secure or guarantee by mortgages, charges, or otherwise the performance and discharge of any contract, obligation or liability of Castleford Ltd. or of any other

person or corporation with whom or which Castleford
Ltd. has dealings or having a business or undertaking in
which Castleford Ltd. is concerned or interested whether
directly or indirectly."

Castleford Ltd. was one of a large group of companies
headed by Pomeroy Developments Ltd., referred to as
Pomeroy, and trading as property developers. All the companies, though not subsidiaries of Pomeroy Ltd., had a
common shareholding, directorate and office. Mr. Oscar
Alexander Pomeroy owned all the issued shares in Castleford Ltd. except one, which was owned by Mrs. Pomeroy.
They were also the sole directors. Pomeroy Ltd., which was
almost wholly owned by Mr. Pomeroy, supervised the
activities of all the companies, provided the office services
and finance and carried out the acquisition and development of the sites. A separate company was incorporated
to deal with each particular site acquired.

In 1956 certain land was leased to Castleford Ltd. for
999 years. Pomeroy Ltd. guaranteed performance by
Castleford Ltd. of its covenants and paid the rent due
from Castleford Ltd. In 1960 the accounts of Pomeroy
Ltd. and two other companies in the group with the defendant, Lloyds Bank Ltd., were overdrawn, the over-
drawings being in excess of the bank's permitted limit.
The bank pressed for security and a chain of guarantees
was given to the bank by Mr. Pomeroy and various companies in the group. Castleford Ltd. guaranteed payment
on demand of all moneys owing by Pomeroy Ltd. to the
bank up to a limit of £30,000, and deposited with the bank
the title deeds of the leasehold property.

In 1961 Castleford Ltd. took a first mortgage from Askinex, borrowing £14,813, against a covenant to repay
£18,147 in 1962. With the consent of the bank, the title
deeds were handed over to Askinex. The proceeds of that
mortgage were paid to the bank in reduction of Pomeroy
Ltd.'s overdraft but it increased again, and following pressure by the bank a legal charge was executed by Castleford
Ltd. in 1962 charging the leasehold property to the bank,
subject to the mortgage in favour of Askinex. Neither the
officers of the group nor the bank at the time of the transaction considered the interest of Castleford Ltd. separately
from that of the group.

Later in 1962 Castleford Ltd. agreed to sell the property
to Charterbridge Corporation Ltd., the plaintiff company,
for over £30,000. Charterbridge Corporation Ltd. paid
£20,000 on account, almost the whole of which was applied
in discharging the Askinex mortgage, leaving the bank
as first mortgagee. Charterbridge Corporation Ltd. then
paid a further £10,000 on account in four instalments,
which were not paid to the bank. In 1964 the bank demanded repayment by Castleford Ltd. of a stated amount
and threatened to realise the security.

Charterbridge Corporation Ltd. took out a writ seeking
a declaration that the legal charge was created for purposes outside the scope of Castleford Ltd.'s business and
was *ultra vires* and void, and claiming an injunction to
restrain the bank from selling the leasehold premises in
exercise of their powers as mortgagees.

PENNYCUICK J.: . . . It will be borne in mind that the present
action is based exclusively upon the contention that it was
ultra vires Castleford, *i.e.* outside its corporate powers, to give
the guarantee and legal charge. On this footing the guarantee
and legal charge were a nullity.

Apart from authority, I should feel little doubt that where a
company is carrying out the purposes expressed in its memorandum, and does an act within the scope of a power expressed
in its memorandum, that act is an act within the powers of the
company. The memorandum of a company sets out its objects
and proclaims them to persons dealing with the company
and it would be contrary to the whole function of a memorandum that objects unequivocally set out in it should be subject to some implied limitation by reference to the state of
mind of the parties concerned.

Where directors misapply the assets of their company, that
may give rise to a claim based on breach of duty. Again,
a claim may arise against the other party to the transaction, if
he has noticed that the transaction was effected in breach of
duty. Further, in a proper case, the company concerned may
be entitled to have the transaction set aside. But all that
results from the ordinary law of agency and has not of itself
anything to do with the corporate powers of the company.

... In my judgment, the state of mind of the directors of Castleford and of the bank's officers is irrelevant upon this issue of *ultra vires*.

That is sufficient to dispose of the action; but in case I am wrong on my view of the law, I must proceed to express a conclusion upon the contention that in creating the guarantee and legal charge, the directors were not acting with a view to the benefit of Castleford. That is a question of fact, and the burden of proof lies on the plaintiff company. As I have already found, the directors of Castleford looked to the benefit of the group as a whole and did not give separate consideration to the benefit of Castleford. ... Each company in the group is a separate legal entity and the directors of a particular company are not entitled to sacrifice the interest of that company. ... The proper test, I think, in the absence of actual separate consideration, must be whether an intelligent and honest man in the position of a director of the company concerned, could, in the whole of the existing circumstances, have reasonably believed that the transactions were for the benefit of the company. If that is the proper test, I am satisfied that the answer here is in the affirmative.

... For the reasons which I have given, this action fails.

IV. THE ARTICLES OF ASSOCIATION

1. The Company's Power to Alter its Articles

**Allen *v.* Gold Reefs of West Africa, Limited. [1900]
1 Ch. 656**

A company's statutory power to alter its articles is limited only by the provisions contained in the Companies· Acts and the conditions contained in its memorandum of association. Like all other powers, it must be exercised bona fide *for the benefit of the company as a whole, and the rights of shareholders under the articles are limited as to their duration by the duration of the articles which confer them.*

The defendant company, the Gold Reefs of West Africa, Limited, was incorporated on 2nd July 1895 under the *Companies Acts*, 1862 to 1890. Article 29 of its articles of association provided "that the company shall have a first and paramount lien for all debts, obligations and liabilities of any member to or towards the company upon all shares (not being fully paid) held by such member."

Article 74 provided that notice of general meetings should be given to members. The articles contained no special provision for service of notices in the case of a deceased member, but Article 45 provided that a person becoming entitled to shares in consequence of the death of any member should not be entitled to receive notice of meetings unless or until he should have become a member in respect of them.

Shares, both fully paid up and not fully paid up, were issued by the company. One Emilio Zuccani, as the nominee of the vendor to the company, had a number of fully paid up shares allotted to him by way of purchase-money for the property acquired by the company under their memorandum of association, and he held 27,885 of these shares at the time of his death, these shares being his own property. It did not appear that when Zuccani took these shares he entered into any special bargain conferring upon him any special rights in respect of them.

In addition to these fully paid up shares, Zuccani applied for and had allotted to him 60,000 ordinary 5s. shares, not paid up. These were applied for and allotted on the terms of the company's prospectus and articles of association. Calls were from time to time made in Zuccani's lifetime on these unpaid-up shares, but he did not pay the calls when they became due, and as early as May 1896 and thenceforward during his life letters were sent to him pressing for payment of his arrears. Although he did not pay his calls, he constantly paid up quantities of shares in full before their amounts had been called up: in other words, he from time to time not only paid all the calls due on some of his shares, but also prepaid the uncalled-up amounts of the same shares. He did this constantly all through 1896, and in that way he was able to sell and transfer the shares so paid up free from all liability to calls and from all lien in favour of the company. From the money so obtained he made remittances to the company on account of his calls in arrear. His object in fully paying up batches of these shares in this way was to obtain shares which he could put on the market free from all claims and demands by the company. This the directors allowed him to do as a favour. All the shares thus paid up were transferred by him in his lifetime; he did not hold any of them at the time of his death.

Zuccani died on 4th February 1897 leaving a will which was proved by the plaintiffs, his executors. At the time of his death he was the registered holder of the 27,885 fully paid-up vendor's shares, and also of 36,435 other shares partly paid up, and he owed the company £6,072 10s. for calls in respect of these, besides interest to a considerable amount.

The plaintiffs did not get themselves registered as members of the company in respect of any of Zuccani's shares, and they had not sufficient assets to answer his liabilities. Steps were taken to have his estate administered in the Chancery Division, but the company, instead of electing to carry in a proof for its debt, proceeded to take more summary measures.

In the first place, on 9th February 1897 a notice was sent out of an extraordinary general meeting of the company to be held on 18th February for the purpose of passing a special resolution to alter article 29 of the articles of association by omitting the words "not being fully paid." This notice was posted to Zuccani at his registered address, although the directors were then aware of his death. The meeting was held, and the special resolution passed.

Thereupon notice of a confirmatory meeting to be held on 8th March was, as before, sent to Zuccani's registered address. Both notices, addressed to Zuccani personally, came to the knowledge of the plaintiffs. On 8th March the confirmatory meeting was held and the resolution confirmed. Thus the company claimed to extend their lien to all fully paid-up shares. There were in fact no fully paid-up shares except those belonging to Zuccani.

The next step the company took was this. On 4th June 1897 the directors posted to Zuccani at his registered address a notice requiring payment by 21st June of the £6,072 10s. due for calls on the 36,435 shares, a sum of £804 6s. 11d. for interest on arrears of calls and further interest from the date of the notice; the notice also stating that in the event of non-payment by the time appointed those shares would be liable to be forfeited. This notice was sent also to the plaintiffs, who had not then lodged the probate of his will with the company for registration. The amounts demanded were not paid, and on 23rd June the directors passed a resolution purporting to forfeit the 36,435 shares.

The plaintiffs brought an action to obtain a declaration that the defendant company had no lien upon the fully paid-up shares, and an injunction to restrain the forfeiture of the partly paid-up shares.

In the High Court KEKEWICH J. held that the notice threatening forfeiture was bad upon the grounds that, as the company or its directors were aware of Zuccani's death at the time they served the notice addressed to him, this service was not sufficient to bind his estate, and that the service of the notice upon his executors was also ineffectual, an executor of a deceased member of a company not being a "member," unless duly registered as such.

He also held that the notices of the meeting of the company to pass the resolution altering article 29 were ineffectual as having been addressed to Zuccani after the directors had become aware of his death. He therefore considered it unnecessary to decide the further question whether the company could alter its articles so as to create a lien upon Zuccani's fully paid-up shares. He accordingly granted an injunction restraining the defendant company from enforcing the lien.

From that judgment the company appealed.

In the Court of Appeal their Lordships held that owing to mistakes on the part of the company there had been no effective forfeiture of the unpaid-up shares, and on that point affirmed the judgment of KEKEWICH J. They then considered the question of whether the company had power to alter its articles by giving itself a lien upon Zuccani's fully paid-up shares.

LINDLEY M.R.: . . . The directors desired to extend the lien . . . to Zuccani's fully paid-up shares. I say, to his shares, for he was the only person entitled to fully paid-up shares from whom any calls were due. Accordingly steps were taken to pass a special resolution to alter art. 29 by striking out the words "not being fully paid," and a resolution to that effect was passed on February 18, 1897, and was confirmed on March 8, 1897. Notice convening these meetings was sent addressed to Zuccani at his registered place of address; and the notice came to the knowledge of his executors. The directors knew that he was dead; but I cannot agree with the learned judge that the resolution is invalid by reason of any defect in the notice. Notices of meetings have only to be given to members, and the executors were not members. If no notice at all had been sent to the executors or to Zuccani's registered address, the omission would not, in my opinion, have affected the propriety of holding the meetings or the validity of the resolutions passed at them. Art. 45 expressly provided that notices of meetings need not be sent to executors who had not become members. To hold that meetings of companies could not be properly held unless the notices convening them were given to the unregistered legal personal representatives of all deceased members would be to paralyse the transaction of business, and would be contrary to the ordinary principles applicable to corporate bodies. . . . The regularity of the proceedings to alter the articles by no means, however, disposes of the matters in controversy between the parties. . . .

The articles of a company prescribe the regulations binding on its members. . . . They have the effect of a contract; but the exact nature of this contract is even now very difficult to define. Be its nature what it may, the company is empowered by the statute to alter the regulations contained in its articles from time to time by special resolutions; and any regulation or article purporting to deprive the company of this power is invalid on the ground that it is contrary to the statute: *Walker* v. *London Tramways Co.* (1879).

The power thus conferred on companies to alter the regulations contained in their articles is limited only by the provisions contained in the statute and the conditions contained in the company's memorandum of association. Wide, however, as the language of S.50 [*now S.10, Companies Act, 1948*] is, the power conferred by it must, like all other powers, be exercised subject to those general principles of law and equity which are applicable to all powers conferred on majorities and enabling them to bind minorities. It must be exercised, not only in the manner required by law, but also *bona fide* for the benefit of the company as a whole, and it must not be exceeded. These conditions are always implied, and are seldom, if ever, expressed. But if they are complied with I can discover no ground for judicially putting any other restrictions on the power conferred by the section than those contained in it. How shares shall be transferred, and whether the company shall have any lien on them, are clearly matters of regulation properly prescribed by a company's articles of association. This is shown by Table A. . . . Speaking, therefore, generally, and without reference to any particular case, the section clearly authorizes a limited company, formed with articles which confer no lien on fully paid-up shares, and which allow them to be transferred without any fetter, to alter those articles by special resolution, and to impose a lien and restrictions on the registry of transfers of those shares by members indebted to the company.

But then comes the question whether this can be done so as

to impose a lien or restriction in respect of a debt contracted before and existing at the time when the articles are altered. Again, speaking generally, I am of opinion that the articles can be so altered, and that, if they are altered *bona fide* for the benefit of the company, they will be valid and binding as altered on the existing holders of paid-up shares, whether such holders are indebted or not indebted to the company when the alteration is made.

. . . The answer to the argument that the company could not alter existing rights is that, within the limits set by the statute and the memorandum of association, the rights of shareholders in limited companies, so far as they depend only on the regulations of the company, are subject to alteration by S.50 [*now S.10 Companies Act, 1948*] of the Act. . . . Such rights are in truth limited as to their duration by the duration of the articles which confer them.

But, although the regulations contained in a company's articles of association are revocable by special resolution, a special contract may be made with the company in the terms of or embodying one or more of the articles, and the question will then arise whether an alteration of the articles so embodied is consistent or inconsistent with the real bargain between the parties. A company cannot break its contracts by altering its articles, but, when dealing with contracts referring to revocable articles, and especially with contracts between a member of the company and the company respecting his shares, care must be taken not to assume that the contract involves as one of its terms an article which is not to be altered.

It is easy to imagine cases in which even a member of a company may acquire by contract or otherwise special rights against the company, which exclude him from the operation of a subsequently altered article. . . .

I take it to be clear that an application for an allotment of shares on the terms of the company's articles does not exclude the power to alter them nor the application of them, when altered, to the shares so applied for and allotted. To exclude that power or the application of an altered article to particular shares, some clear and distinct agreement for that exclusion must be shown, or some circumstances must be proved conferring a legal or equitable right on the shareholder to be treated by the company differently from the other shareholders.

This brings me to the last question which has to be considered, namely, whether there is in this case any contract or other circumstance which excludes the application of the altered article to Zuccani's fully paid-up vendor's shares.

First, let us consider the shares. I am unable to discover any difference in principle between one fully paid-up share and another. Whether a share is paid for in cash or is given in payment for property acquired by the company appears to me quite immaterial for the present purpose. In either case the shareholder pays for his share, and in either case he takes it subject to the articles of association and power of altering them, unless this inference is excluded by special circumstances.

Next let us consider whether a vendor who makes no special bargain except that he is to be paid in fully paid-up shares is in any different position from other allottees of fully paid-up shares. I fail to see that he is, unless he stipulates that his share shall be specially favoured. Zuccani bargained for fully paid-up shares and he got them. The imposition of a lien on them did not render them less fully paid-up than they were before. They remained what they were. Zuccani did not bargain that the regulations relating to paid-up shares should never be altered, or that, if altered, his shares should be treated differently from other fully paid-up shares. I cannot see that the company broke its bargain with him in any way by altering its regulations or by enforcing the altered regulations as it did. . . . The fact that Zuccani's executors were the only persons practically affected at the time by the alterations made in the articles excites suspicion as to the *bona fides* of the company. But, although the executors were the only persons who were actually affected at the time, that was because Zuccani was the only holder of paid-up shares who at the time was in arrear of calls. The altered articles applied to all holders of fully paid shares, and made no distinction between them. The directors cannot be charged with bad faith.

. . . I have come to the conclusion that the appeal from the decision of the learned judge, so far as it relates to the lien created by the altered articles, must be allowed.

VAUGHAN WILLIAMS L.J.: I do not know that I differ from my brethren as to the law of this case. We are all agreed that there was power in the shareholders to pass the resolution which they did pass. . . .

We are further all agreed that a company cannot contract itself out of the statutory power of alteration conferred by S.50 [*now S.10, Companies Act, 1948*]; and the alteration of the articles in the present case involves no contravention of the memorandum of association. But I think that we are all agreed that cases might occur in which a member might have acquired, by contract or otherwise, special rights against the company which would exclude him from the operation of the altered article. . . . A resolution may alter the regulations of a company but cannot retrospectively affect existing rights. I also take it to be clear that the alteration must be made in good faith; and I take it that an alteration in the articles which involved oppression of one shareholder would not be made in good faith.

The result is that we have to consider in the present case whether the alteration, if enforced against Zuccani's executors, would defeat existing rights or operate oppressively. On this point I confess that I have much more doubt than my brethren seem to have. It is of course true that Zuccani, when he took these shares as the price of the property which he was selling, knew or must be taken to have known of the statutory power of alteration; but it does not seem to me that it follows that the company could make alterations which would alter the value, according to the articles in force, of the consideration which they were giving for the property purchased.

. . . The present case is that the company by the articles then in force reserved to themselves a lien upon all shares not being fully paid, and then purchased a property by the issue of fully paid shares. . . . I think that, notwithstanding the statutory powers of alteration, the basis of the contract of purchase was that the property should be paid for in marketable shares. I think that the very object of the exception in art. 29 of fully paid shares from lien was to render those shares marketable, and, as they chose to pay for the property in shares thus made marketable, I think that to allow the company to subject the vendor's shares to a lien would be to make the alteration of the articles retrospectively affect existing rights. I think moreover, that the resolution was not passed in good faith, being really passed merely to defeat the existing rights of an individual shareholder.

ROMER L.J.: . . . A company such as this may undoubtedly by its articles of association provide for a lien on the shares of its shareholders in respect of any debts for the time being due from them to the company, and, if the original articles do not provide for the lien, the company may subsequently, by duly altering its articles, give itself such a lien; and the fact that the original articles did not provide for a lien would be in itself no ground justifying a shareholder who was indebted when the articles were altered in saying that he contracted the debt or that he took his shares in reliance on there being no lien, and that the new articles must not operate so as to make the lien thereby given extend to his existing debt. A shareholder must be taken to have known that the articles might be so altered as to give the lien. And certainly a shareholder could not say as against the company that he was entitled to special rights because he did not pay his debts. And the same considerations apply to the case where the original articles give only a limited lien, as, for example, a lien limited to debts due for unpaid calls. The company might by subsequent articles extend the lien, and a shareholder would have no right to object to the extended lien because he happened to be indebted to the company. . . .

I will now consider the circumstances of the case before us. And the first question is as to the meaning and effect of art. 29 of the company. In my opinion that article merely provides for a limited lien—that is to say, it limits the lien so as to exclude fully paid-up shares. There is nothing in the memorandum of association of the company to prevent that lien being subsequently extended to fully paid-up shares by an alteration in the articles. There is nothing in the company's original articles of association to prevent such extension of the lien. Nor was any shareholder justified in assuming from art. 29 that fully paid-up shares would never be made subject to the lien by an alteration in the articles. No one was justified in assuming from it that the company thereby held out, in favour of any person acquiring fully paid-up shares, that those shares should never be made subject to a lien by an alteration of the articles. If art. 29 had gone on to state expressly that the lien thereby provided might be extended later on by an alteration of the articles, no one could venture to doubt what was the true meaning and effect of the article. But such a statement is implied though not expressed. It was not, in my opinion, necessary for the article to say at the end, "Caution—remember the power of the company to alter its articles by extending its lien," or any words to that effect.

. . . [I]n my opinion, Mr. Zuccani's shares became bound by the company's alteration of its articles unless he can show some special bargain with the company, or some special obligation incurred towards him by the company, in respect of his fully paid-up shares. He fails to establish any such special bargain or obligation. . . . Mr. Zuccani, in respect of all his fully paid-up shares, whether allotted as paid up or not, in fact has obtained and enjoyed all the advantages with regard to lien which the company ever impliedly or expressly promised him— that is to say, the right to deal with the shares without their being subject to any lien so long as the articles remained un-altered and did not extend the lien to fully paid-up shares.

Something was said on behalf of the respondents as to want of good faith on the part of the company in altering the articles. I fail to see any want of good faith. . . . [I]f the company in the present case had, as I think it had, the legal right to alter its articles so as to give it the lien it now claims, I cannot see why, in exercising that legal right, it should be accused of want of good faith. That the reason for the alteration was the very existence of the large debt due from Mr. Zuccani, and that the company had principally in mind this large debt when it made the alteration in the articles, is no ground for impeaching the action of the company. It appears to me the shareholders were acting in the truest and best interests of the company in exercising the legal right to alter the articles so that the company might as one result obtain payment of the debt due from Mr. Zuccani. The shareholders were only bound to look to the interests of the company. They were not bound to consult or consider Mr. Zuccani's separate or private interests.

Further, I may say that the alteration of the articles giving the extended lien was, in my opinion, in no true sense retrospective. The lien given was not made to take effect before the date of the alteration. It operated only from and after that date.

Again, the alteration of the articles cannot be impeached as being one not binding on all shareholders alike. It purports to bind, and does bind, all the shareholders without exception. An article giving a lien cannot be objected to as made in favour of or against a special class of shareholders merely because some shareholders only are or may become indebted to the company.

. . . [I]n the result, I can find no good or sufficient ground on which to hold that the lien given by the amended articles was not good against Mr. Zuccani's executors; and accordingly, I think that the appeal should be allowed.

Sidebottom *v*. Kershaw, Leese and Company, Limited. [1920] 1 Ch. 154

Anything which would be valid if contained in the original articles may properly be inserted later by way of alteration of the articles, provided it is done bona fide *for the benefit of the company as a whole. An alteration may be* bona fide *for the benefit of the company as a whole even though it is to the disadvantage of an individual shareholder, provided it is not actuated by personal motives against him.*

Kershaw, Leese & Co., Ltd., a private company, was incorporated in June 1894 to acquire as a going concern the goodwill, etc., of an existing business of cotton spinners at Heaton Norris in the county borough of Stockport. The nominal capital of the company was £80,000 divided into 4,000 preference and 4,000 ordinary shares of £10 each, both classes of shareholders having the same voting power

—namely, one vote for each share. The total number of shares issued was 7,620, of which 4,396 were held by the directors and 711 by the plaintiffs.

At meetings of the company held on 6th June and 24th June 1919, a special resolution was passed and confirmed to the effect that a certain document be adopted as the articles of the company in substitution for and to the exclusion of the existing articles. At each of the meetings the resolution was carried by a majority larger than sufficient to meet the statutory requirements, the only members voting against it being the plaintiffs.

Of the proposed new articles, article 40, the one complained of, was in the following terms:

"In every case where shares are held by a person who carries on any business which is in direct competition with the business of the company, or who is a director of any company carrying on such business, the directors may at any time give to such person notice requiring him forthwith to transfer all such shares, and he shall thereupon be bound, upon payment of the fair value of the shares to be ascertained as stated in art. 38, to transfer the shares to such person or persons as the directors shall nominate."

The plaintiffs carried on business in Manchester as merchants and shippers under the style of G. I. Sidebottom & Co. Their business was in direct competition with the business of the company. Both the plaintiffs' firm and the company dealt in similar kinds of cloth in the same localities in this country and abroad. The plaintiffs accordingly brought an action for a declaration that the resolution was invalid and for an injunction to restrain the company from giving effect to it.

The directors, however, in their evidence stated that they had never considered that the firm of G. I. Sidebottom & Co. was a firm competing in any way with the defendant company, and that they had no present intention of applying article 40 to expropriate the plaintiffs. They said that the only case they had in contemplation in voting for the adoption of the new article 40 was the case of a Mr. Bodden, who held seventy shares in the company, and who was interested in two businesses which were in constant and keen competition with the company.

The Vice-Chancellor of the County Palatine of Lancaster held that the power conferred by S.13, *Companies (Consolidation) Act*, 1908, *(see now S.10 Companies Act, 1948)* upon a company to alter or add to its articles was qualified by this, that a proposed alteration capable of being enforced upon a minority of the shareholders must be within the ordinary principles of justice, and must be for the benefit of the company as a whole; and, applying that test, he held that the proposed new article was invalid, inasmuch as it would enable the directors, who, in this case, held the majority of the shares, to compulsorily expropriate a competing shareholder.

From this decision the company appealed, and the case accordingly came before the Court of Appeal.

Lord Sterndale M.R.: I do not say this is an entirely easy case, but I have come to the conclusion that the appeal must be allowed.

The question is as to the validity or invalidity of an alteration in the articles of association of the company. There were several articles that were altered, but there is only one in respect to which any question arises on this appeal, and that is art. 40. I need not consider the way in which the value is to be ascertained, because it was not argued that if the altered article were otherwise valid there was anything unfair in the method of the ascertainment of the value which would make it objectionable. . . . [T]he plaintiffs, as I have said, were a competing firm. The directors of the defendant company did not introduce this alteration in the article with any view of using it against the plaintiff firm, but they did introduce it with the view of using it if necessary against Mr. Bodden. Now it does not seem to me to matter, as to the validity of this altered article, whether it was introduced with a view of using it against the plaintiff firm or not, except to this extent, that it might be that if it had been introduced specially for the purpose of using it against the plaintiffs' firm some question of *bona fides* might possibly have arisen, because it might have been argued that it was introduced to do them harm, and not to do the company good. That is the only way in which it seems to me to be relevant. The same seems to me to be the case with regard to the position of Mr. Bodden. If the alteration were proposed with the intention of injuring Mr. Bodden only, or getting Mr. Bodden out of the company only, without any reasonable ground, and not for the benefit of the company, then again there would be, as it seems to me, a lack of *bona fides*, and in that way and in that way only Mr. Bodden's position is of importance. . . . [I]f by reason of the relative position of Mr. Bodden and the defendant company's directors this was invalid against Mr. Bodden, it is invalid altogether. The question is whether it is invalid. It introduces a new power which did not exist in the original articles at all—a power to buy out on the terms mentioned in the article any shareholder who was engaged in a competing business. . . . [A] power such as this is a perfectly valid power in the case of original articles, and it seems to me that prima facie if it could be in the original articles, it could be introduced into the altered articles provided only it is done *bona fide* for the benefit of the company as a whole. . . .

In my opinion, the whole of this case comes down to rather a narrow question of fact, which is this: When the directors of this company introduced this alteration giving power to buy up the shares of members who were in competing businesses did they do it *bona fide* for the benefit of the company or not? It seems to me quite clear that it may be very much to the benefit of the company to get rid of members who are in competing businesses. . . . I think there can be no doubt that a member of a competing business or an owner of a competing business who is a member of the company has a much better chance of knowing what is going on in the business of the company, and of thereby helping his own competition with it, than if he were a non-member. . . . I think, looking at the alteration broadly, that it is for the benefit of the company that they should not be obliged to have amongst them as members persons who are competing with them in business, and who may get knowledge from their membership which would enable them to compete better.

That brings me to the last point. It is said that that might be so were it not for the fact that the directors and the secretary have said: "This is directed against Mr. Bodden," and therefore it is not done *bona fide* for the benefit of the company, but it is done to get rid of Mr. Bodden. If it were directed against Mr. Bodden from any malicious motive I should agree with that—the thing would cease to be *bona fide* at once; but . . . it was directed against every competing person, and Mr. Bodden was only the occasion of the passing of the alteration of the article. . . .

[T]his resolution was passed *bona fide* for the benefit of the company—not directed from any personal motives against Mr. Bodden, but Mr. Bodden being merely in the position, as I have said, of the occasion which gave rise to the alteration.

For these reasons I think this is a valid article. I think the alteration was within the competence of the company, and therefore this appeal must be allowed. . . .

WARRINGTON L.J.: I am of the same opinion.

. . . It may be that a particular course may be to the disadvantage of some individual shareholder; but, notwithstanding that, it might still be for the benefit of the company at large that that course should be pursued. But it is then said that this step was taken with the special object of ridding the company of a particular shareholder, whose name is given in the affidavits, who was known to be a competitor, and that for that reason the resolution was not passed *bona fide*. I am entirely unable to follow that. I have no doubt that the fact that there was this competitor, and probably the knowledge that he was doing harm to the company, awoke the directors to the disadvantage in which they were placed by having such a man as one of their shareholders; that may well be, and that they passed this resolution having had their attention called to it by the position of Mr. Bodden; but that is a very different thing from saying that they passed this resolution with the *mala fide* and dishonest intention of getting rid of a shareholder whom they did not wish to remain in the company. That was not so at all, and I think that the fact that Mr. Bodden was in their minds when they proposed this alteration does not in the least prevent it from still being passed *bona fide* for the benefit of the company. . . .

The result is in my opinion this appeal succeeds. . . .

Eve J.: I am of the same opinion.

. . . I think . . . that the suggestion that this resolution, because it was aimed at a particular shareholder, was passed *mala fide* fails, and that with that goes the substratum of the argument on behalf of the respondents.

I agree that this appeal should be allowed. . . .

Shuttleworth *v.* Cox Brothers and Company (Maidenhead), Limited. [1927] 2 K.B. 9

A contract which derives its force and effect from the articles alone is not an absolute but a conditional contract, since it is subject to alteration of the articles. Thus provided the alteration is made bona fide *for the benefit of the company, there is no breach of contract. Whether the alteration is for the benefit of the company is a question solely for the shareholders acting in good faith, not for the court, for it is not the business of the court to manage the affairs of the company.*

The defendant company was incorporated on 21st May 1921 to acquire and take over as going concerns and carry on the business of English and foreign timber merchants and builders' merchants then belonging to John Beare, Ernest Burton Norris and John Edward Shuttleworth (the plaintiff), under the style of Cox Brothers and Company. The capital of the company was £25,000 divided into 25,000 shares of £1 each. The greater number of these shares were held by the directors.

By article 17 the number of the directors was to be not less than three nor more than seven. By article 18 the following persons were to be the first directors of the company: John Beare, Ernest Burton Norris, John Edward Shuttleworth (the plaintiff), Thomas Norris and Harry Legassicke Fritche. The article proceeded:

 "They shall be permanent directors of the company, and each of them shall be entitled to hold such office so long as he shall live unless he shall become disqualified from any of the causes specified in article 22 hereof."

By article 22:

> "The office of a director shall be vacated:
> (a) if he become bankrupt or insolvent or compound with his creditors;
> (b) if he become of unsound mind or be found a lunatic;
> (c) if he be convicted of an indictable offence;
> (d) if he cease to hold the necessary share qualification or do not obtain the same within one month from the date of his appointment;
> (e) if he absent himself from the meetings of directors for a period of six calendar months without special leave of absence from the other directors;
> (f) if he give the directors one calendar month's notice in writing that he resigns his office."

In June 1921 the plaintiff was appointed the works manager at a salary of £420 a year. Subsequently by a resolution his appointment was made terminable on three months' notice.

As manager it was his duty to keep a credit sales book and a cash sales book and to hand over to the company at the end of the week all sums received by him. Between 21st November 1923 and 4th July 1924 he received twenty-two payments varying between £13 and 5s. 10d. and amounting to £76 9s. 1d., but made no entries of these payments in the cash book and had not at the date of the writ duly accounted for them. On 22nd August 1924 at a meeting of the directors, the plaintiff was summarily dismissed from the position of works manager. At an adjourned meeting held on or about 29 August he was asked to resign his office of director, but refused to do this.

On 9th September 1924 he issued a writ against the company and the four other directors, claiming an injunction restraining the defendants from dismissing him from his offices of director and works manager. On 10th September he applied for the injunction. BRANSON J., the judge in chambers, dismissed the application, and this decision was afterwards affirmed by the Court of Appeal on 11th December 1924.

On 24th October 1924 at a meeting of the directors, the defendant T. Norris, the chairman of the company, proposed and the defendant H. L. Fritche seconded a resolution, which was carried, that an extraordinary general meeting should be called for the purpose of considering and, if thought fit, of passing the following resolution:

"That the following paragraph be added to art. 22 of the articles of association of the company after paragraph (*f*): '(*g*) if he be requested in writing by all the other directors to resign his office.' "

On 25th October the plaintiff received the notice of a general meeting of shareholders to be held on 7th November. The proposed meeting was not held on account of the interlocutory proceedings mentioned above.

By his statement of claim, which was delivered on 6th November and redelivered as amended on 27th November, the plaintiff in addition to the injunction claimed by the writ prayed a declaration that he was a permanent director. He also sought an injunction restraining the defendants from holding any meeting of the company to pass a special resolution altering the articles so as to enable the defendants to exclude him from the office of director otherwise than in accordance with the articles. He also claimed damages for wrongful dismissal from the post of works manager.

On 3rd February 1925 notice was given to the members that an extraordinary general meeting would be held on 13th February 1925 to consider and, if thought fit, to pass the resolution mentioned in the notice of 24th October 1924. This resolution was carried by the requisite majority at a meeting duly held on 13th February and was confirmed at a meeting held on 5th March.

The defence to the action was delivered on 31st March 1925. By it the defendants pleaded that they were justified in dismissing the plaintiff from the post of works manager, and that in accordance with S.13 of the *Companies* (*Consolidation*) *Act*, 1908 (*see now S.10, Companies Act, 1948*),

they had on 25th March 1925 as they were lawfully entitled
to do, altered article 22 of the articles of association by
adding thereto para. (*g*), and that the alteration was *bona
fide* and for the benefit of the defendants as a whole. They
counterclaimed the sum of £76 9*s*. 1*d*., which the plaintiff
had not accounted for, and a further sum of £44 14*s*. 4*d*.
for goods sold and delivered.

On 6th February 1926 the plaintiff was requested in
writing by all the other directors to resign his office of
director.

AVORY J. at the trial asked the jury two questions,
which, with the answers of the jury, were as follows:

    (1) "Was the conduct of the plaintiff such as to justify
        his dismissal without notice?" "No."
    (2) "Was the alteration in the articles made in good faith
        for the benefit of the company?" (*a*) "No." (*b*) "In-
        cidentally, yes."

Upon the first finding judgment was entered for the plaintiff against the company for an agreed sum of £105. The
defendants appealed from that judgment, and the Court of
Appeal dismissed the appeal, being of opinion that there
were grounds to support the verdict.

Upon the second finding AVORY J. held that there was
no evidence on which the jury could find that the alteration
in the articles was not *bona fide*, and gave judgment for the
defendants.

From this judgment the plaintiff appealed, and the case
accordingly came before the Court of Appeal on this point.

BANKES L.J.: . . . At the trial the jury were . . . asked to consider the plaintiff's complaint that he had been wrongfully
deprived of his position of permanent director. He contended
that the alteration of art. 22 was invalid and that the amendment was not *bona fide* for the benefit of the company as a
whole. He also contended that it amounted to a breach of a
contract to be implied from the articles that he should be a
permanent director of the company as long as he should live
unless he became disqualified from any of the causes specified
in art. 22 as it originally stood. In this case the contract, if any,
derives its force and effect from the articles themselves, which

may be altered. It is therefore not an absolute but a conditional contract; and the question of the plaintiff's rights under it depends, as do the other questions raised, upon whether the alteration of art. 22 was validly made.

The power to alter articles of association is conferred by S.13 of the *Companies* (*Consolidation*) *Act*, 1908 [*see now S.10 Companies Act, 1948*]. . . . There is no question here of the formalities required by law. What is said is that this resolution is invalid because it is not *bona fide* for the benefit of the company as a whole. . . . It seems to me that these defendants were anxious throughout to take a charitable view of the plaintiff's conduct. There is not a trace of any vindictiveness or wrong motive. They thought that in the interest of the company the plaintiff should cease to be a director, but in the circumstances of this case that fact does not suggest want of good faith, and in my opinion the evidence directly negatives any such suggestion.

The jury were also asked to give their opinion upon the further question whether the alteration of the articles was for the benefit of the company. They answered that it was incidentally for the benefit of the company. What they meant exactly I do not know. . . . [T]he test is whether the alteration of the articles was in the opinion of the shareholders for the benefit of the company. By what criterion is the Court to ascertain the opinion of the shareholders upon this question? The alteration may be so oppressive as to cast suspicion on the honesty of the persons responsible for it, or so extravagant that no reasonable men could really consider it for the benefit of the company. In such cases the Court is, I think, entitled to treat the conduct of shareholders as it does the verdict of a jury, and to say that the alteration of a company's articles shall not stand if it is such that no reasonable men could consider it for the benefit of the company. . . . In the present case it seems to me impossible to say that the action of these defendants was either incapable of being for the benefit of the company or such that no reasonable men could consider it for the benefit of the company. It is idle to say that their action was directed against the plaintiff, because the more outrageous the conduct of a director the more

certain it is that his removal will be *bona fide* for the benefit of
the company, and the more certainly will the efforts of the
shareholders, acting *bona fide* and for the benefit of the company, be directed against him, because it is necessary to protect
the company against such conduct for the future. For these
reasons I am of opinion that this appeal must be dismissed.

SCRUTTON L.J.: I am of the same opinion. . . .
In my opinion AVORY J. was right in holding that there was
no evidence on which a reasonable jury could find that the
directors acted otherwise than in good faith. . . . If there was
no evidence of lack of good faith, the other finding of the jury
makes an end of this appeal. That finding is that the alteration
of the article was for the benefit of the company. It is true they
say it was "incidentally" for the benefit of the company. That
must mean, I suppose, that the shareholders were primarily
actuated by malice and that they were maliciously doing a
thing which was for the benefit of the company. But now it
must be taken that there was no evidence of malice, and so
there still remains a finding that the action of the shareholders
was for the benefit of the company. That would apparently
conclude this case but for one point . . . namely, that art. 22
in its original form constituted a contract between the company
and the plaintiff, that he should be a permanent director for
life, except in the events specified in that article, a contract
which could not be varied without the consent of both parties;
and that the plaintiff never consented to the article in its altered
form. That argument would be sound if he could show a contract outside the articles; for then an alteration of the articles
would not affect the contract. . . . But if a contract is contained
in the articles it must be, as the articles themselves are, subject
to alteration. . . . Consequently the plaintiff's contract, if any,
is not a contract constituting him a permanent director uncon-
ditionally, but is a contract constituting him a permanent
director subject to the power of terminating his appointment in
accordance with the articles or any modification of the articles
sanctioned by the *Companies Act*. So far, therefore, the appeal
fails.

Then Mr. Porter [*leading counsel for the appellant*] contended that the question is not what the shareholders think, but what the Court thinks is for the benefit of the company. . . . Now when persons, honestly endeavouring to decide what will be for the benefit of the company and to act accordingly, decide upon a particular course, then, provided there are grounds on which reasonable men could come to the same decision, it does not matter whether the Court would or would not come to the same decision or a different decision. It is not the business of the Court to manage the affairs of the company. That is for the shareholders and directors. The absence of any reasonable ground for deciding that a certain course of action is conducive to the benefit of the company may be a ground for finding lack of good faith or for finding that the shareholders, with the best motives, have not considered the matters which they ought to have considered. On either of these findings their decision might be set aside. But I should be sorry to see the Court go beyond this and take upon itself the management of concerns which others may understand far better than the Court does. . . . I think the appeal fails and must be dismissed.

ATKIN L.J.: I agree. . . .

The first question is whether the original articles constituted a contract between the company and the plaintiff making him a permanent director, in which case the alteration of art. 22, being inconsistent with the contract, would not be permitted by the Court and would be invalid. That depends upon whether there was such a contract as would be broken by the alteration of the article. . . . In these circumstances the proper inference appears to be that there was a contract that the plaintiff should be a permanent director, but a contract contained in articles which could be altered by a special resolution of the company in accordance with the provisions of the *Companies Act*. . . . In other words, it is a contract made upon the terms of an alterable article, and therefore neither of the contracting parties can complain if the article is altered. Consequently I cannot find that there has been any breach of contract in making the alteration.

The only other question is whether the article is upon general principles objectionable as being not honestly made within the powers of the company. Here the limits to the power of a company to alter its articles have to be considered. . . . The only question is whether or not the shareholders, in considering whether they shall alter articles, honestly intend to exercise their powers for the benefit of the company. If they do then, subject to one or two reservations which have been explained, the alteration must stand. It is not matter of law for the Court whether or not a particular alteration is for the benefit of the company; nor is it the business of a judge to review the decision of every company in the country on these questions. And even if the question were not for the shareholders themselves, but for some other body, it must be a question of fact. . . . In my view the question is solely for the shareholders acting in good faith. . . .

I should like to add a word upon the finding of the jury that the company did not act in good faith. I am satisfied that there was no evidence on which they could properly come to that conclusion. The alteration of art. 22 empowered the directors to act not only against one particular member of the board; all the directors were thereby exposed to the exercise of the new power. And it was eventually exercised not by reason only of the events which led to the alteration but because of another set of circumstances arising independently some ten months after the alteration. I think therefore that the plaintiff's appeal fails.

2. The Legal Effect of the Articles

Eley *v*. The Positive Government Security Life Assurance Company, Limited. (1876) 1 Ex. D. 20, 88

The articles are a contract between the shareholders inter se, *but cannot give a right of action to any person who is not a party to them, even though named therein.*

In 1869 one Baylis, who was endeavouring to form a joint stock insurance company, applied to the plaintiff William

Eley to make advances to the extent of £200 to meet the expenses of forming such a company, and it was arranged between them that, in the event of the plaintiff making such advances and the company being formed, the plaintiff should be appointed permanent solicitor to the company. The defendant company was formed, and the plaintiff made advances to the extent of £200. The money was paid to Baylis, and by him applied to purposes of the company. The last of the advances was made in May 1870.

The memorandum and articles of association of the company were prepared by the plaintiff and signed by seven persons, each holding five shares, and were duly registered on 27th January 1870, pursuant to the *Companies Act*, 1862.

Clause 118 of the articles of association was as follows:

"Mr. William Eley, of No. 27, New Broad Street, in the City of London, shall be the solicitor to the company, and shall transact all the legal business of the company, . . . for usual and accustomed fees and charges, and shall not be removed from his office except for misconduct."

In December 1870 the company allotted to the plaintiff 200 shares of £1 each, and the plaintiff accepted the same in repayment of his advances, and so became and remained a member of the company.

From the time of the incorporation of the company down to the latter end of 1871 the plaintiff was employed by the company as their solicitor, and transacted all their legal business except some which was transacted by a firm of solicitors in Manchester in or about October 1871, and which formed the subject of a correspondence between the plaintiff and the directors. The plaintiff insisted upon his right to be employed as the sole solicitor of the company, and to transact all their legal business unless he misconducted himself; but he intimated that he would not stand upon what he considered his strict right as regarded the business transacted by the Manchester firm. The directors, on the other hand, insisted that the plaintiff was in error, and that he had no such rights as he alleged.

On 2nd February 1870 at a meeting of the directors, a resolution was passed appointing Mr. Baylis permanent manager of the company. In the minute of the proceedings at that meeting there was the following entry:

"Mr. Eley, solicitor to the company, present."

No resolution was ever passed by the directors appointing the plaintiff as solicitor to the company, neither was he ever appointed as such at any meeting of the company, nor by any instrument bearing the corporate seal of the company.

Early in the year 1871 the directors published a prospectus, in which the plaintiff's name was inserted under the heading "Solicitor."

Subsequently they published other prospectuses, in all of which, under the head of "Solicitors," several names appeared, but the plaintiff's name appeared in two only.

The plaintiff from time to time protested against the appointment of any person besides himself as solicitor of the company; nevertheless the company, by their directors, in and after January 1872 employed several of the persons whose names appeared on the various prospectuses to transact legal business for them, but they had not employed the plaintiff to transact business for them since 1871.

On 8th February 1873 the plaintiff brought an action against the company for breach of contract in not employing him as solicitor on the terms of the articles.

AMPHLETT B.: . . . Under these circumstances it could not, in my opinion, be successfully contended that the 118th clause of the articles of association created any contract between the plaintiff and the company.

The articles, taken by themselves, are simply a contract between the shareholders *inter se*, and cannot, in my opinion, give a right of action to a person like the plaintiff, not a party to the articles, although named therein. . . . [N]or is there any room for the application of the doctrine of ratification, since the arrangement between the plaintiff and Mr. Baylis is not noticed in the articles, and is not found in the case to have been at any time communicated or known to a single shareholder or director, or, except themselves, to any officer of the company.

This being so, and the contract sued upon not being under the seal of the company, it is not binding upon the company, unless it falls within the 37th section of the *Companies Act*, 1867, that is to say, unless it was made by the directors under the express or implied authority of the company.

. . . But, do the facts found by the case prove conclusively . . . that any such special contract was entered into? No written document passed between them, nor is there any entry or notice of such special contract in the minute book of the directors or in any book of the company. All that appears is that the directors allowed the plaintiff to attend their first meeting, and afterwards employed him as the solicitor of the company, which, as between themselves and the company, though not as between themselves and the plaintiff, they were bound by the articles to do. But how does that show that they entered into a special contract with him, that he should not only receive the ordinary remuneration for his services, but transact all the future business of the company, and not be removed from his office unless for misconduct? At the same meeting, when the plaintiff attended as solicitor, and must be taken to have been recognised and employed as solicitor of the company, an entry was made in the minute book of the appointment of Mr. Baylis as permanent . . . manager of the company; why was there not an entry made of this special and most onerous contract with the plaintiff? I think it highly probable that the true explanation is that the plaintiff, who prepared the articles and inserted the 118th clause in his own favour, thought he was safe under the clause itself, and therefore did not think it necessary . . . to ask the directors to enter into any such strange and special contract with him. He was, however, in my judgment, mistaken in that respect; but, of course, such mistake cannot create any special contract between him and the company, or between him and the directors. All that can be said is that he intended that the company should be bound hand and foot to himself, but from a mistaken view of the law he has, most fortunately for the company, failed to carry such intention into effect. The act of the directors in employing another solicitor was, no doubt, as between themselves and the company, a violation of the 118th clause; but that might have been condoned by the company, and if the plaintiff, as a member of the company, had called that act into question at a general meeting, I do not think it difficult to guess what the result would have been. For these reasons, I think that there was no contract at all between the plaintiff and the company. . . .

CLEASBY B.: I agree in the result arrived at by my Brother AMPHLETT. . . . I am of opinion that clause 118 of the articles cannot by itself be taken to operate as a contract between the solicitor and the company.

KELLY C.B.: I also think the defendants are entitled to the judgment of the Court.

> KELLY C.B. declined to give any opinion on whether the articles constituted a contract between the plaintiff and the company, but based his judgment on the absence of a note or memorandum in writing as then required by S.4 of the *Statute of Frauds*.
> From this decision of the Exchequer Division the plaintiff appealed, and the case accordingly came before the Court of Appeal.

LORD CAIRNS L.C.: . . . This case was first rested on the 118th Article. Articles of association, as is well known, follow the memorandum, which states the objects of the company, while the articles state the arrangement between the members. They are an agreement *inter socios*, and in that view, . . . it [*article 118*] becomes a covenant between the parties to it that they will employ the plaintiff. Now, so far as that is concerned, it is *res inter alios acta*, the plaintiff is no party to it. No doubt he thought that by inserting it he was making his employment safe as against the company; but his relying on that view of the law does not alter the legal effect of the articles. This article is either a stipulation which would bind the members, or else a mandate to the directors. In either case it is a matter between the directors and shareholders, and not between them and the plaintiff.

The matter has been put in another way. It is said, this, though not an agreement in itself, is at all events a statement of what had been agreed upon; it must have been intended to be

brought to the plaintiff's knowledge, he has accepted and acted
upon it, and therefore it is evidence of another agreement on
which he can rely. Now it may be considered that Article 118
would have warranted the directors in entering into an agreement with the plaintiff by which they should contract to employ
the plaintiff; but I ask, was such a contract ever made? A joint
stock company may act under their seal, or by the signature of
their directors, which may have equal effect as their seal, or
possibly by a resolution of the board. Nothing of the kind
exists here; and if the article is not an agreement on which the
plaintiff can rely, there is nothing in the case before us but the
fact of his employment, and that would entitle him to remuneration only for work he has done. This seems to us to dispose of
the whole of the case; and I think that . . . the judgment of the
Court below must be affirmed.

LORD COLERIDGE C.J. and MELLISH L.J. concurred.

Rayfield v. Hands and Others. [1960] Ch. 1

*An article purporting to impose on directors of a company an
obligation to buy the shares which any member wishes to sell
creates a contract between the would-be seller as a member and
the directors as members where those directors are already shareholders in the company.*

The plaintiff, Frank Leslie Rayfield, was the registered
holder of 400 shares out of an issued capital of 2,900 £1
shares in Field-Davis Ltd. The defendants, Hands, Scales
and Davies, were the sole directors of the company. Article
11 provided: "Every member who intends to transfer
shares shall inform the directors who will take the said
shares equally between them at a fair value . . ." In accordance with this article the plaintiff so notified the directors,
who contended that they need not take and pay for his
shares, on the ground that the articles imposed no such
liability upon them. The plaintiff sought an order that the
directors should purchase his shares at a fair value.

VAISEY J.: . . . It is admitted that the words "every member

. . . shall inform" the directors does create an obligation but it is argued by the defendants that the words "the directors . . . will take the shares" imports in some way the idea of an option or choice or volition on the part of the directors having regard to the inherent difference (not always observed) in the English language between the words "shall" and "will."

I appreciate the force of that argument, but I cannot accept it. In this context, while the word "shall" clearly imports compulsion and obligation, the word "will" indicates as it seems to me a resultant prospective eventuality, in which the member has to sell his shares and the directors have to buy them, each being under an obligation to bring that eventuality into effect. I think there is thus in the language of Art. 11 a mutual obligation. . . . In my judgment, the article ought not to be invalidated for the purposes of a case (such as this) where it is perfectly easy to give effect to it.

. . . The next and most difficult point taken by the defendants, as to which it would appear that there is no very clear judicial authority, is that Art. 11 . . . does not do what it looks like doing, that is, to create a contractual relationship between the plaintiff as shareholder and vendor and the defendants as directors and purchasers. This depends on S.20 (1) of the *Companies Act*, 1948.

. . . Now the question arises at the outset whether the terms of Art. 11 relate to the rights of members *inter se* . . . or whether the relationship is between a member as such and directors as such. . . . In my judgment, the relationship here is between the plaintiff as a member and the defendants not as directors but as members. . . . This is in words a contract or quasi-contract between members, and not between members and directors.

On the whole, if the proper way to construe the articles of association of a company is as a commercial or business document to which the maxim "validate if possible" applies, I think that the plaintiff in this action ought to succeed. Not one of the judges in . . . *Dean* v. *Prince* showed any signs of shock or surprise in the assumption there made of a contract between directors being formed by the terms of a company's articles. I am encouraged . . . to find in this case a contract similarly formed between a member and member-directors in relation to their holdings of the company's shares in its articles. The conclusion to which I have come may not be of so general an application as to extend to the articles of every company, for it is, I think, material to remember that this private company is one of that class of companies which bears a close analogy to a partnership.

. . . Nobody, I suppose, would doubt that a partnership deed might validly and properly provide for the acquisition of the share of one partner by another partner on terms identical with those of Art. 11 in the present case.

Re Richmond Gate Property Company, Ltd. [1965] 1 W.L.R. 335

Where a company is governed by Table A, Article 108 of Table A applies to a managing director, however appointed. The effect of an article appointing a person managing director, coupled with Article 108, coupled with the fact that that person is a member of the company, is to create a contract of employment between him as managing director and the company.

The Richmond Gate Property Company Ltd. was incorporated on 19th January 1962 and by its articles of association Table A of the *Companies Act*, 1948, was adopted in so far as it was not specifically excluded by or in conflict with the company's articles. By article 9 of the company's articles Herbert Leslie Brock Walker, the applicant, who was one of the two subscribers to the memorandum of association, was appointed joint managing director with one Derek Gordon Clancy, both to hold office for life.

The applicant was not employed in any other capacity than as managing director, and the only mention of remuneration in that capacity was in article 108 of Table A, which had been incorporated into the company's articles as above, but at no time did the directors determine his remuneration pursuant to that article, or otherwise.

On 20th September 1962 the directors resolved that the company should be wound up, a declaration of solvency was filed and the company went into voluntary liquidation.

The applicant lodged a proof in the liquidation claiming £400 for remuneration as managing director either on the basis of a contract with the company or under a *quantum meruit*. The liquidator rejected his claim.

The applicant appealed against the rejection of his claim.

PLOWMAN J.: Mr. Drake [*counsel for the respondent liquidator*] submitted that article 108 was applicable only to a managing director appointed by the board under the provisions of article 107. I do not accept that submission. It seems to me that article 108 is a separate, independent article providing for the remuneration which a managing director is to receive, whether as managing director appointed by the articles or as a managing director appointed by the board under article 107.

The effect of article 9 of the articles, coupled with article 108 in Table A, coupled with the fact that Walker was a member of the company, in my judgment, is that a contract exists between himself and the company for payment to him of remuneration as managing director, and that remuneration depends on article 108 of Table A and is to be such amount "as the directors may determine;" in other words, the managing director is at the mercy of the board, he gets what they determine to pay him, and if they do not determine to pay him anything he does not get anything. That is his contract with the company, and those are the terms on which he accepts office.

Since there is an express contract with the company in regard to the payment of remuneration it seems to me that any question of *quantum meruit* is automatically excluded.

It was submitted to me . . . on behalf of Walker, that *Craven-Ellis* v. *Canons Ltd.* was authority for the proposition that he was entitled to remuneration on the basis of a *quantum meruit*. . . .

When one comes to look at that case two matters, I think, at once distinguish it from the present case. The first is this, that the claim which was being made in that case for remuneration was not a claim for remuneration as managing director at all. It is quite clear, first of all, looking at the argument for the appellant—that is, the man who was claiming remuneration— "The work done for which remuneration is claimed was not done by the appellant *qua* director but as a valuer." . . .

In the present case Walker himself stated in the witness-box that he was never employed by the company except as managing director, so that in the present case the only claim I am concerned with is a claim for a *quantum meruit* as managing director. The second point which I think at once distinguishes *Craven Ellis* v. *Canons Ltd.* from the present is that in that case there was no contract, because the only contract which could have been prayed in aid was held to be void. . . .

In the present case there was an express contract which relates to payment of remuneration, and the only question with which I am concerned is: according to the terms of that express contract, is any sum payable for remuneration? When one finds that the express contract is that the remuneration payable is such sum as the directors may determine that the managing director shall have, and that the directors have not determined that any sum is to be payable to the managing director, it seems to me to follow as a necessary consequence that no remuneration can be claimed. . . . In the result I must dismiss this summons.

V. THE PROMOTERS OF A COMPANY

Emile Erlanger and Others *v*. The New Sombrero Phosphate Company and Others. (1878) 3 A.C. 1218

A promoter is in a fiduciary relation to the company, and if he sells his own property to it is under a duty to ensure that through its directors it is able to form an intelligent and independent judgment as to the value of that property. If he does not fulfil this duty, the company may set the sale aside.

A syndicate (or partnership), of which Emile Erlanger, a Paris banker, was the head, purchased for £55,000 from the liquidator of an insolvent company the lease of the island of Sombrero in the West Indies, said to contain valuable mines of phosphates. Erlanger, who managed this purchase, prepared to get up a company to purchase the lease from his syndicate and work the mines. The syndicate named five persons as directors, two of them, M. Drouyn de Lhuys and Mr. Eastwick, were abroad. Of the three others, John Marsh Evans, Rear-Admiral Macdonald and Alderman Dakin, Evans and Macdonald were entirely under Erlanger's control, and were furnished by him with their qualification shares.

The company was registered on 20th September 1871, and the contract for the purchase of the lease by the company from the syndicate was dated that day. It purported to be made between John Marsh Evans, as the vendor, and Francis Pavy, as the purchaser on behalf of the company. The price to the company was to be £110,000, of which £80,000 was to be paid down, and the remaining £30,000 to be satisfied by fully-paid-up shares in the new company. The money was to be obtained by the subscriptions for the shares, which were to be 13,000 in number, of £10 each.

The first meeting of directors took place on 29th September 1871. Three were present, Dakin, who sat as chairman, Evans, and Macdonald. It was resolved "that the said contract be approved and confirmed." A prospectus of the company was produced. It was intended to be issued to the public. After its publication the number of applications for shares became considerable.

The first general meeting of the company took place on 2nd February 1872. At that meeting, presided over by Dakin, a Mr. Stephenson stated that he had heard a rumour that what the company was to buy at £110,000 had, but a few days before, been sold to the person who were now the vendors to the company, for £55,000, and he alluded to a person, one of the directors, as one of the persons who had made the original purchase. Dakin said that he had heard some such rumours; that he was told that Mr. Evans, with other gentlemen, had bought this fully a month before the company was thought of or projected; that it appeared to him that the contract between Evans and Pavy was fully stated in the prospectus; that whether it cost £50,000 or £110,000 was not material to the question; that "it was not bought by one of our members. The gentleman was not a director then, but bought in concert with other people." He added that what it was bought for he, Dakin, did not know.

The annual general meeting was held on 19th June 1872 with Evans in the chair. The company had not been successful, and the shareholders passed resolutions appointing a committee of investigation, and adjourned the meeting for six weeks. The committee reported, recommending the removal of the original directors and the appointment of others, with authority to take such proceedings as they might be advised for the purpose of recovering the difference between the sums given on the first and second purchase. New directors were appointed at a meeting of 29th August 1872.

A correspondence then ensued with Erlanger and the other members of the syndicate. Erlanger denied all legal liability, but offered to give the company the benefit of the full amount of profit which his firm derived in cash and shares from the transaction. The other members of the syndicate did not answer.

On 24th December 1872 a bill was filed against Erlanger, Evans, Dakin, Macdonald, and others (afterwards amended by the addition of all the members of the syndicate), praying that the contract of 20th September 1871 might be set aside; that the members of the syndicate might repay to the company the £110,000 with interest, the company delivering up the island and accounting for profits made by working it; or that the members of the syndicate might be ordered to repay the difference, £55,000, between the sum paid by the syndicate and that paid by the company.

The answer of Dakin was directed to exonerate himself from any imputation of having known the real facts and having in any way misled the company by misrepresenting them. The answers of the members of the syndicate denied that they stood in any way in a fiduciary position towards the company, insisted on the fairness of the transaction, and imputed the failure of the concern to causes over which they had no control, such as the conduct of the company in working the mines. The delay of the company in claiming relief was also insisted on.

The case was heard before VICE-CHANCELLOR MALINS in March and April 1876 and the bill was ordered to be dismissed. The plaintiff company appealed against this decree, and in the Court of Appeal the contract was ordered to be rescinded. This appeal to the House of Lords was then brought.

LORD PENZANCE: . . . The syndicate had bought the property in question, and it is probable that they bought it with the intention of getting up a company which should buy it off them at an increased price. Baron Erlanger, who acted for the syndicate, took steps for that purpose within a few days of the purchase, and there is no proof that any steps were even considered, much less adopted, for dealing with the property in any other way. No time was lost in carrying this intention into effect. The solicitor of the syndicate is set to work—he prepares articles of association and a prospectus. The articles provide that five gentlemen by name shall be the first directors of the company, and that any two of them shall be a quorum to bind the company. They also provide that without any farther authority from the shareholders, these five directors or any two of them may sanction and accept, on the part of the company, a certain contract bearing even date with the articles for the purchase by the company of the property in question. This contract had been prepared by the syndicate themselves, and was on the face of it a contract between Evans as the vendor, and Pavy, on behalf of the future company, as vendee. Both Evans and Pavy were persons who had no interest in the property, and were the nominees of the syndicate, and remunerated by them for their trouble. In this contract the syndicate fixed their own price at which the future company was to buy, this price being in round numbers double what they had given for it some days before.

The articles of association were therefore so drawn by the solicitor for the syndicate, that the syndicate had it in their power to select, and did select, the five persons, any two of whom were to become the acting agents of the company for the acceptance or rejection of this bargain, by which the syndicate were to obtain for the property double what they had given for it. In exercising this selection they chose first two gentlemen of high standing, one of whom resided abroad, and the other of whom was about to leave England forthwith for Canada, but neither of whom would be expected to take part in the decision as to whether this bargain, advantageous as it was to the syndicate, was also advantageous to the company. Of the other three persons nominated, one (Evans) was a person residing in Paris, who acted in the matter at the desire of Baron Erlanger, and who was remunerated by him with the gift of 100 paid-up shares in the company. Another, Admiral Macdonald, was a personal friend of Baron Erlanger, to whom the office of director was offered by him as a pecuniary benefit, and an entrance into business affairs, while the third, Sir Thomas Dakin, was the Lord Mayor of London, against whose capacity, honesty, and independence, nothing can, I think, be said. . . .

Can a contract so obtained be allowed to stand? The bare statement of the facts is, I think, sufficient to condemn it. From that statement I invite your Lordships to draw two conclusions: first, that the company never had an opportunity of exercising, through independent directors, a fair and independent judgment upon the subject of this purchase; and, secondly, that this result was brought about by the conduct and contrivance of the vendors themselves. It was the vendors, in their character of promoters, who had the power and the opportunity of creating and forming the company in such a manner that with adequate disclosures of fact, an independent judgment on the company's behalf might have been formed. But instead of so doing they used that power and opportunity for the advancement of their own interests. Placed in this position of unfair advantage over the company which they were about to create, they were, as it seems to me, bound according to the principles constantly acted upon in the Courts of Equity, if they wished to make a valid contract of sale to the company, to nominate independent directors and fully disclose the material facts. . . . [T]here is certainly no proof that in the selection of the directors who were to be the company's agents for accepting and affirming the proposed purchase, the vendors used their power as promoters in such a way as to create an independent body capable of acting impartially in defence of the company's interests.

A contract of sale effected under such circumstances is, I conceive, upon principles of equity liable to be set aside.

The principles of equity to which I refer have been illustrated in a variety of relations, none of them perhaps precisely similar to that of the present parties, but all resting on the same basis, and one which is strictly applicable to the present case. The relations of principal and agent, trustee and cestui que trust, parent and child, guardian and ward, priest and penitent, all furnish instances in which the Courts of Equity have given protection and relief against the pressure of unfair advantage resulting from the relation and mutual position of the parties, whether in matters of contract or gift; and this relation and position of unfair advantage once made apparent, the Courts have always cast upon him who holds that position, the burden of showing that he has not used it to his own benefit.

. . . I must advise your Lordships to reject this appeal.

The Lord Chancellor, Lord Cairns: My Lords, the Appellants in this case complain of a decree of the Court of Appeal which has set aside a sale made to the Sombrero Company, of the island of Sombrero, and ordered repayment and re-transfer by the Appellants of large sums of money and shares which had passed to them from the company on the occasion of the sale.

. . . [T]he lease of the island came in 1871 to be sold. The Appellants . . . wished to buy the lease, and for this purpose they formed what is called a syndicate or partnership, and ultimately, on the 30th of August, 1871, did agree to buy the lease by private contract.

. . . I think it to be clear that the syndicate in entering into this contract acted on behalf of themselves alone, and did not at that time act in, or occupy, any fiduciary position whatever. It may well be that the prevailing idea in their mind was, not to retain or work the island, but to sell it again at an increase of price, and very possibly, to promote or get up a company to purchase the island from them; but they were, as it seems to me, after their purchase was made, perfectly free to do with the island whatever they liked; to use it as they liked, and to sell it how, and to whom, and for what price they liked. The part of the case of the Respondents which, as an alternative, sought to make the Appellants account for the profit which they made on the re-sale of the property to the Respondents, on an allegation that the Appellants acted in a fiduciary position at the time they made the contract of the 30th of August, 1871, is not, as I think, capable of being supported, and this, as I understand, was the view of all the Judges in the Courts below.

. . . [I]t is now necessary that I should state to your Lordships in what position I understand the promoters to be placed with reference to the company which they proposed to form. They stand, in my opinion, undoubtedly in a fiduciary position. They have in their hands the creation and moulding of the company; they have the power of defining how, and when, and in what shape, and under what supervision, it shall start into existence and begin to act as a trading corporation. If they are doing all this in order that the company may, as soon as it starts into life, become, through its managing directors, the purchaser of the property of themselves, the promoters, it is, in my opinion, incumbent upon the promoters to take care that in forming the company they provide it with an executive, that is to say, with a board of directors, who shall both be aware that the property which they are asked to buy is the property of the promoters, and who shall be competent and impartial judges as to whether the purchase ought or ought not to be made. I do not say that the owner of property may not promote and form a joint stock company, and then sell his property to it, but I do say that if he does he is bound to take care that he sells it to the company through the medium of a board of directors who can and do exercise an independent and intelligent judgment on the transaction, and who are not left under the belief that the property belongs, not to the promoter, but to some other person.

LORD CAIRNS proceeded to hold that the contract would have been voidable for lack of the exercise upon it of the intelligent judgment of an independent executive, had there not been such delay on the part of the company in seeking relief as to deprive them of their remedy.

He concluded:

Under these circumstances, looking to the very peculiar nature of the property, and the utter impossibility of restoring the property, and the commercial undertaking connected with it, to the vendors in the state in which it was when the company took possession of it, looking to the amount of notice which the company had by the prospectus, and to the knowledge which they might have obtained by pursuing the inquiries which the prospectus ought to have suggested, I should be of opinion that it would be contrary to the principles of equity to give to the company the relief which, at an earlier period, they might have obtained.

LORD HATHERLEY: . . . There are three particular classes of cases of what the Court terms fraud which may be pointed to as having some analogy with, or some bearing upon, the present case. The first is as between vendor and purchaser; the next is as between partner and co-partner; and the third is the case in which an agent for a purchaser receives a gratuity from the vendor. As to the first of these, a vendor need not do what was at one time asserted by this bill, namely, disclose what he has paid in effecting his own anterior purchase before asking an enhanced price from him to whom he seeks to sell the property; but he must not be guilty of any conduct which amounts to unfair concealment on his part of the real facts of the case, which ought in common fairness to be disclosed to a person seeking to purchase or entering into a treaty with him for that purpose. As regards partners, there is no doubt that one partner is bound to exercise *uberrima fides* with regard to any transactions in which the partners may be engaged in common. There is another class of cases well known in Courts of Equity which has some bearing upon the case before us, and that is where a person acting as agent for a purchaser, that is to say for a person who is minded to purchase, receives a gratuity or a bribe of some description from the intending vendor. In that case again the Courts interfere and say that a negotiation carried on between the agent for the purchaser and the vendor as principal, in which the agent for the purchaser receives benefits or advantages of any kind from the intending vendor, is one which can be impeached, and which would be set aside in a Court of Equity.

LORD HATHERLEY then proceeded to deal with the question of laches, concerning which he came to the following conclusion:

I do not see . . . that amount of laches which would induce your Lordships to say that the right which, as every Court and every Judge before whom the case has come agrees, once clearly existed, was waived and lost in consequence of the neglect of the company to take steps in due time to free themselves from the contract. . . . [T]he appeal ought to fail, and should be dismissed. . . .

LORD O'HAGAN: . . . The original purchase of the island of Sombrero was perfectly legitimate—and it was not less so because the object of the purchasers was to sell it again, and to sell it by forming a company which might afford them a profit on the transaction. The law permitted them to take that course, and provided the machinery by which the transfer of their interest might be equitably and beneficially effected for themselves and those with whom they meant to deal. But the privilege given them for promoting such a company for such an object, involved obligations of a very serious kind. It required, in its exercise, the utmost good faith, the completest truthfulness, and a careful regard to the protection of the future shareholders. The power to nominate a directorate is manifestly capable of great abuse, and may involve, in the misuse of it, very evil consequences to multitudes of people who have little capacity to guard themselves. Such a power may or may not have been wisely permitted to exist. I venture to have doubts upon the point. It tempts too much to fraudulent contrivance and mischievous deception; and, at least, it should be watched with jealousy and restrained from employment in such a way as to mislead the ignorant and the unwary. In all such cases the directorate nominated by the promoters should stand between them and the public, with such independence and intelligence, that they may be expected to deal fairly, impartially, and with adequate knowledge in the affairs submitted to their control.

. . . I think that the promoters in this case failed to remember the exigencies of their fiduciary position, when they appointed directors who were in no way independent of themselves, and who did not sustain the interests of the company with ordinary care and intelligence.

. . . If the directors had been nominated merely to ratify any terms the promoters might dictate, they discharged their function; if it was their duty, as it certainly was, to protect the shareholders, they never seem to have thought of doing it. Their conduct was precisely that which might have been anticipated from the character of their selection, and taking that conduct and character together, I concur in, I believe, the unanimous opinion of your Lordships that such a transaction ought not to be allowed to stand.

The promoters, who so forgot their duty to the company they formed, as to give it a directorate without independence of position or vigilance and caution in caring for its interests, must take the consequences. And this without the necessary imputation or evil purpose or conscious fraud. The fiduciary obligation may be violated though there may be no intention to do injustice. If the protection, proper and needful for a person standing at disadvantage in relation to his guardian or his solicitor, or to the promoters of a company, be withheld, the guardian, the solicitor, or the promoters, cannot sustain a contract equitably invalidated by the want of it, merely because it may be impossible to prove that he is impeachable with indirect or improper motives.

LORD O'HAGAN then proceeded to deal with the question of laches, and concluded:

In matters of this kind, every case must be judged according to its own circumstances. In each, the question must be one of degree—of more or less—and the delay which might be sufficient to bar relief, in one condition of things, may be without any effect in another. But it is notable that in none of the cases has laches been imputed without a lapse of time very much greater than that which we have to consider. All along, for many months, the shareholders had pressed for a return of the £55,000. They do not seem to have been advised to seek rescission of the contract until a late period: but a temporary mistake of the remedy does not extinguish the right to one. As soon as they were fully informed, the proper demand was made and the suit was instituted; and, as I have said, in my opinion, without such delay as disentitled them to maintain it. . . . I am of opinion that the decree should be affirmed and the appeal dismissed.

LORD SELBORNE: . . . I think that the decision of the Court of Appeal in Chancery was correct and ought to be affirmed.

LORD BLACKBURN: . . . Throughout the *Companies Act*, 1862, the word "promoters" is not anywhere used. It is, however, a short and convenient way of designating those who set in motion the machinery by which the Act enables them to create an incorporated company.

Neither does this Act in terms impose any duty on those promoters to have regard to the interests of the company which they are thus empowered to create. But it gives them an almost unlimited power to make the corporation subject to such regulations as they please, and to create it with a managing body whom they select, having powers such as they choose to give to those managers, so that the promoters can create such a corporation that the corporation, as soon as it comes into being, may be bound by anything, not in itself illegal, which those promoters have chosen. And I think those who accept and use such extensive powers, which so greatly affect the interests of that corporation when it comes into being, are not entitled to disregard the interests of that corporation altogether. They must make a reasonable use of the powers which they accept from the Legislature with regard to the formation of the corporation, and that requires them to pay some regard to its interests. And consequently they do stand with regard to that corporation when formed, in what is commonly called a fiduciary relation to some extent. . . .

Where, as in the present case, the company is formed for the purpose of becoming purchasers from the promoters as vendors, the interests of the promoters and of the company clash. It is the vendor's interest to get as high a price as possible, and they have a strong bias to overvalue the property which they are selling; it is the purchasers' interest to give as low a price as possible, and to secure that the price actually given is not more than the property is really worth to them.

. . . What I shall do is to inquire what, on the evidence, appears to have been done in this case, and then to confine myself to saying whether, on the facts of this particular case, it appears that an unreasonable use has been made of that confidence which the company did not indeed place in the promoters, for the company did not then exist, but which the Legislature did place in them for the company when it gave the promoters power to create it.

. . . Some things are to my mind clear. The contract was not void, but only voidable at the election of the company.

LORD BLACKBURN then proceeded to discuss the question of laches, concerning which he concluded:

I can find no case in which even a private individual has been precluded by mere delay, except where the delay has been very much greater than in this case. . . .

I am of opinion that the judgment below should be affirmed. . . .

LORD GORDON: . . . I agree with your Lordships in thinking that the promoters failed in their duty, . . . and that the company was not put in a position for forming an intelligent and independent judgment as to the contract between the promoters and the company; and that if the contract had been challenged by the company in proper time it might have been set aside.

The only questions of difficulty in the case are whether the contract has been challenged in due time; or whether there has been such laches on the part of the shareholders as to prevent their now demanding the rescission of their contract. . . . I think that the Appellants have failed to show that there have been such laches on the part of the company. And therefore I am of opinion that the judgment appealed against is right, and should be affirmed.

The Emma Silver Mining Company, Limited *v.* Lewis & Son. (1879) 4 C.P.D. 396

A promoter has duties towards the company before it is incorporated, and may continue to be in a fiduciary relation to it after incorporation. He cannot retain a profit which he has not disclosed to the company.

In 1871 the Emma Silver Mine in America was in the possession of Trevor William Park and others, who wished to sell it. Prior to July 1871 the defendants, metal brokers at Liverpool, had been selling about one-half of the produce of the mine for the usual commission on sales for American companies of $2\frac{1}{2}$ per cent.

On 17th July the defendant Arthur Lewis, then in America, wrote from the neighbourhood of the mine to his father, the defendant James Lewis, stating that he contemplated giving assistance to mine owners in selling their mines to companies. A number of confidential letters passed between father and son from which it appeared that Arthur Lewis visited the Emma Mine and ascertained that it was of doubtful character; that a Professor Silliman who had given a favourable opinion of it was in popular opinion not trustworthy; that he, Arthur Lewis, was asked by Park to report on it and help place it on the English market in return for which Park promised liberal remuneration.

The defendants agreed. Park went to London where the defendant James Lewis introduced him to a prospective purchaser and was promised £5,000 at least for his trouble and if Park sold the mine at his own price, £10,000. This purchase never took place.

On 8th November 1871 the plaintiff company was registered. The memorandum of association stated the first of the objects for which it was established to be "the carrying out of an agreement dated the 4th of November, 1871, between Trevor William Park of the one part and George Henry Dean of the other part." The capital of the company was £1,000,000 in 50,000 shares of £20 each. By the agreement of 4th November Dean, as trustee for the intended company, agreed on behalf of the company to purchase the mine for £1,000,000 of which £500,000 were to be paid in cash and the residue in shares of the company. This agreement was mentioned in the articles of association as being adopted by the company.

On 9th November the prospectus of the company was issued. It stated that the defendants would be ready to answer any inquiries relating to the ores and the mine, one of their firm having been at the mine for some time. The defendants swore that they gave no express authority for this use of their names, but on 11th November James Lewis wrote to Arthur Lewis in America sending a paper with the prospectus and saying that he was writing to Park to let him have half the amount promised in paid-up shares.

Between 11th and 23rd November several letters passed between James Lewis and persons who had received the prospectus. In answer to inquiries whether Lewis & Son believed all that was stated in the prospectus, James Lewis replied to the effect that the figures given in the prospectus as to the quality of the ore sold and the amount realised were perfectly correct, but that he could guarantee nothing further and the persons inquiring must act upon their own judgment as to whether they applied for shares. His replies enclosed a copy of the prospectus and a copy of a report by Professor Silliman as to the mine, and stated that "the future of the mine entirely depended on the full realisation of the report" as to whether it was a true fissure vein or merely a deposit.

On 23rd November a minute was entered in the company's books stating that the defendants should be metal brokers to the company at the usual English commission of 1 per cent. The defendants in the course of their evidence said that the remuneration to be received by their firm for their assistance was in consideration of the loss they would be put to by only receiving 1 per cent commission instead of $2\frac{1}{2}$ per cent on the sale of the ore.

The purchase-money was paid, and £500,000 value in shares allotted to the vendors, including 250 which were afterwards transferred from Park to Arthur Lewis. These 250 were sold for the defendants who received £5,968 15s. of the proceeds. This sum and dividends upon 250 shares and interest the plaintiffs claimed to recover as money received by the defendants as trustees for the company since no disclosure of this transaction had been made to the company.

DENMAN J. gave judgment for the plaintiffs, but a rule *nisi* was granted. The Court consisted of LORD COLERIDGE C.J., DENMAN J., and LINDLEY J., and the judgment was delivered by LINDLEY J.

LINDLEY J.: . . . It is said that there was no evidence to go to the jury of the defendants being promoters of the company, in the proper sense of that expression; that there was no sufficient explanation of the proper meaning of the word given to the jury; and that the defendants were entitled to judgment, or, at all events, to have a new trial.

With respect to the word "promoters," we are of opinion that it has no very definite meaning. . . . As used in connec-

tion with companies the term "promoter" involves the idea
of exertion for the purpose of getting up and starting a company (of what is called "floating" it) and also the idea of some
duty towards the company imposed by or arising from the
position which the so-called promoter assumes towards it.
It is now clearly settled that persons who get up and form a
company have duties towards it before it comes into existence. . . .

Moreover, it is in our opinion an entire mistake to suppose
that after a company is registered its directors are the only
persons who are in such a position towards it as to be under
fiduciary relations to it. A person not a director may be a
promoter of a company which is already incorporated, but
the capital of which has not been taken up, and which is not
yet in a position to perform the obligations imposed upon it
by its creators.

The defendants say they owed no duty to this company.
But in our opinion this contention cannot be supported. In
the first place, the defendants left Park to get up the company
upon the understanding that they as well as he were to profit
by the operation; they were behind him; they were in the
position of undisclosed joint adventurers; and in respect of
their interest his obligations and theirs are in our opinion
undistinguishable. The defendants in fact were, partly by
assisting Park and partly by leaving him to do the best he
could for them as well as himself, in the position of promoters
of the company.

In the next place, the defendants became the metal brokers
of the company; and it became their duty not to take from the
company for their appointment or services a greater remuneration than the company knew they were getting. The company
agreed to pay the usual commission of 1%, and had no idea
that the defendants were getting £5,000 in addition to a bonus.
Whether this bonus was for services to Park in assisting him in
getting up the company or for loss of commission, or partly
for one and partly for the other, seems to us immaterial. In
any view, the defendants, being agents of the mine, obtained
a large profit from the company through the instrumentality

of Park. This profit was concealed from the company, and cannot be retained by the defendants.

Again, the acceptance by the defendants of the reference to them in the company's prospectus, imposed upon the defendants a duty to the company to answer candidly such inquiries as might be made by intending applicants for shares. The defendants by this acceptance undertook the duty of assisting to float the company, by answering the inquiries of persons proposing to take shares in it; and they did in fact answer inquiries in such a way as to allay suspicion.

Upon these grounds we are of opinion that there was ample evidence to warrant the finding and verdict of the jury. . . .

It has, however, been urged that the company have not rescinded their contract with Park; and that so long as that contract remains unrescinded the shares given by him to the defendants must be treated as having been his to give, and that the company cannot claim them. But the moment it is proved, as in this case it is, that the £1,000,000 paid by the company, although nominally paid for the mine, was only colourably so; that some portion of that sum, say £5,000, was not for the mine at all, as the company supposed, but was for something very different, *e.g.*, the remuneration of the Messrs. Lewis, and that the company was, without knowing it, really paying them for, *inter alia*, their acceptance of the office of metal brokers, and for concealing their own misgivings as to the mine, and when it is further proved, as it is, that the shares paid to the defendants were created for the purpose of paying them, and the company was never informed of this, it follows in our opinion that the company can recover from the defendants what they have thus obtained, without rescinding its contract with Park. . . . For the reasons we have given we think that the verdict was right; that judgment ought not to be entered for the defendants; that there ought to be no new trial, and that the rule ought to be discharged. . . .

Whaley Bridge Calico Printing Company Ltd. *v.* Green and Smith. (1879) 5 Q.B.D. 109

The company can compel a promoter who makes a secret profit to pay over that profit to the company. Where the contract is still unexecuted, the company as principal may stand in the agent's shoes and compel a payment of money to be made directly to itself.

The facts sufficiently appear from the judgment.

BOWEN J.: This is an action brought by the Whaley Bridge Calico Printing Company, Ltd., against Robert Ellis Green, the vendor to the company of certain works and premises. John Smith, a defendant joined in the suit, did not appear to defend, and the present question arises wholly between the defendant Green and the company.

In or about May, 1876, the defendant Green purchased certain calico printing works and premises situate at Whaley Bridge, near Buxton, for the sum of £15,000. The defendant John Smith was the manager in Mr. Green's employment at the time, and various negotiations took place between Green and Smith as to the working of the premises for Green himself, and as to their resale to some company. Ultimately, on the 13th of October, 1876, the plaintiff company was incorporated for the purpose of purchasing and working these works, and on the 2nd of February, 1877, the premises were conveyed to the company by Smith and Green for the sum of £20,000, Green having previously purported to sell the premises to Smith for £20,000 by a contract of the 19th of September, which the jury found was a sham contract, and which (if a sham contract) was obviously intended to be used for the purpose of the negotiations with the company.

The immediate question in the present case turns upon the following findings of the jury:

1. That Green was a promoter of the company from the 29th of August.

2. That before the 2nd of February the board of directors

knew that Green had previously purchased the property for £15,000 only.

3. That at the date of the incorporation of the company there was an agreement between Smith and Green that Smith should have £3,000 out of the purchase-money paid by the plaintiff company.

. . . The first claim put forward on behalf of the plaintiff company was to have refunded to them the £5,000, the difference between the £20,000 purchase-money and the price at which Green himself had bought.

This claim, in my opinion, cannot be sustained. The company bought with their eyes open as to the price. They knew Green had in fact given only £15,000 for the works. A fraud was no doubt practised upon them in respect of the contract of the 19th of September, assuming the finding of the jury to be correct, for it is clear that Green and Smith induced the company to suppose that there was a genuine contract of sale for £20,000, under which Smith had become the purchaser. In reality, this contract was a mere sham, and Green, by the agreement referred to in the last finding of the jury, had arranged with Smith to pay him back £3,000 out of the £20,000 purchase-money. It is true that the property in question appears upon the evidence to be fully worth £20,000, but this does not prevent the use made of the sham contract from having been fraudulent. In any action for deceit based on this ground a jury might perhaps have assessed at £3,000 the damages recoverable by the company against Smith and Green, should the jury have thought that this sham contract induced the company to give £3,000 more than they otherwise need have done.

The plaintiffs, however, have not asked for damages to be assessed in this manner. What they desire is to enforce against Green the secret agreement to pay over £3,000 to Smith, upon the ground that they are entitled to treat this contract with Smith as made for the profit of the plaintiff company and not for Smith.

The relief afforded by equity to companies against promoters, who have sought improperly to make concealed profits out of the promotion, is only an instance of the more general principle upon which equity prevents the abuse of undue influence and of fiduciary relations. The term promoter is a term not of law, but of business, usefully summing up in a single word a number of business operations familiar to the commercial world by which a company is generally brought into existence. In every case the relief granted must depend on the establishment of such relations between the promoter and the birth, formation and floating of the company, as render it contrary to good faith that the promoter should derive a secret profit from the promotion. A man who carries about an advertising board in one sense promotes a company, but in order to see whether relief is obtainable by the company what is to be looked to is not a word or name, but the acts and the relations of the parties. In the present instance, Green and Smith agreed to, and did bring out the present company for the purpose of purchasing the chemical works and premises on their own terms. The board of directors consisted of their nominees, and in order to make the purchase run more smoothly a sham contract of purchase was on the 19th of September flashed before the eyes of the directors as if it were a real contract by both Smith and Green. The relation in which Smith by these acts placed himself towards the company is one in which equity will not allow him to retain any secret advantage for himself. He had a perfect right to agree with Green that he should be remunerated to the extent of £3,000 provided such agreement was made with the knowledge and assent of the company. But the company have a clear right to treat all profit made by Smith out of such a transaction as profit belonging to them, and it was hardly disputed, and in my opinion cannot be successfully denied, that if Green had actually paid the £3,000 to Smith, Smith might be compelled to pay over to the company the clear profit left after deducting what he had expended in the promotion. But it is said that the contract cannot be enforced against Green so far as it remains still unexecuted, that there is no instance which can be found in the books in which a company has been allowed

to recover for its own benefit on a similar unexecuted contract
and that as Smith could not enforce against Green a contract
based on an illegal consideration, so neither can the company.

This objection seems to me unfounded. There is, in the first
place, nothing illegal in the contract that Smith should receive
£3,000 out of the sale, provided it was not to be kept secret
from the company when the company was induced to negotiate
for the purchase. It is said, indeed, that the agreement for the
£3,000 was anterior in date to the beginning of the promotion
of this particular company. This may have been so; but the
agreement, as the jury have found, was continued and applied
to the formation of this particular company. As soon as Smith
and Green formed the company and nominated its board,
it became their duty, in my opinion, to inform the company
of this private arrangement between them. Thereupon the
company might either, at its option, decline the proposed
purchase or accept it, claiming the benefit of Smith's bargain,
or, might, if they thought it reasonable, sanction the agreement
and allow Smith to retain the profit himself. The company
cannot be worse off because the existence of this contract was
concealed from them. The contract, it is true, has not been
as yet fully executed, but nothing remains to be done under it
except the payment of money, and the right to this is a profitable right, of which the company are entitled to insist on
availing themselves. It does not lie in Green's mouth to say
that his own bargain with Smith was a fraudulent one and
therefore cannot be enforced: *Allegans suam turpitudinem non
est audiendus*. In order to recover against Green, the company
do not indeed require to prove that Green was fraudulent. It
is enough to show that this is a profit coming to their agent
to the benefit of which they are entitled. It is not, perhaps,
every contract which a cestui que trust even under similar
circumstances, could in this manner enforce. In many unexecuted contracts the principal could not substitute himself
in the agent's place, as the person for whose benefit the
contract was to be performed, without altering substantially
the character of the contract. But where nothing has to be
done under the contract but payment of money to the agent, I

think that the principal, under circumstances such as these, is entitled to stand in the agent's shoes and compel a payment of money directly to himself.

. . . The plaintiffs therefore must have judgment. . . .

Gluckstein v. Barnes. [1900] A.C. 241

A promoter has no right to retain an undisclosed profit, and where there is no independent board of directors disclosure must be made to the intended shareholders.

Barnes as liquidator of Olympia, Limited had taken out a summons against Gluckstein before WRIGHT J. who dismissed it.

The Court of Appeal reversed the decision and ordered Gluckstein to pay £6,341 with interest whereupon Gluckstein appealed to the House of Lords.

The other facts sufficiently appear from the judgments.

EARL OF HALSBURY L.C.: My Lords, in this case the simple question is whether four persons, of whom the appellant is one, can be permitted to retain the sums which they have obtained from the company of which they were directors by the fraudulent pretence that they had paid £20,000 more than in truth they had paid for property which they, as a syndicate, had bought by subscription among themselves, and then sold to themselves as directors of the company. If this is an accurate account of what has been done by these four persons, of course so gross a transaction cannot be permitted to stand. That that is the real nature of it I now proceed to show.

In the year 1892 the freehold grounds and buildings known as "Olympia" were the property of a company which in that year was being wound up. That company had issued debentures to the extent of £100,000 as a first charge and a mortgage as a second charge for £10,000. The four persons in question knew that the property would have to be sold, and they combined to buy it in order that they might resell it to a company to be formed by themselves. The combination . . . proceeded to buy up so far as they could the incumbrances on the property called "Olympia." They expended £27,000 in buying debentures. These, of course, were very much depreciated in value, and they gave £500 for the mortgage of £10,000. As soon as this transaction had been completed they . . . proceeded to form a company, and it was of course necessary that the company should be willing to help, and accordingly the four persons in question were made by the articles of association the first directors.

The property was sold on February 8 . . . for £140,000, and the syndicate purchased nominally for that sum, but, by reason of the arrangement to which I have referred, that sum was less by £20,734 6s 1d than what they appeared to give. On March 29 they completed as directors the purchase of the property for £180,000, and they as directors paid to themselves as members of the syndicate £171,000 in cash and £9,000 in fully paid-up shares—in all £180,000.

The prospectus by which money was to be obtained from the public disclosed the supposed profit which the vendors were making of £40,000, while in truth their profit was £60,734 6s 1d and it is this undisclosed profit of £20,000, and the right to retain it, which is now in question.

My Lords, I am wholly unable to understand any claim that these directors, vendors, syndicate, associates, have to retain this money. I entirely agree with the Master of the Rolls that the essence of this scheme was to form a company. It was essential that this should be done, and that they should be directors of it, who would purchase. The company should have been informed of what was being done and consulted whether they would have allowed this profit. . . . When they did afterwards sell to a company, they took very good care there should be no one who could ask questions. They were to be sellers to themselves as buyers, and it was a necessary provision to the plan that they were to be both sellers and buyers, and as buyers to get the money to pay for the purchase from the pockets of deluded shareholders.

My Lords, I decline to discuss the question of disclosure to the company. It is too absurd to suggest that a disclosure to the parties to this transaction is a disclosure to the company of which these directors were the proper guardians and trustees.

They were there by the terms of the agreement to do the work of the syndicate, that is to say, to cheat the shareholders. . . .

I do not discuss either the sum sued for, or why Gluckstein alone is sued. The whole sum has been obtained by a very gross fraud, and all who were parties to it are responsible to make good what they have obtained and withheld from the shareholders.

I move your Lordships that the appeal be dismissed.

LORD MACNAGHTEN: . . . For my part, I cannot see any ingenuity or any novelty in the trick which Mr. Gluckstein and his associates practised on the persons whom they invited to take shares in Olympia, Limited. It is the old story. It has been done over and over again.

These gentlemen set about forming a company to pay them a handsome sum for taking off their hands a property which they had contracted to buy with that end in view. They bring the company into existence by means of the usual machinery. They appoint themselves sole guardians and protectors of this creature of theirs, half-fledged and just struggling into life, bound hand and foot while yet unborn by contracts tending to their private advantage, and so fashioned by its makers that it could only act by their hands and only see through their eyes. They issue a prospectus representing that they had agreed to purchase the property for a sum largely in excess of the amount which they had, in fact, to pay. On the faith of this prospectus they collect subscriptions from a confiding and credulous public. And then comes the last act. Secretly, and therefore dishonestly, they put into their own pockets the difference between the real and the pretended price. After a brief career the company is ordered to be wound up. In the course of the liquidation the trick is discovered. Mr. Gluckstein is called upon to make good a portion of the sum which he and his associates had misappropriated. Why Mr. Gluckstein alone was selected for attack I do not know any more than I know why he was only asked to pay back a fraction of the money improperly withdrawn from the coffers of the company.

However that may be, Mr. Gluckstein defends his conduct, or, rather I should say, resists the demand, on four grounds. . . . In the first place, he says that he was not in a fiduciary position towards Olympia, Limited, before the company was formed. Well, for some purposes he was not. For others he was. A good deal might be said on the point. But to my mind the point is immaterial, for it is not necessary to go back beyond the formation of the company.

In the second place, he says, that if he was in a fiduciary position he did in fact make a proper disclosure. [T]hat seems to me to be absurd. "Disclosure" is not the most appropriate word to use when a person who plays many parts announces to himself in one character what he has done and is doing in another. To talk of disclosure to the thing called the company, when as yet there were no shareholders, is a mere farce. To the intended shareholders there was no disclosure at all. On them was practised an elaborate system of deception.

The third ground of defence was that the only remedy was rescission. That defence, in the circumstances of the present case, seems to me to be as contrary to common sense as it is to authority. . . .

The last defence of all was that, however much the shareholders may have been wronged, they have bound themselves by a special bargain, sacred under the provision of the *Companies Act*, 1862, to bear their wrongs in silence. In other words, Mr. Gluckstein boldly asserts that he is entitled to use the provisions of an Act of Parliament, which are directed to a very different purpose, as a shield and shelter against the just consequences of his fraud. . . . The prospectus, I am sorry to find, was prepared in the office of a well-known solicitor. I wish I could say that it displays the simplicity and candour which some persons perhaps might expect from such an origin. . . .

My Lords, it is a trite observation that every document as against its author must be read in the sense which it was intended to convey. And everybody knows that sometimes half a truth is no better than a downright falsehood. Is the statement in the prospectus . . . as to the price which the vendors had to pay for the property true or false? In the letter it is true. The vendors had bid £140,000 for the property, and had formally agreed to pay that sum for it. But for all that, the sum of £140,000 was not the sum they were going to pay, and they knew that well enough. They had provided themselves with counters, obtained at little cost, which in reckoning the price would be taken, as they knew, at their face value, so that the price of the property to them would be only about £120,000. Is that what Mr. Gluckstein and his associates meant the public to understand? . . . "But then," says Mr. Gluckstein, "there is something in the prospectus about 'interim investments,' and if you had only distrusted us properly and read the prospectus with the caution with which all prospectuses ought to be read, and sifted the matter to the bottom, you might have found a clue to our meaning. You might have discovered that what we call 'interim investments' was really the abatement in price effected by purchasing charges on the property at a discount." My Lords, I decline altogether to take any notice of such an argument. I think the statement in the prospectus as to the price of the property was deliberately intended to mislead the shareholders and to conceal the truth from them. . . .

There are two things in this case which puzzle me much, and I do not suppose that I shall ever understand them. . . . I do not understand why Mr. Gluckstein and his associates were not called upon to refund the whole of the money which they misappropriated. What they did with it, whether they put it in their own pockets or distributed it among their confederates, or spent it in charity, seems to me absolutely immaterial. In the next place, I do not understand why Mr. Gluckstein was only charged with interest at 3%. I should have thought it was a case for penal interest.

In these two matters Mr. Gluckstein has been in my opinion extremely fortunate. But he complains that he may have a difficulty in recovering from his co-directors their share of the spoil, and he asks that the official liquidator may proceed against his associates before calling upon him to make good the whole amount with which he has been charged. My Lords, there may be occasions in which that would be a proper course to take. But I cannot think that this is a case in which any indulgence ought to be shown to Mr. Gluckstein. He may or may not be able to recover a contribution from those who joined with him in defrauding the company. He can bring an action at law if he likes. If he hesitates to take that course or takes it and fails, then his only remedy lies in an appeal to that sense of honour which is popularly supposed to exist among robbers of a humbler type.

I agree that the appeal must be dismissed. . . .

LORD ROBERTSON: My Lords, I am satisfied of the liability of the appellant. . . .

The facts here are that the company had been so far organised that its executive was provisionally appointed. The directors of a company are its executive organ; to them its interests are confided; and in the present instance the company, even in this, its inchoate stage, was identifiable through its executive. I hold that from the moment this step was taken the coming directors stood in a fiduciary relation to the company whose interests were to be in their sole hands.

. . . But, in the present case, the company was paralysed so far as vigilance and criticism were concerned; for the board-room was occupied by the enemy. Now, the question whether adequate disclosure has been made to a company by a vendor bound to do so must necessarily depend upon the intelligence brought to bear on the information. And if, by his own act, the promoter has weakened, or, as here, has annulled the directorate, his case on disclosure becomes extremely arduous—for he has to make out such disclosure to shareholders as makes directors unnecessary. How this could be done we have no occasion to consider, for the appellant is not within sight of doing it.

. . . I consider the liability of the appellant . . . to be the necessary result of the ground of judgment which I adopt.

Re Leeds and Hanley Theatres of Varieties, Limited. [1902] 2 Ch. 809

Where a promoter buys property with the intention of selling it to the company at a profit, and then on the sale to the company does not disclose that profit, he will, where rescission is impossible, be liable to the company in damages. The measure of damages is the amount of the profit.

The Consolidated Exploration and Finance Company, Limited, who were the promoters of the Leeds and Hanley Theatres of Varieties, Limited, heard that the Leeds and Hanley music-halls were for sale and agreed with the proprietors of the halls to form a company to take over the halls. On 21st December, 1896, the board of the Finance Company resolved to take over the two music-halls on the terms of a draft contract then approved.

The contract referred to the intended Theatres Company as the intended ultimate purchaser, and provided for part of the purchase-money (£7,000 in one case and £9,000 in the other) being left on mortgage of the halls, if the intended company should so require; but upon the company obtaining three-fourths of its capital from public subscription it was to pay off the mortgages.

The contract for the purchase of the Hanley music-hall for £10,500 was signed by George Rands, a trustee for the Finance Company, on the same day and a deposit of £1,000 was paid by the Finance Company out of their own money. Afterwards a similar contract for the purchase of the Leeds music-hall for £13,500 was signed and a deposit paid.

On 1st February 1897 Rands entered into a contract by which he purported to sell the two halls to W. O. Carter as trustee for the intended company for £75,000. In the meantime the Finance Company had settled the memorandum and articles of association of the Theatres Company, and had registered it on 2nd February, the signatories to the memorandum being provided, paid, and indemnified by the Finance Company. On 3rd February Rands executed a declaration of trust in favour of the Finance Company. On 4th February the directors of the Theatres Company, who had been appointed by the Finance Company, and some of whom had received their qualification shares from that company, held their first meeting and approved the prospectus and adopted the purchase by the trustee. The prospectus did not disclose the fact that the Finance Company were the real vendors to the Theatres Company, or that they were making a large profit upon the sale. Afterwards the arrangement was completely carried out.

The music-halls were worked at a loss and the Theatre Company was ordered to be wound up. By that time the Finance Company was also in liquidation. The liquidator of the Theatres Company applied for a declaration that the Finance Company were liable to contribute to the assets of the Theatres Company the amount of the secret profit made by them in connection with the promotion of the Theatres Company, and in the sale to that company of the two music-halls. Alternatively, he sought a declaration that the Finance Company were liable to contribute to the assets of the Theatres Company compensation for their misfeasance in inducing the Theatres Company to purchase the two music-halls without proper disclosure, and at a fraudulent over-value. The Finance Company were charged with having bought the two halls for £24,000, and having, without disclosing that as the price paid, sold them to the Theatres Company for £75,000; also with having issued a fraudulent prospectus.

WRIGHT J.: Under these circumstances, what were the duties of the respondents to the company which they had projected and promoted? Plainly they were bound to disclose to the company that they were the real vendors, and the price at which they had bought and the profit which they were to make, and, failing such disclosures, the company would have been entitled to rescission of the contract of purchase, and the respondents must then have returned the price paid by the company, if rescission had been possible. Rescission is not now possible, because the mortgagees of the halls have enforced their security, and have sold to persons out of whose hands the halls cannot now be taken. But it seems to me clear on the facts of this case that the respondents ought to be held to have bought the halls as agents or trustees for the intended company, with whose money the purchase-money was to be paid. They never intended to buy the halls for themselves, or to pay for them out of their own money. They always intended to act for the projected company, and the purchase was never completed until that company had been formed, and had been caused by the respondents to adopt the purchase and to provide most of the means for completion.

I think, therefore, that they must account to the company for the profit received on a purchase made on its behalf and at its cost.

Further, I think that the respondents are liable on the ground that they imposed on the company directors of the respondents' own selecting, and through these directors caused the company to agree to pay an excessive price, without any disclosure that the directors were of their own selection, and without any disclosure to the company of the facts necessary to enable a judgment to be formed upon the question of price. An independent board informed of the facts would certainly not have adopted the purchase. The respondents made it impossible for the company to obtain independent advice, and imposed their own terms, concealing the material facts. They must, therefore, disgorge to their cestuis que trust the benefit which they have extorted from them by taking an undue advantage of their position and influence.

Another ground of liability is that a prospectus of the company was prepared and issued for it by the respondents, containing material representations which were false, or false and fraudulent, and which were part of the inducement to purchase. For the damages sustained by reason of these misrepresentations the respondents may be liable to an extent not necessarily limited by the benefit which they have received. There was a representation that Rands, an impecunious clerk who acted as vendor for a customary fee of £5, was the real vendor. . . .

On these grounds the company could, irrespectively of the fraud, have repudiated its purchase, if it had known the facts in time, and it could now maintain a common law action for damages for the deceit, in which the measure of damages would presumably be the amount of the damage which the company had sustained in consequence of the fraud, and the measure of that damage as against the wrong-doer would probably be prima facie the whole cost to the company of its purchase, less any benefit which it can be shown to have received.

The assets of the respondents available to answer the applicant's claim do not, as I understand, exceed £12,000.

On either view of the case their liability exceeds that amount, and the order will be that they make compensation to that amount.

From this decision of WRIGHT J. the liquidator of the Finance Company appealed and the case accordingly came before the Court of Appeal.

VAUGHAN WILLIAMS L.J.: . . . I do not propose to base my judgment upon the hypothesis that the Finance Company at the moment of the purchase were acting as the agents of or the trustees for the company which was about to be created. . . .

The conclusion at which I arrive, taking all the facts together, is, that from first to last the Finance Company were promoters; that from first to last their intention was to buy the music-halls for the purpose of selling them to a company which they should create. They intended from the first to do that which they ultimately did—to create a board of directors which should be under their control and carry out their desire, which it is abundantly clear upon the evidence was to sell the music-halls which they had bought for £24,000 at an inflated price.

Now, if I am right in saying that the Finance Company were promoters from first to last of the Theatres Company, it follows that the Finance Company throughout this period stood in a fiduciary relation towards the Theatres Company. At first there were only four directors, who had been nominated and some of whom were qualified by the Finance Company, and the seven necessary signatories of the memorandum of association. When it is said that the promoters stood in a fiduciary position towards the company, that does not mean that they stood in such a relation to these directors and these seven signatories. It means that they stood in a fiduciary relation to the future allottees of shares—to the persons who were invited to come and take up the shares of the company. . . .

This, then, being the position of the Finance Company, and these being the persons to whom they stood in this fiduciary position, what duty did that position involve? In the first place, in my judgment, it was their plain duty to disclose the fact that they themselves were interested as the beneficial vendors of the music-halls. . . . What, then, did the prospectus disclose to the future allottees? . . . [I]t seems to me that this prospectus proves up to the hilt, not only that there was no disclosure of the interest of the Finance Company or that they were really the vendors, but a positive *suggestio falsi* in the statements made in relation to the interest of Rands.

There being then this breach of duty, the next question is whether under these circumstances the Theatres Company are now entitled to a remedy as against the company which thus acted in relation to the promotion. In my judgment, they are entitled to a remedy, but I think it is a remedy in the nature of damages. To put it in a short common law form, I am not sure that the Theatres Company can, in reference to this breach of fiduciary duty by their promoters, maintain an action in the nature of an action for money had and received. I think the safer way of putting it is to say that their remedy is in damages. The authorities are not all perfectly conclusive that there is no remedy by way of an account of profits, but I prefer to say that there is a remedy in the shape of damages.

. . . [I]t would have been impossible to rescind the contract. They could not replace things *in statu quo*. But, in my judgment, although the Theatres Company cannot give back the property and ask that their money should be returned *in toto*, they are entitled to damages for this breach of duty.

Let us first see what injury has been really done to the Theatres Company by this course of conduct. They have purchased for a total sum . . . of £75,000 that which the Finance Company purchased for £24,000. . . . [O]f course large deductions must be made for the money which had to be expended by the promoting company, partly in promotion expenses and partly in redecorating the halls and such like.

But it is agreed that the cash difference is something over £40,000; and under these circumstances, how can it possibly be said that WRIGHT J. was not justified by the evidence when he fixed the difference at £12,000? . . .

In my judgment, there has been a clear breach of the fiduciary duty of the promoting company; . . . and I think there is sufficient evidence of money damage sustained by the Theatres Company, and that the estimate of £12,000 made by WRIGHT J. is amply supported by the evidence.

ROMER L.J.: . . . Now, in the first place, it is clear that the Finance Company were the promoters of the Theatres Company, and on the evidence taken as a whole I think it is established that the prospectus which was issued, and which induced the shareholders of the Theatres Company to take shares in that company, was prepared, printed, and issued under such circumstances as to make the Finance Company responsible for its issue and contents. . . .

Then, when I look at the prospectus I am satisfied that it was fraudulent. It not only concealed the fact that the Finance Company, who were the promoters of the Theatres Company, were the real vendors of the property, but it contained actual misrepresentations. . . . To my mind this was a most fraudulent prospectus, and intentionally so on the part of those who were responsible for it; and under the circumstances it was a fraud perpetrated by the Finance Company upon the Theatres Company. It was the duty of the Finance Company, as promoters, under the circumstances of this case, to take care that an independent board of directors was provided on behalf of the company which it was bringing into existence. There were four directors, and it appears that none of those four ever took any share or interest in the Theatres Company. Two of the directors were qualified, or, in other words, bribed, by the Finance Company, one of them being a director of the Finance Company. . . .

Then, I ask, What was the result of this fraud? . . . [I]f it be proved that the two properties so obtained by the Theatres Company were at that time worth substantially less than the property which they parted with as the consideration, then, in my opinion, the difference in value is the damage suffered by the Theatres Company in consequence of the fraud of the Finance Company for which that company is liable. . . .

I think . . . that the evidence is sufficient to prove the fact of damage suffered by the Theatres Company by reason of the fraud of the Finance Company; and it further proves this, that the amount of that damage is certainly not less than either of the two sums I am about to mention: First, the amount of the profit made in the transaction by the Finance Company, treating the purchase and the resale of the property as one transaction; secondly, the sum of £12,000 mentioned in the order of WRIGHT J. . . .

I think, therefore, . . . the appeal fails and should be dismissed. . . .

STIRLING L.J.: I am of the same opinion, and substantially for the same reasons.

In my judgment it has been established, first, that the Finance Company have as promoters of the Theatres Company committed a misfeasance in the nature of a breach of trust; and, secondly, that by reason of that misfeasance the Theatres Company has sustained loss to at least the amount of £12,000. . . .

For these reasons I think that the appeal fails.

VAUGHAN WILLIAMS L.J.: We are all of opinion that the true measure of the damages is the amount of the profit which was made by the promoting company. . . .

VI. THE PROSPECTUS

Re South of England Natural Gas and Petroleum Company, Limited. [1911] 1 Ch. 573

A document inviting applications for shares or debentures which is sent only to shareholders in certain gas companies is an offer to the public, even though marked "For private circulation only."

The omission of a matter required by the Companies Act to be stated in the prospectus does not entitle the allottee to rescind his contract, though he may have a remedy in damages against the directors and other persons responsible for the prospectus.

The South of England Natural Gas and Petroleum Company was incorporated on 30th January 1909 with a capital of £20,000 divided into 10,000 preference shares of £1 each and 10,000 ordinary shares of £1 each. On 21st February 1910 a prospectus was issued marked "For private circulation only," but also containing a statement "This prospectus has been filed with the Registrar of Joint Stock Companies." It offered for subscription 7,000 preference shares, 9,000 ordinary shares, and £5,000 debentures and stated that the minimum subscription upon which the directors might proceed to allotment was fifty shares.

The prospectus was sent, it was stated, only to shareholders in certain gas companies in which Eaton, the promoter of the company who undertook the distribution of the prospectus, was interested. The issue was not publicly advertised and only 3,000 copies were sent out. Only 200 shares were applied for, and of these 180 were applied for by the directors of the company.

In March 1910 the company applied for and obtained a certificate from the Registrar of Joint Stock Companies that they were entitled to commence business. Upon this application the managing director made a statutory declaration that the prospectus fixing £50 as the minimum subscription had been issued to the public.

On 3rd April 1910 a prospectus was issued offering 8,000 preference and 8,000 ordinary shares and some debentures.

This prospectus was publicly advertised and issued in the ordinary way. It did not contain a statement of the amount offered for subscription or the amount allotted on the previous allotment as required by S.81 (*d*), *Companies (Consolidation) Act*, 1908, [*see now para. 6, 4th Schedule, Companies Act, 1948*].

On this issue 1,150 ordinary and 943 preference shares were applied for and allotted. C. P. Byrne applied for and was allotted 200 preference shares; he paid £50 allotment money, but died on 28th June without having paid £150 which had by that time become due. His executors moved to rectify the register of shareholders by removing his name on the ground of the omission in the prospectus.

In answer to this application the managing director filed an affidavit that the earlier issue was private only, and not an offer to the public, and therefore did not need to be mentioned in the second prospectus.

SWINFEN EADY J.: . . . I am satisfied that the first prospectus did offer shares to the public, and none the less because copies were sent only to shareholders in gas companies who were the most likely subscribers. It follows that the second prospectus contained a subsequent offer and did not comply with S.81 (*d*).

Then the question is what is the remedy of the shareholder? Is he entitled to rescind his contract and have his money back? . . . There is no provision of that kind in S.81, nor in any other section relating to the omissions relied on in this case. But the section does contemplate a liability in damages on the part of the "directors and other persons responsible for the prospectus," for sub. s. (6) exonerates such persons from liability if they can prove certain matters [*see now S.38 (4) Companies Act, 1948*]. That is equivalent to saying that they are liable if they cannot prove them. In my opinion the allottee is not entitled to rescind his contract because of any breach of the statutory requirements, which extend to such

comparatively unimportant matters as the names and addresses of the company's auditors. His remedy is against the directors and other persons responsible for the prospectus.
. . . The motion therefore fails.

Governments Stock and Other Securities Investment Company Ltd. *v.* Christopher and Others. [1956] 1 W.L.R. 237

The word "prospectus" in S.37 and S.38 Companies Act, 1948, has the same meaning as in S.455.

Unissued shares cannot be the subject of an offer for "purchase," and the word "subscription" means taking shares for cash.

Where the letters of allotment to be issued are non-renounceable, the document inviting applications for the shares falls within S.55 (2) Companies Act, 1948, and is not distributed to the public.

By a circular dated 12th November 1955 and issued by the British and Commonwealth Shipping Co. Ltd. (hereinafter called "the new company"), the new company offered to acquire the whole of each class of preference and ordinary shares and stock in the issued capitals of the Union-Castle Mail Steamship Co. Ltd. and the Clan Line Steamers, Ltd. and to issue its own shares in exchange therefor.

The circular was sent to all members of Union-Castle and Clan Line together with a form headed "Form of acceptance and transfer." The offer was expressed to be conditional on acceptance on or before 30th December 1955, or such later date not after 29th February 1956 as the new company might allow, by the holders of not less than 90 per cent of every class of issued capital of Clan Line and Union-Castle, or such less percentage as the new company might elect to accept, and on permission to deal and to quote being granted by the council of the Stock Exchange before the dispatch of letters of allotment.

The plaintiff company contended, *inter alia,* that the circular was a "prospectus" to which S.38 of the *Companies Act,* 1948, applied, and that as such it did not comply with the requirements of the Act. On behalf of itself and other shareholders of Union-Castle, it moved for an injunction against seven directors of Union-Castle and against Union-Castle to restrain the carrying out of the above scheme.

WYNN-PARRY J.: . . . I think that in order to understand and consider the attacks which the plaintiff company makes on the circular, I should first consider its nature. It is alleged by the plaintiff company that it is a prospectus to which S.38 of the *Companies Act*, 1948 applies, and that as such it does not comply with the requirements of the Act.

The word "prospectus" is defined in S.455 of the *Companies Act*, 1948. . . . It is argued that "prospectus" in S.38 of the *Companies Act*, 1948 has a wider meaning than in S.455, the reason put forward being that in subsection (3) reference is made to the issue of "A form of application," and that there being nothing in the subsection to limit the issue of the form of application to an allotment and issue for cash, it must apply where the consideration is a consideration other than cash. This, it is said, constitutes a context requiring the word "prospectus" to cover documents not included in the definition in S.455. I do not accept this view. S.38 follows S.37, which appears under the heading "prospectus." There is no ground whatsoever for giving the word "prospectus" in S.37 any more extended meaning than it has in S.455, and it would be strange if in the very next section "prospectus" were to be found to have a wider meaning. I can see no need to attribute any other meaning to "prospectus" in S.38 than that given in S.455. The reference in subsection (3) to a form of application means only a form of application in connection with a prospectus offering shares for subscription or purchase.

It is clear that the circular does not involve an offer for the purchase of any shares. The shares in question are unissued shares of the new company, so they cannot be the subject of an offer for purchase.

It becomes necessary, therefore, to consider the word "subscription" in the definition of "prospectus." In my view the word means: taking or agreeing to take shares for cash.

It imports that the person agreeing to take the shares puts himself under a liability to pay the nominal amount thereof in cash. . . . Paras. 4, 5, 6, and 7 of Part I of Schedule 4 to the Act clearly require that "subscription" and "subscribe" involve the notion of payment in cash. The circular in this case does not invite subscription for shares in cash. For these reasons I am of opinion that the circular is not a prospectus within the meaning of that word as used in the *Companies Act*, 1948. . . . I am further of opinion that the circular was not distributed to the public. I accept the proposition . . . that the test is not who receives the circular, but who can accept the offer put forward. In this case it can only be persons legally or equitably interested as shareholders in the shares of Union-Castle or Clan. In the case of those who accept non-renounceable letters of allotment will be issued. In these circumstances the case appears to me to fall within S.55 (2) of the *Companies Act*, 1948.

. . . [T]he circular is not a prospectus, but what it purports to be, namely, the communication of an offer to exchange shares in the new company for shares in Union-Castle or Clan as the case may be.

. . . In the result, in my judgment, the plaintiff company is not entitled to any of the injunctions for which it asks, and consequently the motion must be dismissed.

VII. PAYMENT FOR SHARES

Spargo's Case. (1873) L.R. 8 Ch. 407

Any transaction which would in law support a plea of payment in cash amounts to payment in cash within the meaning of the Companies Act. Thus where there are two debts payable immediately, one by the company to the shareholder, and the other by the shareholder to the company in respect of his shares, the setting-off of those debts against each other will constitute payment in cash for the shares.

Michell and Stevens were licensees of a sett for twelve months from 28th January 1871, with the right at any time within that period to call for a lease of twenty-one years. They and Thomas Spargo entered into arrangements for promoting a company to work this mine, and determined that its capital should be £3,200 in sixty-four shares of £50 each; £16 per share to go for working capital and £34 per share for the purchase of the mine, treating it as worth £2,176. A company for that purpose was accordingly registered on 9th March 1871. Spargo subscribed the memorandum for thirty-one shares, two other persons for two shares each, and the remaining four subscribers for one share each. Neither Michell nor Stevens was a subscriber.

On 16th March 1871 a meeting was held at which it was unanimously resolved, *inter alia*, that the sum of £2,176 should be credited to Mr. Thomas Spargo for the lease of the property, and that the same should be paid out of the share capital of the company. Then followed, first, the names of the seven subscribers to the memorandum, with the numbers of shares for which they had respectively subscribed it set against their respective names; next, the names of three persons who had applied for shares, amounting to five in all; and lastly, the name of Spargo, with the balance of twenty shares set against it.

From the account kept in the books of the company

it appeared that all the shares except Spargo's were fully paid up in cash in March 1871.

After the above meeting Spargo, at different times, disposed of a number of his shares at a premium. No lease was ever granted, difficulties having been raised as to its form on the part of the lessees. The company having proved a failure, an order for winding it up was obtained on 21st December 1871. Spargo was placed on the list of contributories for nine shares, which were all that were standing in his name at the commencement of the winding-up.

In February 1872 the liquidator applied for an order for Spargo to pay into court £1,633, alleged to have been retained by him out of the assets of the company, and the above-mentioned sum of £2,176. The Vice-Warden of the Stannaries refused the application, and there was no appeal from his decision.

The liquidator then applied for an order upon Spargo to pay into Court £450, being £50 per share on the nine shares in respect of which he was on the list of contributories; and also to pay into Court £893, being the balance of £50 per share on the forty-two other shares taken by Spargo, after deducting £1,207, the amount of the moneys which the liquidator computed to have been paid by Spargo on behalf of the company.

The Vice-Warden made the order asked for, and Spargo appealed.

Sir W. M. James, L.J.: I am of opinion in this case that the order of the Vice-Warden cannot stand.

The question turns upon what is the true intent and meaning of the 25th section of the *Companies Act*, 1867, which we had to consider very fully in *Fothergill's Case*. . . . In that case no doubt it was not necessary for us to lay down what would amount to "payment in cash," . . . but it was said by the Lord Chancellor, and we entirely concurred with him, that it could not be right to put any construction upon that section which would lead to such an absurd and unjustifiable result as this, that an exchange of cheques would not be payment in cash, or that an order upon a banker to transfer money from the account of a man to the account of a company would not

be a payment in cash. In truth, it appeared to me that anything which amounted to what would be in law sufficient
evidence to support a plea of payment, would be a payment in
cash within the meaning of this provision. . . . [I]f a transaction resulted in this, that there was on the one side a bona
fide debt payable in money at once for the purchase of property, and on the other side a bona fide liability to pay money
at once on shares, so that if bank notes had been handed from
one side of the table to the other in payment of calls, they might
legitimately have been handed back in payment for the property, it did appear to me in *Fothergill's Case*, and does appear
to me now, that this Act of Parliament did not make it necessary that the formality should be gone through of the money
being handed over and taken back again; but that if the two
demands are set off against each other the shares have been
paid for in cash. If it came to this, that there was a debt in
money payable immediately by the company to the shareholders, and an equal debt payable immediately by the
shareholders to the company, and that each was accepted in
full payment by the other, the company could have pleaded
payment in an action brought against them, and the shareholder could have pleaded payment in cash in a corresponding
action brought by the company against him for calls. Supposing the transaction to be an honest transaction, it would in a
court of law be sufficient evidence in support of a plea of payment in cash, and it appears to me that it is sufficient for this
Court sitting in a winding-up matter. Of course, one can easily
conceive that the thing might have been a mere sham, or
evasion, or trick, to get rid of the effect of the Act of Parliament, but any suggestion of sham, or fraud, or deceit seems to
be entirely out of the question in this case, because everybody
in the company knew of the transaction; every shareholder of
the company was present, and was a party to the resolution;
there was no deceit practised on any creditor, nor was there
any registration of these shares, except as shares paid up.
This seems to me to dispose of the case. It was argued, however, that the payment by the company was made for a consideration which has absolutely failed. If however the payment was

made, the subsequent failure of the consideration could not prevent its being a payment, nor prevent its repayment by the shareholders from being a payment in full of the shares, though there· might be an action. . . . by the company either for the return of the money or for damages, in case there was a subsequent failure to do something in respect of the property. But I see no trace whatever, no shadow of anything like what may be called a failure of consideration. What the parties were dealing with was a license or sett for a year, with a right to get a licence or sett for twenty-one years. That was the property which the parties undertook to deal with. The company, with knowledge of all this, not only paid the £2,176 . . . to the Appellant, but afterwards made arrangements with him for satisfying the two other persons who were interested with him for their proportion of the property. After this disputes arose, not between this gentleman and themselves, but between the intending lessors and themselves; not as to the right of one to have the lease and the obligation of the other to grant a lease, but as to what would be the proper conveyancing language in which that lease was to be expressed. It appears to me that it would be an abuse of language to say that there was anything like a failure of consideration on the part of Mr. Spargo, which is to entitle the company to treat that payment as a payment never made, and to insist that the shares remain unpaid to this day. This applies to the forty-two shares as well as the nine shares. . . .

I am of opinion that the order of the Vice-Warden ought to be discharged. . . .

Sɪʀ G. Mᴇʟʟɪsʜ, L.J.: I am of the same opinion. . . .

Ooregum Gold Mining Company of India v. Roper. [1892] A.C. 125

The liability of a shareholder is limited to the amount unpaid on his shares, from which it follows that he is liable up to that amount. The amount of these shares must be fixed by the memorandum of association, and it is unlawful for a company to issue shares at a discount.

Payment for shares need not be in cash, but may be in property, goods or services.

The Ooregum Gold Mining Company, Limited, was incorporated in October 1880 under the *Joint Stock Companies Acts* 1862 to 1880. The memorandum of association stated that the capital of the company was £125,000 divided into 125,000 shares of £1 each, and that the shares of which the original or increased capital might consist might be divided into different classes and issued with such preference, privilege or guarantee as the company might direct. Forty thousand of the shares were allotted to the vendors to the company, the residue were issued to the public, and the full amount paid thereon.

The operations of the company were not, in the first instance, successful, and a winding-up order was obtained. An application was subsequently made to the Court for an order to stay the winding-up, with a view to the introduction of fresh capital and a resumption of mining operations, and an order was made accordingly. In pursuance of this policy an extraordinary general meeting of the company was summoned in 1885, at which it was resolved that the capital should be increased by the issue of 120,000 preference shares of £1 each, to be credited in the capital and books of the company as having the sum of 15s. per share paid thereon, such preference shares carrying the right to a non-cumulative preference dividend up to 10 per cent on the nominal amount of such preference capital out of the profits of the undertaking each year, and to equal participation with the ordinary shares in such further profits as should remain for distribution each year after the payment of the above 10 per cent preference dividend. At this time the market value of the ordinary shares was only 2s. 6d. per share.

Upwards of 100,000 of these preference shares were allotted, with 15s. credited as paid thereon. A contract to this effect was registered under S.25 of the *Companies Act*, 1867. The capital raised by means of the issue of the preference shares sufficed to discharge the obligations of the company, to extricate it from its difficulties, and to give it a new start. Gold to a considerable amount was shortly afterwards raised from the mines, and the company prospered, the market value of the ordinary shares rising to about 40*s*.

In February 1889 the respondent, George Roper, purchased on the stock exchange and paid for ten fully paid-up ordinary shares in the company. On 15th July following, on behalf of himself and the other ordinary shareholders, Roper brought an action against the company to have it declared that the issue by the company of the 120,000 preferred shares, at a discount of 15*s*. per share, was *ultra vires*, and to have the register rectified accordingly. NORTH J. made an order declaring that the issue of the preferred shares of £1 each at a discount of 15*s*. per share was beyond the powers of the company, and that the said shares were held subject to the liability of the holders to pay to the company in cash so much of the £1 per share as had not been paid on the same; and ordering that the company do rectify the register accordingly.

This order was affirmed by the Court of Appeal. The company thereupon appealed to the House of Lords.

LORD HALSBURY L.C.: . . . My Lords, the whole structure of a limited company owes its existence to the Act of Parliament, and it is to the Act of Parliament one must refer to see what are its powers, and within what limits it is free to act. Now, confining myself for the moment to the Act of 1862, it makes one of the conditions of the limitation of liability that the memorandum of association shall contain the amount of capital with which the company proposes to be registered, divided into shares of a *certain fixed amount*. It seems to me that the system thus created by which the shareholder's liability is to be limited by the amount unpaid upon his shares, renders it impossible for the company to depart from that requirement, and by any expedient to arrange with their shareholders that they shall not be liable for the amount unpaid on the shares, although the amount of those shares has been, in accordance with the Act of Parliament, fixed at a certain sum of money. It is manifest that if the company could do so the provision in question would operate nothing. . . .

I think . . . that the question which your Lordships have

to solve is one which may be answered by reference to an
inquiry: What is the nature of an agreement to take a share in
a limited company? and that that question may be answered
by saying, that it is an agreement to become liable to pay to the
company the amount for which the share has been created. That
agreement is one which the company itself has no authority
to alter or qualify, and I am therefore of opinion that . . . the
company were prohibited by law, upon the principle laid down
in *Ashbury* v. *Riche*, from doing that which is compendiously
described as issuing shares at a discount.

The question remains whether S.25 of the Act of 1867 has
made any difference. . . . That section prescribes that every
share in any company shall be deemed and taken to have been
issued and to be held *subject to the payment* of the whole
amount thereof *in cash*, unless the same shall have been
otherwise determined by contract duly made in writing, and
filed with the Registrar of Joint Stock Companies at or before
the issue of such shares. Two things are manifest in this
provision. The share is to be held subject *to payment*, and the
payment is to be *in cash*. The amount is to be paid and the
whole amount to be paid *in cash*, and to me it appears, looking
at the latter part of the section, whereby a contract made and
filed may qualify and cut down the form of payment, and that
it may be in goods or in value received in some form, instead
of in cash, it must nevertheless be payment. . . . [T]here is
nothing in the section which justifies the notion that that which
the statute required to be paid in cash, subject to qualification
of a mode of payment, should not be paid at all.

. . . [I]t seems to me that, although not directly in point,
the principle laid down by your Lordships' House in *Trevor*
v. *Whitworth* would render it extremely difficult to so read the
sections to which I have referred as to justify the appellants'
contention.

. . . Accordingly, I move your Lordships that the order
appealed from be affirmed, and the appeal dismissed. . . .

LORD WATSON: My Lords, can a company limited by shares,
formed and registered under the Act of 1862, issue its shares

as fully paid up, for a money consideration less than their nominal value? . . . [T]he statutory liability of each shareholder is for the difference between the amount fixed by the memorandum and the sum which has actually been paid upon his shares. Consequently, if shares are issued against money, it appears to me that any payment to the company less than the nominal amount of the share must, by force of the statute, and notwithstanding any agreement to the contrary, be treated as a payment to account, the member remaining liable to contribute the balance, when duly called for.

A company is free to contract with an applicant for its shares; and when he pays in cash the nominal amount of the shares allotted to him, the company may at once return the money in satisfaction of its legal indebtedness for goods supplied or services rendered by him. That circuitous process is not essential. It has been decided that, under the Act of 1862, shares may be lawfully issued as fully paid up, for considerations which the company has agreed to accept as representing in money's worth the nominal value of the shares. I do not think any other decision could have been given in the case of a genuine transaction of that nature where the consideration was the substantial equivalent of full payment of the shares in cash. The possible objection to such an arrangement is that the company may over-estimate the value of the consideration, and, therefore, receive less than the nominal value for its shares. The Court would doubtless refuse effect to a colourable transaction, entered into for the purpose or with the obvious result of enabling the company to issue its shares at a discount; but it has been ruled that, so long as the company honestly regards the consideration given as fairly representing the nominal value of the shares in cash, its estimate ought not to be critically examined. . . . The rule is capable of being abused, and I have little doubt that it has been liberally construed in practice.

. . . In all such cases, the clause [*S.25 of the Companies Act, 1867*] provides that the contract, if not duly filed with the registrar, shall be of no effect, and that the shareholder shall remain liable for the value of his shares in money. The obvious purpose of the enactment is to enable persons dealing with the company to judge for themselves what may be the value of the consideration given as representing capital. . . .

In my opinion, . . . the register of the company is erroneous, in so far as it bears that these additional shares have been fully paid up; and the order appealed from . . . ought to be affirmed. . . .

I . . . concur in the judgment which has been moved by the Lord Chancellor.

LORD HERSCHELL: My Lords, this case raises the important question whether a company incorporated with limited liability can issue its shares at a discount.

. . . If it had been determined that under the *Companies Act* a shareholder was in all cases liable to pay the whole of the nominal value of a share in cash, I should have had less difficulty in adhering to the judgment of the Court below. But the contrary has been determined. And not only may a share be allotted as fully paid up in respect of property, goods or services received by the company, but the Courts will not inquire into the adequacy of the consideration, and certainly have not required it to be proved that the consideration given was equivalent in cash value to the nominal amount of the share. . . .

I cannot myself place any great weight on the requirement of S.8 [*of the Companies Act, 1862*], that the amount of capital with which the company proposes to be registered is to be divided into shares "of a certain fixed amount." The provision was, of course, necessary in introducing a scheme of limited liability. But it does not, of itself, determine anything as to the extent of liability. Had it stood alone, the shareholders would have been liable, on general principles, to the extent necessary to discharge all the obligations of the industrial partnership. The limitation of liability arises from the provision of S.38 [*see now S.212 (1) (d) Companies Act, 1948*], that in case the company is wound up an individual shall only be liable "to the amount, if any, unpaid on the shares in respect of which he is liable as a present or past member." This must be regarded as by implication enacting that he shall be liable to that extent.

... [W]hilst goods or services given or taken in lieu of payment in cash may be regarded as in a sense payment, it is difficult to say that payment of a portion of a sum is payment of the whole. Although, therefore, my mind has not been free from doubt, I am not prepared to differ from the Court below, and from those of your Lordships who entertain that view, in thinking that a company cannot issue its shares at a discount so as to exonerate those taking the shares from the liability, in case the company be wound up, to pay the amount not already paid on the shares.

> LORD HERSCHELL then went on to say that, had the point been argued in the present case, he would have thought that since the company was not being wound up, the company were not entitled to call upon the preference shareholders for any further payment beyond that agreed upon, and that he saw nothing in the *Companies Acts* which would render such an agreement invalid [*see now S.57 Companies Act, 1948*].

LORD MACNAGHTEN: My Lords, your Lordships are called upon to determine whether it is or is not competent for a company limited by shares to issue shares at a discount so as to relieve persons taking shares so issued from liability to pay up their amount in full. . . .

The question turns upon the construction of the *Companies Act*, 1862. The provisions of the Act are, I think, plain enough if one bears in mind the condition of things which existed before the principle of limited liability was introduced in 1855. Before that time there was no way known to the law by which persons trading in partnership could restrict their liability. They were liable to the uttermost farthing. At last the legislature intervened and authorised persons who proposed to trade in partnership to form themselves into a registered company with a declared capital and shares of a fixed amount, and then limited the liability of the partners as members of the company to the amount unpaid upon their shares.

But all this legislation proceeds on the footing of recognising and maintaining the liability of the individual members to the company until the prescribed limit is reached. The memorandum of association of a company limited by shares must contain "the amount of capital with which the company proposes to be registered divided into shares of a certain fixed amount." It must also contain "a declaration that the liability of the members is limited." Neither the liability nor the limitation is defined in the memorandum itself. And so the declaration carries you back to the earlier part of the section, where you are told what is meant by "a company limited by shares." It is a company "formed on the principle of having the liability of its members limited to the amount unpaid upon their shares." That must mean that the liability of a member continues so long as anything remains unpaid upon his shares. Nothing but payment, and payment in full, can put an end to the liability . . . Whether this liability is one of "the conditions of the memorandum," within the meaning of that expression in the Act of 1862, . . . or a condition attached by the Act to a company limited by shares and of the essence of such a company, though it may not be found contained within the four corners of the memorandum, is a matter of little or no importance. In either view of the case it is plain that the condition is one which cannot be dispensed with by anything in the articles of association, or by any resolution of the company, or by any contract between the company and outsiders who have been invited to become members of the company and who do come in on the faith of such a contract. . . .

In the present case, I regret that I am compelled to say that in my opinion the transaction cannot stand. The course which the directors took probably saved the company. All parties concerned acted in a perfectly open and honest manner. But it seems to me that the requirements of the *Companies Act*, 1862 have been contravened, and, therefore, I think that the appeal must be dismissed.

LORD MORRIS: My Lords, the Act of 1862 enabled a company to be formed on the principle of having the liability of its members limited to the amount unpaid on their shares; it did not impose a liability—on the contrary, it limited liability to the extent of the amount of the share; but there is no power given that I can see to further limit liability by not paying that amount. Has that position been varied by S.25 of the Act of 1867? . . . That section appears to me plainly to refer to and deal only with the mode of payment—prima facie, the payment of the whole amount is to be in *cash*, but with a power given of contracting for something other than cash to be taken in payment, but payment in meal or malt is clearly contemplated —the amount of the shares must be paid. A company can only do what it is authorised to do, and not that which it is only not prohibited from doing. I can find no authority to issue a pound share but that only 5*s*. is to be paid of the pound.

For these reasons I concur in the judgment which has been moved by the Lord Chancellor.

Mosely *v*. Koffyfontein Mines, Ltd. [1904] 2 Ch. 108

An issue of debentures at a discount giving the holder an immediate right to convert his debentures into fully paid shares of the same nominal value is void, since it is capable of being used as a means of issuing shares at a discount.

A company proposed to issue to its shareholders debentures at a discount of 20 per cent, repayable on 1st November, 1909, upon the terms of a circular. By the circular the registered holder was to have the right at any time prior to 1st May 1909 to exchange his debentures for fully paid shares in the company at the rate of one £1 fully paid share for every £1 of the nominal amount of the debentures; and by the conditions of the debentures, in the event of the debenture-holder giving to the company a written demand for shares in exercise of this right, the principal moneys were to become immediately repayable.

The plaintiff, Mr. Mosely, was the largest shareholder in the company, and he applied for an injunction to restrain the company and its directors from carrying into effect the proposed allotment of debentures on the ground that the transaction involved the issuing of shares at a discount.

BUCKLEY J. refused to grant an injunction, and Mr.

Mosely appealed from his decision. The case accordingly came before the Court of Appeal.

VAUGHAN WILLIAMS L.J.: . . . There is, of course, no doubt about the obligation of a shareholder to pay to the company the full amount of his shares . . . continuing as long as anything remains unpaid on his shares, but the liability . . . can be discharged by payment in money, or (with the consent of the company) by payment in money's worth, and the Court will not, if there is a valid contract . . . by the company for the acceptance of something of substantial value as money's worth, inquire into the adequacy of the consideration. But the cases decide that a man must really pay for the shares. And, further, that, if the contract makes it manifest on its face that the taker of the shares is paying less than their nominal cash value, he may be liable for the balance. If the consideration is illusory, or if it permits an obvious money measure to be made shewing that discount was allowed, or if the shares are openly issued at a discount, the shareholder may be called on to pay the balance in cash.

. . . Now it seems to me in the present case that the immediate consideration for the issue of shares to a debenture-holder demanding such allotment in exchange for, or in satisfaction of his debenture, is clearly the surrender of the debenture, and the mere fact that the debenture was purchased at a discount of 20% will not afford an obvious money measure shewing that a discount was allowed in the price of the shares. Test it in this way. Suppose the debentures to have been issued at a discount of 20%, and subsequently, quite independently of any contract at the time of the issue of the debentures, the company is minded to buy up as many of the debentures as the debenture-holders will sell, allotting 100 £1 shares in exchange for a £100 debenture, could it possibly be said that those shares were issued at an obvious discount? I think not. . . . The question therefore arises, Does it make any difference that the bargain to issue the 100 £1 shares in exchange for the £100 debenture issued at the price of £80 was part and parcel of the consideration for the issue of the £100 debenture at the price of £80? It seems to me that such a bargain might be a very good bargain for a company to make who wished to borrow on debentures a large sum of money required for the development of the enterprise of the company. It is true, however, that it might be a very bad bargain for the company, and, what is really essential, such a bargain might enable the debenture-holders who claim the allotment of shares to escape the statutory obligation to pay the full nominal amount of their shares. If the debentures were exchanged for shares immediately after the issue of the debentures, the practical result would be that the shares, although nominally issued in exchange for the surrender of debentures, would really be issued at a discount—*i.e.* 100 £1 shares for a payment of £80. . . .

I think that the real question is, Does this bargain give to the company that which the company as business men might fairly regard as money's worth for the full nominal value of the shares? It is not sufficient for the company to say the bargain was made in good faith. The company must at least establish that there is no obvious money measure on the face of this bargain shewing that the shares were issued at a discount. . . .

The appeal must be allowed.

I wish to add one word before I leave this case. It was established long ago that the obligation of a shareholder to pay the full nominal value of his shares need not be satisfied in cash, but might be satisfied in money's worth. It has also been held that the Court will not, if it is satisfied that there is an honest bargain under which the money's worth is paid, inquire into the adequacy of the consideration. These two propositions have been affirmed by the highest tribunal, and I am not suggesting for a moment that the cases which established them were not properly decided, having regard to the terms of the *Companies Act*, 1862; but I hope that the day may come when it will be gravely considered by the Legislature whether it is not for the advantage of the community, and in particular of the commercial community, that an Act should be passed that in all cases the full nominal value of the shares shall be paid in cash and nothing else. I am satisfied from my own judicial experience in the administration of companies that such a law would have a tendency to benefit the companies themselves, and also to check a great deal of unwholesome speculation on the Stock Exchange which is largely fed and supported by operations undertaken by vendors, promoters, and others, for the purpose of unloading fully paid shares which they have been allowed to satisfy by giving what is called money's worth instead of making a cash payment.

COZENS-HARDY L.J.: This appeal raises a highly important and very difficult question. Is it competent for a limited company in consideration of £80 to contract to issue a fully paid share of £100 whenever requested so to do? Put in that bare form, the answer to the question admits of no doubt. The transaction would result in the issue of shares at a discount. . . . I do not think we ought to consider the motive or intention of the company in issuing the debentures in this form. . . . I assume in favour of the directors that, from a business point of view, the transaction is expedient, but that is unimportant if the transaction is contrary to the policy of the Act of Parliament. . . . In my opinion, an injunction ought to be granted to restrain the directors from carrying into effect the proposed allotment of debentures . . . on this short and simple ground—that the directors propose thereby to confer an immediate right to demand a £100 share in consideration of a cash payment of £80 only. I desire to guard myself against the supposition that the conclusion at which I have arrived involves the proposition that under no circumstances can a debenture be issued at a discount which may confer a right *at some future date* to demand a fully paid share in exchange for the debenture. It is sufficient to say that whenever such a question comes before the Court it will be discussed and decided with the care and deliberation which its importance demands.

VIII. THE PRESERVATION OF THE COMPANY'S SHARE CAPITAL

Trevor and Another *v*. Whitworth and Another. (1887) 12 A.C. 409

It is unlawful for a company to purchase its own shares, since this involves a reduction of capital.

James Schofield and Sons Ltd. were incorporated in 1865 under the *Companies Act*, 1862. The objects as stated in the memorandum of association were to acquire and carry on the business of certain flannel manufacturers and any other businesses and transactions which the company might consider to be in any way conducive or auxiliary thereto, or proper to be carried on in connection therewith.

The memorandum did not authorise the company to purchase its own shares. Several of the articles of association, however, dealt with the purchase of shares by the company. Article 179 provided: "Any share may be purchased by the company from any person willing to sell it, and at such price, not exceeding the then marketable value thereof, as the board think reasonable." Article 181 provided: "Shares so purchased may at the discretion of the board be sold or disposed of by them or be absolutely extinguished, as they deem most advantageous for the company."

In 1884 the company went into liquidation in the Court of Chancery of the County Palatine of Lancaster, whereupon the respondents as the executors of Robert Whitworth, a deceased shareholder, made a claim against the company for the balance of the price of Whitworth's shares sold by the executors to the company in 1880 and not wholly paid for. The appellants, the official liquidators, took out a summons to determine whether the claim ought to be allowed and the Vice-Chancellor of the County Palatine made an order that it ought not.

The Court of Appeal reversed this decision and allowed the claim, whereupon the liquidators appealed to the House of Lords.

LORD HERSCHELL: . . . I pass now to the main question in this case, which is one of great and general importance, whether the company had power to purchase the shares. The result of the judgment in the . Court below is certainly somewhat startling. The creditors of the company which is being wound up, who have a right to look to the paid-up capital as the fund out of which their debts are to be discharged, find coming into competition with them persons who, in respect only of their having been, and having ceased to be, shareholders in the company, claim that the company shall pay to them a part of that capital.

. . . It cannot be questioned, since the case of *Ashbury Railway Carriage and Iron Co.* v. *Riche*, that a company cannot employ its funds for the purpose of any transactions which do not come within the objects specified in the memorandum, and that a company cannot by its articles of association extend its power in this respect.

. . . The *Companies Act* 1862 requires (S.8) that in the case of a company where the liability of the shareholders is limited, the memorandum shall contain the amount of the capital with which the company proposes to be, registered, divided into shares of a certain fixed amount; and provides (S.12) that such a company may increase its capital and divide it into shares of larger amount than the existing shares, or convert its paid-up capital into stock, but that "save as aforesaid, no alteration shall be made by any company in the conditions contained in its memorandum of association." [*see now S.2 (4) (a) and S.61 (1) (a), (b) and (c) Companies Act, 1948.*]

. . . What is the meaning of the distinction thus drawn between a company without limit on the liability of its members and a company where the liability is limited, but, in the latter case, to assure to those dealing with the company that the whole of the subscribed capital, unless diminished by expenditure upon the objects defined by the memorandum, shall remain available for the discharge of its liabilities? The capital may, no doubt, be diminished by expenditure upon and reasonably incidental to all the objects specified. A part of it may be lost in carrying on the business operations authorised. Of this all persons trusting the company are aware, and take the risk. But I think they have a right to rely, and were intended by the Legislature to have a right to rely, on the capital remaining undiminished by any expenditure outside these limits, or by the return of any part of it to the shareholders.

Experience appears to have shown that circumstances might occur in which a reduction of the capital would be expedient. Accordingly, by the Act of 1867 provision was made enabling a company under strictly defined conditions to reduce its capital [see now S.66 Companies Act, 1948). Nothing can be stronger than these carefully-worded provisions to show how inconsistent with the very constitution of a joint stock company, with limited liability, the right to reduce its capital was considered to be.

Let me now invite your Lordships' attention to the facts of the present case. The company had purchased, prior to the date of the liquidation, no less than 4142 of its own shares; that is to say, considerably more than a fourth of the paid-up capital of the company had been either paid, or contracted to be paid, to shareholders, in consideration only of their ceasing to be so. I am quite unable to see how this expenditure was incurred in respect of or as incidental to any of the objects specified in the memorandum. And, if not, I have a difficulty in seeing how it can be justified. If the claim under consideration can be supported, the result would seem to be this, that the whole of the shareholders, with the exception of those holding seven individual shares, might now be claiming payment of the sums paid upon their shares as against the creditors, who had a right to look to the moneys subscribed as the source out of which the company's liabilities to them were to be met. And the stringent precautions to prevent the reduction of the capital of a limited company, without due notice and judicial sanction, would be idle if the company might purchase its own shares wholesale, and so effect the desired result. I do not think it was disputed that a company could not enter upon such a transaction for the purpose of reducing its capital, but it was suggested that it might do so if that were not the object, but it was considered for some other reason desirable in the interest of the company to do so. To the creditor, whose interests, I think, S.8 and S.12 of the *Companies Act* were intended to protect, it makes no difference what the object of the purchase is. The result to him is the same. The shareholders receive back the moneys subscribed, and there passes into their pockets what before existed in the form of cash in the coffers of the company, or of buildings, machinery, or stock available to meet the demands of the creditors.

What was the reason which induced the company in the present case to purchase its shares? If it was that they might sell them again, this would be a trafficking in the shares, and clearly unauthorised. If it was to retain them, this would be to my mind an indirect method of reducing the capital of the company. The only suggestion of another motive . . . is that this was intended to be a family company, and that the directors wanted to keep the shares as much as possible in the hands of those who were partners, or who were interested in the old firm, or of those persons whom the directors thought they would like to be amongst this small number of shareholders. I cannot think that the employment of the company's money in the purchase of shares for any such purpose was legitimate. The business of the company was that of manufacturers of flannel. In what sense was the expenditure of the company's money in this way incidental to the carrying on of such a business, or how could it secure the end of enabling the business to be more profitably or satisfactorily carried on? I can quite understand that the directors of a company may sometimes desire that the shareholders should not be numerous, and that they should be persons likely to leave them with a free hand to carry on their operations. But I think it would be most dangerous to countenance the view that, for reasons such as these, they could legitimately expend the moneys of the company to any extent they please in the purchase of its shares. No doubt if certain shareholders are disposed to hamper the proceedings of the company, and are willing to sell their shares, they may be bought out; but this must be done by persons, existing shareholders or others, who can be induced to purchase the shares, and not out of the funds of the company.

It is urged that the views I have expressed are inconsistent with the forfeiture and surrender of shares in a company. I do not think so. The forfeiture of shares is distinctly recognised by the *Companies Act*, and by the articles contained in the schedule, which in the absence of other provisions regulate the management of a limited liability company. It does not involve any payment by the company, and it presumably exonerates from future liability those who have shown themselves unable to contribute what is due from them to the capital of the company. Surrender no doubt stands on a different footing. But it also does not involve any payment out of the funds of the company. If the surrender were made in consideration of any such payment it would be neither more nor less than a sale, and open to the same objections. If it were accepted in a case when the company were in a position to forfeit the shares, the transaction would seem to me perfectly valid. There may be other cases in which a surrender would be legitimate. As to these I would repeat what was said by the late Master of the Rolls in *In re Dronfield & Co.*: "It is not for me to say what the limits of surrender are which are allowable under the Act, because each case as it arises must be decided upon its own merits."

. . . I move your Lordships that the judgment appealed from be reversed, and the judgment of the Vice-Chancellor restored.

LORD WATSON: . . . One of the main objects contemplated by the legislature, in restricting the power of limited companies to reduce the amount of their capital as set forth in the memorandum, is to protect the interests of the outside public who may become their creditors. In my opinion the effect of these statutory restrictions is to prohibit every transaction between a company and a shareholder, by means of which the money already paid to the company in respect of his shares is returned to him, unless the Court has sanctioned the transaction. Paid-up capital may be diminished or lost in the course of the company's trading; that is a result which no legislation can prevent; but persons who deal with, and give credit to a limited company, naturally rely upon the fact that the company is trading with a certain amount of capital already paid, as well as upon the responsibility of its members for the capital remaining at call; and they are entitled to assume that no part of the capital which has been paid into the coffers of the company has been subsequently paid out, except in the legitimate course of its business.

. . . When a company, in order to get rid of a troublesome shareholder, buys his shares and continues to hold them, . . . the object may be different, but the result, so far as regards the capital of the company, is precisely the same as if it had purchased the shares as an investment. If the shares are purchased with the view of being re-sold, that is simply a speculation with the funds of the company. If they are purchased with the view of their being retained by the company, that is a permanent withdrawal of the money invested in them from the trading capital of the company. I do not agree . . . that if such a transaction is invalid no forfeiture or surrender could be supported. When shares are forfeited or surrendered and not re-issued, that affects only the nominal amount of the shares so far as unpaid; when they are bought and not re-issued that diminishes the paid-up as well as the nominal capital.

Notwithstanding the general prohibition of alterations upon the memorandum of association which diminish the capital, whether paid-up or nominal, of a company limited by shares, the *Companies Acts* contemplate the possibility of diminution of unpaid capital in certain cases, although the memorandum remains unaltered. S.26 of the Act of 1862 and the regulations of Table A . . . show plainly that the legislature intended companies to have the power of forfeiting shares. There is no reference in the Acts to surrenders of shares; but these have been admitted by the Courts upon the principle . . . that they have practically the same effect as forfeiture, the main difference being that the one is a proceeding *in invitum*, and the other a proceeding taken with the assent of the shareholder, who is unable to retain and pay future calls on his shares. Whatever may be the case with regard to surrender, I do not think the purchase of its own shares by a company bears any analogy to forfeiture. It appears to me that a transaction by which, as in this case, . . . the company gave back his money to the shareholder, and accepted and held the shares in his stead, in point of fact operates as a diminution of its paid-up as well as of its nominal capital; and I have been unable to discover any good reason why such a diminution should be held to be legal in the face of statutory enactment to the contrary.

. . . In the present case I should have been of the opinion . . . that the purchase of the respondents' 533 shares was a transaction *ultra vires* of the company . . . It was not an isolated transaction with a single troublesome shareholder who was obstructing the business of the company, but was part and parcel of a scheme carried out by the directors under the articles of association, by which they acquired for the company more than one-fourth of the whole shares of its undertaking, and returned to the shareholders from whom they purchased more than one-fourth of its paid-up capital. It does not appear to have formed any part of the scheme to re-sell or re-issue the shares; and matters stood in the position I have described at the date of the liquidation. I do not doubt that . . . the object of the directors was to keep James Schofield & Sons Limited as a sort of family concern, which was a perfectly lawful object if pursued by legitimate means. But the directors and shareholders of a company limited by shares who desire to have the concern in the hands of themselves and their friends, and to keep its shares out of the market, ought to use their own money for that purpose and not the trading capital of the company. In my opinion the application of the company's funds in furtherance of any such object is altogether illegitimate, because it is foreign to the proper business of the company and in violation of statute law.

. . . I concur, therefore, in the judgment which has been moved.

LORD MACNAGHTEN: My Lords, the learned counsel for the appellants raised three points for your Lordships' consideration.

. . . The third point is one of general importance. It raises the question whether it is competent for a company formed under the Act of 1862, on the principle of limited liability, to purchase its own shares when it is authorised by its articles to do so. The consideration of that question, as it appears to me, necessarily involves the broader question whether it is competent for a limited company under any circumstances to invest any portion of its capital in the purchase of a share of its own capital stock, or to return any portion of its capital to any shareholder without following the course which Parliament has prescribed. . . . It appears to me that the notion of a limited company taking power to buy up its own shares is contrary to the plain intention of the Act of 1862, and inconsistent with the conditions upon which, and upon which alone, Parliament has granted to individuals who are desirous of trading in partnership the privilege of limiting their liability.

The Act of 1862 requires that the objects for which a limited company is established shall be stated in its memorandum. Those objects cannot be enlarged by anything to be found in the articles, or by anything outside the memorandum. Whatever may fairly be regarded as incidental to the objects stated in the memorandum, the company is authorised to do. Everything beyond that is prohibited. Further, every limited company is required to state in its memorandum the amount of capital with which it proposes to be registered, divided into shares of a certain fixed amount. That is equivalent to a declaration that the capital is to be devoted to the objects of the company.

. . . Your Lordships asked in what case, and under what circumstances, such a purchase could be said to be incidental to the objects of a limited company. In answer to that question the learned counsel . . . suggested that at any rate it might be so when the power was used as an incident of domestic management to buy out shareholders whose continuance in the company was undesirable. . . . But I would ask, Is it possible to suggest anything more dangerous to the welfare of companies and to the security of their creditors than such a doctrine? Who are the shareholders whose continuance in a company the company or its executive consider undesirable? Why, shareholders who quarrel with the policy of the board, and wish to turn the directors out; shareholders who ask questions which it may not be convenient to answer; shareholders who want information which the directors think it prudent to withhold. Can it be contended that when the policy of directors is assailed they may spend the capital of the company in keeping themselves in power, or in purchasing the retirement of inquisitive and troublesome critics?

. . . [The purchase] must involve the employment of funds which have been dedicated to other purposes, and the use or misuse of which concerns other persons besides the shareholders. Nor can it be considered incidental to the objects of the company merely because it may be very convenient. After all, the inconvenience sought to be avoided arises either from restrictions which Parliament has thought right to impose, or from the common misfortune of having to pay for what one wants out of one's own purse, when there is no other way of getting it. If the capital proposed to be expended in the purchase of its shares is "in excess of the wants of the company," the transaction may be carried out under the provisions of the Acts . . . If the capital of the company is not in excess of the company's wants, it certainly ought not to be diverted from its proper objects. But even then there is no reason why there should be a deadlock. The end in view may still be attained by means to which no exception can be taken. If shareholders think it worth while to spend money for the purpose of getting rid of a troublesome partner who is willing to sell, they may put their hands in their own pockets and buy him out, though they cannot draw on a fund in which others as well as themselves are interested. That, I think, is the law, and that is the good sense of the matter.

. . . It seems to me that if a power to purchase its own shares were found in the memorandum of association of a limited company, it would necessarily be void. . . . When Parliament sanctions the doing of a thing under certain conditions and with certain restrictions, it must be taken that the thing is prohibited unless the prescribed conditions and restrictions are observed.

. . . One word with regard to powers of forfeiture and surrender of shares. . . . Forfeiture is contemplated by the Act of 1862. . . . There can be no question as to the power of a company in a proper case to forfeit shares. Surrender of shares stands on a different footing. It is not mentioned in the *Companies Acts*, but I conceive there can be no objection to the surrender of shares which are liable to forfeiture. A surrender of shares in return for money paid by the company is a sale, and open to the same objections as a sale, whatever expression may be used to describe or disguise the transaction.

. . . I am of opinion that the judgment of the Court of Appeal should be reversed, and the appeal allowed.

Bellerby *v.* Rowland & Marwood's Steamship Company, Limited. [1902] 2 Ch. 14

A surrender of shares is lawful only where the circumstances would justify a forfeiture.

The Rowland and Marwood's Steamship Company, Limited, was incorporated in May 1890 with a capital of £275,000 divided into 25,000 shares of £11 each. Its objects were to acquire steamships and vessels of every description, and to carry on the business of shipowners. By clause 37 of the articles of association the directors were authorised to accept from any member the surrender of his shares, or any part thereof.

In 1893 the plaintiffs, Bellerby, Moss, and Marwood, were, with William Wright and John Rowland (both since deceased), the directors of the company. Bellerby, Moss and Marwood were at the date of the action still three of the directors. In that year a steamship called the *Golden Cross*, belonging to the company, was, owing to the depressed conditions of the shipping trade, sold at a loss of over £4,000.

The directors agreed to bear that loss between them, and, with the object of relieving the company from the loss, it was arranged that each of the directors should surrender to the company eighty-three of his shares in the company. At this time £10 per share had been paid up, £1 per share remaining uncalled.

By resolutions of the board of 29th and 30th June 1893 the transaction was confirmed, and the certificates for the shares surrendered were cancelled, new certificates being issued to the directors for the balances of their respective holdings. The intention of the directors was that the shares should become vested in the company, and that the directors should not remain liable for the £1 per share at that time unpaid.

Since 1893 the business of the company had become more prosperous, and at general meetings of the shareholders, held on 20th September 1899 and 19th September 1900, the view was expressed that the prosperity of the company warranted the restoration of their shares to the former directors and the representatives of the two who had died. As the result of a further meeting of the shareholders held on 10th October 1900 an action was brought against the company by the three surviving directors and the executors of the two who had died, claiming a declaration that the surrender of the shares and the acceptance thereof by the company was *ultra vires* and inoperative, and that the register of members might be rectified accordingly by inserting the names of the plaintiffs as shareholders in respect of the surrendered shares with the sum of £10 paid up on each share.

The surrendered shares had not been reissued or in any way dealt with by the company.

KEKEWICH J. held that the surrender was illegal and null and void, but he dismissed the action on the ground that it was in substance an application under S.35 of the *Companies Act*, 1862, for the rectification of the company's register (*see now* S.116 *Companies Act, 1948*), and that after the lapse of time the plaintiffs had no equity to justify the interference of the Court.

From this decision the plaintiffs appealed and the case accordingly came before the Court of Appeal.

COLLINS M.R.: . . . Since *Trevor* v. *Whitworth* it is clear law that a limited company incorporated under the *Joint Stock Companies Acts* cannot purchase its own shares, unless it does so by way of reduction of capital with the sanction of the Court. . . . Is then the transaction in this case a purchase by the company of its own shares? It was certainly intended by the parties who carried it out to involve the release by the company to the surrenderors of the right to call up the unpaid balance of £1 on each share, and was, therefore, not a gratuitous surrender. There was an exchange of real consideration of the parties, and, therefore, it ought to be described perhaps more accurately as a sale and purchase than as a surrender. But, assuming that it can be properly described as a surrender, although it involves a consideration given out of the assets of the company to the party surrendering, it remains to consider whether there is any legal ground upon which it can be taken out of the principle of *Trevor* v. *Whitworth*. It seems to me that there is not. . . .

I can see no distinction in principle between returning to a shareholder a part of the paid-up capital in exchange for his shares and wiping out his liability for the uncalled-up sum payable thereon. Both methods involve a reduction of the capital which, as LORD WATSON pointed out in *Trevor* v. *Whitworth*, persons dealing with the company are entitled to rely upon as existing, either as paid up or as still to be called up, and such a reduction, therefore, can only hold good if sanctioned under the conditions prescribed.

. . . I think the reasoning in *Ooregum Gold Mining Company of India* v. *Roper* establishes that to release a shareholder from any part of his obligation to pay the uncalled-up balance on his shares is an *ultra vires* act on the part of the company. . . . The justification of forfeitures rests upon the statute itself, and I think that since *Trevor* v. *Whitworth* no authority can be relied on as justifying a surrender having the effect of reducing capital which cannot be supported as a form of forfeiture. . . . I am of opinion, therefore, that KEKEWICH J. was right in his decision on the principal question in the case.

Upon the second point, however, he has held that, notwithstanding that the surrender of the shares was void as being an act *ultra vires*, still the application to restore the plaintiff to the register must be treated as being made under S.35 of the Act of 1862, and that he was not satisfied of the justice of the case within that section, and he therefore refused to make the order. The learned judge relied on the fact that so much time had elapsed since the surrender, and that it was conceivable that some persons might have altered their position on the footing that the capital of the company had been reduced, and . . . he held that the plaintiffs had shown no equity in their favour to disturb the existing state of things, and he therefore refused to rectify the register at their instance. The application in this case is not in fact made under S.35 (if anything turns upon that), but is an action, asserting the legal right of the plaintiffs to be on the register, on the ground that the act whereby they were removed from it was *ultra vires*, and, therefore, a nullity. . . . Here it seems to me that in point of law the plaintiffs never ceased to be the legal owners of the shares, and therefore they are not obliged to rely upon an equity to have the register rectified. Nor, on the other hand, can the company set up lapse of time or acquiescence as validating that which was in its essence incapable of being made valid, being . . . void and not voidable only. . . . It seems to me, therefore, that the learned judge's decision on this part of the case cannot be supported, and that the appeal must be allowed.

STIRLING L.J.: On the first of the two points decided by KEKEWICH J. I have arrived at the same conclusion as the learned judge, though not without some doubt. . . . I think the weight of authority is in favour of the view that forfeiture, which is specifically mentioned in the Act of 1862, stands on a special footing, and that surrenders can only be supported in circumstances which would justify forfeiture. . . .

On the second point, I think that the decision of KEKEWICH J. cannot be sustained. . . . The surrender is an isolated transaction, and it is neither alleged nor proved that any one has altered his position by reason of it. . . . I think, therefore, that the appeal should be allowed.

COZENS-HARDY L.J.: . . . I assume that the arrangement entered into in 1893 was a highly beneficial arrangement for the company. The question remains, however, whether it was not *ultra vires*. . . .

Two propositions may be asserted without doubt. First, a company may forfeit shares. This is recognised by S.26 of the *Companies Act*, 1862, as well as by Table A. Secondly, it is not competent to a company to purchase its own shares, and any such transaction is *ultra vires*. I think *Trevor* v. *Whitworth* also decides that, under circumstances which would entitle a company to forfeit shares for non-payment of calls, the same result may be attained by means of a voluntary surrender. In the case of forfeiture the statute treats the forfeited shares as being the property of the company, and it may well be that the acquisition of this property by the company is equally lawful, whether it is acquired by hostile proceedings in the nature of forfeiture, or by a voluntary transaction producing the same result. There is no infringement of the statutory provisions in either case. There is merely an unimportant difference in form. When, however, the transaction involves, as in the present case, the release by the company to the shareholders of uncalled capital on their shares, it seems to me that it is, within *Trevor* v. *Whitworth*, a reduction of capital not sanctioned by law.

The decision of the House of Lords in the *Ooregum Case*, that shares in a limited company cannot be issued at a discount, involves the principle, that the company cannot by any device relieve a shareholder from the liability to pay the full amount due on his shares. This would be the result, if the shares had been retained by the plaintiffs, instead of being surrendered to the company. But the fact that in consideration of the release the shares were surrendered seems to me to render the transaction no better. Uncalled capital is part of the assets of the company. It may be mortgaged. . . . And, by clause 107 (8) of the defendant company's articles of association, a mortgage of its uncalled capital is expressly authorised. The company, therefore, parted with £415, a portion of its assets, in consideration of the acquisition of the shares. This was a purchase of the shares, and is directly within the authority of *Trevor* v. *Whitworth*.

[T]he real objection to a surrender of shares does not lie in the fact that money has been paid by the company to acquire the shares. The objection is founded on a larger proposition. A company cannot be a shareholder in itself. Every surrender of shares, whether fully paid up or not, involves a reduction of capital, which is unlawful, except when sanctioned by the Court. . . . Forfeiture is a statutory exception, and is the only exception. For I regard a surrender, under circumstances which would justify a forfeiture, as merely equivalent to a forfeiture.

KEKEWICH J. while holding that the surrender was *ultra vires* and void, yet refused to restore the plaintiffs to the register. In this respect I am unable to follow his view. If the plaintiffs are, as I hold they are, still shareholders, it seems to me that their names ought to be upon the register, so as to give them the full status and advantage of shareholders, unless something has happened to deprive them of that right. . . . If . . . the transaction, though honest, was illegal and void, and if no Statute of Limitations applies, I fail to see what answer can be made to the plaintiffs' claim. If the company were wound up, I think the liquidator might put their names on the register, and hold them liable as contributories for £1 per share. . . . Upon the whole, therefore, I think that the plaintiffs are entitled to the relief sought.

Rowell v. John Rowell and Sons, Limited. [1912] 2 Ch. 609

A surrender of fully paid shares in exchange for other fully paid shares of the same nominal value, though with different dividend rights, is valid since it does not involve any reduction of capital.

The company, John Rowell and Sons, Ltd., was incorporated in 1894 with a memorandum of association which provided that its capital was £75,000 divided into 2,500 preference shares and 5,000 ordinary shares, all of £10 each. The preference shares were entitled to a cumulative preferential dividend of 6 per cent per annum on the amount paid thereon, and with certain preferential rights as regards repayment of capital.

Clause 34 of the articles of association authorised the board of directors, where the law permitted, to accept a surrender of any shares from any holder on such terms as the board might determine, and to extinguish or cancel such shares, or re-issue them.

Of the 2,500 preference shares 1,000 only were issued and in 1896 those were all fully paid. There were also issued 2,000 ordinary shares. In 1896 it was desired to increase the capital by the creation of additional preference shares and also to increase the borrowing powers of the company; and for the purpose of carrying this into effect it was decided to reduce the dividend on the preference shares from 6 per cent to 5 per cent by obtaining a surrender of the existing 1,000 6 per cent preference shares, and issuing in lieu of them to the then holders 1,000 preference shares bearing a 5 per cent dividend, but in all other respects exactly in the same position as the original 1,000 preference shares.

A special resolution was passed by which the capital of the company was increased by the creation of 3,000 shares of £10 each, to be called first preference shares, bearing a cumulative preferential dividend of 5 per cent per annum and to have a first preference in capital as well as in dividend; these shares were to be offered either to the original preference shareholders or to the public, on such terms and at such times as the board of directors might determine and as should be approved in writing by the holders of at least three fourths of the original preference shares. Any original preference shares when surrendered should be subject to reissue by the board.

In pursuance of this resolution, the company accepted the surrender by the existing preference shareholders of the 1,000 6 per cent preference shares, and issued to each holder of those shares a corresponding number amounting altogether to 1,000 5 per cent preference shares. On 27th July 1906 an agreement in writing providing that the shares so to be issued should be taken to be fully paid up was duly filed with the Registrar of Joint Stock Companies pursuant to S.25 of the *Companies Act*, 1867.

Two holders of 5 per cent first preference shares later brought an action against the company on behalf of themselves and all other holders of 5 per cent first preference shares, claiming (1) a declaration that the issued 6 per cent preference shares were validly surrendered in the year 1896, and (2) a declaration that the 5 per cent first preference shares allotted in 1896 in exchange for 6 per cent preference shares were fully paid up and that there was no liability in respect of them.

WARRINGTON J.: . . . The case involves two questions—first, whether a surrender of fully-paid shares in consideration of the issue of shares to precisely the same nominal amount is or is not *ultra vires* the company, and, secondly, whether the shares issued in exchange are properly to be treated as fully paid. . . .

The company is now desirous of taking certain steps with regard to its capital, which require or may require the assent of the preference shareholders, and the question has been raised whether what is required to be done can be done without the assent of the holders of the previously existing first preference shares; in other words, whether there are now any holders of those first preference shares, or whether the holders of preference shares at the present time are the holders only of the 5 per cent. preference shares created in 1896; and a further question has been raised whether the new shares are to be treated as fully paid up.

Now the case with which I have to deal is the surrender of shares fully paid up and therefore not involving the release of the shareholder from any liability. That is an extremely important consideration, and, in fact, it is the determining consideration in the present case, and one which in my opinion distinguishes the present case from *Bellerby* v. *Rowland & Marwood's Steamship Co.*

. . . Now I have carefully looked through the speeches of the learned Lords in *Trevor* v. *Whitworth*. . . . With reference to the surrender of shares each of the learned Lords expressed his opinion that a surrender of shares under the circumstances which would entitle the company to forfeit the shares, and which therefore merely takes the place of a proceeding *in invitum*,—substituting a voluntary proceeding for a proceeding *in invitum*—would be valid; but I cannot find that any one of them expressed any opinion in reference to the validity or invalidity of any other possible surrender of shares. In fact Lord Herschell was very careful to reserve power to deal with

any question of surrender when it might arise. The result is that
I do not think that in *Trevor* v. *Whitworth* the House of Lords
expressed any opinion against the validity of a surrender of
fully-paid shares in exchange for other fully-paid shares. So
matters rested until . . . *Bellerby* v. *Rowland & Marwood's
Steamship Co.* came before the Court of Appeal in 1902. . . .
[T]wo of the judges of the Court of Appeal expressed certain
opinions which were not necessary for the decision of the case,
and both those opinions, if read literally, are certainly against
the validity of such a surrender as that with which I have to
deal in the present case. . . . The generality of the proposition . . . on which COZENS-HARDY L.J. founds his dictum as
to the invalidity of every surrender of shares, except where it
takes the place of a forfeiture, seems to me to be a matter of
some doubt, because he is clearly referring in his judgment to
surrenders which involve reduction, and not to surrenders
which do not involve reduction. . . . I have here . . . a surrender which in my opinion does not involve any reduction
of capital. . . . In my opinion, therefore, I must hold that the
surrender in the present case was a valid surrender.
　. . . The other question is, Are these shares fully paid up?
In my opinion they are. . . . I hold, therefore, that the plaintiffs
are entitled to the two declarations which they claim.

Victor Battery Company, Ltd. *v.* Curry's Ltd. and Others. [1946] Ch. 242

*The word "security" in S.54 Companies Act, 1948 means
"valid security," and a debenture giving a charge on the company's assets in breach of the section is not invalidated by it.*

Mr. Jaina was a director of and principal shareholder in
the British Lion Battery Co. Ltd. and Princely Battery Co.
Ltd. He agreed to buy from certain vendors for £15,000
the issued share capital of Victor Battery Co. Ltd., the
plaintiff company. He could himself pay in cash only
£6,000. Curry's Ltd., the defendant company, was willing
to help him to complete the purchase by lending £6,000
to British Lion Co., £2,000 to Princely Battery Co. and

£2,000 to Victor Battery Co., out of which the balance of the purchase money was to be provided.

The purchase was completed and Victor Battery Co. issued a debenture secured by a charge on its assets for £10,000 to a nominee of Curry's Ltd.

Later, a receiver was appointed by the debenture holder out of court and Victor Battery Co. subsequently brought an action for a declaration that the debenture was void and of no effect, as having been issued in contravention of S.45 *Companies Act*, 1929 (*now S.54*) *Companies Act, 1948*).

ROXBURGH J.: . . . Mr. Slade, for the plaintiff company, contended that the law is that, if the debenture holder knows that the company, by the debenture, is giving even the least financial assistance to any person in connection with the purchase of any of its shares, the debenture will be invalid, even though the amount involved in the purchase of the shares may be £50 or less, and that secured by the debenture £100,000 or more. He contended that applying well-settled principles of law to the interpretation of S.45 [*now S.54*], I am driven to hold that, although in terms it imposes on the actual doer of the prohibited act a maximum penalty of £100, it may impose on a person whose offence is knowledge of what the principal offender is doing what, in effect, is a penalty with no fixed upper limit. If those contentions are correct, the section may, indeed, prove a positive boon to the principal offender. In the present case the plaintiff company would obtain, at the expense of the defendant company and at none to itself, a sum much greater than any fine which could be imposed on it under the section. If that is the law, the defendant company has involuntarily made a present to Mr. Jaina of shares which cost it £9,000 and a present of £1,000 to the plaintiff company.

In my judgment, however, there are two answers to Mr. Slade's contention. The first is in the construction of S.45. S.45—in marked contrast to S.79 [*now S.95 Companies Act, 1948*]—does not indicate an intention to avoid the security to which it refers. . . . The section provides, not that it shall not be lawful for a company to provide a security in order to give financial assistance, but that it shall not be lawful for a company by means of the provision of security to give any financial assistance. In my judgment, "security" prima facie means "valid security," although I do not say that it must mean that. Moreover, the words of the section are not "purport to give financial assistance" but "give financial assistance" and I cannot see how an invalid debenture could give any financial assistance.

. . . The second answer to Mr. Slade's contentions for the plaintiff company is in the passage to which he referred me in Anson on Contracts. . . . For the purposes of that second answer it must be assumed, contrary to my holding above, that the debenture is properly to be described as an illegal contract. The passage in Anson is: "It remains to consider whether a party to an illegal contract can under any circumstances make it a cause of action. The rule is clear that a party to such a contract cannot come into a court of law and ask to have his illegal object carried out; nor can he set up a case in which he must necessarily disclose an illegal transaction as the groundwork of his claim; and this rule holds good although neither party had any intention of breaking the law. The rule is expressed in the maxim, 'in pari delicto potior est conditio defendentis.' But there are exceptional cases in which a man may be relieved of an illegal contract into which he has entered; cases to which the maxim just quoted does not apply. They fall into four classes: (1) the contract may be of a kind made illegal by statute in the interests of a class of persons of whom the plaintiff is one. . . ."

Mr. Slade for the plaintiff company, contends that the plaintiff company is one of that class of persons and therefore comes within that exception. . . . Mr. Slade contended . . . that, notwithstanding that in S.45 the only persons singled out by name for punishment are the company and its officers the primary class of persons for whose protection the illegality of the contract was created—assuming it to be illegal—is companies. . . . I cannot hold that the plaintiff company has been shown to come within the exception. Accordingly, it is put out of court by the application of the general principle—which Mr. Slade did not dispute—and the action is dismissed.

Heald and Another v. O'Connor. [1971] 1 W.L.R. 497

A debenture giving a charge on the company's assets in breach of S.54 Companies Act, 1948 is void. It follows that a guarantee of the moneys due under that debenture is a nullity, since no moneys can be due under a void debenture.

The plaintiffs, Douglas Ernest Heald and Margaret Joyce Heald, by a written agreement dated 1st October 1968 agreed to sell to the defendant, Patrick George O'Connor, all the shares in D. E. Heald (Stoke-on-Trent) Ltd. for the sum of £35,000.

By clause 7 of the agreement the plaintiffs undertook to lend to O'Connor the sum of £25,000, repayable at the rate of £5,000 a year and secured by a floating charge on the assets of the company. By the same clause O'Connor was to give a personal guarantee of repayment of the loan.

On 23rd December 1968 the company issued a debenture to the plaintiffs acknowledging that it was indebted to them in the sum of £25,000. The debenture was duly endorsed by the defendant O'Connor with his personal guarantee to pay the moneys due under the debenture if the company defaulted in payment.

The company defaulted and the plaintiffs claimed from O'Connor under the guarantee the balance of the moneys owing, a sum of £21,700. Judgment for the sum claimed was entered for the plaintiffs by the district registrar at Stoke-on-Trent, whereupon O'Connor appealed, contending that the debenture and the guarantee were void as being in breach of S.54 *Companies Act*, 1948.

FISHER J.: . . . The defendant says that the company gave, by means of the provision of security, financial assistance for the purpose of or in connection with the purchase by the defendant of its shares. The defendant says that this not only rendered the company liable to a fine of £100 but made the debenture illegal and void and that therefore the guarantee also is void and unenforceable. . . .

I proceed to consider the question of law on the assumption that the debenture was given to secure the repayment of the sum of £25,000 lent by the plaintiffs to the defendant in order to enable him to pay for the shares and that without such security the plaintiffs would not have been willing to make the loan. On this assumption I am satisfied that the company did give financial assistance within the words of S.54. Some meaning has to be given to the words in the section "give financial assistance by means of the provision of security" and the meaning must be such as to cover some matter not already covered by the other words "loan" and "guarantee." It seems to me that a usual way, and maybe the only way, in which a company could give financial assistance by means of the provision of a security in circumstances which would not amount to the giving of financial assistance by means of a loan or guarantee would be by entering into a debenture such as the one in the present case.

Is the debenture for this reason illegal and void? In *Victor Battery Co. Ltd.* v. *Curry's Ltd.* ROXBURGH J. held that a debenture given by a company as security for moneys lent to enable a person to purchase shares in the company was not illegal and void. He was impressed by the apparent injustice if the debenture were held to be illegal: the company which had contravened the section would benefit and the lender would suffer a loss which might greatly exceed the maximum penalty of £100. He held that the word "security" in S.54 must mean a "valid security." . . .

The reasoning and conclusion of ROXBURGH J. in that case have been questioned in Palmer's Company Law, 21st ed. (1968), p. 447, and in three Commonwealth decisions, *Dressy Frocks Pty. Ltd.* v. *Bock* (1951) N.S.W.S.R. 390; *Shearer Transport Co. Pty. Ltd.* v. *McGrath* [1956] V.L.R. 316 and *E. H. Dey Pty. Ltd.* v. *Dey* [1966] V.R. 464, and more recently by Ungoed-Thomas J. in *Selangor United Rubber Estates Ltd.* v. *Cradock* (*No. 3*) [1968] 1 W.L.R. 1555, 1656 to 1659. I am impressed by these criticisms and I propose to adopt them and to find in the contrary sense to ROXBURGH J. . . .

In summary, my reasoning is as follows: by the provision of a security in the circumstances in *Victor Battery Co. Ltd.* v. *Curry's Ltd.* and of this case the company undoubtedly gives financial assistance to the purchaser of the shares whether the security is valid or not. All that is necessary to make the financial assistance effective is that the lender should believe the security to be valid and on the strength of it make the loan. The apparent injustice which is the common result of the statutory prohibition of these particular kinds of transaction is not sufficient warranty for declining to apply the well-settled principle of law. The application of this principle in such circumstances as the present is likely to deter potential lenders from lending money on security which might be held to contravene the statute and is likely to be more efficacious in achieving the policy of the sections than the very small maximum penalty on the company. . . .

Is a guarantee void and unenforceable if the agreement imposing liability on the principal debtor is void as being prohibited by statute? . . . [T]he promise made by the guarantor in the present case was . . . to pay the principal moneys which had become due under the debenture if the company did not. If the debenture was void, then no moneys could become due under it. . . .

IX. DIVIDENDS

Verner v. General Commercial Investment Trust. [1894] 2 Ch. 239

The excess of current receipts over current payments may be distributed by way of dividend despite a loss of fixed capital. Circulating capital, however, must be kept up to its original value.

The General and Commercial Investment Trust was registered as a limited company on 26th January 1888. Its objects were to invest its capital in securities of various descriptions. The articles of association provided for the appointment of a body of trustees, who occupied the same position as that usually occupied by directors.

The capital of the company was £1,200,000 divided into 120,000 shares of £10 each, to be converted when fully paid up into equal moieties of preferred stock and deferred stock. Sixty thousand shares in the company were taken and fully paid up, and each share was converted, as to one-half into preference stock, and as to the other half into deferred stock.

The company issued £300,000 debenture stock, bearing interest at 4 per cent per annum; and the £300,000 received for it as well as the £600,000 paid on the shares was invested in securities authorised by the memorandum.

On 28th February 1894 on which day the financial year of the company ended, the state of the company's affairs was as follows: the income received during that year from the company's investments, after payment of the interest on the debenture stocks and of all expenses, left a balance of upwards of £23,000. On the other hand, some of the investments had turned out utterly worthless and the market price of most of the others had declined; so that the value of the investments had decreased by at least £250,000.

An action was brought by one of the trustees of the company, on behalf of himself and the stockholders except the defendants, against the company and the other trustees, to have it decided whether under the above circumstances a dividend could lawfully be declared. The plaintiff moved for an injunction to restrain the defendants from declaring and paying any dividend in respect of the year ending 28th February 1894.

STIRLING J. held that a dividend could lawfully be declared, and from his decision the plaintiff appealed. The case accordingly came before the Court of Appeal.

LINDLEY L.J.: The judgment I am about to deliver is the joint judgment of the LORD JUSTICE A. L. SMITH and myself.

The broad question raised by this appeal is, whether a limited company which has lost part of its capital can lawfully declare or pay a dividend without first making good the capital which has been lost. I have no doubt it can—that is to say, there is no law which prevents it in all cases and under all circumstances. Such a proceeding may sometimes be very imprudent; but a proceeding may be perfectly legal and may yet be opposed to sound commercial principles. We, however, have only to consider the legality or illegality of what is complained of.

As was pointed out in *Lee* v. *Neuchatel Asphalte Company*, there are certain provisions in the *Companies Acts* relating to the capital of limited companies; but no provisions whatever as to the payment of dividends or the division of profits. Each company is left to make its own regulations as to such payment or division. The statutes do not even expressly and in plain language prohibit a payment of dividend out of capital. But the provisions as to capital, when carefully studied, are wholly inconsistent with the return of capital to the shareholders, whether in the shape of dividends or otherwise, except, of course, on a winding-up, and there can, in my opinion, be no doubt that even if a memorandum of association contained a provision for paying dividends out of capital such provision would be invalid. The fact is that the main condition of limited liability is that the capital of a limited company shall be applied for the purposes for which the company is formed, and that to return the capital to the shareholders either in the shape of dividend or otherwise is not such a purpose as the Legislature contemplated.

But there is a vast difference between paying dividends out of capital and paying dividends out of other money belonging to the company, and which is not part of the capital mentioned in the company's memorandum of association. The capital of a company is intended for use in some trade or business, and is necessarily exposed to risk of loss. As explained in *Lee* v. *Neuchatel Asphalte Company*, the capital even of a limited company is not a debt owing by it to its shareholders, and if the capital is lost, the company is under no legal obligation either to make it good, or, on that ground only, to wind up its affairs. If, therefore, the company has any assets which are not its capital within the meaning of the *Companies Acts*, there is no law which prohibits the division of such assets amongst the shareholders. Further, it was decided in that case, and, in my opinion, rightly decided, that a limited company formed to purchase and work a wasting property, such as a leasehold quarry, might lawfully declare and pay dividends out of the money produced by working such wasting property, without setting aside part of that money to keep the capital up to its original amount.

There is no law which prevents a company from sinking its capital in the purchase or production of a money-making property or undertaking, and in dividing the money annually yielded by it, without preserving the capital sunk so as to be able to reproduce it intact either before or after the winding-up of the company.

A company may be formed upon the principle that no dividends shall be declared unless the capital is kept undiminished, or a company may contract with its creditors to keep its capital or assets up to a given value. But in the absence of some special article or contract, there is no law to this effect; and, in my opinion, for very good reasons. It would, in my judgment, be most inexpedient to lay down a hard and fast rule which would prevent a flourishing company, either not in debt or well able to pay its debts, from paying dividends so long as its capital sunk in creating the business was not represented by assets which would, if sold, reproduce in money the capital sunk. Even a sinking fund to replace lost capital by degrees is not required by law.

It is obvious that dividends cannot be paid out of capital which is lost; they can only be paid out of money which exists and can be divided. Moreover, when it is said, and said truly, that dividends are not to be paid out of capital, the word "capital" means the money subscribed pursuant to the memorandum of association, or what is represented by that money. Accretions to that capital may be realised and turned into money, which may be divided amongst the shareholders, as was decided in *Lubbock* v. *British Bank of South America.*

But, although there is nothing in the statutes requiring even a limited company to keep up its capital, and there is no prohibition against payment of dividends out of any other of the company's assets, it does not follow that dividends may be lawfully paid out of other assets regardless of the debts and liabilities of the company. A dividend presupposes a profit in some shape, and to divide as dividend the receipts, say, for a year, without deducting the expenses incurred in that year in producing the receipts, would be as unjustifiable in point of law as it would be reckless and blameworthy in the eyes of business men. The same observation applies to payment of dividends out of borrowed money. Further, if the income of any year arises from a consumption in that year of what may be called circulating capital, the division of such income as dividend without replacing the capital consumed in producing it will be a payment of a dividend out of capital within the meaning of the prohibition which I have endeavoured to explain.

It has been already said that dividends presuppose profits of some sort, and this is unquestionably true. But the word "profits" is by no means free from ambiguity. The law is much more accurately expressed by saying that dividends cannot be paid out of capital, than by saying that they can only be paid out of profits. The last expression leads to the inference that the capital must always be kept up and be represented by assets which, if sold, would produce it; and this is more than is required by law. Perhaps the shortest way of expressing the distinction which I am endeavouring to explain is to say that fixed capital may be sunk and lost, and yet that the excess of current receipts over current payments may be divided, but that floating or circulating capital must be kept up, as otherwise it will enter into and form part of such excess, in which case to divide such excess without deducting the capital which forms part of it will be contrary to law. . . .

It follows from what has been said above that the proposed payment of dividend in this particular case cannot be restrained . . . .There is no suggestion of any improper juggling with the accounts, and there is no payment of dividend out of capital. There is no insolvency, and we have not to deal with a petition to wind up. Some capital is lost, but that is all that can be truly said, and that is not enough to justify such an injunction as is sought. The appeal must be dismissed. . . .

KAY L.J. was of the same opinion.

Foster *v*. New Trinidad Lake Asphalt Company, Limited. [1901] 1 Ch. 208

Although an appreciation in total value of capital assets may in a proper case be distributed by way of dividend, a realised accretion to the estimated value of one item of the capital assets cannot be regarded as distributable profit without reference to the result of the whole accounts fairly taken.

In 1894 an American company, the Trinidad Lake Asphalt Company, Limited, acquired the stock and bonds of the New York and Bermudez Company, and also a debt of $100,000 due from the latter company to the former company and secured by promissory notes.

In 1897 the defendant company, an English company, purchased the property and assets of the old Trinidad Company including the debt.

On 31st December 1899 the New York and Bermudez Company gave to the defendant company new promissory notes for $127,355, being the amount of the said debt of $100,000 with accrued interest thereon. The notes for this sum were then paid off, and the defendant company, through their directors, proposed, without reference to their other business or assets, to treat the whole sum, amounting to £26,258 16s. in English currency, as assets available for dividends, and to distribute it accordingly.

The debenture-holders and a shareholder in the New Trinidad Lake Asphalt Company, Limited, applied for an injunction to restrain the company and its directors from treating this sum of money in the proposed manner.

BYRNE J.: . . . No question is raised as to so much of the sum as represents interest, the point at issue being as to the amount representing principal of the debt. There is no doubt that the debt formed part of the assets originally purchased by the defendant company, and as such, part of its original capital assets, but it is argued that as the debt was not regarded or treated as an asset of any value upon the purchase, and as it has not appeared in the former balance-sheet as part of the assets of the company, and as the only entry in relation to it in the books of the company is a journal entry carrying the notes to a profit-and-loss account, it ought to be regarded as a windfall in the nature of an unexpected profit, and as divisible accordingly amongst the shareholders. I cannot accept this view . . . [T]he amount of this debt is a distinct item of the property purchased which has since been realised by payment. It appears to me that the amount in question is prima facie capital, and that I have no evidence which would justify me in saying that it has changed its character because it has turned out to be of greater value than had been expected. . . . I think that I ought to grant an injunction to restrain the defendants from distributing the $100,000 as dividend without reference to the other business or assets of the defendant company. I must not, however, be understood as determining that this sum or a portion of it may not properly be brought into profit-and-loss account or be taken into account in ascertaining the amount available for dividend. That appears to me to depend upon the result of the whole accounts for the year. It is clear, I think, that an appreciation in total value of capital assets, if duly realised by sale or getting in of some portion of such assets, may in a proper case be treated as available for purposes of dividend. . . . If I rightly appreciate the true effect of the decisions, the question of what is profit available for dividend depends upon the result of the whole accounts fairly taken for the year, capital, as well as profit and loss, and although dividends may be paid out of earned profits in proper cases, although there has been a depreciation of capital, I do not think that a realised accretion to the estimated value of one item of the capital assets can be deemed to be profit divisible amongst the shareholders without reference to the result of the whole accounts fairly taken.

Dimbula Valley (Ceylon) Tea Company Ltd. *v.* Laurie and Another. [1961] Ch. 353

Where a company has fluid assets available for payment of a dividend, those assets may be used for that purpose, and as a matter of account the dividend may be treated as paid out of a capital surplus resulting from an appreciation in value of unrealised fixed assets. Since such a capital surplus is distributable, it follows that it can be capitalised.

The plaintiff, the Dimbula Valley (Ceylon) Tea Company Ltd., was incorporated in 1896 with an original authorised capital of £200,000, divided into 10,000 preference shares, 20,000 ordinary shares and 10,000 unclassified shares which might be issued as ordinary, preference or deferred shares as required, all of £5 each.

The original articles of association contained no capitalisation clause, but in 1920 the company by special resolution adopted a new article authorising capitalisation of undivided profits. On 14th April of that year the company increased its share capital to £250,000 by the creation of 50,000 ordinary shares of £1 each. On the same day it capitalised a sum of £42,044 in the form of ordinary shares distributed amongst the ordinary shareholders credited as fully paid. The amount so capitalised then stood to the credit of the general reserve of the company and represented accumulated revenue.

In 1946 the company adopted a new set of articles including a capitalisation article 140 which read:

"The company in general meeting may at any time pass a resolution that any sum not required for the payment of any fixed preferential dividend and (A) standing to the credit of any reserve fund or reserve account of the company, including premiums received on the issue of any shares or debentures, or any sum arising from any operation creating an excess of assets on capital account, or (B) being undivided net profits, be capitalised, and that such sum be appropriated as capital amongst the shareholders who would have been entitled thereto if the same had been distributed by way of dividend in the shares and proportions in which they would have been so entitled."

Later the company took out a summons for the determination, *inter alia*, of the question whether it had power to allot to the ordinary shareholders credited as fully paid up shares by way of capitalisation of (*i*) credit balance on profit and loss account and other revenue reserves, (*ii*) reserves resulting from the realisation of capital profits, (*iii*) reserves resulting from the revaluation of capital assets, or (*iv*) share premium account.

The first defendant was a representative preference shareholder, and the second defendant a representative ordinary shareholder. It was conceded that the company had power to capitalise credit balance on profit and loss account and other revenue reserves, reserves resulting from the realisation of capital profits, and share premium account.

BUCKLEY J.: . . . I come now to the question of the effect of the capitalisation article, article 140 in the company's new articles of association. . . . The question raised by the originating summons in respect of article 140 involves first the consideration of whether under the terms of that article amounts standing to the credit of all, or some, and if so which, of the accounts referred to . . . can be capitalised, and secondly the consideration of whether the power to capitalise so construed conflicts with any right of the preference shareholders. . . . As a general rule only that which could be distributed in dividends can be capitalised. . . . The exception to this general rule is that a sum standing to the credit of a share premium account or of a capital redemption reserve fund may not be distributed, except as provided by S.56 (1) or S.58 (1) of the *Companies Act*, 1948, but may be capitalised under S.56 (2) or S.58 (5). The Court of Appeal has held that, if a share premium account is distributed with the sanction of the court, the distribution must be treated as though it were not a distribution of profit but a repayment of paid-up capital: *In re Duff's Settlements*. A share premium account and a capital redemption reserve fund are, however, statutory creatures and these statutory provisions governing their distribution are of a special and artificial character. This exception to the general rule which I have formulated accordingly does not, in my judgment, in any way discredit the rule.

. . . It has, I think, long been the generally accepted view of the law in this country (though not established by judicial authority) that, if the surplus on capital account results from a valuation made in good faith by competent valuers, and is not likely to be liable to short-term fluctuations, it may properly be capitalised . . . For myself, I can see no reason why, if the valuation is not open to criticism, this should not be so, or even why, in any case in which the regulations of the company permit the distribution by way of dividend of profit on capital account, a surplus so ascertained should not be distributed in that manner. After all, every profit and loss account of a trading concern which opens and closes with a stock figure necessarily embodies an element of estimate. The difference between ascertaining trading profits by, amongst other things, estimating the value of the stock in hand at the beginning and end of the accounting period, and ascertaining capital profits by comparing an estimated value of the assets with their book value, appears to me to be a difference of degree but not of principle. Moreover, if a company has fluid assets available for payment of a dividend, I can see nothing wrong in its using those assets for payment of a dividend, and at the same time, as a matter of account, treating that dividend as paid out of a capital surplus resulting from an appreciation in value of unrealised fixed assets. The proper balance of the company's balance-sheet would not be disturbed by such a course of action. The company would be left with assets of sufficient value to meet the commitments shown on the liabilities side of its balance-sheet, including paid-up share capital. A company is not required by law to keep any part of its assets in any particular form. I do not say that in many cases such a course of action would be a wise commercial practice, but for myself I see no ground for saying that it is illegal. . . .

For these reasons I reach the conclusion that, unless it conflicts with the rights of the preference shareholders, article 140 authorises capitalisation of a reserve resulting from the revaluation of capital assets.

As, for the same reasons, I have also reached the conclusion that the company could legitimately distribute a capital surplus of this nature by way of dividend, that is to say, exclusively amongst the ordinary shareholders at any time when the preference dividend has been paid in full, a capitalisation exclusively for the benefit of the ordinary shares in similar circumstances could not, in my opinion, encroach upon the rights of the preference shareholders.

Accordingly, I declare that the company has power pursuant to article 140 of its present articles of association to capitalise under all the heads set out in . . . the originating summons.

[In this case a further question came before the court for determination, namely, the construction of the article setting out the rights of the preference shareholders to participation in surplus assets in a winding up.

Since this is a matter of particular rather than general interest, it has not been included here, but a considerable portion of the judgment of BUCKLEY J. was concerned with it.]

X. THE AUDITORS OF A COMPANY

Re Kingston Cotton Mill Company (No. 2). [1896] 2 Ch. 279

It is the duty of an auditor to show reasonable skill, care and caution, but what is reasonable skill, care and caution depends on the circumstances of each case. He is not bound to be suspicious as distinguished from reasonably careful, nor is he liable for not tracking out ingenious and carefully laid schemes of fraud when there is nothing to arouse his suspicion.

For some years before the company was ordered to be wound up the directors published to the shareholders balance-sheets signed by the auditors, Messrs. Pickering and Peasegood, in which to an increasing extent in each year the value of the stock-in-trade at the end of the year was grossly overstated.

Dividends were declared and paid for several years on the footing that these balance-sheets were correct, whereas if the true values of the stock-in-trade had been given it would have appeared that there were no profits.

The auditors relied on the certificates of the manager, Mr. Jackson, who was also a director, as to the value of the stock-in-trade and in each case the amount was entered in the balance-sheet "as per manager's certificate."

If the auditors had added to the alleged value of the stock-in-trade at the beginning of any of these years the amount spent in purchasing raw materials during the year, and had deducted the amount of the year's sales, it would have been seen that the statement of the value of the stock-in-trade at the end of the year required explanation; but they did not enter into any such inquiry. The manager was a man of great business ability and of high repute, and up to the stoppage of the company was trusted by every one; but he had designedly exaggerated the value of the stock-in-trade in order to make the company appear prosperous.

VAUGHAN WILLIAMS J. held that it was the duty of the

auditors to test the accuracy of the manager's certificate by a comparison of the figures in the books, and that they were liable to the liquidator for the dividends which had been paid in consequence of the erroneous balance-sheets.

The auditors appealed from this decision, and the case accordingly came before the Court of Appeal.

LINDLEY L.J.: . . . I come now to the real question in this controversy, and that is, whether the appellants have been guilty of any breach of duty to the company. To decide this question it is necessary to consider (1) what their duty was; (2) how they performed it, and in what respects (if any) they failed to perform it. The duty of an auditor generally was very carefully considered by this Court in *In re London and General Bank*, and I cannot usefully add anything to what will be found there. It was there pointed out that an auditor's duty is to examine the books, ascertain that they are right, and to prepare a balance-sheet showing the true financial position of the company at the time to which the balance-sheet refers. But it was also pointed out that an auditor is not an insurer, and that in the discharge of his duty he is only bound to exercise a reasonable amount of care and skill. It was further pointed out that what in any particular case is a reasonable amount of care and skill depends on the circumstances of that case; that if there is nothing which ought to excite suspicion, less care may properly be considered reasonable than could be so considered if suspicion was or ought to have been aroused. These are the general principles which have to be applied to cases of this description. I protest, however, against the notion that an auditor is bound to be suspicious as distinguished from reasonably careful. To substitute the one expression for the other may easily lead to serious error.

. . . Auditors are, however, in my opinion bound to see what exceptional duties, if any, are cast upon them by the articles of the company whose accounts they are called upon to audit. Ignorance of the articles and of exceptional duties imposed by them would not afford any legal justification for not observing them. . . .

I pass now to consider the complaint made against the auditors in this particular case. The complaint is that they failed to detect certain frauds. There is no charge of dishonesty on the part of the auditors. They did not certify or pass anything which they did not honestly believe to be true. It is said, however, that they were culpably careless. . . . I confess I cannot see that their omission to check [the manager's] returns was a breach of their duty to the company. It is no part of an auditor's duty to take stock. No one contends that it is. He must rely on other people for details of the stock-in-trade on hand. In the case of a cotton mill he must rely on some skilled person for the materials necessary to enable him to enter the stock-in-trade at its proper value in the balance-sheet. In this case the auditors relied on the manager. He was a man of high character and of unquestioned competence. He was trusted by every one who knew him. The learned judge has held that the directors are not to be blamed for trusting him. The auditors had no suspicion that he was not to be trusted to give accurate information as to the stock-in-trade in hand, and they trusted him accordingly in that matter. But it is said they ought not to have done so, and for this reason. The stock journal showed the quantities —that is, the weight in pounds—of the cotton and yarn at the end of each year. Other books showed the quantities of cotton bought during the year and the quantities of yarn sold during the year. If these books had been compared by the auditors they would have found that the quantity of cotton and yarn in hand at the end of the year ought to be much less than the quantity shown in the stock journal, and so much less that the value of the cotton and yarn entered in the stock journal could not be right, or at all events was so abnormally large as to excite suspicion and demand further inquiry. This is the view taken by the learned judge. But, although it is no doubt true that such a process might have been gone through, and that, if gone through, the fraud would have been discovered, can it be truly said that the auditors were wanting in reasonable care in not thinking it necessary to test the managing director's return? I cannot bring myself to think they were, nor do I think that any jury of business men would take a different view. It is not sufficient to say that the frauds must have been detected if the entries in the books had been put together in a way which never occurred to any one before suspicion was aroused. The question is whether, no suspicion of anything wrong being entertained, there was a want of reasonable care on the part of the auditors in relying on the returns made by a competent and trusted expert relating to matters on which information from such a person was essential. I cannot think there was. The manager had no apparent conflict between his interest and his duty. His position was not similar to a cashier who has to account for the cash which he receives, and whose own account of his receipts and payments could not reasonably be taken by an auditor without further inquiry. The auditor's duty is not so onerous as the learned judge has held it to be. The order appealed from must be discharged. . . .

LOPES L.J.: . . . [I]n determining whether any misfeasance or breach of duty has been committed, it is essential to consider what the duties of an auditor are. . . . Shortly they may be stated thus: It is the duty of an auditor to bring to bear on the work he has to perform that skill, care, and caution which a reasonably competent, careful, and cautious auditor would use. What is reasonable skill, care, and caution must depend on the particular circumstances of each case. An auditor is not bound to be a detective, or, as was said, to approach his work with suspicion or with a foregone conclusion that there is something wrong. He is a watch-dog, but not a bloodhound. He is justified in believing tried servants of the company in whom confidence is placed by the company. He is entitled to assume that they are honest, and to rely upon their representations, provided he takes reasonable care. If there is anything calculated to excite suspicion he should probe it to the bottom; but in the absence of anything of that kind he is only bound to be reasonably cautious and careful. . . .

It is not the duty of an auditor to take stock; he is not a stock expert; there are many matters in respect of which he must rely on the honesty and accuracy of others. He does not guarantee the discovery of all fraud. I think the auditors were justified in this case in relying on the honesty and accuracy of Jackson, and were not called upon to make further investigation. . . .

The duties of auditors must not be rendered too onerous. Their work is responsible and laborious, and the remuneration moderate. I should be sorry to see the liability of auditors extended any further than in *In re London and General Bank*. . . . Auditors must not be made liable for not tracking out ingenious and carefully laid schemes of fraud when there is nothing to arouse their suspicion, and when those frauds are perpetrated by tried servants of the company and are undetected for years by the directors. So to hold would make the position of an auditor intolerable. The appeal will be allowed.

KAY L.J.: . . . It is of the highest importance that auditors, particularly, perhaps, in the case of joint stock companies, whose shareholders are dependent chiefly on their intelligence and vigilance, should perform their duty with scrupulous care. But if they have conducted their work with that amount of skill and care which can reasonably be expected from men of business in their position, is there any rule of law by which they can be made liable?

If it was the duty of the auditors to test the statements of the manager in the manner suggested, or, indeed, in any manner, they were certainly guilty of negligence, for they made no attempt whatever to test them. The question is, was it their duty?

Upon the best consideration I can give to the case, I come to the conclusion that this was not their duty; and I therefore think that the decision of the learned judge should be reversed.

Dean *v.* Prince and Others. [1954] Ch. 409

Where an auditor is required by the articles of a company to value its shares, he need give no reasons for his valuation. If, however, he gives his reasons, then the court may consider them.

The paid-up capital of the company consisted of 200 shares of £1 each, of which 140 were held by the late Mr. Dean and thirty each by the two defendants, Prince and Cowen. All three of these men were working directors.

Article 9 (*g*) of the company's articles of association provided: "In the event of the death of any member his shares shall be purchased and taken by the directors at such price as is certified in writing by the auditor to be in his opinion the fair value thereof at the date of death. . . . Unless otherwise agreed the directors shall take such shares equally between them."

On the death of Mr. Dean, the auditor Mr. Jenkinson who was a member of a firm of chartered accountants, made the valuation and subsequently stated the basis on which he had arrived at it. Mrs. Dean, as her late husband's personal representative, sought to have the valuation reopened, whereupon the defendants contended that the auditor's certificate was conclusive and binding on her, and that as it was not wrong on the face of it the court was not entitled to go behind it and look at the reasons subsequently offered.

HARMAN J.: . . . [Article 9 (*g*)] is a very unusual type of article, because, instead of entitling the directors to take shares it is mandatory upon them to do so. Whether that is a right which the personal representative of the deceased member could enforce against the directors seems to me a matter of great doubt, but it is one which does not fall to me at this stage to determine. I see great difficulty in any such action, but it was assumed that the directors here . . . would take these shares, and steps were immediately taken to that end. The auditors assumed the burden of certifying in writing their opinion as to their fair value.

The plaintiff was extremely dissatisfied with that valuation. She would, in my judgment, nevertheless have been powerless in the matter if the auditors had declined to expand their views. They should have remembered that silence is golden in a matter of this kind and that, short of fraud or dishonesty, which no one attributed to the auditors in this case, there was no way of questioning that certificate if the auditors declined to give reasons for the result at which they had arrived. It was their opinion. Opinions may differ, but the members of this company had committed themselves, maybe unwisely, to be bound by the opinion of the auditors; and, if those auditors gave an

234 CASES IN COMPANY LAW

opinion which the members disliked or distrusted, so much the
worse for them; they had made their bed and must lie on it.
But, unfortunately for the defendants, the auditors did not
keep quiet. . . .

By way of preliminary point in this case, I was asked to hold
that the court could not look at those points but was bound by
the certificate . . . and that, therefore, there was no cause of
action. I held that that was not so, the case being analogous to
the well-known cases where directors refuse to accept transfers
when, as everyone knows, if they maintain silence no one can
question their refusal if it is honest, but directly they give
reasons, those reasons can be impeached. So here the court is
entitled to look at, and the plaintiff is entitled to bring to the
court's notice, the reasons which have been given and to
criticise them as being bad. . . .

> No appeal on this point was brought, but HARMAN J.
> then proceeded to discuss the auditor's valuation which he
> declared had been made on a wrong basis and therefore
> was not binding on the plaintiff.
>   The defendants appealed on the question of the valua-
> tion alone, and the Court of Appeal reversed the decision
> of HARMAN J. on that point and declared the auditor's
> valuation to be correct.

XI. SHARES

The Bradford Banking Company, Limited *v*. Henry Briggs, Son & Co., Limited. (1885) 29 Ch.D 149 (1886) 12 A.C. 29

Where a company acquires an equitable interest in the shares of a member under its lien, that interest will rank after any prior equitable interest in those shares of which the company has notice. "Notice" here is not used in the sense of notice of a trust, which under S.117 is not permitted, but in the sense of knowledge in their capacity of traders.

The articles of association of Henry Briggs, Son & Co., Ltd., a company registered under the *Companies Act*, 1862, provided that the company should have "a first and permanent lien and charge, available at law and in equity, upon every share for all debts due from the holder thereof."

On 6th November 1879 Mr. John Faint Easby, a shareholder, deposited his share certificates with the Bradford Banking Co., Ltd. as security for the balance due and to become due on his current account, and on 13th November 1879 the bank gave the company notice of the deposit. The certificates stated that the shares were held subject to the articles of association, and at this time Easby owed the company £206 4*s*. 2*d*.

In June 1881 Easby deposited with the bank the certificates of some more shares in the company as security for the balance of his current account, and again on 20th June 1881 the bank gave the company notice of the deposit.

On 22nd June 1881 the company acknowledged receipt of the notice in a letter informing the bank at the same time that Easby was indebted to the company, and that under the articles the company had a first and permanent lien upon all his shares.

In September 1881 Easby repaid what he owed the company. On 31st December 1883 he filed a liquidation petition. At that time he again owed the company money —the sum of £1,593 5*s*. 3*d*. After 22nd June 1881 he received no further advances from the bank but at that time owed them a large sum.

The bank brought an action for an account of what was due to them and to have their securities realised by foreclosure or sale, claiming that their securities as equitable mortgagees by deposit had priority over the company's lien.

FIELD J.: I have come to the conclusion that the plaintiffs are right in their contention, and that they are entitled to priority over any debts which became due from the shareholders to Briggs & Co. subsequently to the receipt by them of notice of the plaintiffs' advance. . . . When a charge is created by equitable deposit, the substantial owner of the property is the mortgagee, though the actual owner is the mortgagor. If the property is worth considerably more than the charge, the mortgagor is the substantial owner, and it is exceedingly important that, if a man has a valuable property, he should be able to take it into the market and convert it into money by means of obtaining advances upon it. We know that at the present day enormous sums of money are constantly advanced on deposit of deeds and share certificates and things of that kind, and this is a very healthy operation of commerce. . . . A mortgagee who is not bound to make further advances may never advance another penny, he may always refuse to do so, and, if another person lending money to the mortgagor could not obtain priority over further advances made by the first mortgagee, the mortgagor would practically never be able to borrow any money at all. That is precisely the state of things here. For what purpose does the shareholder have the certificates of his shares in his possession? Is it to be imagined for a moment that he will keep them locked up in a box? He may be a trader whose life consists in his being able to get money for the purpose of his business. Is he to have no power of obtaining any advance at all on his shares, because he may hereafter become indebted to the company? It would be very unreasonable so to hold. . . . I remain unconvinced that it was the intention of the parties to this contract that the company's lien should be a lien not only for the debts which should be due to them from the shareholder at any particular time, but also for any debts which should thereafter become due, although the company might have had notice of an advance by another person. I do not think that the words "first and permanent" can be enlarged by any fair construction into that meaning.

The company had a first charge upon the shares for any debts which should become due to them by the shareholder, but, after that charge had been created, and before any of the debts now sought to be recovered by the company were incurred, the shareholder exercised his right of borrowing money upon the shares by means of an absolute charge on them to the bank. The company had notice of that charge, and I think that from that time they had no power to make advances to the shareholders so as to rank in priority to the debts due to the bank.

The decision of FIELD J. was reversed by the Court of Appeal. The Bradford Banking Co., Ltd. then appealed to the House of Lords, who reversed the decision of the Court of Appeal and restored the judgment of FIELD J.

In the House of Lords the effect of S.30, *Companies Act, 1862* [*now S.117 Companies Act, 1948*] was discussed. Of this section LORD BLACKBURN there said:

I do not think that the appellants in this case seek to affect the respondents with a trust; they seek no more than to affect them, in their capacity of traders, with knowledge of their [the appellants'] interest.

Simpson v. Molsons' Bank. [1895] A.C. 270

The effect of a provision comparable with S.117 Companies Act, 1948, is that in the absence of actual knowledge of a breach of trust, a company is not concerned with the execution of a trust and has no duty to inquire into it.

This was an appeal to the Judicial Committee of the Privy Council from a decree of the Court of Queen's Bench, Lower Canada.

The facts sufficiently appear from the judgment, which was delivered by LORD SHAND.

LORD SHAND: The Honourable John Molson died on the 12th of July, 1860, leaving a will dated the 20th of April of that year, and this appeal from a judgment of the Court of Queen's Bench for Lower Canada relates to 640 shares in the Molsons' Bank, Canada, which formed part of the residue of his estate. The complaint of the appellants is that the bank, the respondents, wrongfully registered in the books of the bank a transfer of these shares granted by William Molson and Alexander Molson, executors under the will, in favour of Alexander Molson, the testator's son, to the loss and injury of the appellants, as having right to have the shares secured to them under a substitution in favour of Alexander Molson's children contained in the will of their grandfather John Molson. Their claim of damages has arisen in consequence of the insolvency of Alexander Molson who transferred the shares in question to third parties who cannot be affected by the substitution founded on. . . .

The argument of the appellants involves the consideration of two questions; first, whether the bank had any notice, and if so what notice, of the trust created by the testator's will; . . . and, secondly, whether if the bank had notice it was such as to make it the duty of the bank to refuse to register the transfer in question. . . .

The statute incorporating the Molsons' Bank (18 Vict. c. 202) contains this provision in S.36, *viz.*, "The bank shall not be bound to see to the execution of any trust whether express, implied or constructive to which any of the shares of the bank may be subject." [*cf. S.117, Companies Act, 1948*]. This language is general and comprehensive. It cannot be construed as referring to trusts of which the bank had not notice, for it would require no legislative provision to save the bank from responsibility for not seeing to the execution of a trust, the existence of which had not in some way been brought to their knowledge. The provision seems to be directly applicable to trusts of which the bank had knowledge or notice; and in regard to these the bank, it is declared, are not to be bound to see to their execution.

Apart from the provision of the statute, it may be that notice to the bank of the existence of a trust affecting the shares would have cast upon them the duty of ascertaining what were the terms of the trust; and that in any question with the beneficiaries, whose rights had been defeated by the absolute transfer in favour of Alexander Molson, the bank, whether they had inquired or not, might have been held to have constructive knowledge of all the trust provisions. Assuming this point in favour of the appellants, their Lordships, however, see no reason to doubt that by the clause in question the bank are relieved of the duty of making inquiry, and that they cannot be held responsible for registering the transfer, unless it were shown that they were at the time possessed of actual knowledge which made it improper for them to do so until at least they had taken care to give the beneficiaries an opportunity of protecting their rights. In the present case their Lordships are satisfied that at the date of the transfer the bank had not any notice which could warrant the inference that they were aware that a breach of trust was intended or was being committed. What amount of knowledge would be sufficient to imply that the bank must know that a transfer is in breach of trust is a question which must depend on the circumstances of each case. In the present case, their Lordships do not find it necessary to consider what might be the legal effect of their having such knowledge, because they are satisfied that at the date of the transfer in favour of Alexander Molson the bank had not any notice which was sufficient to bring to their knowledge, or to lead them to believe, that any breach of trust was being committed or intended by the trustees or executors under the will.

The bank had notice that the shares in question were acquired and held by William Molson and Alexander Molson in the character of trustees and executors for the execution of trust purposes. The entry of the transfer of the shares by transmission was made in their names as executors in the bank's books, and the will of the testator, in virtue of which the transfer entry was made, directly gave, devised, and bequeathed the shares to them as trustees and executors for the execution of trust purposes. But it was maintained by the appellants that the bank had further notice, not only of the general trust created by the will, but of the terms of the particular trust in favour of Alexander Molson's children directed by the testator to be provided for by the trustees by way of substitution of them to their father, Alexander Molson.

Their Lordships are, however, of opinion that it has not been proved that the bank had any notice of this particular trust purpose, or at least any notice which could affect them with knowledge of the way in which it ought to have been executed by the trustees. The facts alleged and relied on by the appellants as proof of such notice were (1) that a copy of [the] will was in the possession of the bank; (2) that in the case of the families of three of the testator's children notice of the substitution of grandchildren was contained in the transfers by the executors registered in the bank's books in April, 1871; and (3) that William Molson, the testator's brother and one of the executors, was president of the bank, while Mr. Abbott, the law agent of the executors, was also the bank's law agent, and as both of these gentlemen must be taken to have been fully aware of the detailed provisions of the testator's will, the bank through them, as its officers, had full knowledge of the trust. It is clear, however, that these facts are quite insufficient to prove the alleged notice.

The evidence does not clearly show how the bank came into possession of the copy of the testator's will. . . . It may have been left with the bank, as evidence of the title of the executors to receive the dividends on the shares which were paid to them from the first after the testator's death, or it may have been given to the bank six years afterwards when the executors desired to have their title as owners by transmission registered in the bank's books. . . . The production of the will or probate at that time would be in accordance with the usual practice, which entitles the bank to require evidence by production of the title in virtue of which the entry of any transfer of shares in the bank's books is asked. But the only question with which the bank were concerned was that of the legal title. They had to satisfy themselves only that the will gave a right to the shares which entitled the executors to be registered as owners. They were not called upon, on an application to enter a transfer by

transmission of the bank's shares, to examine the will with
reference to an entirely different matter which did not concern
them, namely, the testator's directions as to the ultimate
destination and disposal of his estate; and there is no reason
to suppose that anything more was done on this occasion than
is usual in such cases. Again, the entries of transfers in favour
of other members of the testator's family, in terms differing
from that in favour of Alexander Molson, was not a circumstance calling in any way for the notice or attention of the bank,
and even if observed these gave no notice to the bank that the
shares transferred to Alexander Molson and to his brother
John were held under similar trusts, to which effect should be
given. It might well be that in the allocation and distribution
of the residue entirely different arrangements would be in
compliance with the testator's directions. Nor can the knowledge of Mr. William Molson as a trustee and executor, and of
Mr. Abbott as law agent in the execution of the testamentary
directions of the deceased, and the execution of the transfer in
question, be imputed to the bank so as to affect them with
liability. It is not proved that these gentlemen or either of them
intervened in any way in reference to the registration of the
transfer in favour of Alexander Molson. But, apart from this,
their knowledge was not that of the directors or manager of
the bank. They were clearly not agents of the bank, so that
notice to them could be regarded as notice to the bank.

Their Lordships will on these grounds humbly advise Her
Majesty that the appeal ought to be dismissed. . . .

Bloomenthal *v.* Ford. [1897] A.C. 156

*When a company issues a share certificate, that certificate creates
an estoppel so that the company cannot afterwards deny, as
against a person who has acted on the faith of it, the truth of the
matters stated in it.*

The company, Veuve Monnier et ses Fils, Limited, was
registered in 1890 under the *Companies Acts* as a company
limited by shares. In February 1894 the appellant Frederick Bloomenthal, a stationer in the city of London, who

had supplied the company with stationery and printed for them, was asked to lend the company £1,000. He verbally agreed with the secretary and the managing director to lend that sum upon the terms that he should have the company's acceptance for £1,000, and as collateral security 10,000 of the company's fully paid shares of £1 each, and that if the company should wish to pay off any part he should return a proportionate part of the shares.

The appellant advanced the company £1,000 and afterwards received a letter from the company enclosing the company's acceptance for £1,000 and ten certificates. Each certificate stated that the appellant was the registered proprietor of 1,000 cumulative preference shares of £1 each in the company, and "that on each of such shares the full amount has been paid."

In April 1894 the appellant made a further advance of £600 and received 6,000 shares under precisely similar circumstances. In November the company sold by auction 200 of the above shares at 17s. 6d. each. The appellant returned to the company one of the certificates, executed a transfer of the 200 shares to the purchaser, authorised the auctioneers to pay the purchase-money to the company, and received from the company £20 in reduction of the loan.

In 1895 the company was ordered to be wound up and the appellant was placed by the liquidator, James Ford, on the list of contributories in respect of 16,000 shares. Upon the hearing before VAUGHAN WILLIAMS J. of an application by the appellant to strike his name out of the list, he said that he did not know that the shares handed to him were part of the unissued shares for which the public had not applied, and that he always believed they were fully paid up until December 1894 when he was told by a friend that they were not; that he then gave notice of an application to remove his name from the register of shareholders, but the winding-up supervened.

VAUGHAN WILLIAMS J. refused the application, and this decision was affirmed by the Court of Appeal.

From these decisions the appellant then appealed to the House of Lords.

LORD HALSBURY L.C.: . . . In arriving at a conclusion upon

this question of fact, like every other question of fact, all the circumstances must be considered. A statement may be made so preposterous in its nature that nobody could believe that any one was misled; . . . but once the conclusion is arrived at that the belief was induced, and intentionally induced, and by a mis-statement of fact intended to operate upon the mind of another, upon which the man has acted, then I do not think any case can be found in the books in which it has been suggested that the legal consequence does not follow, namely, that there is estoppel, and that it is open to the person who has made the representation to say, "I told you so-and-so; but you ought not to have believed me. You were too great a fool. I had a right to mislead you because you were too great a fool." I do not believe that any such case can be brought forward, or that there is any authority for such a proposition.

Now, my Lords, dealing with it as a question of fact, . . . I come to an exactly opposite conclusion from that which the learned judges in the Court below have arrived at. The circumstances are simple; they speak for themselves: *res ipsa loquitur*. Here is a company, which is not too flush of money, applying to their stationer and printer for a loan of money. Can anybody believe that if he had known the true state of the facts, namely, that instead of getting a security he was getting a liability to the extent of £16,000, he would have lent the money? . . . He agrees to give a loan if he gets "fully paid-up shares." . . . I do not know why people should not mean what they say when they speak of fully paid-up shares. People who know anything about limited liability companies know that there is a certain liability upon their shares, and that from time to time the company calls up such and such a proportion of the money due upon those shares, and I should have thought, without being a lawyer or discussing questions which have been raised in the courts, that a person would ordinarily understand that fully paid-up shares mean shares upon which the whole amount that could be called up had been called up. . . .

Then, my Lords, this case appears to have been started by the liquidator under the impression that this gentleman had received express notice of the actual state of things, and I think one of the learned judges says in terms that it was not a question of constructive notice, but that he had received express notice. All I can say is that the appellant himself absolutely denies it, and he is not cross-examined in any sense which in my opinion ought to shake his evidence: his *bona fides* has at least been affirmed by three judges. . . .

If that is the state of the facts at which one arrives in considering the evidence in this case, the legal conclusion cannot be doubted. . . . [I]f you induce a man to act upon a statement of yours, meaning him to act upon it, and that statement is untrue, and he does act upon it because he believes it, it is not competent then for the person who has made the representation to say afterwards, "I will show another state of facts than that which I represented, and you ought not to have believed it." . . . [I]t would be a very lamentable thing indeed for the course of business—and indeed for the course of human life—if the law did not recognise the responsibility of persons who make statements and induce others to act upon them, so that they should not afterwards be permitted to turn round and say that what they stated was untrue, having altered the position of those whom they deceived by the statements they made.

Under those circumstances I move your Lordships that the appeal be allowed.

LORD HERSCHELL: My Lords, I am of the same opinion.

In differing, as I do with all respect, from the learned judges in the Court below, I do not think that I am differing from them upon any question of law. The doctrine of estoppel to which my noble and learned friend has alluded appears to be entirely admitted by the learned judges in the Court of Appeal. The decision against the appellant has arisen from the conclusion that the doctrine of estoppel does not apply in the present case so as to preclude the company, or the liquidator representing the company, from contending that the liability upon these shares exists.

Now, this is not the case of an application to a company by a member of the public for an allotment of shares and the acceptance of an allotment under the impression that it created no liability, when in truth according to law it did create a liability. The transaction was one of loan to the company, and for that loan the company were to give as security "fully paid-up shares." I do not think it can be doubted that the company represented to the appellant that the shares which they were handing to him, by means of the certificate, in return for his loan, and which he was to receive as security, were fully paid-up shares. . . . That he acted upon that representation there can equally be no doubt. He was not content to lend his money without security. . . . The money was lent, and under those circumstances, if the representation in the sense in which it would be naturally understood and was understood by the appellant was untrue, then all the elements of an estoppel appear to me to be present.

. . . Now, the statement having been made that he was to receive "fully paid-up shares" in exchange for his money, he gets a certificate, on the face of which it is stated that on each of such shares the full amount has been paid. It was argued . . . that the money was parted with by the appellant on the faith of the statement that the shares were fully paid up, and that he could not rely upon the form of words to be found in the certificate . . . I do not think that in any case that contention could be maintained, because, although it is quite true that he parted with his money in exchange for this certificate, and lent the money before he actually got the certificate, yet the loan in the first instance was only for a limited period. A bill was given which fell due in the month of August, and that bill was renewed, and he most assuredly acted upon representations he had received prior to that time, or the effect produced by them, by leaving his money, as he was not bound to do, for a considerable time after that, as a loan to the company. . . . [I]t is stated in the affidavit that both bills were renewed in the month of November. Therefore, I do not think there is anything in the point sought to be made that you are not entitled to look at the certificate as part of the inducement by the company to let them have or retain his money; at all events, the certificate can be looked at for the purpose of seeing what was the meaning or what was regarded as the meaning of "fully paid-up shares," because the representation to him having been that the shares he was to get were fully paid up, the certificate distinctly and unequivocally represents that on each of them the full amount had been paid. Now, in point of fact they were not fully paid up—they were not paid up at all—and he is sought to be made liable for the whole amount.

It is said that he is under this liability, and that the law of estoppel does not apply, because if he had thought the matter out, . . . he would have seen and must have seen that the shares were not fully paid up. My Lords, I cannot myself think that, where an unequivocal statement is made by one party to another of a particular fact, the party who made that statement can get rid of the estoppel which arises from another man acting upon it by saying that if the person to whom he made the statement had reflected and thought all about it he would have come to see that it could not be true. Of course, if the person to whom the statement was made did not believe it, and did not act on the belief induced by it, there is no estoppel. But supposing he did believe it and did act on the belief induced by it, then it seems to me you do not get rid of the estoppel by saying, "If you had thought more about it you would have seen it was not true." The very person who makes a statement of that sort has put the other party off making further inquiry. He has produced on his mind an impression as a result of which further inquiry is thought to be unnecessary or useless. Therefore I confess I do not think that it is legitimate to speculate what is the conclusion at which a man would have arrived if he had put together . . . all the considerations that might have occurred to a reflective mind cogitating on the whole subject, and then to say that because he would have come to the conclusion that the statement made to him could not have been true, he is not entitled to act upon it as if it had been true, when in point of fact he did not enter into those considerations, but did believe it and did act upon it. . . . What the appellant in effect says is quite satisfactory to my mind: that he did not think about it at all; he was told these shares were fully paid up; he believed it, and that was enough for him; he did not care to inquire or to think; on that belief he acted; that belief was a false belief; that false belief was induced by the company. If so, you have every element necessary to make an estoppel and justify the appellant in this appeal.

LORD MACNAGHTEN: My Lords, I am of the same opinion . . . I agree in thinking that the appeal ought to be allowed.

LORD MORRIS: My Lords, I am of the same opinion.

LORD SHAND; My Lords, . . . in my opinion the appeal should be allowed.

Galloway *v*. Hallé Concerts Society. [1915] 2 Ch. 233

Prima facie it is improper for directors to make a call on some members only of a class of shareholders without making a similar call on the other members of that class.

The defendant society was formed for the purpose of taking over the undertaking of the Hallé Concerts in Manchester. It was incorporated in 1899 under the *Companies Acts* as a company limited by guarantee omitting, pursuant to licence of the Board of Trade, the word "Limited" as part of its name, on the usual condition that no portion of its income and property should be paid or transferred by way of dividend, or otherwise by way of profit, to its members.

The memorandum of association provided that every member should contribute to its assets, in the event of the society's being wound up, for payment of its debts, winding-up expenses and the adjustment of the rights of the contributories among themselves, such amount as might be required not exceeding £5; and also that, if on winding up, after payment of all debts, there remained any property, this should not belong to the members but should be handed over to some kindred institution.

Clause 7 of the articles of association provided:

"Each member shall be liable to contribute, and shall, when demanded, pay to the committee, any sum or sums, not exceeding in the aggregate the sum of £100, which is hereafter referred to as the contribution. The liability to the contribution shall be additional to and without prejudice to any liability in case of winding-up under the guarantee clause in the memorandum of association.

The committee may from time to time make such calls as they think fit upon each member in respect of all moneys unpaid on his contributions, and each member shall pay the amount of every call so made upon him to the persons in the manner and at the times and places appointed by the committee."

The plaintiffs, William Johnson Galloway and Oliver Standbrooke Holt, were members of the society, and for some time past had objected to its general policy, and in particular to certain calls on the members, one for £7 and the other for £3. They ultimately paid these calls, but as regards the call of £3 only after proceedings had been taken in the county court. A third call for £10 was made in June 1914 and at the date of the resolution next mentioned had not been paid by them.

On 31st March 1915 the committee passed the following resolution:

"The secretary reported that there were certain guarantors who had not paid the call of £10 made in June last. He desired especially to call attention to the cases of Mr. W. J. Galloway and Mr. O. S. Holt, who had refused to pay the call of £3 made in June, 1913, and had even gone so far as to allow themselves to be sued in Court for the amount. As it was evident that they did not intend to pay the call of £10 made in June, 1914, the society would have the trouble of again suing them for the amount, and it was resolved therefore that the sum of £80 be called up in respect of the contribution of Mr. W. J. Galloway and £75 in the case of Mr. O. S. Holt, respectively, this amount to be in addition to the sum of £10 owing in respect of the call made in June, 1914."

These two sums of £80 and £75 represented the whole of the uncalled liability of the two plaintiffs. No similar call was made on the other members of the society.

The plaintiffs on 5th May 1915, issued a writ claiming (1) a declaration that the resolution was invalid and *ultra vires* and that the calls made in pursuance thereof were not enforceable against the plaintiffs, and (2) an injunction to restrain the society from enforcing by action at law or otherwise the said calls.

SARGANT J.: . . The question now arises whether the society is entitled to call up the full amount uncalled in respect of the contributions of the plaintiffs, while making no similar call in respect of the contributions of the other members of the society for the reason that these two members have given trouble to the society in the past in securing and enforcing payment of the previous calls made by the society. . . . There is no doubt that prima facie . . . there is by virtue of the ordinary law of partnership an implied condition of equality between shareholders in a company, and that prima facie it is entirely improper for the directors to make a call on some members of a class of shareholders who stand in the same relation to the company as the other members of the class without making a similar call on all the other members of that class. . . . Is it right to make this call on these two persons alone for this large amount merely because they have been dilatory in the payment of previous calls? It is said that expense is caused to the society by the necessity of enforcing these repeated calls against them and that less expense will be caused if the amounts can be called up in a lump sum. In my opinion that is not a sufficient reason. . . . In the present case the result might be more unfair to the plaintiffs than in an ordinary case, because, so far as I can see, in case of a winding up of the company there is no certainty at all under the memorandum of association that the sums of £80 and £75 in question would come back to the plaintiffs in priority to the payments that would have to be made to the other members of the society. However that may be, it seems to me that the reason given by the committee of the society for making the calls on these two persons separately from any similar calls on the other members of the society is altogether insufficient, and accordingly I propose to make a declaration substantially to the effect claimed by the writ.

Re Copal Varnish Company, Limited. [1917] 2 Ch. 349

Where a director refuses to attend a board meeting so that a quorum cannot be reached, and consequently the consent of the board to registration of share transfers cannot be obtained, the court will order that the transferee should be entered on the register.

The Copal Varnish Company, Limited, was incorporated in 1883 for the purpose of carrying on the business of manufacturing copal varnish. The issued share capital consisted of sixty ordinary shares of £10 each, of which twenty-eight were registered in the name of Ernest Randall, twenty-eight in the name of his brother Percy Randall, and the four remaining shares in the names of four other persons.

In addition there were 541 preference shares of £10 each, of which 105 were registered in the name of Ernest Randall, 105 in the name of Percy Randall and the remaining 331 in their joint names, being held by them on certain trusts in favour of their sisters. As the name of Ernest Randall stood first in the register, he had, under the articles of association, the sole voting power in respect of these shares. By the articles every member was entitled to one vote for every share held by him.

In 1908 the company was by special resolution converted into a private company under the provisions of the *Companies Act*, 1907. On this occasion the following words were by special resolution added to article 17, namely: "No share shall be transferred to any person who is not already a member of the company without the consent of the directors."

There were only two directors, Ernest Randall and Percy Randall, and the quorum of directors was two. Ernest Randall was the chairman and in the case of an equality of votes the chairman had a second or casting vote.

Without first obtaining the consent of the board of directors, Ernest Randall executed transfers of twelve of his shares to twelve persons who were not members of the company. These transfers were sent to the company for registration, and a meeting of the directors was summoned by a notice stating, among the agenda, "transfer of shares."

After the meeting had been postponed to meet the convenience of Percy Randall he wrote to the secretary of the company that, having regard to the addition made to article 17, he was "advised that the transfers of shares of which notice has been given to you are invalid, as the consents of the directors have not been obtained. As that is the only business on the agenda I do not propose to attend." This refusal was subsequently persisted in by his solicitors.

The transferees of the shares in question accordingly commenced proceedings against the company, under S.32 of the *Companies (Consolidation) Act*, 1908 [*see now S.116 Companies Act, 1948*], for rectification of the register of members by inserting their names as holders of the shares in the place of the name of Ernest Randall.

EVE J.: ... The only point which I have to consider is what are the legal rights of the persons who are now applying to have the register rectified. In order that there may be no doubt as to the standpoint from which I approach this question, I wish to say that, alike in a public and a private company, a shareholder has in my opinion, to use the language of LORD COZENS-HARDY M.R. in *In re Bede Steam Shipping Co.*, "a property in his shares, a property which he is at liberty to dispose of, subject only to any express restriction which may be found in the articles of association of the company." That statement is, I think, as applicable to a private company as to a public one, subject only to this observation, that, whereas in a public company it is not necessary that there should be any agreement *inter socios* operating as a restriction of the right of transfer, in the constitution of a private company some restriction must be found. It follows that in the present case Ernest Randall had a property in his shares of which he had a right to dispose subject only to any express restriction in the articles of association. Those express restrictions are to be found in article 17. ... [I]t is said that the addition to the article ... imposes upon an intending vendor of shares an obligation to obtain the consent of the directors to the reception into the company of the proposed purchaser before he can proceed with the transaction to the point of executing the transfer. ... The operation of legally transferring a share is indeed one of some complexity. In the first place there is the contract of sale followed by the execution of an instrument of transfer containing an agreement by the purchaser to accept the shares subject to the several conditions on which the vendor held the same immediately prior to the execution of the transfer—that is to say, subject, amongst other things, to the conditions imposing restrictions on the vendor's right to transfer to that particular purchaser. Up to this point all that has been done is to pass an equitable interest in the shares to the transferee. There has been no legal assignment completed; indeed, the most crucial point in the transaction has not been reached—the acceptance of the transfer by the board of directors and the passing of it for registration; and even then the matter is not completed, because until the actual entry of the name of the transferee on the register the transferor remains the legal holder of the share. Such being the successive operations by which alone a legal transfer can be effectuated, what is there in the wording of the clause . . . which imposes upon an intending transferor any obligation to approach the directors and ask them if they will approve of an intended transferee before executing the document, which is only one of the series of operations, and creates no title in the transferee of which the company can take any note until the directors have sanctioned its registration? I cannot see anything in the article which imposes any such obligation, and I think it would be an unreasonable construction to hold that there is an obligation to apply for the consent before the transfer is tendered for acceptance and registration. So long as prior to the completion of the transaction an opportunity is given to the directors sitting as a board to determine whether the proposed transferee is a person whom they are prepared to admit as a member of the company, the conditions imposed by the article are, in my opinion, complied with, and the contract into which the vendor on becoming a shareholder entered with his co-shareholders is sufficiently discharged. . . .

In my opinion Percy Randall has taken up an attitude in this dispute which is untenable.

> EVE J. then proceeded to make an order directing the company to rectify the register by giving effect to the transfers, as requested by the transferees.

XII. THE DIRECTORS OF A COMPANY

1. Directors as Agents of the Company

**The Royal British Bank *v*. Turquand. (1855) 5 E. & B. 248
(1856) 6 E. & B. 327**

*Where the directors, as the company's agents, act within their
apparent authority, even though exceeding their actual authority,
the company, as their principal, will be bound to the third party.*

The defendant company, Cameron's Coalbrook, Steam,
Coal and Swansea and London Railway Company, of
which Turquand was at the time of the action the official
manager, was registered under the *Joint Stock Companies
Act*, 1844. It was formed for the working of certain mines
and collieries and making a railway between specified places.

Its registered deed of settlement (corresponding to the
memorandum and articles of association) authorised the
directors, under certain circumstances, to give bills, notes,
bonds or mortgages; and one clause provided that the
directors might borrow on bond such sums as should, from
time to time, by a resolution passed at a general meeting
of the company, be authorised to be borrowed.

On 6th March 1850 a bond was signed by two directors
under the seal of the company, whereby the company
acknowledged themselves to be bound to the plaintiff, who
was a banker, in the sum of £2,000. There had been no
resolution authorising the making of the bond as required
by the deed of settlement. The sum lent was not repaid
to the plaintiff.

Lord Campbell C.J.: In this case the bond sued upon is
allowed to be under the seal of the company, and to be their
deed. A prima facie case therefore is made for the plaintiffs.
. . . Here the defendants, having executed the bond, and having
no defence under the plea of *non est factum*, the onus is cast
upon them of showing that the bond is unlawful and void.

No illegality appears on the face of the bond or condition. A good plea, therefore, must allege facts to establish illegality. . . . But this plea makes no charge of fraud against the plaintiffs, and states no facts from which fraud can be inferred: it shows no immorality nor breach of common law or statute law. It alleges that, as between the directors and the shareholders, the directors exceeded their authority in executing the bond, but without adding that this was known to the plaintiffs, or that it was to the prejudice of the shareholders. Looking to the business to be carried on by this company, it might well be presumed that opening such an account and carrying on such dealings with a banking house as are described in the conditions would be within the authority of the directors, and would be for the benefit of the shareholders. A mere excess of authority by the directors, we think, of itself would not amount to a defence. The bond being under the seal of the company, the gist of the defence must be illegality. If the directors had exceeded their authority to the prejudice of the shareholders by executing the bond, and this had been known to the obligees, illegality, we think, would have been shown. The obligors in executing, and the obligees in accepting, the bond might be considered as combining together to injure the shareholders; the two parties would have been *in pari delicto*: and the action could not have been maintained. In such circumstances *potior est conditio defendentis*. But without the *scienter*, and without prejudice to the shareholders or any others whatsoever, illegality is not established against the obligees. If no illegality is shown as against the party with whom the directors contract under the seal of the company, excess of authority is a matter only between the directors and the shareholders.

. . . [W]e think that the bond cannot be rendered illegal and void from any irregularity in the proceedings of the company, nor even by an excess of authority, the plaintiffs having acted with good faith, and the shareholders not being prejudiced. The plaintiffs have *bona fide* advanced their money for the use of the company, giving credit to the representations of the directors that they had authority to execute the bond; and

the money which they advanced, and which they now seek to
recover, must be taken to have been applied in the business of
the company and for the benefit of the shareholders. If the
plaintiffs must be presumed to have had notice of the contents
of the registered deed of settlement, there is nothing there to
show that the directors might not have had authority to execute
the bond as they asserted.

. . . We are therefore of opinion that there ought to be judgment for the plaintiffs.

> From this decision of the Court of Queen's Bench the case
> came before the Court of Exchequer Chamber.

JERVIS C.J.: I am of opinion that the judgment of the Court of
Queen's Bench ought to be affirmed. We may now take for
granted that the dealings with these companies are not like
dealings with other partnerships, and that the parties dealing
with them are bound to read the statute and the deed of
settlement. But they are not bound to do more. And the party
here, on reading the deed of settlement, would find, not a prohibition from borrowing, but a permission to do so on certain
conditions. Finding that the authority might be made complete
by a resolution, he would have a right to infer the fact of a
resolution authorising that which on the face of the document
appeared to be legitimately done.

POLLOCK C.B., ALDERSON B., CRESSWELL J., CROWDER J.
and BRAMWELL B. concurred.

Mahony *v.* East Holyford Mining Company, Ltd. (1875) L.R. 7 H.L. 869

A company is bound to bona fide *third parties by the acts of
persons who have been permitted by the shareholders to occupy
the position of* de facto *directors.*

> Erwin Harvey Wadge was the proprietor of a publication
> called the *Industrial Magazine*, published in Dublin. He
> had several employees, among whom were Tully,
> McKenna, Murphy and Hughes.
> In July 1866 he decided to form a limited company called

the East Holyford Mining Company. Two of his friends, Hoare and Wall, joined him and, with the four employees mentioned above and a seventh person, Thomas McNally, signed the memorandum and articles of association. Wadge neither signed the memorandum nor subscribed for shares in the company.

The company was duly registered and many persons applied for shares. Nearly £4,000 was obtained as capital, which was paid into the National Bank in College Green where an account was opened. The bank manager afterwards received a note, signed by Wall as secretary and headed with the company's name, stating that enclosed was a copy of a resolution relating to the bank account, and Wadge's and McNally's signatures, with Hoare's signature to follow. The enclosed resolution requested the bank to pay all cheques signed by any two of the following three directors, namely, McNally, Wadge and Hoare, and countersigned by the secretary. The genuine signatures of Wadge and McNally were appended, and a few days later Hoare's was sent as well.

Shortly afterwards several cheques were sent, generally payable to Wadge and signed and countersigned in accordance with the resolution. No meeting of shareholders was ever held, but Wadge, Hoare and Wall were constantly at the company's office in Grafton Street and transacted all the business done there.

The articles authorised the directors to adopt a contract made by Wall and Hoare for the purchase of a lease of the East Holyford Mine in Tipperary for £10,000. Wadge was the owner of the lease. The articles also contained, in Article 85, a clause equivalent to S.180 *Companies Act* and a clause in Article 53 which stated that the subscribers to the memorandum were to appoint the directors.

Eventually all the money paid into the bank was drawn out, except for about £55. The company was ordered to be wound up and the liquidator, on behalf of the shareholders, brought an action against the bank to recover the money subscribed by them. The bank's defence was that all the money except for £55 had been duly paid out on cheques of the directors, and the £55 was paid to the liquidator.

It was contended for the liquidator that there had been

no sufficient authority for the payments on the cheques, as there was no evidence that Wadge, Hoare and McNally had ever been appointed directors. McNally stated at the trial that he was not aware that he was ever appointed a director or in fact was a director of the company, that he never acted as such, that he never attended any meeting of directors or shareholders, or got any notice of such meetings, and that he signed the documents at the request of Wadge. This was the only act which he had done in relation to the company and he thought that he had done it as a shareholder.

The jury found as a fact that no directors had been appointed, and no meeting of directors held, and that the bank had acted on the faith of Wall's letter, believing it to be accurate.

The Court of Common Pleas gave judgment for the bank, but this decision was reversed in the Exchequer Chamber, whereupon the case came before the House of Lords.

THE LORD CHIEF BARON (SIR FITZROY KELLY): . . . The bankers paid to the liquidator £55 2s. 4d., and asserted that as to the remainder of the moneys received by it, amounting to £3,915, they had a discharge good against the company, and consequently good against the . . . liquidator. . . .

The only real issue between the parties was whether payments made on account of these cheques were valid discharges to the bankers as against the company. . . . The jury found . . . that the bankers altogether acted on the faith of Mr. Wall's letter, believing it to be accurate.

If this had been all, it would not give a sufficient discharge to the bankers; for, no doubt, a plausible swindler might induce his dupes to believe a statement that he was secretary to a company, and that his accomplices were directors of the company, though there was no colour of truth in either assertion, and nothing done or permitted by the company to give colour to either assertion. It was therefore necessary for the bankers to prove more. . . .

We think that the jury ought to have been directed . . . that, if the shareholders and members of the company permitted Wadge, McNally and Hoare to act as directors, to have possession of the office of the company, and of the books of the company, to transact, as directors, all such business as required to be transacted, such shareholders knowing, as from the articles of association they must have known, that from the moment the company was incorporated, directors could be appointed at once by the first seven members, or a majority of them; and that there was business which required the immediate action of directors, and such shareholders yet taking no steps themselves to appoint any directors *de jure* to transact that business;—the jury might and should find that the shareholders permitted these persons to be *de facto* in possession of the office of directors; and that if they did so they were bound, at least as to innocent third persons, by the acts of those directors *de facto*, just as if they had been regularly appointed by the majority of the seven.

We wish not to be understood as saying that all these facts are requisite to bind the shareholders; probably less would do, but as we are quite prepared, as jurors, to find that every one of those facts did here exist, we think it enough to say, as Judges, that, at least, where all those facts do exist, the company is bound by the acts of the *de facto* directors, at least as to those who had no notice that they were not properly and duly installed in their offices.

. . . There was very strong evidence that this was a conspiracy to defraud the public, Wadge and Wall being the prime conspirators, and the other six, Hoare, Tully, McKenna, Murphy, Hughes, and McNally, lending themselves with a guilty knowledge to aid that conspiracy. But there is no evidence . . . that the managers of the bank had any knowledge that it was a conspiracy.

. . . [T]he evidence . . . in our opinion, shows that the three persons who signed these cheques as directors, *viz.*, Wadge, Hoare, and McNally, were permitted by the company to take possession of the position of directors *de facto*. As the directors appoint the secretary, they, if installed in the office of directors, though irregularly, could appoint Wall to act as secretary. . . .

It seems, therefore, to be a proper inference from these facts that there was an actual appointment of these three as directors,

though a very informal one; and so literally came within
Article 85.

But we think it quite enough, these men being thus permitted
to be in actual possession of the directorship, to make their
acts valid as regards third persons with persons who dealt
bona fide with persons who may be termed *de facto* directors,
and who might, as far as they could tell, have been directors
de jure.

Objection was made to the form of the letter . . . which does
not in distinct terms say that the resolution was passed by the
directors, but documents on which men are to act in the course
of business are not to be criticised too closely. No one could
fail to understand the letter as meaning that there was such a
resolution. It is found by the jury that there was no such
resolution; but the bankers did not know that the statement was
false, and, as is found by the jury, believed it was accurate; and,
according to the decision in *Royal British Bank* v. *Turquand,*
were not called upon to inquire whether it was true or false.
They were told by the persons who alone acted as directors,
and who alone had authority to pass any resolution, that it had
been passed, and that they, the directors, were acting on the
authority given to them by that resolution.

. . . We think it enough to say that (assuming that those who
signed had authority to draw for the company) the bankers
have a sufficient voucher when they produce an order to pay
the money, really signed by those persons, really acting under
their authority, though, it may be, that that authority was
exercised in an informal manner.

Upon these grounds, we are of opinion that the verdict
should be entered for the defendant.

THE LORD CHANCELLOR (LORD CAIRNS): . . . [T]he bankers
could have no certainty of the truth of what was stated to them
unless they had themselves attended the meetings of the directors, and heard what was done there—a course which I need
hardly say it would be impossible for men of business to take.
It appears to me that this is exactly such a case as the 85th
section of the articles . . . is meant to meet. There is no regular

appointment of directors, and the persons so acting may perhaps have been disqualified; but the acts done by them are to be taken as being as valid as if they had been duly appointed and qualified.

. . . I have no hesitation in advising your Lordships . . . that you should now hold that there having been *de facto* directors of the company, who were suffered and permitted by the majority of those who signed the articles . . . to occupy the position of and act as directors, and the bankers having, in the full belief that these persons were directors, as they were represented to be, honoured the cheques drawn by them, the payment of these cheques is an answer to the action of the liquidator . . ., and that the judgment in the action ought to be entered for the defendant. . . .

LORD CHELMSFORD: . . . The bankers . . . having acted *bona fide*, and dealing with persons acting as directors, without any reason to believe they were unauthorised so to act . . ., they are, in my opinion, entitled to judgment, notwithstanding the two other findings, as to the non-appointment and absence of assent to the appointment of directors, and to there being no such resolution by the directors as that mentioned in Wall's letter.

LORD HATHERLEY: My Lords, it appears to me also that the judgment in this case should be entered for the defendant. . . . [W]hen there are persons conducting the affairs of the company in a manner which appears to be perfectly consonant with the articles of association, then those so dealing with them, externally, are not to be affected by any irregularities which may take place in the internal management of the company. They are entitled to presume that that of which only they can have knowledge, namely, the external acts, are rightly done, when those external acts purport to be performed in the mode in which they ought to be performed. For instance, when a cheque is signed by three directors, they are entitled to assume that those directors are persons properly appointed for the purpose of performing that function, and have properly performed the function for which they have been appointed. . . .

And, my Lords, I apprehend we are quite justified in holding that the 85th clause of the articles of association covers any defect there might have been in that appointment.

LORD PENZANCE: . . . I do not differ in the slightest degree from any of the principles that I have heard enunciated, or from the application which has been made of those principles to the circumstances of this case. . . .

It seems to me . . ., my Lords, that we have here the case of three individuals being *de facto* directors, and one being *de facto* secretary. . . .

My Lords, the question is a very broad one whether a bank, having a written authority of a *de facto* secretary, is bound, before it acts upon that authority, to ascertain whether he is the properly constituted secretary of the company or not, and not only that, but whether any resolution, of which he forwards a copy, was properly passed by the directors. Now, my Lords, the case of *Royal British Bank* v. *Turquand* distinctly lays down the proposition that the bank is not bound to make any such inquiry, but that it is justified in acting upon a letter such as that to which reference has been made, provided that the transaction which appears upon that letter is one which might legally have taken place, and been legally consummated under the articles of association. Upon this simple ground, my Lords, it seems to me that your Lordships would be perfectly justified in directing the judgment in this case to be entered for the defendant.

. . . I have not heard any argument . . . which has satisfied me that the 85th clause of the articles of association was not sufficient to cover the defect of appointment of these directors. The words of that clause are extremely large; the substance of it is that, if the directors act, and third persons deal with those directors, the acts of the directors shall be valid, although they have not been properly appointed. In this case, no doubt, they were not properly appointed; they appear to have had either the formal, or informal, assent of three out of the four persons who would have constituted the majority necessary to make a proper appointment; but, nevertheless, although not properly

appointed, they would seem to have their acts validated under
the 85th clause.

Craven-Ellis *v*. Canons, Limited. [1936] 2 K.B. 403

An implied promise to pay for goods or services on a quantum
meruit *basis can arise only in the absence of a binding contract.
It is based on the inference drawn by the law from the provision
of those goods or services by one party and the acceptance of
them by the other.*

*S.180 Companies Act, 1948, does not enable a director who
is not properly appointed or qualified to do anything which a
properly appointed and qualified director could not do.*

In 1927 Sir Arthur du Cros and his son, Mr. Phillip du
Cros, became interested in the development of a building
estate known as Canons Estate, which became vested in
Pard Estates, Ltd.

They got into communication on the subject with the
plaintiff Mr. Craven-Ellis, a valuer and estate agent, and he
in letters to them stated the terms on which he was willing
to act in connection with the development of the estate.
Terms were eventually agreed and the engagement was to
be for three years.

On 15th August 1928 the defendant company was
formed to purchase the Canons Park Estate from Pard
Estates, Ltd., and the plaintiff continued to do work
for the defendant company of which he became a director.
The du Cros' and a Mr. Wheeler were the other directors.
Under the articles of the defendant company the directors
could act without qualification for two months, but after
that time they became incapable of acting, as none of them
in fact acquired the necessary qualification.

On 14th April 1931 an agreement was executed under
the seal of the defendant company setting out the terms
on which the plaintiff was to act as managing director of
the company, its seal being affixed by resolution of the
unqualified directors. The plaintiff then sought to recover
the remuneration set out in this agreement for work done
and services rendered under and in pursuance of it and,
alternatively, the same sum on a *quantum meruit*.

By their defence the defendant company said that the written agreement relied upon by the plaintiff was made in purported confirmation of his appointment as managing director of the company upon the terms and conditions therein contained, including an undertaking by him to place at the company's disposal his expert skill as a land and estate agent. By reason of his appointment as managing director the defendant company said that it was the plaintiff's duty to acquire the share qualification required by the company's articles; that he never acquired the requisite share qualification; that the acts and matters in respect of which payment was claimed were illegal, being in breach of the provisions of S.73 of the *Companies (Consolidation) Act*, 1908, and S.141 of the *Companies Act*, 1929 [*now S.182, Companies Act, 1948*], and therefore that the plaintiff's claim was unenforceable in law.

In his reply the plaintiff relied upon article 18 of the defendant company's articles of association. By this it was provided that the office of a director should be vacated if he ceased to hold his qualification, but that any act done in good faith by a director whose office was vacated should be valid unless prior to the doing of such act written notice should have been served upon the director or an entry made in the minute book that such director had ceased to be a director of the company; and that no such notice was served upon him or any entry made in the directors' minute book stating that the plaintiff had ceased to be a director. The plaintiff contended that the defendant company having, with full knowledge of the facts, taken the benefit of his services were precluded and estopped from disputing liability to pay for the same.

In the High Court GODDARD J. in his judgment said that the plaintiff never was a director at all, and although he might be liable to a penalty it was contended on his behalf that the statute did not debar him from acting as a director. In his Lordship's view all the authorities were against that construction. It was then said that in any event the plaintiff was entitled to recover on a *quantum meruit*; but in his Lordship's opinion such a cause of action depended on an implied request, and an express request negatived an implied request. He held therefore that the plaintiff's claim failed.

From this decision the plaintiff appealed, and the case accordingly came before the Court of Appeal.

GREER L.J.: . . . As regards the services rendered between December 31, 1930, and April 14, 1931, there is, in my judgment, no defence to the claim. These services were rendered by the plaintiff not as managing director or as a director, but as an estate agent, and there was no contract in existence which could present any obstacle to a claim based on a *quantum meruit* for services rendered and accepted.

As regards the plaintiff's services after the date of the contract, I think the plaintiff is also entitled to succeed. The contract, having been made by directors who had no authority to make it with one of themselves who had notice of their want of authority, was not binding on either party. It was in fact, a nullity, and presents no obstacle to the implied promise to pay on a *quantum meruit* basis which arises from the performance of the services and the implied acceptance of the same by the company.

It was contended . . . on behalf of the respondents that, inasmuch as the services relied on were purported to be done by the plaintiff under what he and the directors thought was a binding contract, there could be no legal obligation on the defendants on a *quantum meruit* claim. . . . This would certainly be strictly logical if the inference of a promise to pay on a *quantum meruit* basis were an inference of fact based on the acceptance of the services or of the goods delivered under what was supposed to be an existing contract; but in my judgment the inference is not one of fact, but is an inference which a rule of law imposes on the parties where work has been done or goods have been delivered under what purports to be a binding contract, but is not so in fact.

. . . In [*Lawford* v. *Billericay Rural District Council*] the work in respect of which the plaintiff sued was done in pursuance of express instructions given by the defendant council, but the contract purported to be so made was not binding on the defendants because no agreement had been executed under their seal. It was impossible to say as a matter of logical inference from the facts that by accepting the advantage of the plaintiff's work they had promised to pay him a reasonable sum therefor. Both parties assumed that there was a contract between them, and the acceptance of the work by the defendants could not in fact give rise to the inference of a promise to pay the reasonable value. For these reasons this case seems to me to show that the obligation is one which is imposed by law in all cases where the acts are purported to be done on the faith of an agreement which is supposed to be but is not a binding contract between the parties. . . . In my judgment, the obligation to pay reasonable remuneration for the work done when there is no binding contract between the parties is imposed by a rule of law, and not by an inference of fact arising from the acceptance of services or goods. It is one of the cases referred to in books on contracts as obligations arising *quasi ex contractu*. . . .

I accordingly think that the defendants must pay on the basis of a *quantum meruit* not only for the services rendered after December 31, 1930, and before the date of the invalid agreement, but also for the services after that date. I think the appeal should be allowed, and judgment given for such a sum as shall be found to be due on the basis of a *quantum meruit* in respect of all services rendered by the plaintiff to the company until he was dismissed. The defendants seem to me to be in a dilemma. If the contract was an effective contract by the company, they would be bound to pay the remuneration provided for in the contract. If, on the other hand, the contract was a nullity and not binding either on the plaintiff or the defendants, there would be nothing to prevent the inference which the law draws from the performance by the plaintiff of services to the company, and the company's acceptance of such services, which, if they had not been performed by the plaintiff, they would have had to get some other agent to carry out.

The appeal will be allowed.

GREENE L.J.: In my opinion, the agreement of April 14, 1931, in so far as it purports to appoint the plaintiff managing director of the company, was altogether void. The only power which is given to directors to appoint a managing director is a power to appoint one of their number, that is to say, a person who is a director: see art. 17 and cl. 72 of Table A in the First Schedule to the *Companies (Consolidation) Act*, 1908 [*now cl. 107 of Table A, Companies Act, 1948*]. The appointment as managing director of a person not a director would have been *ultra vires* a properly constituted board, and the circumstance that both such a board and the appointee thought that the appointee was a director would not, in my judgment, affect the matter. If this view be right, the position is not made any better by cl. 94 of Table A of the *Companies (Consolidation) Act*, 1908 [*now cl. 105 of Table A, Companies Act, 1948*] or by S.143 of the *Companies Act*, 1929 [*now S.180 Companies Act, 1948*]' since those provisions . . . do not empower a *de facto* board to do what a *de jure* board is incapable of doing.

There is also, I think, another ground for saying that the contract is void. At the date when it was executed, both parties believed that the plaintiff was a director and was capable of continuing to act as a director. This belief was essential to the making of the agreement and formed the basis upon which the parties purported to contract. The agreement was accordingly void *ab initio* on well-recognised principles. I may quote as an accurate statement of the law a passage on p. 296 of Salmond and Winfield's Principles of the Law of Contracts: "The contract was entered into under a mistake as to the present existence of an essential fact recognised by the law as the foundation of the contract, and by its non-existence the contract is invalidated accordingly."

. . . The plaintiff's claim, therefore, in so far as it relates to services rendered after the date of the agreement can only succeed upon the basis of a *quantum meruit*. . . .

The question remains, however, whether the facts that the parties thought that there was a valid agreement and that the services rendered and accepted were performed under a supposed agreement precludes a claim upon a *quantum meruit*. . . .

I agree with the order proposed by GREER L.J.

TALBOT J. concurred in the above judgments.

Rama Corporation, Ltd. *v.* Proved Tin and General Investments Ltd. [1952] 2 Q.B. 147

A person contracting with a company without any knowledge of the company's articles cannot rely on those articles as conferring ostensible or apparent authority on the agent with whom he deals. The doctrine of constructive notice operates against the person who has failed to inquire, but does not operate in his favour.

Ostensible or apparent authority is a form of estoppel, and a person cannot call in aid estoppel without: (i) a representation, (ii) a reliance on the representation, and (iii) an alteration of his position resulting from that reliance. It is possible to have ostensible or apparent authority apart from the articles, though not where it is inconsistent with them.

On 21st March 1949, Rama Corporation Ltd., through their director Mr. Wedderburn, purported to enter into an agreement with Mr. Titley, a director of Proved Tin and General Investments Ltd., purporting to act on behalf of that company. Under the agreement Rama was to contribute £2,000 and Proved Tin £5,000 to a fund which was to be applied on behalf of the two companies to financing the sales of a telephone directory holder manufactured by R.B.K. Products Ltd. Proved Tin were to administer the fund and periodically account to Rama for it.

Rama claimed an account of moneys from Proved Tin under this agreement. Proved Tin denied that they had entered into the agreement, or that Mr. Titley had any authority, express, implied or apparent, to enter into it.

Article 119 of the articles of association of Proved Tin provided that the directors might delegate any of their powers to a committee consisting of such members of their body as they thought fit. Rama submitted that Proved Tin were estopped from denying that Mr. Titley had authority to enter into the agreement because the articles showed that he was capable of being so authorised.

SLADE J.: The material facts for the purposes of my judgment are as follows: (1) that Wedderburn trusted Titley completely; (2) that he had never heard of the defendant company before March 21, 1949; (3) that the whole bargain was concluded . . .

in Wedderburn's office on March 21, 1949, and that on that date Wedderburn had no knowledge of the contents of the defendant company's articles of association. I find as a fact that Wedderburn did not rely on any power contained in those articles of association to delegate the powers of the defendant company's board to a committee of their number (who might in law be a committee of one), and I find further that Titley never at any time disclosed to his fellow members of the board of the defendant company anything whatever about the transaction which he purported to enter into on its behalf with Wedderburn on behalf of the plaintiff company on March 21, 1949.

In my judgment I am bound by the decision of the Court of Appeal in *Houghton & Co.* v. *Nothard, Lowe & Wills Ltd.* [1927] 1 K.B. 246 to hold that a person who, at the time of making a contract with a company . . ., has no knowledge of the company's articles of association, cannot rely on those articles as conferring ostensible or apparent authority on the agent with whom he dealt, and by the same authority I am constrained to hold that the doctrine of constructive notice . . . of a company's registered documents, such as its memorandum of association, its articles of association, its special resolutions, etc., does not operate against a company, but only in its favour. Put in the converse way, the doctrine of constructive notice operates against the person who has failed to inquire, but does not operate in his favour. There is no positive doctrine of constructive notice; it is a purely negative one.

I am also bound by the same authority to hold that a person cannot set up an ostensible or apparent authority unless he relied on it in making the contract. . . . Ostensible or apparent authority which negatives the existence of actual authority is merely a form of estoppel, indeed, it has been termed agency by estoppel, and you cannot call in aid an estoppel unless you have three ingredients: (*i*) a representation, (*ii*) a reliance on the representation, and (*iii*) an alteration of your position resulting from such reliance. . . .

It is possible to have ostensible or apparent authority, apart from the articles of association. You cannot have one inconsistent with the articles of association or beyond the articles of association, but a company can hold out by correspondence a person as holding authority which he does not, in fact, possess, to third persons dealing with him in good faith.

. . . I have already found as a fact there was no actual authority, express or implied, and I find . . . that there was no apparent or ostensible authority on which the plaintiff company, or Wedderburn, was entitled to rely. Ostensible or apparent authority must be something emanating from the company and not from the person who seeks to defraud it. In the result there will be judgment for the defendants.

Freeman and Lockyer *v*. Buckhurst Park Properties (Mangal), Ltd. and Another. [1964] 2 Q.B. 480

When the agent of a company makes a contract on its behalf without actual authority to do so, the other party can hold the company bound by such contract on the grounds that the agent had apparent authority to make it only if four conditions are satisfied:

(a) a representation that the agent had authority to make contracts of that kind was made to him;

(b) the representation was made to him by persons with actual authority to manage the company's business, or the relevant part of it;

(c) he relied on the representation;

(d) the memorandum and articles of the company did not deprive the company of the capacity to make the contract, or of the power to delegate authority to make it to an agent.

Mr. Kapoor was a property developer. In September 1958 he entered into a contract for the purchase of Buckhurst Park Estate for the sum of £75,000, but had not sufficient money to complete the purchase.

He sought assistance from a Mr. Hoon, who was willing to advance a sum of approximately £40,000. They formed a private limited company, Buckhurst Park Properties (Mangal), Ltd., with a share capital of £70,000 which they subscribed in equal shares. The directors of the company were Mr. Kapoor and Mr. Hoon themselves and a nomi-

nee of each of them, making four in all. The company's
articles incorporated Article 107 of Table A authorising the
directors to appoint one of their number to be managing
director.

Mr. Hoon went abroad and was at all material times out
of the country. Mr. Kapoor, to the knowledge of the other
directors, acted throughout as managing director although
none was ever appointed. After the Buckhurst Park
Estate was duly conveyed to the company it was Mr.
Kapoor who, on behalf of the company, sought a purchaser
for it and instructed Freeman and Lockyer, a firm of archi-
tects and surveyors, to apply for planning permission,
prepare plans and define the estate boundaries.

When the fees due to Freeman and Lockyer for this work
were not paid, they brought an action claiming payment of
£291 6s. In the County Court an order was made that they
should recover this sum from the defendant company.
The company appealed against this order, contending that
the liability was not theirs but that of Mr. Kapoor, and the
case accordingly came before the Court of Appeal.

WILLMER L.J.: . . . The plaintiffs admittedly executed the work
which they were employed to do, and there is no dispute as to
the quantum of the fees earned by them, namely, £291 6s. The
question is whether the liability in respect of those fees is that
of the defendant company or that of the second defendant,
Kapoor. . . .

The plaintiffs contended (1) that . . . Kapoor had actual
authority to engage the plaintiffs on behalf of the defendant
company; alternatively (2) that Kapoor was held out by the
defendant company as having ostensible authority, so that the
latter is estopped from denying responsibility for his acts. . . .
The judge found that Kapoor, although never appointed as
managing director, had throughout been acting as such . . .,
and that this was well known to the board. In the light of this
finding he gave judgment in favour of the plaintiffs. . . . I take
this to be a finding, not that Kapoor had actual authority to
employ the plaintiffs, but that in doing so he was acting within
the scope of his ostensible authority.

In this court the plaintiffs have adhered to their contention that Kapoor had actual authority to employ the plaintiffs. But I do not think that this view can be supported. Actual authority might, of course, be either express—for example, if Kapoor were specifically authorised to engage the plaintiffs—or it might be implied—for example, if Kapoor had been appointed to some office which carried with it authority to make such a contract on behalf of the defendant company. There is certainly no resolution of the board specifically authorising Kapoor to engage the plaintiffs. . . . I can find no record in writing of Kapoor ever being appointed to any office which would carry with it authority to engage the plaintiffs. In these circumstances I think it is hopeless to contend that Kapoor was ever clothed with actual authority to do what he did.

The real question to be determined is whether the judge was right in finding that Kapoor had ostensible authority to engage the plaintiffs. This is partly a question of fact and partly one of law. . . . I can see no good ground for interfering with the judge's finding of fact that Kapoor was, to the knowledge of the board, acting as managing director of the defendant company. . . . The doctrine of ostensible authority in relation to a limited company necessarily gives rise to difficult legal problems. For a company can act only through its officers, and the powers of its officers are limited by its articles of association. It is well established that all persons dealing with a company are affected with notice of its memorandum and articles of association, which are public documents open to inspection by all; see *Mahony* v. *East Holyford Mining Co.* (1875). But by the rule in *Royal British Bank* v. *Turquand* (1856), re-affirmed in *Mahony's* case, it was also established, in the words of LORD HATHERLEY in the latter case, "that, when there are persons conducting the affairs of the company in a manner which appears to be perfectly consonant with the articles of association, then those so dealing with them, externally, are not to be affected by any irregularities which may take place in the internal management of the company." Thus in *Biggerstaff* v. *Rowatt's Wharf Ltd.* (1896), where the articles of association conferred power to appoint a managing director, the company was held bound by the act of a person who purported to contract as its managing director though he had never been formally appointed as such.

LOPES L.J. said that ". . . a company is bound by the acts of persons who take upon themselves, with the knowledge of the directors, to act for the company, provided such persons act within the limits of their apparent authority; and that strangers dealing *bona fide* with such persons, have a right to assume that they have been duly appointed." In the same case LINDLEY L.J. said: "The persons dealing with him" [the apparent managing director] "must look to the articles, and see that the managing director might have power to do what he purports to do, and that is enough for a person dealing with him *bona fide.*" . . . Consequently, if in that case the articles of association had conferred no power to appoint a managing director, the plaintiffs could not have been heard to say that the person with whom they contracted had been held out by the company as its managing director.

. . . [A] party who seeks to set up an estoppel must show that he in fact relied on the representation that he alleges, be it a representation in words or a representation by conduct. . . .

In the present case the plaintiffs do not have to rely on the articles of association of the defendant company in order to establish their claim. . . . The plaintiffs here rely on the fact that Kapoor, to the knowledge of the defendant company's board, was acting throughout as managing director, and was therefore being held out by the board as such. The act of Kapoor in engaging the plaintiffs was clearly one within the ordinary ambit of the authority of a managing director. The plaintiffs accordingly do not have to inquire whether he was properly appointed. It is sufficient for them that under the articles there was in fact power to appoint him as such.

In my judgment the judge here . . . rightly applied the principle enunciated by LOPES L.J. in *Biggerstaff's* case. I think that he came to the right conclusion, and I would accordingly dismiss the appeal.

PEARSON L.J.: . . . In my view the decision of the judge was correct. On the facts as found the plaintiffs were entitled to rely on Kapoor's ostensible authority to give them instructions on behalf of the company because there was a holding out of Kapoor by the company as its agent to conduct its business within the ordinary scope of that business. The expressions "ostensible authority" and "holding out" are somewhat vague. The basis of them . . . is an estoppel by representation. The agent professes to act on behalf of the company, and he thereby impliedly represents and warrants that he has authority from the company to do so. . . . In this case the company has known of and acquiesced in the agent professing to act on its behalf, and thereby impliedly representing that he has the company's authority to do so. The company is considered to have made the representation, or caused it to be made, or at any rate to be responsible for it. Accordingly, as against the other contracting party, who has altered his position in reliance on the representation, the company is estopped from denying the truth of the representation.

The identification of the persons whose knowledge and acquiescence constitute knowledge and acquiescence by the company depends upon the facts of the particular case. In one case those persons were the shareholders and subscribers of the company's memorandum and articles of association who permitted the *de facto* directors and *de facto* secretary to carry on the company's business: *Mahony* v. *East Holyford Mining Co.* (1875). More frequently those persons are the directors: *Biggerstaff's* case.

. . . The plaintiffs are not seeking to rely on any provision in the company's articles of association, but on things done by Kapoor within the ordinary scope of the company's business, and with the knowledge and acquiescence of the company through its other directors. It is true that the plaintiffs in this case did not look at the company's articles of association; it would have been surprising if they had done so. . . .

Rama Corporation, Ltd. v. *Proved Tin and General Investments Ltd.* (1952) was another case of an unusual transaction, and it was decided on the ground that the plaintiffs, having no knowledge of the defendant company's articles of association, could not claim to have acted in reliance on a provision for delegation contained therein. . . . In my view the judgment cannot reasonably be regarded as saying . . . that a person dealing with a director of a company in a normal transaction within the ordinary scope of the company's business is not protected by the director's ostensible authority unless that person obtained and studied the company's articles of association and the incorporated provisions of Table A and made sure that the directors had power to delegate to a single director. Such a requirement would be an absurd example of legal pettifoggery. There is no difficulty in applying the principle of *Rama's* case to any case where there is an unusual transaction outside the scope of the ordinary business which the single director is . . . held out by the company as authorised to conduct on its behalf.

In my judgment . . . the appeal must be dismissed.

DIPLOCK L.J.: . . . We are concerned in the present case with the authority of an agent to create contractual rights and liabilities between his principal and a third party whom I will call "the contractor". . . .

It is necessary at the outset to distinguish between an "actual" authority of an agent on the one hand, and an "apparent" or "ostensible" authority on the other. Actual authority and apparent authority are quite independent of one another. Generally they co-exist and coincide, but either may exist without the other and their respective scopes may be different. . . . [I]t is upon the apparent authority of the agent that the contractor normally relies in the ordinary course of business when entering into contracts.

An "actual" authority is a legal relationship between principal and agent created by a consensual agreement to which they alone are parties. Its scope is to be ascertained by applying ordinary principles of construction of contracts, including any proper implications from the express words used, the usages of the trade, or the course of business between the parties. To this agreement the contractor is a stranger; he may be totally ignorant of the existence of any authority on the part of the agent. Nevertheless, if the agent does enter into a contract pursuant to the "actual" authority, it does create contractual rights and liabilities between the principal and the contractor. . . . [T]his rule relating to "undisclosed principals" . . . is peculiar to English law. . . .

An "apparent" or "ostensible" authority, on the other hand, is a legal relationship between the principal and the contractor created by a representation, made by the principal to the contractor, intended to be and in fact acted upon by the contractor, that the agent has authority to enter on behalf of the principal into a contract of a kind within the scope of the "apparent" authority, so as to render the principal liable to perform any obligations imposed upon him by such contract. To the relationship so created the agent is a stranger. He need not be (although he generally is) aware of the existence of the representation but he must not purport to make the agreement as principal himself. The representation, when acted upon by the contractor by entering into a contract with the agent, operates as an estoppel, preventing the principal from asserting that he is not bound by the contract. It is irrelevant whether the agent had actual authority to enter into the contract.

In ordinary business dealings the contractor at the time of entering into the contract can in the nature of things hardly ever rely on the "actual" authority of the agent. His information as to the authority must be derived either from the principal or from the agent or from both, for they alone know what the agent's actual authority is. All that the contractor can know is what they tell him, which may or may not be true. In the ultimate analysis he relies either upon the representation of the principal, that is, apparent authority, or upon the representation of the agent, that is, warranty of authority. . . .

In applying the law . . . to the case where the principal is not a natural person, but . . . a corporation, two further factors arising from the legal characteristics of a corporation have to be borne in mind. The first is that the capacity of a corporation is limited by its constitution . . .; the second is that a corporation cannot do any act, and that includes making a representation, except through its agent.

Under the doctrine of *ultra vires* the limitation of the capacity of a corporation by its constitution to do any acts is absolute. This affects the rules as to the "apparent" authority of an agent of a corporation in two ways. First, no representation can operate to estop the corporation from denying the authority of the agent to do on behalf of the corporation an act which the corporation is not permitted by its constitution to do itself. Secondly, since the conferring of actual authority upon an agent is itself an act of the corporation, the capacity to do which is regulated by its constitution, the corporation cannot be estopped from denying that it has conferred upon a particular agent authority to do acts which, by its constitution, it is incapable of delegating to that particular agent.

To recognise that these are direct consequences of the doctrine of *ultra vires* is, I think, preferable to saying that a contractor who enters into a contract with a corporation has constructive notice of its constitution, for the expression "constructive notice" tends to disguise that constructive notice is not a positive, but a negative doctrine, like that of estoppel of which it forms a part. It operates to prevent the contractor from saying that he did not know that the constitution of the corporation rendered a particular act or a particular delegation of authority *ultra vires* the corporation. It does not entitle him to say that he relied upon some unusual provision in the constitution of the corporation if he did not in fact so rely.

The second characteristic of a corporation, namely, that unlike a natural person it can only make a representation through an agent, has the consequence that in order to create an estoppel between the corporation and the contractor, the representation as to the authority of the agent which creates his "apparent" authority must be made by some person or persons who have "actual" authority from the corporation to make the representation. Such "actual" authority may be conferred by the constitution of the corporation itself, as, for example, in the case of a company, upon the board of directors, or it may be conferred by those who under its constitution have the powers of management upon some other person to whom the constitution permits them to delegate authority to make representations of this kind. It follows that where the agent upon whose "apparent" authority the contractor relies has no "actual"

authority from the corporation to enter into a particular kind
of contract with the contractor on behalf of the corporation,
the contractor cannot rely upon the agent's own representation
as to his actual authority. He can rely only upon a representation by a person or persons who have actual authority to
manage or conduct that part of the business of the corporation
to which the contract relates.

The commonest form of representation by a principal
creating an "apparent" authority of an agent is by conduct,
namely, by permitting the agent to act in the management or
conduct of the principal's business. Thus, if in the case of a
company the board of directors who have "actual" authority
under the memorandum and articles of association to manage
the company's business permit the agent to act in the management or conduct of the company's business, they thereby represent to all persons dealing with such agent that he has authority
to enter on behalf of the corporation into contracts of a kind
which an agent authorised to do acts of the kind which he is in
fact permitted to do usually enters into in the ordinary course
of such business. The making of such a representation is
itself an act of management of the company's business. *Prima
facie* it falls within the "actual" authority of the board of
directors, and unless the memorandum or articles of the company either make such a contract *ultra vires* the company or
prohibit the delegation of such authority to the agent, the
company is estopped from denying to anyone who has entered
into a contract with the agent in reliance upon such "apparent"
authority that the agent had authority to contract on behalf of
the company.

If the foregoing analysis of the relevant law is correct, it can
be summarised by stating four conditions which must be fulfilled to entitle a contractor to enforce against a company a
contract entered into on behalf of the company by an agent
who had no actual authority to do so. It must be shown:

(1) that a representation that the agent had authority to
enter on behalf of the company into a contract of the kind
sought to be enforced was made to the contractor;

(2) that such representation was made by a person or persons who had "actual" authority to manage the business of the company either generally or in respect of those matters to which the contract relates;

(3) that he (the contractor) was induced by such representation to enter into the contract, that is, that he in fact relied upon it; and

(4) that under its memorandum or articles of association the company was not deprived of the capacity either to enter into a contract of the kind sought to be enforced or to delegate authority to enter into a contract of that kind to the agent.

The confusion which . . . has sometimes crept into the cases is in my view due to a failure to distinguish between these four separate conditions, and in particular to keep steadfastly in mind (a) that the only "actual" authority which is relevant is that of the persons making the representation relied upon, and (b) that the memorandum and articles of association of the company are always relevant (whether they are in fact known to the contractor or not) to the questions (i) whether condition (2) is fulfilled, and (ii) whether condition (4) is fulfilled, and (but only if they are in fact known to the contractor) may be relevant (iii) as part of the representation on which the contractor relied. . . .

In the present case the findings of fact by the county court judge are sufficient to satisfy the four conditions, and thus to establish that Kapoor had "apparent" authority to enter into contracts on behalf of the company for their services. . . .

I think the judgment was right, and would dismiss the appeal.

2. The Fiduciary Duty of Directors

Re Forest of Dean Coal Mining Company. (1878) 10 Ch.D 450

Although the position of a director is in some ways analogous to that of a trustee, he is not a trustee of unpaid debts owed to the company, and has a discretion as to whether to sue for them or not.

He is under no duty after becoming a director to communicate to the shareholders knowledge acquired before becoming a director of misconduct on the part of other persons.

S.333 is procedural only and does not create any new liability. It merely provides a summary method of enforcing existing liabilities, and therefore cannot apply where there is none.

The Forest of Dean Coal Mining Company was formed in 1873 for the purchase of certain collieries of which J. F. Corbett was the owner.

In the negotiations for the purchase in 1872, it was agreed that the purchase-money for the collieries should be £35,000, to be paid by the company partly in money and partly in shares; and it was agreed between Corbett and J. F. Johnson, the promoter of the company, that Johnson and his nominees should receive out of the purchase-money £10,000 for its promotion, which sum was subsequently paid to them.

At that time Osman Barrett had a mortgage on the collieries for £7,000, and it was agreed that he should join in the conveyance and take a fresh mortgage for the same amount. The property was accordingly conveyed to the trustees of the company and a fresh mortgage executed.

Barrett was informed by Corbett at the time of these transactions of the payment of the said sum of £10,000, but he was not then a shareholder in the company nor one of the proposed directors. He afterwards qualified and in December 1875 he became a director, but he did not take any steps towards recovering for the company the said sum of £10,000.

In 1877 an order was made for winding up the company, and the liquidator applied to make Johnson and his nominees liable to repay to the company the said sum, and also to make Barrett liable for his alleged misfeasance in not taking steps to recover the money of the payment of which he was cognisant.

JESSEL M.R.: I am quite clear about this case. One must be very careful in administering the law of joint stock companies not to press so hardly on honest directors as to make them liable for these constructive defaults, the only effect of which would be to deter all men of any property, and perhaps all men who have any character to lose, from becoming directors of companies at all. On the one hand, I think the Court should do its utmost to bring fraudulent directors to account, and, on the other hand, should also do its best to allow honest men to act reasonably as directors.

Wilful default no doubt includes the case of a trustee neglecting to sue, though he might by suing earlier have recovered a trust fund —in that case he is made liable for want of due diligence in his trust. But I think directors are not liable on the same principle. Directors have sometimes been called trustees, or commercial trustees, and sometimes they have been called managing partners, it does not much matter what you call them so long as you understand what their true position is, which is that they are really commercial men managing a trading concern for the benefit of themselves and of all the other shareholders in it. They are bound, no doubt, to use reasonable diligence having regard to their position, though probably an ordinary director, who only attends at the board occasionally, cannot be expected to devote as much time and attention to the business as the sole managing partner of an ordinary partnership, but they are bound to use fair and reasonable diligence in the management of their company's affairs, and to act honestly.

But where without fraud and without dishonesty they have omitted to get in a debt due to the company by not suing within time, or because the man was solvent at one moment and became insolvent at another, I am of opinion that it by no means follows as a matter of course, as it might in the case of ordinary trustees of trust funds or of a trust debt, that they are to be made liable. Traders have a discretion as to whether they shall sue their customers, a discretion which is not vested in the trustee of a debt under a settlement.

. . . Such a case as this has, in my opinion, no direct relation to the rule which makes it incumbent on a trustee to sue a debtor at once under pain of having the liability for the debt afterwards thrown upon him, on the ground that if he had sued he could have got the money. . . . [I]n my opinion no such liability attaches to directors of joint stock companies. They must, as ordinary managing partners of a trading concern, be allowed a discretion, and not be too much interfered with by the Court, or have inquiries made by the Court as to whether the debtor could have paid at a particular moment a larger or a smaller amount if he had been sued. So much with regard to ordinary debts.

Again, directors are called trustees. They are no doubt trustees of assets which have come into their hands, or which are under their control, but they are not trustees of a debt due to the company. The company is the creditor, and, as I said before, they are only the managing partners. In my opinion it is extravagant to call them trustees of a debt when it has not been received. You may of course have an actual trust of a debt, as . . . where trustees have assigned to them a debt to get in, but that is not the case with directors of a company. A director is the managing partner of the concern, and although a debt is due to the concern I do not think it is right to call him a trustee of that debt which remains unpaid, though his liability in respect of it may in certain cases and in some respects be analogous to the liability of a trustee. So much for the question of unpaid debts.

The next point is this: does that reasoning which applies to a debt apply to a demand of this kind, which is a liability, though not strictly a debt? I do not think it does. There are totally different considerations applicable to this kind of demand or liability from those applicable to an uncontested debt.

Analogy or illustration is sometimes useful. In the case of trustees newly appointed, their liability extends to seeing that they get the trust funds into their hands; but did anybody ever imagine that their liability extended beyond that, or that they are bound to inquire into all the dealings with the trust fund from the origin of the trust, and to pursue every past trustee who might by any means whatever have become liable to pay more than the actual trust funds? . . .

Now, to apply these observations to the actual case before me, I must first of all consider what the position of the Respondent Barrett was here, and I find that he was mortgagee of the vendor . . . for some £7,000. The vendor had a mine worth, to sell, £25,000. A company was formed to buy the mine, and the promoters of the company induced the vendor to do what was no doubt very wrong, and indeed amounted to a fraud on the company, namely, to add nominally £10,000 to the purchase price, so as to make the actual purchase price to the company £35,000 instead of £25,000, so that the company was to pay to the vendor £35,000 in money and shares, and the directors were to divide the plunder or extra sum between themselves and the promoters. Of course as regards all these promoters . . . there can be no question of their liability for what was no doubt a gross fraud. The vendor got nothing by it except this, that he got £25,000 for his mine, which probably was not very readily saleable at that price, and no doubt, therefore, he had an interest in the matter to that extent. But still we must not forget that the company has affirmed the sale for £25,000, taking away the profits of the directors, and it cannot be possible, therefore, for the liquidator to say now that it was not a good sale to the extent of £25,000.

Now, Mr. Barrett as mortgagee knew of the transaction, and he got paid to some extent, not out of the £10,000, because he got none of that, but out of the £25,000. Therefore he did not receive any part of the plunder, and he is not responsible on that ground. . . . But the ground on which it is sought to make Mr. Barrett liable is this:

The transaction took place in 1872, and he became a director of the company in December, 1875. In 1877 the company went into liquidation, and it is said that, having knowledge when he was appointed a director of the company of the facts I have mentioned, it was his duty to communicate that knowledge, acquired by him three years and a quarter before he became a director, to the shareholders of the company; and that it was also his duty to institute, or to endeavour to institute, proceedings against the promoters, in order to obtain the return of this £10,000 of which the company had been defrauded.

And then it is said that, because he did not communicate to the shareholders the knowledge he had acquired previously to becoming a director, and because he took no steps as a director of the company to institute proceedings against the promoters, he is now to be made liable for this £10,000 under the doctrine of wilful default. . . .

In the first place, I have never heard that it has been held to be the duty of a director to communicate to his shareholders knowledge acquired by him years before, as to misconduct with reference to the affairs of the company on the part of other persons for which they may be still liable. . . .

I put a case which perhaps may sound ridiculous, but when you have extravagant propositions to deal with, ridiculous illustrations are really not the worst mode of meeting propositions of such a character. Suppose the case of a company dealing with a man for butter, and one of the directors of the company had, three years before he became a director, purchased the butterman's business, and had discovered that that butterman had been in the habit of supplying the company for some years, and had also discovered from the books of his vendor that he had supplied the company with butter at short weight, and had already defrauded the company of £1,000— he himself, of course, not continuing the system—would he, under such circumstances, be liable to the company for not disclosing to the shareholders that he had ascertained that this retired butterman had in this way defrauded the company of £1,000, for which he or his estate might be made liable? It would be obviously, to my mind, an extravagant proposition that that director could be made liable for not disclosing the knowledge so acquired by him at so long a period before he became a director of the company.

. . . [T]his is a case where the man derived no benefit whatever from the frauds of the promoters. It appears to me that I should not be expounding or applying the law, but that I should be making new law, if I were to hold directors liable for withholding their knowledge from shareholders under such circumstances.

Then is Mr. Barrett liable in this case for not taking proceedings? . . . I do not think it is for this Court to say that a man is to be made liable simply because he does not choose to sue, or does not take steps to sue under such circumstances.

That being so, I think he is not under any legal liability at all; but even if he were, he could not be considered liable for the whole £10,000; he could only be held liable for what was lost by his not suing. . . . I am not at all satisfied that there was anything really lost by their not suing, and therefore the notion that this gentleman is to be made liable on that ground is entirely unreasonable.

Then the next question is, whether the 165th section of the Act [now S.333 *Companies Act, 1948*] applies to such a case as this. . . . Now Mr. Barrett is not liable under the first part of the section at all. It was not money in his hands; he is not liable for money of the company, because the money had gone long ago, and, therefore, if he is liable at all, it is for misfeasance or breach of trust in relation to the company, and misfeasance or breach of trust means here either non-communication of his knowledge to the shareholders or not endeavouring to institute proceedings. . . .

Of course, if I had arrived at the opinion that the man was liable as for a breach of trust, I have jurisdiction under that clause [S.333 (1)] to make him pay, but it must be a liability for breach of trust or under the word "misfeasance." But I should be very sorry to hold that under those words I have a summary jurisdiction to inquire whether a man had or had not properly exercised his discretion as a director as to suing or not suing a debtor to the company, even where the debt was not disputed, and *a fortiori* where it is a demand of this kind. I do not think the section . . . could have been meant to apply to such a case as I have now before me. . . .

I do not think myself that the section applies to anything but what I may call fairly plain and ordinary cases of misconduct, . . . or that it was intended to go beyond what was the settled law on the subject before the statute was passed, so as to make that a case of misfeasance or breach of trust which would not have rendered a man liable as a trustee before the passing of the Act.

The summons as against Barrett will be dismissed.

Re Cape Breton Company. (1885) 29 Ch.D. 795

When a director sells to the company, without disclosing his profit on the transaction, property which he acquired before he became in a fiduciary relation towards it, the sole remedy available to the company is rescission of the contract.

In April 1871 six persons, of whom Fenn was one, purchased three coal areas in Nova Scotia for £5,500, and the legal estate was vested in Gisborne as a trustee for them, the trust not being disclosed.

In November 1873 the Cape Breton Company was formed for the purpose of acquiring the property of three previously existing companies, and also the coal areas in question. Fenn was one of the first directors of this company. In December 1873 Gisborne agreed to sell these coal areas to the company for £42,000, to be paid £12,000 in cash and £30,000 in fully paid-up £10 shares. Fenn was present at the meeting of the directors at which the seal of the company was affixed to the agreement, but did not disclose the fact, nor did his co-directors know, that he was a part owner of the property.

The sale was completed, and Fenn received for himself and his partner, who was another of the six owners, £4,525 in cash, and 810 shares.

In 1875 an order was made to wind up the company. In 1878, by which time the shareholders knew of Fenn's interest in the property, a meeting of contributories was called at which two rival schemes were brought forward, one for repudiating the purchase of the coal areas, the other for adopting the purchase and selling the property. The former scheme was negatived and the latter adopted and confirmed by the Court. Accordingly, in 1880 these coal areas along with the other property of the company were sold by the liquidator for £14,500, the three areas selling for much less than the company had given.

After this, the appellant, who was one of the contributories, took out a summons under S.165 of the *Companies Act*, 1862 (*now S.333 of the Companies Act, 1948*) to make Fenn liable for misfeasance as a director in allowing the seal of the company to be affixed to the agreement of December 1873.

PEARSON J. dismissed the summons, holding that though the company would have been entitled to rescind the contract, yet as rescission had become impossible no relief could be given against Fenn; that as Fenn when he acquired his interest in the property was not a trustee for the company, he could not be treated as having purchased on behalf of the company at the price he gave, and therefore was not chargeable with the difference between the price at which he bought and the price paid by the company, and that he could not be charged with the difference between the price paid by the company and the value of the property when the company bought it, as this would be making a new contract between the parties.

From this decision an appeal was brought, and the case accordingly came before the Court of Appeal.

COTTON L.J.: . . . I need not go into the terms of S.165, for the effect of that section was settled long ago. Mr. Cookson [*leading counsel for the appellant*], if I rightly understood him, put his case under that section too high, as though it gave him some new right. His junior took what I think is the correct view, that it only gives a summary method of enforcing rights which exist independently of that section, but does not create any new right.

. . . At the time when Mr. Fenn acquired an interest in these properties he was not in any way acting as a director of the Cape Breton Company, and that company was not formed until long after he had acquired his interest. Nor was it suggested that he was in such a position that he could when the company was formed be considered as being a trustee of these properties for the company which was in the course of formation.

. . . The property unfortunately sold for very much less than had been given for it by the company. On the 6th of December, 1882, this summons was taken out in order to recover from Mr. Fenn either the whole amount which had been given by the company for the property, or to recover the profit which it was said he had made by the transaction.

In the first place, the application was treated by the Appellant as an action for damages, because that was the only way in which the whole amount of purchase-money could be recovered. . . . This is the case of a shareholder who says he represents the company, and in fact is bringing an action for damages on behalf of the company. . . . [I]n my opinion such an action could not be maintained. There could be no action at law, and it cannot be considered that a contributory can acquire a right to bring in substance such an action, by taking out a summons under S.165. . . . [A]ssuming that the whole circumstances were not in fact known to the board and to the company at the time of the purchase, the company, if so minded, might have set aside this purchase altogether. Where a trustee, purchasing on behalf of his cestui que trust, purchases his own estate without disclosing his own interest in it, the cestui que trust, when he discovers the fact, may, if he pleases, set aside the contract altogether, but then he must return that which has been purchased. The same rule applies, in the case of a purchase by a director on behalf of a company, of property in which he has any interest: if the company repudiates the contract, the property must be returned. In this case a return of the property is impossible after what was done in 1878. The resolution of the shareholders to sell the property was passed in 1878, and the company having determined to adopt, and not to set aside, this contract of purchase, it is too late now to seek to do so.

Then it was said that if there can be no action for damages yet that this shareholder, on behalf of the company, is entitled to get the difference between what was paid by Mr. Fenn for his share of the property and his share of the purchase-money which he got. No authority has been cited for that proposition. Numerous cases have been brought before the Court, but none of them are like the present, because, in all the cases where relief was given, the case was that of a trustee or a director who had sold to his cestuis que trust, the company, at an enhanced price, property which he had acquired when he was a trustee or a director, and he was held to be liable for the difference on the ground that at the time he acquired his interest in the property he was in the position of a trustee. The principle of those cases is very clear. It is this, that having bought the property while he was a director, and so in the position of a trustee for the company, and having afterwards made it over to the company without disclosing his interest, he was stopped from saying that he originally bought the property on his own behalf, or otherwise than for and on behalf of the company. When, therefore, he pays a large additional sum of money out of the coffers of the company for the property, he is putting into his own pocket a sum of money by way of purchase-money paid by the company for that which was already their own. . . . How, then, can Mr. Fenn be made answerable for what is called 'the profit, if at the time when he acquired the property he was not trustee for the company, or in any fiduciary position towards the company. . . . What is really profit made by a trustee? It is the difference between the value of the property at the time of the purchase being made by the company, and the price which the company gave. It is not the difference between the price that the trustee gave when he was in no way a trustee for the company and that which he got from the company. . . . The company have, with the knowledge of the facts, determined to hold the property which they only acquired by agreeing to pay a certain price, and although they may have been entitled to set that agreement aside, yet I think that as they, with knowledge of all the facts, elected to retain the property, it would be wrong to require the trustee to hand over to them that money which was the only consideration upon which he agreed to give the property.

. . . [T]here is no decision which in any way favours the view of the Appellant. His counsel have been unable to refer to any decided case in which where an agent has bought his own property on behalf of his principal, that principal has been allowed to retain the property and charge the agent with the difference between the price the agent gave for it, and the price at which he sold it to his principal. This appeal therefore fails.

BOWEN L.J. dissented, saying that he was unable to follow the decision of PEARSON J.

FRY L.J.: The facts of the present case appear to me to amount shortly to these:—that Mr. Fenn was the agent of the company to purchase a specific property in which, before the commencement of his agency, he had acquired an interest, that Mr. Fenn did purchase it for the company without disclosing to the company his interest in the property, and that after the purchase the facts were fully disclosed to the company, and, with the knowledge so acquired, the company elected to retain the property. Upon that state of facts arises the question, whether Mr. Fenn was liable to the company for any sum, by reason of fraud or breach of trust or duty.

Now, let me in the first place say what this case is not. This case is not the case of an agent who, after he has accepted the agency, has acquired property, the purchase of which was within the scope of his agency, and then has resold that property to his principal at a larger sum, in which case it is obvious that the principal may say that the original purchase by the agent at a smaller price was a purchase on behalf of the principal. Nor is this the case of a man who accepts an agency to buy some article in the market, and then sells to his principal his own goods, in which case it may be that the agent is liable for not performing his agency by purchasing in the market, supposing it was possible for him so to do. This case is distinguished from that, by there being a direction to buy a specific property. Nor, again, is this the case of an agent who, by any subsequent acts of his own, has rendered the rescission of the contract by his principal impossible. I express no opinion whether or no, in that case, the principal would have a right against the agent, notwithstanding the non-rescission of the contract. This is a case in which the agent, before accepting the agency, had an interest in the property, and during the agency sold that property to his principal without disclosing his interest. That in such a case the principal would have a right to rescind there can be no doubt. The option which the principal had, has in this case been exercised by confirming the contract with knowledge of the facts, and the question is whether, after that affirmance, the agent is liable in any sum to his principal. There is no authority which determines this point, and it, therefore, is to be determined upon principle.

. . . I think that the case is one in which the adoption of the contract by the principal puts an end, and ought to put an end, to any further rights against the agent. It appears to me that to allow the principal to affirm the contract, and after the affirmance to claim, not only to retain the property, but to get the difference between the price at which it was bought and some other price, is, however you may state it, and however you may turn the proposition about, to enable the principal, against the will of his agent, to enter into a new contract with the agent, a thing which is plainly impossible, or else it is an attempt on the part of the principal to confiscate the property of his agent on some ground which, I confess, I do not understand.

It is said that, notwithstanding the ratification of the contract, the principal may claim some profits from the agent because those profits were made surreptitiously or clandestinely. It appears to me that the answer to that is this, that whatever the profits are, and however they are to be measured, those profits result, not from the original contract, but from the affirmance of the contract by the principal, and that, therefore, the profits which are made by the agent are neither clandestine nor surreptitious. I can conceive two possible claims being made. The one would be on the view that the profits were the difference between the purchasing and the selling price in the hands of the agent, but . . . that cannot possibly be the measure of the claim of the principal, because at the date when the agent purchased he was not the agent of the principal, and the principal, therefore, had no right to go back to that date and fix it as the time at which he acquired a right to retain the property at the price paid for it by the agent. The other claim would be on the view that the profits were the difference between the real value, or the market value, if a market value exist, and the actual price at which the property was sold by the agent to the principal. I think the principal cannot claim that difference, because it appears to me that in such a case as this, where the principal had no right to claim the property as having been purchased on his behalf at the smaller price, the voluntary ratification of the purchase by the principal is equivalent for this purpose to a new sale by the agent to the principal after the relation between them had ceased, and that it is only in consequence of that ratification or adoption that any profits remain in the hands of the agent. In other words, therefore, I think it is not a case of profits made clandestinely or surreptitiously, because those profits have not arisen from the original transaction alone but from the adoption of it by the principal. I think, therefore, that the decision of PEARSON J. is right, and that this appeal must be dismissed.

The decision of PEARSON J. and the Court of Appeal was affirmed in the House of Lords sub. nom. *Cavendish-Bentinck* v. *Fenn* (1887) 12 A.C. 652, but on different grounds—namely, insufficiency of the evidence.

Percival *v.* Wright. [1902] 2 Ch. 421

Directors must act bona fide *in the interests of the company, but are not in a fiduciary position towards individual shareholders.*

The plaintiffs were the joint registered owners of 253 shares of £10 each (with £9 8s. paid up) in a colliery company called Nixon's Navigation Company, Limited. The objects of the company as defined by the memorandum of association included the disposal by sale of all or any of the company's property. The board of directors were empowered to exercise all powers not declared to be exercisable by general meetings; but no sale of the company's collieries could be made without the sanction of a special resolution.

The shares of the company, which were in few hands and were transferable only with the approval of the board of directors, had no market price and were not quoted on the stock exchange.

On 8th October 1900 the plaintiffs' solicitors wrote to the secretary of the company asking if he knew of anyone disposed to purchase shares. On 15th October 1900, in answer to the secretary's inquiry as to what price they were prepared to accept, the plaintiffs' solicitors wrote stating that the plaintiffs would be disposed to entertain offers of £12 5s. per share. This price was based on a valuation which the plaintiffs had obtained from independent valuers some months previously.

On 17th October 1900 the chairman of the company wrote to the plaintiffs' solicitors stating that their letter of 15th October had been handed to him, and that he would take the shares at £12 5s.

On 20th October 1900, the plaintiffs' solicitors having taken a fresh valuation, replied that the plaintiffs were prepared to accept £12 10s. per share. On 22nd October 1900 the chairman wrote accepting that offer and stating that the shares would be divided into three lots. On 24th October the chairman wrote stating that eighty-five shares were to be transferred to himself, and eighty-four shares apiece to two other named directors. The transfers having been approved by the board, the transaction was completed.

The plaintiffs subsequently discovered that, prior to and during their own negotiations for sale, the chairman and the board were being approached by one Holden with a view to the purchase of the entire undertaking of the company, which Holden wished to re-sell at a profit to a new company. Various prices were successively suggested by Holden, all of which represented considerably over £12 10s. per share; but no firm offer was ever made which the board could lay before the shareholders, and the negotiations ultimately proved abortive.

The plaintiffs brought an action against the chairman and the two other purchasing directors, asking to have the sale set aside on the ground that the defendants as directors ought to have disclosed the negotiations with Holden when treating for the purchase of the plaintiffs' shares.

SWINFEN EADY J.: . . . Directors must dispose of their company's shares on the best terms obtainable, and must not allot them to themselves or their friends at a lower price in order to obtain a personal benefit. They must act *bona fide* in the interest of the company.

The plaintiffs' contention in the present case goes far beyond this. It is urged that the directors hold a fiduciary position as trustees for the individual shareholders, and that, where negotiations for sale of the undertaking are on foot, they are in the position of trustees for sale. The plaintiffs admitted that this fiduciary position did not stand in the way of any dealing between a director and a shareholder before the question of sale of the undertaking had arisen, but contended that as soon as that question arose the position was altered. No authority was cited for that proposition, and I am unable to adopt the view that any line should be drawn at that point. It is contended that a shareholder knows that the directors are managing the business of the company in the ordinary course of management, and impliedly releases them from any obligation to disclose any information so acquired. That is to say, a director purchasing shares need not disclose a large casual profit, the discovery of a new vein, or the prospect of a good dividend in the immediate future, and similarly a director selling shares need not disclose losses, these being merely incidents in the ordinary course of management. But it is urged that, as soon as negotiations for the sale of the undertaking are on foot, the position is altered. Why? The true rule is that a shareholder is fixed with knowledge of all the directors' powers, and has no more reason to assume that they are not negotiating a sale of the undertaking than to assume that they are not exercising any other power. It was strenuously urged that, though incorporation affected the relations of the shareholders to the external world, the company thereby becoming a distinct entity, the position of the shareholders *inter se* was not affected, and was the same as that of partners or shareholders in an unincorporated company. I am unable to adopt that view. I am therefore of opinion that the purchasing directors were under no obligation to disclose to their vendor shareholders the negotiations which ultimately proved abortive. The contrary view would place directors in a most invidious position, as they could not buy or sell shares without disclosing negotiations, a premature disclosure of which might well be against the best interests of the company. I am of opinion that directors are not in that position.

There is no question of unfair dealing in this case. The directors did not approach the shareholders with the view of obtaining their shares. The shareholders approached the

directors, and named the price at which they were desirous of
selling. The plaintiff's case wholly fails. . . .

Regal (Hastings), Ltd. *v.* Gulliver and Others. [1967] 2 A.C. 134

*The equitable rule that a director who uses his fiduciary position
and knowledge to make a profit is liable to account for that profit
to the company does not depend on fraud, or on whether the
profit would otherwise have gone to the company, or on whether
the company was damaged or benefited by his action. The
liability arises from the mere fact that a profit was made.*

Regal (Hastings) Ltd., the appellant company, owned a
cinema in Hastings. With a view to selling it as a going
concern, they wished to acquire two other cinemas called
the Elite and the De Luxe, and for this purpose they formed
a subsidiary company, Hastings Amalgamated Cinemas,
Ltd., the directors of which were the same as those of Regal
with the addition of Mr. Garton, the solicitor to Regal.

They were offered a lease of the two cinemas, but the
landlord required a guarantee of the rent by the directors
unless Hastings Amalgamated Cinemas had a paid-up
capital of £5,000. The directors were unwilling to provide
a guarantee, so the required £5,000 capital was subscribed
as follows: Regal took up 2,000 £1 shares at par, the most
it could provide; the chairman of the directors, Mr.
Gulliver, found three other persons who took up 500 £1
shares between them; the remaining £2,500 was found by
the subscription for 500 shares each by Mr. Garton and the
four other directors.

The transaction was ultimately carried through, not by
the sale of the property as a going concern, but by the sale
of all the shares in both Regal and Hastings Amalgamated
Cinemas to a purchaser, as a result of which Regal came
under the management of a new board of directors.

The new board issued a writ against all six of the directors of Hastings Amalgamated Cinemas, claiming recovery
of the sum of £8,412 10*s*., being the profit made by these
directors on the sale of the 3,000 shares in Hastings Amal-

gamated Cinemas for which they had between them subscribed at par. It was found as a fact that all the defendants had acted *bona fide*.

WROTTESLEY J. gave judgment for the defendants and Regal accordingly appealed. The Court of Appeal dismissed the appeal. Regal appealed to the House of Lords.

VISCOUNT SANKEY: . . . In my view, the respondents were in a fiduciary position and their liability to account does not depend upon proof of *mala fides*. The general rule of equity is that no one who has duties of a fiduciary nature to perform is allowed to enter into engagements in which he has or can have a personal interest conflicting with the interests of those whom he is bound to protect. If he holds any property so acquired as trustee, he is bound to account for it to his *cestui que trust*. The earlier cases are concerned with trusts of specific property: *Keech* v. *Sandford*. . . . The rule, however, applies to agents, as, for example, solicitors and directors, when acting in a fiduciary capacity.

. . . I will deal first with the respondents, other than Gulliver and Garton. . . . It was . . . argued that it would have been a breach of trust for the respondents, as directors of Regal, to have invested more than £2,000 of Regal's money in Amalgamated, and that the transaction would never have been carried through if they had not themselves put up the other £3,000. Be it so, but it is impossible to maintain that, because it would have been a breach of trust to advance more than £2,000 from Regal and that the only way to finance the matter was for the directors to advance the balance themselves, a situation arose which brought the respondents outside the general rule and permitted them to retain the profits which accrued to them from the action they took. At all material times they were directors and in a fiduciary position, and they used and acted upon their exclusive knowledge acquired as such directors. They framed resolutions by which they made a profit for themselves. They sought no authority from the company to do so, and, by reason of their position and actions, they made large profits for which, in my view, they are liable to account to the company.

I now pass to the cases of Gulliver and Garton. . . . Gulliver's case is that he did not take any shares and did not make any profit by selling them. . . . He did, however, find subscribers. . . . The shares were held by them on their own account. When the shares were sold, the moneys went to them, and no part of the moneys went into Gulliver's pocket. . . . In these circumstances, . . . it is clear that he made no profits for which he is liable to account. The case made against him rightly fails, and the appeal against the decision in his favour should be dismissed.

Garton's case is that in taking the shares he acted with the knowledge and consent of Regal, and that consequently he comes within the exception to the general rule as to the liability of the person acting in a fiduciary position to account for profits. . . . It is clear that he took the shares with the full knowledge and consent of Regal and that he is not liable to account for profits made on their sale. The appeal against the decision in his favour should be dismissed.

LORD RUSSELL OF KILLOWEN: . . . The rule of equity which insists on those, who by use of a fiduciary position make a profit, being liable to account for that profit, in no way depends on fraud, or absence of *bona fides*; or upon such questions or considerations as whether the profit would or should otherwise have gone to the plaintiff, or whether the profiteer was under a duty to obtain the source of the profit for the plaintiff, or whether he took a risk or acted as he did for the benefit of the plaintiff, or whether the plaintiff has in fact been damaged or benefited by his action. The liability arises from the mere fact of a profit having . . . been made. The profiteer, however honest and well-intentioned, cannot escape the risk of being called upon to account. . . .

My Lords, I have no hesitation in coming to the conclusion, upon the facts of this case, that these shares, when acquired by the directors, were acquired by reason, and only by reason of the fact that they were directors of Regal, and in the course of their execution of that office.

. . . Directors of a limited company are the creatures of

statute and occupy a position peculiar to themselves. In some respects they resemble trustees, in others they do not. In some respects they resemble agents, in others they do not. In some respects they resemble managing partners, in others they do not. . . .

In the result, I am of opinion that the directors standing in a fiduciary relationship to Regal in regard to the exercise of their powers as directors, and having obtained these shares by reason and only by reason of the fact that they were directors of Regal and in the course of the execution of that office, are accountable for the profits which they have made out of them. . . . They could, had they wished, have protected themselves by a resolution (either antecedent or subsequent) of the Regal share-holders in general meeting. In default of such approval, the liability to account must remain. . . .

The case of the respondent Gulliver, however, requires some further consideration. . . . Gulliver . . . made no profit for which he is accountable. As regards Gulliver, this appeal should, in my opinion, be dismissed.

There remains to consider the case of Garton. He stands on a different footing from the other respondents in that he was not a director of Regal. He was Regal's legal adviser; but, in my opinion, he has a short but effective answer to the plain-tiffs' claim. He was requested by the Regal directors to apply for 500 shares. . . . In law his action, which has resulted in a profit, was taken at the request of Regal, and I know of no principle or authority which would justify a decision that a solicitor must account for profit resulting from a transaction which he has entered into on his own behalf, not merely with the consent, but at the request of his client.

LORD MACMILLAN: . . . The issue, as it was formulated before your Lordships, was not whether the directors of Regal (Hastings), Ltd., had acted in bad faith. Their *bona fides* was not questioned. Nor was it whether they had acted in breach of their duty. They were not said to have done anything wrong. The sole ground on which it was sought to render them accountable was that, being directors of the plaintiff company and therefore in a fiduciary relation to it, they entered in the course of their management into a transaction in which they utilised the position and knowledge possessed by them in virtue of their office as directors, and that the transaction resulted in a profit to themselves. The point was not whether the directors had a duty to acquire the shares in question for the company and failed in that duty. They had no such duty. We must take it that they entered into the transaction lawfully, in good faith and indeed avowedly in the interests of the company. However, that does not absolve them from accountability for any profit which they made, if it was by reason and in virtue of their fiduciary office as directors that they entered into the transaction. . . .

The issue thus becomes one of fact. The plaintiff company has to establish two things: (*i*) that what the directors did was so related to the affairs of the company that it can properly be said to have been done in the course of their management and in utilisation of their opportunities and special knowledge as directors; and (*ii*) that what they did resulted in a profit to themselves. The first of these propositions is clearly established. . . . The second proposition is admitted, except in the case of Gulliver, in whose case I agree that . . . he is not proved to have made any profit personally. The conditions are, therefore, in my opinion, present which preclude the four directors who made a personal profit by the transaction from retaining such profit.

The position of the respondent Garton is quite different. He was the solicitor of the plaintiff company and in no sense a trustee for it. . . . He subscribed for his shares not only with the knowledge, but at the express request, of his clients, and I know of no principle on which he could be held accountable to them for any resultant profit to himself.

Lord Wright and Lord Porter were of the same opinion.

Bamford and Another v. Bamford and Others. [1970] Ch. 212

Where directors do an act which is both intra vires *the company and within their powers under the articles, but for an improper motive and so in breach of their general duty to act* bona fide *in the interests of the company, the company in general meeting may ratify it.*

The defendant company, Bamfords Ltd., was a public company incorporated in 1916 with an authorised capital of £1,000,000 divided into 5,000,000 shares of 4s. each, of which 4,500,000 were issued. By clause 12 of its articles the power to allot the unissued shares was vested in the directors of the company.

The company was based in Uttoxeter in the County of Stafford and was a well-known manufacturer of agricultural implements. Large shareholdings in the company were held by members of the Bamford family. The plaintiffs, Rupert Cyril Bamford and Anthony Paul Bamford, were shareholders in the company. Rupert Bamford was also prior to 20th November 1967 a director of the company, but he resigned on that day after the then other directors, the first three defendants, Henry Vincent Bamford, Richard Hawthorn Bamford and John George Bamford (who were also shareholders) had resolved, pursuant to article 12, to allot the remaining 500,000 unissued shares to Frederick H. Burgess Ltd. at par. Rupert Bamford thought that that issue was inappropriate at that time.

There had been proposals in 1966 by J. C. Bamford (Excavators) Ltd., in which company a cousin of the above members of the Bamford family had a controlling interest, to amalgamate its business, which was manufacturing earth moving equipment, with the agricultural implements business of Bamfords Ltd. Those proposals had not been favourably received by the directors of Bamfords Ltd. Early in November 1967 J. C. Bamford (Excavators) Ltd. made a bid to take over the shares of Bamfords Ltd. at a price of 12s. per share. On 20th November 1967 the directors allotted the 500,000 unissued shares in the company to Frederick H. Burgess Ltd.

at par payable in full on application. The allottee was a principal distributor of the products of Bamfords Ltd., and the directors considered that it would be advantageous for the allottee to have a direct stake in the company.

On 21st November 1967 the plaintiffs (the minority shareholders) issued a writ against the first three defendants, the allottee, and the company, claiming, *inter alia*, a declaration that the allotment was invalid and of no effect on the ground that the directors had made it in bad faith and not *bona fide* in the interests of the company in that it was made as a tactical move to block the takeover bid made by J. C. Bamford (Excavators) Ltd.

As a counter to that writ the directors gave notice convening a general meeting of the shareholders of the company for 15th December 1967, to consider, and, if thought fit, to pass a resolution approving and ratifying the allotment.

On 1st December 1967 the plaintiffs issued a second writ against the company, the first three defendants, Hubert Frederick Burgess and Graham Arthur Rayden, who had since joined the board of the company as directors, claiming, *inter alia*, an injunction restraining the company and the directors from holding the proposed meeting and a declaration that any resolution passed at the proposed meeting would be a nullity.

Application was made for an interlocutory injunction to restrain the holding of the meeting, but that was refused and the meeting was duly held. Over 1,000 of the 2,000 or so shareholders in the company attended the meeting and on a show of hands, 292 were in favour of the allotment and some 800 against it. On a poll there was a substantial majority of votes in favour of the resolution, which was accordingly passed. The 500,000 shares in question were not voted.

The two actions were then consolidated. At the suggestion of the directors the parties agreed that a preliminary point of law should be tried first, since if the directors succeeded on that point, it would dispose of the action. The preliminary point was whether, assuming that the allotment was not made *bona fide* in the interests of the company, it was capable of being ratified and approved by an ordinary resolution of a general meeting.

On the trial of this preliminary point of law, PLOWMAN J. held that it was, and that accordingly the allotment was valid, even if the directors had acted in bad faith and from an improper motive in making it.

He dismissed the action, whereupon the plaintiffs appealed and the case accordingly came before the Court of Appeal.

HARMAN L.J.: . . . It is trite law, I had thought, that if directors do acts, as they do every day, especially in private companies, which, perhaps because there is no quorum, or because their appointment was defective, or because sometimes there are no directors properly appointed at all, or because they are actuated by improper motives, they go on doing for years, carrying on the business of the company in the way in which, if properly constituted, they should carry it on, and then they find that everything has been so to speak wrongly done because it was not done by a proper board, such directors can, by making a full and frank disclosure and calling together the general body of the shareholders, obtain absolution and forgiveness of their sins; and provided the acts are not *ultra vires* the company as a whole everything will go on as if it had been done all right from the beginning. I cannot believe that that is not a commonplace of company law. It is done every day. Of course, if the majority of the general meeting will not forgive and approve, the directors must pay for it. . . .

So it seems to me here that these directors . . . made this allotment in breach of their duty—*mala fide*, as it is said. They made it with an eye primarily on the exigencies of the take-over war and not with a single eye to the benefit of the company, and, therefore, it is a bad allotment. But it *is* an allotment. There is no doubt that the directors had power to allot these shares. There is no doubt that they did allot them. There is no doubt that the allottees are on the register and are for all purposes members of the company. The only question is whether the allotment, having been made, as one must assume, in bad faith, is voidable and can be avoided at the instance of the company—at their instance only and of no one else, because the wrong, if wrong it be, is a wrong done to the company. If that be right, the company, which had the right to recall the allotment, has also the right to approve of it and forgive it; and I see no difficulty at all in supposing that the ratification by the decision of December 15 in the general meeting of the company was a perfectly good "whitewash" of that which up to that time was a voidable transaction. And that is the end of the matter. . . . I would dismiss this appeal.

RUSSELL L.J.: . . . The question of law is whether the allotment . . . was capable of being effectively ratified and/or approved by an ordinary resolution of the company in general meeting.

There is no doubt that the allotment . . . would be voidable as against the allottee without such a resolution, at least if the allottee was aware of the improper purpose, and that the directors could be sued in appropriate proceedings for misfeasance. But unless the allotment is avoided in proceedings it is effective. The question basically is whether the company in general meeting can waive the voidability. . . .

. . . In truth the allotment of shares by directors not *bona fide* in the interests of the company is not an act outside the articles; it is an act within the articles, but in breach of the general duty laid on them by their office as directors to act in all matters committed to them *bona fide* in the interests of the company.

It is true that the point before us is not an objection to the proceedings on *Foss* v. *Harbottle* grounds. But it seems to me to march in step with the principles that underlie the rule in that case. None of the factors that admit exceptions to that rule appear to exist here. The harm done by the assumed improperly motivated allotment is a harm done to the company, of which only the company can complain. It would be for the company by ordinary resolution to decide whether or not to proceed against the directors for compensation for misfeasance. Equally, assuming that the allottee could not rely upon *Royal British Bank* v. *Turquand* it would be for the company to decide whether to institute proceedings to avoid the voidable allotment: and again this decision would be one

for the company in general meeting to decide by ordinary resolution. . . .
. . . I also would dismiss the appeal.

KARMINSKI L.J.: I agree, and have nothing to add.

Industrial Development Consultants, Ltd. *v.* Cooley. [1972] 1 W.L.R. 443

Where a person puts himself in a position in which his fiduciary duty and his interests conflict, he must account to those to whom he owed that duty for any profit made, even if it could never have been obtained by those persons themselves.

The defendant, Neville Cooley, was an architect of considerable distinction. In 1967 he met Mr. Hicks, the chairman and managing director of a group of companies which included the plaintiff company, Industrial Development Consultants, Ltd. Mr. Hicks and Mr. Cooley agreed that the latter should be appointed managing director of the plaintiff company and, although no written agreement was ever signed, Mr. Cooley in fact became managing director with effect from February 1968.

The same month he entered into correspondence with the Eastern Gas Board regarding the design and construction of new depots for that Board by the plaintiff company. His proposals on behalf of the company were rejected by the Board.

In May 1969 the new deputy chairman of the Eastern Gas Board, Mr. Smettom, made an approach to Mr. Cooley in a private capacity regarding the same matter, and the two men met on 13th June. Mr. Cooley realised that if he could release himself from his obligations to the plaintiff company, he stood a good chance of getting a valuable contract from the Board for his own benefit.

On 16th June 1969 Mr. Cooley went to Mr. Hicks and falsely represented that his health prevented him from carrying on as managing director. Mr. Hicks, believing him seriously ill, released him as from 1st August 1969. Mr. Cooley then registered on the Business Names Register a business of consultancy and design under the name of "Design Group for Industry," giving his private address

and stating the date of starting business as 8th June 1969.
By a letter of 17th June he told Mr. Smettom, who had
inquired about his involvement with the plaintiff company,
that he had discussed the matter with Mr. Hicks, who
appreciated his intentions.

On 6th August 1969 he was offered employment for a
large scheme by the Board which was substantially the same
as that which the plaintiff company had been trying to
obtain in 1968: four depots to be constructed at an estimated cost of £1,700,000.

On 2nd December 1969 the plaintiff company issued a
writ against Mr. Cooley claiming a declaration that he was
a trustee for them of all contracts with the Board; an
account of all fees and remuneration in respect of those
contracts; alternatively, damages for breach of duty as a
director.

ROSKILL J.: . . . The first matter that has to be considered is
whether or not the defendant was in a fiduciary relationship
with his principals, the plaintiffs. Mr. Davies [*leading counsel
for the defendant*] argued that he was not because he received
this information which was communicated to him privately.
With respect, I think that argument is wrong. The defendant
had one capacity and one capacity only in which he was carrying on business at that time. That capacity was as managing
director of the plaintiffs. Information which came to him while
he was managing director and which was of concern to the
plaintiffs and was relevant for the plaintiffs to know, was
information which it was his duty to pass on to the plaintiffs
because between himself and the plaintiffs a fiduciary relationship existed. . . .

It seems to me plain that throughout the whole of May,
June and July 1969 the defendant was in a fiduciary relationship with the plaintiffs. From the time he embarked upon his
course of dealing with the Eastern Gas Board . . . he embarked
upon a deliberate policy and course of conduct which put his
personal interest as a potential contracting party with the
Eastern Gas Board in direct conflict with his pre-existing and
continuing duty as managing director of the plaintiffs. That is

something which for over 200 years the courts have forbidden. . . .

Therefore, I feel impelled to the conclusion that when the defendant embarked on this course of conduct . . . he was guilty of putting himself into the position in which his duty to his employers, the plaintiffs, and his own private interests conflicted and conflicted grievously. There being the fiduciary relationship I have described, it seems to me plain that it was his duty once he got this information to pass it to his employers and not to guard it for his own personal purposes and profit. He put himself into the position when his duty and his interests conflicted. . . .

Does accountability arise? It is said: "Well, even if there were that conflict of duty and interest, nonetheless, this was a contract with a third party in which the plaintiffs never could have had any interest because they would never have got it." . . .

The remarkable position then arises that if one applies the equitable doctrine upon which the plaintiffs rely to oblige the defendant to account, they will receive a benefit which . . . it is unlikely they would have got for themselves had the defendant complied with his duty to them. On the other hand, if the defendant is not required to account he will have made a large profit, as a result of having deliberately put himself into a position in which his duty to the plaintiffs who were employing him and his personal interests conflicted. I leave out of account the fact that he dishonestly tricked Mr. Hicks into releasing him on June 16. . . .

When one looks at the way the cases have gone over the centuries it is plain that the question whether or not the benefit would have been obtained but for the breach of trust has always been treated as irrelevant. . . . It is an overriding principle of equity that a man must not be allowed to put himself in a position in which his fiduciary duty and his interests conflict. . . . The facts of this case are, I think, exceptional and I hope unusual. They seem to me plainly to come within this principle. . . .

In my judgment, therefore, an order for an account will be

issued because the defendant has made and will make his profit as a result of having allowed his interests and his duty to conflict.

Howard Smith, Ltd. v. Ampol Petroleum, Ltd. [1974] A.C. 821

Directors must exercise their powers not only bona fide *in the interests of the company as a whole, but also for a proper purpose.*

In May 1972 Ampol Petroleum, Ltd. had acquired 29·8 per cent of the issued share capital of R. W. Miller (Holdings), Ltd. 25·1 per cent of Miller was held by Bulkships, Ltd., so that Ampol and Bulkships together owned about 55 per cent of Miller.

On 15th June 1972 Ampol made an offer for all the issued shares in Miller at $2·27 per share (the par value was $1). A week later another company, Howard Smith, Ltd., announced its intention of making a take-over bid at $2·50 per share. The next day the Miller directors decided to recommend the rejection of the Ampol offer as too low.

On 27th June 1972 Ampol and Bulkships issued a statement saying that they intended to act jointly in relation to Miller and had decided to reject any offer for their shares, whether from Howard Smith or elsewhere.

Under Miller's articles the directors had power to allot unissued shares to such persons on such terms and conditions and at such time as they thought fit. A majority of the Miller directors were in favour of the Howard Smith offer and a scheme was accordingly evolved to make an issue of shares to Howard Smith large enough to turn Ampol and Bulkships combined into minority shareholders. The number of shares was calculated on the basis of Miller's capital requirements, and Miller did in fact require some $10,000,000. It was decided to issue 4,500,000 shares at $2·30 per share, and these shares were allotted to Howard Smith.

On 7th July Ampol commenced proceedings in the Supreme Court of New South Wales to set aside the issue. The trial judge, STREET J., found:

(i) that the allotment had not been made by Miller's directors out of self-interest, and (*ii*) that its primary purpose was not to satisfy Miller's need for capital but to destroy the majority holding of Ampol and Bulkships and procure the continuation of Howard Smith's take-over offer.

Since this was an improper purpose, he ordered that the issue be set aside.

Howard Smith appealed to the Judicial Committee of the Privy Council, contending that once it had been found that the directors were not acting out of self-interest, it was not open to the court to inquire into the validity of their reasons for making the issue.

The judgment of the Judicial Committee was delivered by LORD WILBERFORCE.

LORD WILBERFORCE: . . . In order to assist him in deciding upon the alternative motivations contended for, the judge considered first . . . the objective question whether Millers was in fact in need of capital. This approach was criticised before their Lordships: it was argued that what mattered was not the actual financial condition of Millers, but what the majority directors *bona fide* considered that condition to be. Their Lordships accept that such a matter as the raising of finance is one of management, within the responsibility of the directors: they accept that it would be wrong for the court to substitute its opinion for that of the management, or indeed to question the correctness of the management's decision, on such a question, if *bona fide* arrived at. There is no appeal on merits from management decisions to courts of law: nor will courts of law assume to act as a kind of supervisory board over decisions within the powers of management honestly arrived at.

But accepting all of this, when a dispute arises whether directors of a company made a particular decision for one purpose or for another, . . . the court, in their Lordships' opinion, is entitled to look at the situation objectively in order to estimate how critical or pressing, or substantial or, *per contra*, insubstantial an alleged requirement may have been. . . .

This was, in their Lordships' view the course taken by STREET J. . . . Their Lordships accept that the general financial picture as drawn by the judge was correct.

. . . [T]he issue was clearly *intra vires* the directors. But, *intra vires* though the issue may have been, the directors' power under this article is a fiduciary power: and it remains the case that an exercise of such a power though formally valid, may be attacked on the ground that it was not exercised for the purpose for which it was granted. It is at this point that the contentions of the parties diverge. The extreme argument on one side is that, for validity, what is required is *bona fide* exercise of the power in the interests of the company: that once it is found that the directors were not motivated by self-interest— *i.e.* by a desire to retain their control of the company or their positions on the board—the matter is concluded in their favour and that the court will not inquire into the validity of their reasons for making the issue. . . .

On the other side, the main argument is that the purpose for which the power is conferred is to enable capital to be raised for the company, and that once it is found that the issue was not made for that purpose, invalidity follows. . . .

In their Lordships' opinion neither of the extreme positions can be maintained. It can be accepted, as one would only expect, that the majority of cases in which issues of shares are challenged in the courts are cases in which the vitiating element is the self-interest of the directors, or at least the purpose of the directors to preserve their own control of the management. . . .

Further it is correct to say that where the self-interest of the directors is involved, they will not be permitted to assert that their action was *bona fide* thought to be, or was, in the interest of the company; pleas to this effect have invariably been rejected . . . —just as trustees who buy trust property are not permitted to assert that they paid a good price.

But it does not follow from this, as the appellants assert, that the absence of any element of self-interest is enough to make an issue valid. Self-interest is only one, though no doubt the commonest, instance of improper motive: and, before one can say that a fiduciary power has been exercised for the purpose for which it was conferred, a wider investigation may have to be made. This is recognised in several well-known statements of the law. Their Lordships quote the clearest which has so often been cited:

> "Where the question is one of abuse of powers, the state of mind of those who acted, and the motive on which they acted, are all important, and you may go into the question of what their intention was, collecting from the surrounding circumstances all the materials which genuinely throw light upon that question of the state of mind of the directors so as to show whether they were honestly acting in discharge of their powers in the interests of the company or were acting from some bye-motive, possibly of personal advantage, or for any other reason." (*Hindle* v. *John Cotton Ltd.* (1919) 56 Sc.L.R. 625, *per* VISCOUNT FINLAY.)

On the other hand, taking the respondents' contention, it is, in their Lordships' opinion, too narrow an approach to say that the only valid purpose for which shares may be issued is to raise capital for the company. The discretion is not in terms limited in this way: the law should not impose such a limitation on directors' powers. To define in advance exact limits beyond which directors must not pass is, in their Lordships' view, impossible. This clearly cannot be done by enumeration, since the variety of situations facing directors of different types of company in different situations cannot be anticipated. No more, in their Lordships' view, can this be done by the use of a phrase—such as "*bona fide* in the interest of the company as a whole," or "for some corporate purpose." Such phrases, if they do anything more than restate the general principle applicable to fiduciary powers, at best serve, negatively, to exclude from the area of validity cases where the directors are acting sectionally, or partially: i.e. improperly favouring one section of the shareholders against another. . . .

In their Lordships' opinion it is necessary to start with a consideration of the power whose exercise is in question, in this case a power to issue shares. Having ascertained, on a fair view, the nature of this power, and having defined as can best be done in the light of modern conditions the, or some, limits within which it may be exercised, it is then necessary for the court, if a particular exercise of it is challenged, to examine the substantial purpose for which it was exercised, and to reach a conclusion whether that purpose was proper or not. In doing so it will necessarily give credit to the *bona fide* opinion of the directors, if such is found to exist, and will respect their judgment as to matters of management; having done this, the ultimate conclusion has to be as to the side of a fairly broad line on which the case falls.

. . . [T]he present case, on the evidence, does not . . . involve any considerations of management, within the proper sphere of the directors. The purpose found by the judge is simply and solely to dilute the majority voting power held by Ampol and Bulkships so as to enable a then minority of shareholders to sell their shares more advantageously. So far as authority goes, an issue of shares purely for the purpose of creating voting power has repeatedly been condemned. , . . The constitution of a limited company normally provides for directors, with powers of management, and shareholders, with defined voting powers having power to appoint the directors, and to take, in general meeting, by majority vote, decisions on matters not reserved for management. Just as it is established that directors, within their management powers, may take decisions against the wishes of the majority of shareholders, and indeed that the majority of shareholders cannot control them in the exercise of these powers while they remain in office (*Automatic Self-Cleansing Filter Syndicate Co. Ltd.* v. *Cuninghame* [1906] 2 Ch. 34), so it must be unconstitutional for directors to use their fiduciary powers over the shares in the company purely for the purpose of destroying an existing majority, or creating a new majority which did not previously exist. To do so is to interfere with that element of the company's constitution which is separate from and set against their powers. If there is added, moreover, to this immediate purpose, an ulterior purpose to enable an offer for shares to proceed which the existing majority was in a position to block, the departure from the legitimate use of the fiduciary power becomes not less, but all the greater. The right to dispose of shares at a given price is essentially an individual right to be exercised on individual decision and on which a majority, in the absence of oppression or similar impropriety, is entitled to prevail. Directors are of course entitled to offer advice, and bound to supply information, relevant to the making of such a decision, but to use their fiduciary power solely for the purpose of shifting the power to decide to whom and at what price shares are to be sold cannot be related to any purpose for which the power over the share capital was conferred upon them. That this is the position in law was in effect recognised by the majority directors themselves when they attempted to justify the issue as made primarily in order to obtain much needed capital for the company. And once this primary purpose was rejected, as it was by STREET J., there is nothing legitimate left as a basis for their action, except honest behaviour. That is not, in itself, enough.

Their Lordships therefore agree entirely with the conclusion of STREET J. that the power to issue and allot shares was improperly exercised by the issue of shares to Howard Smith. . . .

Their Lordships will humbly advise Her Majesty that the appeal be dismissed.

3. The Directors' Duty of Care

Re City Equitable Fire Insurance Company, Ltd. [1925] 1 Ch. 407

A director must take the care which an ordinary man might be expected to take in the circumstances on his own behalf. He need not show a greater degree of skill than may reasonably be expected from a person of his knowledge and experience. He is not liable for mere errors of judgment. He is not bound to give continuous attention to the affairs of his company. In respect of all duties which may properly be left to some other official, he is, in the absence of grounds for suspicion, justified in trusting that official to perform such duties honestly.

A person is guilty of wilful negligence if he knows that he is committing, and intends to commit, a breach of his duty, or is recklessly careless in the sense of not caring whether his act or omission is or is not a breach of duty.

In the winding up of the City Equitable Fire Insurance Company by the court it appeared that there was a shortage in its funds of over £1,200,000, due partly to depreciation of investments, but mainly to the instrumentality of the managing director and largely to his deliberate fraud, for which he had been convicted and sentenced.

Article 150 of the company's articles of association provided that none of the directors, auditors, secretary or other officers should be answerable for the acts, receipts, neglects or defaults of the others, or for any bankers or other persons with whom any moneys or effects of the company should be deposited for safe custody, or for deficiency of any security upon which any moneys of the company should be invested, or for any other loss, misfortune or damage which might happen in the execution of their offices or trusts, unless the same should happen through their own wilful neglect or default.

On a misfeasance summons under S.215 *Companies (Consolidation) Act*, 1908 [now S.333 *Companies Act*, 1948], the Official Receiver as liquidator sought to make the directors, all of whom except the managing director had acted honestly throughout, liable for negligence in respect of losses occasioned by investments and loans, and of payment of dividends out of capital.

On the same summons the Official Receiver also sought to make the auditors liable for negligence and breach of duty with respect to the audit of the balance sheets for the three preceding years.

ROMER J.: On 27th June, 1916, Gerrard Lee Bevan became a director of the City Equitable Fire Insurance Company, Ltd. The company at that time was carrying on successfully the business of reinsurance of fire and marine risks, and was in a sound financial condition. On 14th February, 1922, an order was made for the winding up of the company by the Court. A searching investigation of the affairs of the company was then made, and this investigation disclosed a shortage in the funds of which the company should have been possessed of over £1,200,000. This deplorable state of affairs was in no way due to the company's trading operations. . . . Nearly the whole of these enormous losses were brought about through Bevan's instrumentality, and a large part of them by his deliberate fraud. For that fraud he has been tried, and convicted, and is now suffering the just penalty. But the question not unnaturally arises as to whether . . . the other directors and the auditors of the company were properly discharging the duties that they owed to the company's shareholders. The Official Receiver, as the liquidator of the company, alleges that they were not. . . . [W]hilst admitting, and rightly admitting, that they have acted honestly throughout, he claims that they have been guilty of such negligence as to render themselves liable to the company in damages. Whether they are, or are not so liable, is the question that I have to determine. It will be convenient to consider the case of the directors and the case of the auditors separately, and I propose to begin with the directors. . . .

It has sometimes been said that directors are trustees. If this means no more than that directors in the performance of their duties stand in a fiduciary relationship to the company, the statement is true enough. But if the statement is meant to be an indication by way of analogy of what those duties are, it appears to me to be wholly misleading. I can see but little resemblance between the duties of a director and the duties of a trustee of a will or of a marriage settlement. It is indeed impossible to describe the duty of directors in general terms, whether by way of analogy or otherwise. The position of a director of a company carrying on a small retail business is very different from that of a director of a railway company. . . . The larger the business carried on by the company the more numerous, and the more important, the matters that must of necessity be left to the managers, the accountants and the rest of the staff. The manner in which the work of the company is to be distributed between the board of the directors and the staff is in truth a business matter to be decided on business lines. . . .

In order, therefore, to ascertain the duties that a person appointed to the board of an established company undertakes to perform, it is necessary to consider not only the nature of the company's business, but also the manner in which the work of the company is in fact distributed between the directors and the other officials of the company, provided always that this distribution is a reasonable one in the circumstances, and is not inconsistent with any express provisions of the articles of association. In discharging the duties of his position thus ascertained a director must, of course, act honestly; but he must also exercise some degree of both skill and diligence. To the question of what is the particular degree of skill and diligence required of him, the authorities do not, I think, give any very clear answer. . . . The care that he is bound to take has been described by NEVILLE J. in [*Re Brazilian Rubber Plantations and Estates Ltd.*] as "reasonable care" to be measured by the care an ordinary man might be expected to take in the circumstances on his own behalf. . . .

There are, in addition, one or two other general propositions that seem to be warranted by the reported cases: (1) A director need not exhibit in the performance of his duties a greater degree of skill than may reasonably be expected from a person of his knowledge and experience. A director of a life insurance company, for instance, does not guarantee that he has the skill of an actuary or of a physician. . . . It is perhaps only another way of stating the same proposition to say that directors are not liable for mere errors of judgment. (2) A director is not bound to give continuous attention to the affairs of his company. His duties are of an intermittent nature to be performed at periodical board meetings, and at meetings of any committee of the board upon which he happens to be placed. He is not, however, bound to attend all such meetings, though he ought to attend whenever, in the circumstances, he is reasonably able to do so. (3) In respect of all duties that, having regard to the exigencies of business, and the articles of association, may properly be left to some other official, a director is, in the absence of grounds for suspicion, justified in trusting that official to perform such duties honestly. . . .

These are the general principles that I shall endeavour to apply in considering the question whether the directors of this company have been guilty of negligence. But in order to determine whether any such negligence, if established, renders the directors liable in damages, it is necessary to consider the provisions of article 150 of the company's articles of association. . . . [T]he difficulty is not so much in ascertaining the meaning of the adjective "wilful," as in ascertaining precisely what is the noun to which the adjective is to be applied. An act, or an omission to do an act, is wilful where the person of whom we are speaking knows what he is doing and intends to do what he is doing. But if that act or omission amounts to a breach of his duty, and therefore to negligence, is the person guilty of wilful negligence? In my opinion that question must be answered in the negative unless he knows that he is committing, and intends to commit, a breach of his duty, or is recklessly careless in the sense of not caring whether his act or omission is or is not a breach of duty. . . .

I must now turn to the facts of the case for the purpose of ascertaining first, whether in any of the matters charged against them the respondents have been guilty of negligence, and secondly, whether any such negligence was wilful, negligence and default meaning for all practical purposes one and the same thing. That Bevan was guilty not merely of wilful negligence but also of fraud will appear quite clearly. The real question that I have to decide is with reference to his co-directors. . . . I desire to make one general observation. Cases have not been unknown in which a director has lent his name to a company for what may be called window dressing purposes, and has treated himself as having thereby given ample consideration for his remuneration and as being absolved from any further effort towards promoting the welfare of the company. This cannot be said of any one of the respondent directors. . . . I am satisfied from the evidence adduced before me that each one of the respondent directors was willing and anxious to give of his best to the company and at all times took as active a part in the work of the board as circumstances would reasonably permit.

ROMER J. then proceeded to consider the facts of the case in great detail. He concluded:

. . . [T]he case of the Official Receiver fails against all the respondent directors. He is, however, entitled to relief against

Bevan in respect of many of the transactions to which I have referred. . . .

It remains for me to deal with the charges made against the respondents, Messrs. Langton and Lepine, the auditors of the company. . . . [T]he Official Receiver asks for a declaration that these respondents were guilty of negligence in respect of the audit by them of the balance sheets of the company for the years ending 28th February, 1919, 29th February 1920, and 28th February, 1921, respectively, and are liable to pay to the liquidator compensation for the loss sustained by the company by reason of such negligence and breach of duty. . . . [I]n *In re London and General Bank* (*No. 2*) LINDLEY L.J. dealt at some length with the duties of an auditor of a company. He says this: "It is no part of an auditor's duty to give advice, either to directors or shareholders, as to what they ought to do. An auditor has nothing to do with the prudence or imprudence of making loans with or without security. It is nothing to him whether the business of a company is being conducted prudently or imprudently, profitably or unprofitably. It is nothing to him whether dividends are properly or improperly declared, provided he discharges his own duty to the shareholders. His business is to ascertain and state the true financial position of the company at the time of the audit, and his duty is confined to that. But then comes the question, How is he to ascertain that position? The answer is, By examining the books of the company. But he does not discharge his duty by doing this without inquiry and without taking any trouble to see that the books themselves shew the company's true position. He must take reasonable care to ascertain that they do so. . . . An auditor, however, is not bound to do more than exercise reasonable care and skill in making inquiries and investigations. He is not an insurer; he does not guarantee that the books do correctly shew the true position of the company's affairs; he does not even guarantee that his balance sheet is accurate according to the books of the company. If he did, he would be responsible for error on his part, even if he were himself deceived without any want of reasonable care on his part, say, by the fraudulent concealment of a book from him.

His obligation is not so onerous as this. Such I take to be the duty of any auditor; he must be honest—*i.e.* he must not certify what he does not believe to be true, and he must take reasonable care and skill before he believes that what he certifies is true. What is reasonable care . . . must depend upon the circumstances of that case. Where there is nothing to excite suspicion very little inquiry will be reasonably sufficient. . . . Where suspicion is roused more care is obviously necessary; but, still, an auditor is not bound to exercise more than reasonable care and skill, even in a case of suspicion, and he is perfectly justified in acting on the opinion of an expert where special knowledge is required." I must now inquire whether, in the matters complained of, Mr. Lepine fell short of the duty of an auditor as so explained and defined.

ROMER J. then again proceeded to consider the facts of the case in great detail, and concluded:

. . . I have heard Mr. Lepine's evidence in the witness box, and I have inspected many of the numerous documents prepared by him for the purposes of the audits that he conducted. I am convinced that throughout the audits that he conducted he honestly and carefully discharged what he conceived to be the whole of his duty to the company. If in certain matters he fell short of his real duty, it was because, in all good faith, he held a mistaken belief as to what that duty was. As against him and his partner, the application of the Official Receiver must accordingly be dismissed.

The Official Receiver appealed from this decision of ROMER J. so far as it affected the auditors, Messrs. Langton and Lepine, and the case accordingly came before the Court of Appeal on this point. That Court, consisting of POLLOCK M.R., WARRINGTON L.J. and SARGANT L.J., affirmed the decision of the High Court.

4. Directors' Qualification Shares

**Sutton *v*. English and Colonial Produce Company. [1902]
2 Ch. 502**

*Where the articles require a director to hold his qualification
shares "in his own right" he need not be the beneficial owner
of them, but he must hold them in such a way that the company
can safely deal with him as owner.*

The English and Colonial Produce Company, Limited,
was incorporated on 9th November 1901.

The following clauses were contained in its articles of
association:

"35. Any person becoming entitled to a share in
consequence of the death or bankruptcy of any member
may, upon producing such evidence of title as the directors shall require, . . . either be registered himself as
holder of the share or elect to have some person
nominated by him registered as the transferee thereof.

103. The first directors of the company shall be Joseph
Sutton (and four other persons).

104. A director must be a member of the company.
The qualification of a director shall be the holding in
his own right alone, and not jointly with any other
person, 100 shares of £1 each or £100 stock. . . .

116. The office of a director shall be vacated . . . (*d*) if
he cease to hold the qualifying number of shares or
amount of stock."

The plaintiff Joseph Sutton was the registered holder of
1,000 shares in the company. In 1888 he had been adjudicated a bankrupt, and was never discharged.

On 14th April 1902 the trustee in bankruptcy gave notice
to the secretary of the company requiring to have his name
placed on the register of members in regard to the 1,000
shares, and threatened proceedings to enforce the entry of
his name. On 16th April he withdrew this notice by tele-
gram, and then wrote to the secretary referring to the tele-
gram and saying: "I mean by this, that though I claim the
shares as property which is vested in me by law, I will not

ask for the actual transfer for a few days; but I shall be very much obliged if you could supply me by return of post with a list of the names and addresses of the shareholders, as I purpose to offer the shares for sale to the shareholders."

On 25th April 1902 Sutton was excluded from the board of directors upon the ground that he had become disqualified.

On 28th April 1902 a transfer in favour of Sutton of 100 shares was executed and lodged for registration. It came before the board of directors on 1st May. The directors refused to register it upon the ground that if they registered it Sutton's trustee in bankruptcy would be entitled to take the shares.

Sutton moved for an injunction to restrain the company and two of its directors from preventing him from acting as a director of the company, and also that the register of members might be rectified by inserting his name therein as the holder of the 100 shares.

BUCKLEY J.: The effect of what the trustee did, in my opinion, was that he claimed the 1,000 shares as his, but postponed for a few days his decision as to whether under art. 35 he would require to be registered himself or elect to have some person nominated by him registered as transferee. Under these circumstances the question is whether, after April 14 and 16, 1902, the bankrupt continued to hold "in his own right" these 1,000 shares.

Negatively, . . . the holder in his own right need not be beneficial owner. It remains to say what, affirmatively, he must be. . . . He must be a person who holds shares in such a way that the company can safely deal with him in respect of his shares, whatever his interest may be in the shares. Holding in a representative character will not do. Holding as trustee without beneficial ownership will do, but the holder must so hold as that the company can safely deal with him as owner. Turning, then, to the facts of this case, after April 14 and 16, 1902, could this company have safely dealt with the plaintiff in respect of the shares? I think not. The company had received notice from the trustee that he claimed the shares, and that he postponed for a few days stating in which way he would, under art. 35, avail himself of his rights of ownership. After that the company could not have safely dealt with the plaintiff in disregard of the claims of the trustee. In my judgment, therefore, the plaintiff (although he had a beneficial interest in case his estate proved to be solvent) was not on April 25 the holder in his own right of the 1,000 shares. He had become disqualified, and his office of director was vacated.

Subsequently, namely, on April 28, a transfer in his favour of 100 shares was executed and lodged for registration. It came before the board on May 1. The directors refused to register it, and the ground upon which they rely is that, if they had registered it, the trustee in bankruptcy would have been entitled to take the shares. This is not, I think, in the mouth of the company, any answer to a demand for registration of the transfer. It is an effectual transfer. The trustee had not raised, and I see no reason why he should raise, any objection to its registration. The right of the trustee to the shares is in no way defeated, but, on the contrary, is assisted by the company taking the shares out of the name of the transferor and putting them into the name of the transferee. Seeing, however, that the plaintiff had previously become disqualified as a director, and his office had fallen vacant, his subsequent registration as the holder of these 100 shares will not re-establish him in his office.

So far, therefore, as the notice of motion asks an injunction to restrain the defendants from excluding the plaintiff from acting as director, it fails, and I dismiss it. So far as it asks for rectification by inserting the plaintiff's name as the holder of the 100 shares, . . . it succeeds, and I make an order for rectification. . . .

XIII. THE SECRETARY OF A COMPANY

Panorama Developments (Guildford) Ltd. *v.* Fidelis Furnishing Fabrics, Ltd. [1971] 2 Q.B. 711

A company secretary is no longer a mere clerk. He is the chief administrative officer of the company, and as regards matters of administration has ostensible authority to sign contracts on behalf of the company.

The facts sufficiently appear from the judgment of LORD DENNING in the Court of Appeal.

LORD DENNING M.R.: In this case the court has to decide which of two innocent parties is to suffer for the fraud of a third party. One innocent party is Panorama Developments (Guildford) Ltd., the plaintiffs. They run a car hire business which they call the Belgravia Executive Car Rental ("Belgravia"). They have a fleet of imposing cars such as Rolls-Royces and Jaguars. They let them out on hire for the hirers to drive themselves. In short "self-drive" hire.

Fidelis Furnishing Fabrics Ltd., the defendants, are a company of good repute and excellent credit. They have a managing director of unimpeachable integrity—Mr. Mavrogordato. The third party who committed the fraud is a young man aged 28. His name is R. L. Bayne. The Fidelis company appointed him as their secretary some 18 months ago. He practised fraud of this kind: he told Belgravia that he was the secretary of Fidelis Furnishing Fabrics Ltd. He said that his company wanted to hire cars for the company's business. He said that he would drive the cars himself. They were wanted so that he could meet important customers when they arrived at Heathrow and take them to the company's office and to the company's factory in Leeds. On the first transaction he paid the hire by a cheque on his own private account. It was duly met.

(We are told that he probably reimbursed himself from the company's account.) Having thus inspired confidence, he gave them a list of dates on which cars would be needed in the future. He gave some dates on which they would want a Rolls-Royce; other dates for a Jaguar. He asked Belgravia for the cars to be charged to the account of Fidelis Furnishing Fabrics Ltd. Before giving credit, Belgravia asked for references. Mr. Bayne gave references. He wrote on the company's paper and signed himself "Company Secretary." Belgravia took up the references. They came back saying that the Fidelis company were of good standing and honoured their obligations. Being satisfied with the references, Belgravia sent the cars on the dates which Mr. Bayne had given. They sent with each car a printed form of hiring agreement and proposal for insurance. On each form it was stated that the hirer was "R. L. Bayne," who was described as "Company Secretary." Payment was to be "by account." When the car was delivered, Mr. Bayne usually signed the hiring agreement himself in his own name. But sometimes the sales manager signed the name of R. L. Bayne. Mr. Bayne had the cars and used them. But the hire was never paid. Belgravia sent in the account to the Fidelis company. But the company did not pay.

All this was done whilst the managing director of Fidelis, Mr. Mavrogordato, was away. When he came back, he discovered the frauds. Mr. Bayne had told a whole lot of lies to Belgravia. No customers were ever met at Heathrow. The Fidelis company had not got a factory at Leeds. Mr. Bayne got these cars for some purpose of his own, perhaps to let them out on hire himself. He involved the company in other debts too. He has since been prosecuted, convicted, and sentenced to imprisonment. Now Belgravia sues Fidelis for the amount of the hire due—£570 12s. 6d. Fidelis say that Mr. Bayne had no authority to hire them. The Judge has found against Fidelis. He held that they are responsible for what Mr. Bayne did and the orders which he gave. Fidelis now appeal to this court.

Mr. Hames, who appears for the Fidelis company, takes two points. His first point is that the contracts for hire were made with Mr. Bayne personally and not with the company: and so the company are not liable on them. . . . It appears that in these "self-drive hire" transactions, Belgravia, for insurance purposes, always want the driver to be named as the hirer. So they deliberately inserted Mr. Bayne's name as the hirer. Can they now go back on their own documents? Belgravia have to prove that the Fidelis company was in fact the party which hired the cars. For this, they have to go outside their own regular hiring agreements. Can they do this? I think they can. I regard these hiring agreements as part and parcel of a contract contained in correspondence: so much so that you must not look at the hire agreement alone, but at all that took place. . . .

Applying those considerations, it is clear that these cars were hired as a result of letters which described Fidelis Furnishing Fabrics Ltd. as the contracting party. . . . In these circumstances, the hiring agreements were mere machinery for carrying the correspondence into effect. . . . The contract for each of them was with the company and not with Mr. Bayne.

Mr. Hames' second point is this: he says that the company is not bound by the letters which were signed by Mr. Bayne as "Company Secretary." He says that, on the authorities, a company secretary fulfils a very humble role: and he has no authority to make any contracts or representations on behalf of the company. He refers to *Barnett, Hoares & Co.* v. *South London Tramways Co.* (1887), where LORD ESHER M.R. said . . . "A secretary is a mere servant; his position is that he is to do what he is told, and no person can assume that he has any authority to represent anything at all. . . ." Those words were approved by LORD MACNAGHTEN in *George Whitechurch Ltd.* v. *Cavanagh* (1902). They are supported by the decision in *Ruben* v. *Great Fingall Consolidated* (1906). They are referred to in some of the textbooks as authoritative.

But times have changed. A company secretary is a much more important person nowadays than he was in 1887. He is an officer of the company with extensive duties and responsibilities. This appears not only in the modern Companies Acts, but also by the role which he plays in the day-to-day business of companies. He is no longer a mere clerk. He regularly makes representations on behalf of the company and enters into contracts on its behalf which come within the day-to-day running of the company's business. So much so that he may be regarded as held out as having authority to do such things on behalf of the company. He is certainly entitled to sign contracts connected with the administrative side of a company's affairs, such as employing staff, and ordering cars, and so forth. All such matters now come within the ostensible authority of a company's secretary.

Accordingly I agree with the judge that Mr. Bayne, as company secretary, had ostensible authority to enter into contracts for the hire of these cars and, therefore, the company must pay for them. Mr. Bayne was a fraud. But it was the company which put him in the position in which he, as company secretary, was able to commit the frauds. So the defendants are liable. I would dismiss the appeal, accordingly.

SALMON L.J.: . . . Whatever the position of a company's secretary may have been in 1887, I am quite satisfied that it has altered a great deal from what it was then. At the end of the last century a company secretary still occupied a very humble position—very little higher, if any, than that of a minor clerk. Today, not only has the status of a company secretary been much enhanced, but that state of affairs has been recognised by the statutes to which LORD DENNING M.R. has referred. I think there can be no doubt that the secretary is the chief administrative officer of the company. As regards matters concerned with administration, in my judgment, the secretary has ostensible authority to sign contracts on behalf of the company. If a company is ordering cars so that its servants may go and meet foreign customers at airports, nothing, to my mind is more natural than that the company should hire those cars through its secretary. The hiring is part of his administrative functions. Whether the secretary would have any authority to sign a contract relating to the commercial management of the company, for example, a contract for the sale or purchase of goods in which the company deals, does not arise for decision in the present case and I do not propose to express any concluded opinion upon the point; but contracts such as the present fall within the ambit of administration and I entertain no doubt that the secretary has ostensible power to sign on behalf of the company.

I have great sympathy with Mr. Mavrogordato. This man Bayne came to him with the highest references, which no doubt were forged, but of which Mr. Mavrogordato had no reason to be suspicious in any way. . . . But if you employ a company secretary you certainly have to take the risk whether he he is going to be honest in transactions such as the present. Whenever it is a question of which of two innocent parties has to bear a loss caused by a rogue, one cannot help having great sympathy for the man on whose shoulders the burden falls. However that may be, there can be no doubt in this case that there was ostensible authority in Mr. Bayne to sign on behalf of the defendant company and that means that the defendant company must pay.

I agree with LORD DENNING M.R. and the judge. In the result this appeal should be dismissed.

MEGAW L.J.: I agree.

XIV. COMPANY MEETINGS

East *v*. Bennett Brothers, Limited. [1911] 1 Ch. 163

Although in the ordinary way a meeting must consist of more than one person, where one person only is the holder of all the shares of a particular class the word "meeting," as applied to the holders of the shares of that class, includes the case of that single shareholder.

Bennett Brothers, Ltd. was incorporated in May 1904 with a capital of £25,000 divided in 25,000 shares of £1 each, of which 10,000 were 6 per cent cumulative preference shares and 15,000 ordinary shares.

The memorandum of association empowered the company to increase its capital, but provided that no new shares should be issued so as to rank equally with or in priority to the preference shares, unless such issue was sanctioned by an extraordinary resolution of the holders of the preference shares present at a separate meeting of such holders specially summoned for the purpose of considering the question. It further provided that the variation of the rights of any class of shares should be effected by an extraordinary resolution of the holders of the shares of that class passed at a separate meeting of such holders at which there should be present in person or by proxy the holders of not less than three-quarters of the issued shares of that class. The articles of association contained a similar provision regarding variation of class rights.

In June 1904 the company wished to increase its capital by issuing an additional 10,000 6 per cent cumulative preference shares. At that time Joseph Bennett, junior, was the sole holder of all the original 10,000 6 per cent cumulative preference shares.

On 20th June 1904 a company meeting was held at which Bennett took the chair. At that meeting a resolution for

the increase of the company's capital to £40,000 by the
creation of 10,000 6 per cent cumulative preference shares
and 5,000 ordinary shares of £1 each, ranking *pari passu*
in all respects with the existing preference and ordinary
shares, was proposed by Bennett and carried unanimously.
On the same day Bennett signed in the minute-book of the
company a document giving his formal consent as the
holder of all the existing preference shares to the increase
of capital.

At a further company meeting on 5th July 1904 the
resolution was confirmed as a special resolution. The
company then proceeded to issue the new shares.

Later the company was proposing to issue fresh capital,
and the question arose whether the preference shares
issued in 1904 were validly issued. In order to have this
question determined the plaintiff, who was the holder of
400 of these shares, brought an action on behalf of himself
and the other registered holders against the company
claiming that the issue was invalid, and that the register
of members should be rectified by the removal of the names
of the holders.

WARRINGTON J.: The question that I have to determine is
whether what the company did was in effect, although not
perhaps in terms, within the provisions of the memorandum
and articles of association, and, if it was in effect though not in
terms, whether there was a sufficient compliance with the memorandum and articles to render the proceedings valid. Perhaps
I ought to say that the real question is not so much whether
the proceedings were in effect a compliance with the memorandum and articles as whether upon the true construction of
the memorandum and articles they were not really and in terms
a compliance with them. The question resolves itself into this.
On the construction of this particular memorandum and the
particular part of it, can there be such a thing as a meeting
of one shareholder? It is not a question of there being several
shareholders, and one shareholder only attending the so-called
meeting, but where there is only one shareholder, so that a
meeting in the sense of an assembly of persons is impossible.
The object of the provisions in the memorandum is quite

plain. It is to obtain, before the issue of new shares, the assent in a binding and formal manner of the person or persons whose rights are affected.

. . . It is clear that if Bennett can constitute "a meeting" there is no difficulty about the quorum, because the quorum in this case is to be the holders of shares present in person (or represented by proxy) holding not less than three fourths of the issued shares of the class. In an ordinary case I think it is quite clear that a meeting must consist of more than one person. . . .

But now what I have to consider is whether this is not one of the cases . . . in which it may be possible to show that the word "meeting" has a meaning different from the ordinary meaning. For that purpose I think I am entitled to see what is the object of the provision in the memorandum of association. Plainly, as I have already said, that object is that before affecting the rights of the preference shareholders it shall be necessary to obtain and record in a formal manner the assent of the preference shareholders to that course. I think I may take it also that the persons who framed this document may have had, and must be taken to have had, in their minds the possibility at all events that this particular class of shares might fall into the hands of one person. There is nothing to prevent it in the constitution of the company. One must regard the memorandum as far as possible as providing for circumstances which in the ordinary course may arise. That being so, I think I may very fairly say that where one person only is the holder of all the shares of a particular class, and as that person cannot meet himself, or form a meeting with himself in the ordinary sense, the persons who framed this memorandum having such a position in contemplation must be taken to have used the word "meeting," not in the strict sense in which it is usually used, but as including the case of one single shareholder. There is, of course, no difficulty in treating the formally expressed assent of Bennett as a resolution. The only question is the purely technical difficulty arising from the use of the word "meeting" in the memorandum.

I think on the whole that I may give effect to obvious

common sense by holding that in this particular case, where
there is only one shareholder of the class, on the true construction of the memorandum, the expression "meeting" may be
held to include that case. It seems to me, therefore, that the
shares were validly issued, and that there is therefore no
necessity for the rectification of the register. I refuse the motion
on that ground.

Morgan and Another *v.* Gray and Others. [1953] Ch. 83

*Unless there is an express provision to the contrary in the
company's articles, a shareholder who is adjudicated bankrupt
remains a member of the company as long as he is on the register and is therefore entitled to vote, though he must exercise
his vote in accordance with the direction of the persons beneficially entitled to the shares.*

In April 1952 the plaintiff Morgan and the defendant
L. A. Gray were the sole directors and shareholders in
British Ethical Proprietaries Ltd., each holding fifty shares
of £1 out of a total authorised and issued capital of £100.

Article 18 of the company's articles of association provided: "The qualification of a director shall be the holding
of at least 50 shares in the company of an aggregate value
of £50. . . . A director may act before acquiring his qualification." By article 16 the number of directors was to be
not less than two, unless otherwise determined by the
company in general meeting.

On 30th April 1952 Morgan was adjudicated bankrupt
and vacated office as a director by virtue of article 23.

On 6th August 1952 Gray appointed his wife, the second
defendant, to be a director. He then called an extraordinary
general meeting of the company for 29th August for the
purpose of passing a resolution to delete articles 16 and
18. This meeting was attended by Morgan, who sought
to vote and tendered proxies in the alternative on his own
behalf and on behalf of his trustee in bankruptcy, the
second plaintiff. Gray refused to allow Morgan to vote, or
to accept the proxies tendered; acting under article 46 of
Table A of the *Companies Act*, 1929 (*see now article 54 of*

Table A of the Companies Act, 1948), which was largely incorporated in the company's articles, he declared that there was no quorum; adjourned the meeting for one week; and at the adjourned meeting on 6th September declared the resolution carried, again rejecting the plaintiff's vote and proxies.

The annual general meeting of the company was called for 18th October, a notice being sent to the plaintiff trustee. Proxies in the alternative for the plaintiffs were again tendered and were rejected by Gray, who adjourned the meeting for want of a quorum. At the adjourned meeting on 25th October, a resolution was passed purporting to appoint Mrs. Gray a director.

The plaintiffs, who contended that Morgan's votes and proxies had throughout been improperly rejected, brought an action against Mr. and Mrs. Gray and the company, claiming injunctions to restrain the defendants from acting on the purported resolutions deleting articles 16 and 18, and appointing Mrs. Gray as a director.

DANCKWERTS J.: It is claimed on behalf of the plaintiffs that, as the plaintiff Morgan remained on the register of the company throughout the whole of these material dates, he remained entitled to vote at those meetings, and that his vote in person when he was present and his proxies which would have been available if he had been allowed to demand a poll, or if his representatives had been allowed to demand a poll, were improperly disallowed; and, therefore, that the resolutions were not properly passed at the adjourned meetings in those cases.

It is curious that apparently it has never been decided whether, in spite of bankruptcy, a member of a company who remains a registered proprietor of shares on the company's register can continue to vote. It is no doubt the case that, if he can vote, he must exercise those votes in accordance with the direction of the persons beneficially entitled to the shares, which in the present case would, of course, be his trustee in bankruptcy, because the beneficial interest in his shares at any rate would have vested in the trustee in bankruptcy.

. . . It seems to me that, unless there is some provision in the company's articles or in the *Companies Act* which empowers me to say that the bankrupt is no longer a member of the company, and is, therefore, unable to vote, expressly, I must come to the conclusion that the bankrupt still remains a member as long as he is on the register; notwithstanding that by taking appropriate steps under the appropriate provisions the trustee in bankruptcy may be able to secure registration of himself as the proprietor of the shares. Unless and until that is done, and as long as the bankrupt remains on the register of the company, he remains a member in respect of those shares and is entitled, as it seems to me, to exercise the votes which are attributable to that status, notwithstanding that he has no longer any beneficial interest in the shares and that the company is entitled to pay any dividends to his trustee in bankruptcy.

It seems to me, therefore, that at all material times in the present case the person who was the proprietor of the 50 shares not held by Mr. Gray was Mr. Morgan, and that Mr. Morgan was entitled to attend the meetings of the company, even though he might not be able to demand that notices of general meetings should be sent to him and not to his trustee in bankruptcy. If he attended, as long as he was on the register he was entitled to vote; and as long as he was on the register he was entitled to give proxies for somebody else to vote on his behalf.

Accordingly, in my judgment, the resolutions on which the defendant company relies should not have been passed.

I will make an order that the defendants be restrained from acting upon a special resolution that the articles of association of the defendant company be altered by the deletion of articles 16 and 18 therefrom, alleged to have been passed on September 5, 1952; and an order restraining the defendants and each of them from acting upon an alleged resolution at the adjourned annual general meeting of the defendant company confirming the appointment of the defendant Mabel Muriel Gray.

Re West Canadian Collieries Ltd. [1962] Ch. 370

Where a clause in a company's articles of association is in the same terms as article 51 of Table A of the Companies Act, 1948, notice of a meeting is deemed to have been duly given despite an accidental omission to give notice to certain members entitled to it.

The registrar of a company, West Canadian Collieries Ltd., in sending out to members notices of a special resolution for the reduction of capital to be proposed at the annual general meeting, inadvertently omitted to send notices to nine of the members. The omission was due to the fact that the addressograph plates of these nine members were kept in a separate place to ensure that dividend warrants were not sent out to them, since in the past such warrants had either been returned to the company or not been cashed.

Article 75 of the company's articles of association was identical in terms with article 51 of Table A.

The special resolution was passed at the meeting, and the company petitioned the court for confirmation of the re-duction of capital. The petition was unopposed.

PLOWMAN J.: The question which I have to decide is whether the allegation that the special resolution for the reduction of capital was duly passed has been proved, having regard to the events which happened concerning the notices convening the annual general meeting and the omission to send the notices to those nine members. . . .

There appears to be no authority as to the effect of that article [*article 75*] in the circumstances that I am considering, although it is a common form article in identically the same terms as article 51 of the current Table A. The fact that it is a Table A article means that its validity as an article cannot be impugned. . . .

In the first place, I am satisfied that the omission to give notice of the meeting to the nine members in question was "accidental" within article 75. It follows from that that the omission to give notice to the nine members did not—and I

quote the article—"invalidate the proceedings at that meeting."
But the question arises whether the result of this is (a) that
though the proceedings of the meeting were valid, the notice
of the meeting is nevertheless still not deemed to have been
duly given for the purposes of S.141, or (b) that the notice of
the meeting is to be deemed to have been duly given for the
purposes of that section. The latter, in my judgment, is the
true view. It must, I think, be implicit in article 75 that a
meeting, the proceedings of which are to be taken to be valid
notwithstanding the omission to give notice to members, is to
be deemed to have been duly convened for the purposes of the
articles, including in those purposes the manner of convening
the meeting. It seems to me that, in the absence of such an
implication, there would be no meeting the proceedings of
which could be validated by the articles. I say that there would
be no meeting, because it is well settled that as regards a
general meeting failure to give notice to a single person entitled to receive notice renders the meeting a nullity.

I therefore hold that the notice of the meeting was duly
given, and that the resolution in question was duly passed for
the purposes of S.141, and therefore . . . I propose to confirm
the reduction.

Musselwhite and Another *v*. Musselwhite & Son Ltd. and Others.
[1962] Ch. 964

*Omission to give notice of a meeting due to an error of law is
not "accidental" within article 51 of Table A.*

*An unpaid vendor of shares remaining on the register after
the contract for sale retains the prima facie right to vote in
respect of those shares.*

The first defendant was a private company, C. H. Musselwhite & Co. Ltd., which was formed in 1933 with a share
capital of 8,000 £1 shares. 7,200 of these shares were issued
fully paid up. The plaintiffs, Mr. Ross James Musselwhite
and his wife Doris Annie Musselwhite, were the registered holders of 3,599 and one of these shares respectively, and the individual defendants, Mr. John Kenneth
Musselwhite and his wife Laura Amy Musselwhite, were

also the registered holders of 3,599 and one of the shares respectively.

The first plaintiff was the uncle of the male defendant. The plaintiffs and the individual defendants constituted the board, and Mr. Ross James Musselwhite was the managing director and secretary. The company's articles of association incorporated Table A set out in the First Schedule to the *Companies Act*, 1929, article 43 of which is identical to article 51 of Table A set out in the First Schedule to the *Companies Act*, 1948.

Owing to differences on policy between the parties, by an agreement dated 21st May 1958, Mr. Ross Musselwhite agreed on behalf of himself and his wife to sell their shares in the company and another company to Mr. Kenneth Musselwhite for £10,000, of which sum £7,500 was to be paid by three-monthly instalments of £375 over five years. The agreement also provided that transfers of the shares should be executed and that the executed transfers and the relevant share certificates should be deposited with the company's solicitors until payment had been made in full.

In accordance with the agreement, the relevant transfers and certificates were deposited with the solicitors and the plaintiffs resigned as directors and Mr. Ross Musselwhite also resigned as secretary. The plaintiffs remained on the company's register of members as the holders of the shares. The instalments were being duly paid, and at the date of the hearing about £2,600 was still outstanding.

On 30th December 1958 the annual general meeting of the company for the year ending 31st May 1958 was purported to be held. No notice of such meeting was given to either of the plaintiffs. The omission to give such notice resulted from the then directors of the company being under the erroneous impression that the plaintiffs, having executed transfers of their shares to Mr. Kenneth Musselwhite, were no longer members of the company and were not, therefore, entitled to receive such notice.

In October 1959 a further fifty shares of the original share capital were issued to Laura Amy Musselwhite.

In January 1960 the plaintiffs issued a writ claiming (1) a declaration that the meeting was invalid and that every resolution carried thereat was irregular, invalid and of no

effect, and (2) an order that the company convene a fresh
annual general meeting for the year ending 31st May 1958,
and that at the said meeting the members of the company
should have votes in respect only of those shares held
respectively by them on 1st December 1958.

The defendants denied that the plaintiffs were entitled
to the relief claimed, and counterclaimed for an injunction
to restrain the plaintiffs from attending or voting at any
annual general meeting of the company or exercising
any other rights in relation to the shares registered in the
names of the plaintiffs except in accordance with directions given by Mr. Kenneth Musselwhite.

RUSSELL J.: On December 30th, 1958, the annual general
meeting of the company was held. I am not concerned with
what business was before the meeting or what passed. No
notice of the meeting was served on the plaintiffs. Prima
facie the meeting was a nullity for that reason. The defendants,
however, rely on the relevant article 43 [*article 51 of Table A
of the Companies Act, 1948*]. . . . I fail to understand how the
omission to give notice to the plaintiffs was accidental. As Mr.
Dehn for the plaintiffs succinctly put it, it would have been
accidental if a notice had been given to the plaintiffs. It was
argued that an omission founded on a misapprehension of
law, or indeed of fact, was accidental. Reference was made to
the cases of *Barker* v. *Purvis* and *In re Inchcape*. . . . I do not
see how these cases can support the argument that an omission
is accidental because it arises from an error.

. . . Prima facie, therefore, the plaintiffs are entitled to their
declaration that the annual general meeting was a nullity.
On that basis they ask for an order that the annual general
meeting for the year 1957–58, now long overdue, be held. By
itself, this would be unnecessary, even if the court had power
to order it, but in truth, what the plaintiffs wanted was a
declaration that whenever such meeting was held the voting
rights should be on the basis of the state of the share register
at the expiration of the period during which the meeting was
required by law to have been held. The exact date is not
determined, but it would have been prior to a date in October,

1959, when 50 more shares of the original capital were issued and registered in the name of the female defendant, upsetting the balance on the register between the families. . . . I know of no justification for this proposition in authority or statute law, and it seems to me wrong in principle.

. . . The question really, for the purpose of this case, is whether, as between the plaintiffs and the individual defendants, the plaintiffs have the prima facie right to decide how to exercise the voting rights in respect of the shares, or whether the defendants have the prima facie right to direct in all cases how those votes are to be cast. If the former, then there is no justification for not holding a proper meeting: if the latter, there is no point in holding a proper meeting and no justification for this action.

. . . I turn next to the position of an unpaid vendor of shares (still on the register), *vis-à-vis* the purchaser in connection with voting rights. Counsel was not able to find any authority directly on this point. For the plaintiffs it was submitted that such a vendor was in at least no worse position than a mortgagee on the register. For the defendants it was submitted that he was in the position of trustee for the purchaser to whom, on the signing of the contract, the beneficial ownership had passed (contract being specifically enforceable) and that the position of a mortgagee on the register was different.

. . . In my judgment, so far as voting powers are concerned, an unpaid vendor remaining on the register is not to be regarded as in a weaker position, so far as the exercise of voting powers is concerned, than a mortgagee. The purchaser acquires the beneficial interest subject to the vendor's lien: the mortgagor retains the beneficial interest subject to the charge in favour of the mortgagee, in the form of an equity of redemption. In the one case the mortgagee is deliberately put on the register to safeguard his money lent: in the other case the vendor is deliberately left on the register until all is paid to safeguard his purchase-money due.

In my judgment an unpaid vendor of shares remaining on the register after the contract for sale retains *vis-à-vis* the purchaser the prima facie right to vote in respect of those shares.

. . . Accordingly, the plaintiffs are entitled to a declaration in terms of . . . the writ, and the counterclaim must be dismissed.

Re London Flats, Ltd. [1969] 1 W.L.R. 711

As a general rule one member of a company cannot constitute a meeting, so that a meeting terminates on the departure of all the members save one.

The liquidator of a private company in voluntary liquidation died and a meeting of shareholders was called to pass a resolution appointing a successor.

Only two shareholders were present, being the only persons entitled to vote. One of them was proposing to amend the resolution by substituting his own name for the person named therein when the other shareholder left the meeting, pointing out that there was then no quorum. The remaining shareholder then purported to appoint himself as liquidator.

A summons was taken out to determine whether the appointment was valid.

PLOWMAN J.: . . . In the present case I can find no context which enables me to say that a meeting of one member is good enough.

It is true that in *In re Hartley Baird Ltd.* (1955) WYNN PARRY J. held on the construction of the company's memorandum and articles . . . that if a quorum was present at the beginning of a meeting the subsequent departure of a member reducing the meeting below the number required for a quorum does not invalidate the proceedings of the meeting after his departure. But the quorum in that case was 10, and the departure of one member still left nine, so that the point with which I am concerned did not arise. There, the question was quorum or no quorum, while here it is meeting or no meeting.

It is also true that there are certain circumstances in which the *Companies Act*, 1948, enables one member of a company to constitute a meeting. They may be found in S.131 (2) and S.135 (1). But they are exceptional cases which have no application here.

In my judgment, therefore, the respondent's purported appointment of himself as liquidator was a nullity.

Re Duomatic Ltd. [1969] 2 Ch. 365

Where all the shareholders who have a right to attend and vote at a general meeting assent to some matter which a general meeting could carry into effect, that assent is as binding as a resolution in general meeting.

S.191 requires disclosure of payment of compensation for loss of office to all members of the company, whether they have a right to attend and vote at a general meeting or not.

Duomatic Ltd. was incorporated in 1960 with a share capital of 100 £1 ordinary shares and 80,000 £1 non-voting redeemable preference shares. The ordinary shares were held by the three directors in the following proportions: Mr. James Elvins, seventy-six; Mr. William Hanly, twenty-two; and Mr. Patrick East, two. The non-voting preference shares were all held by a Dutch company, A. G. Bondo N.V.

Mr. Hanly quarrelled with his co-directors who were critical of the way in which he performed his duties. They could have voted him off the board, but since he threatened, if dismissed, to sue the company, he was paid £4,000 as an inducement to leave the company without making trouble, although he had no contract of service. On 1st April 1963 he ceased to be a director and the following month transferred his twenty-two shares to Mr. Elvins.

The company's business of selling washing machines was not prospering when in April 1964 Mr. Wood, a representative of Bentworth Credits Ltd., the finance company that was providing the company's hire-purchase business, joined the board. In July 1964 Mr. Elvins transferred thirty-two of his shares to Mr. Wood, and thirty-two shares each to Mr. Weikersheim and Mr. Conisbee, two other officers of the finance company. He was thus left with only two shares.

On 13th August 1964, the capital of the company was increased and thereafter the ordinary shareholders consisted of Mr. Elvins, Mr. East, Mr. Wood, Mr. Weikersheim, Precast Concrete Ltd. and Bentworth Credits Ltd. At the same time Mr. Middleton-Smith joined the board so that thenceforth the board consisted of Mr. Elvins, Mr East, Mr. Wood and Mr. Middleton-Smith.

The articles of the company incorporated by reference article 76 of Table A. However, no resolution was ever passed authorising the directors to receive any remuneration. The directors drew sums from the company in accordance with their personal needs, and at the end of each financial year these drawings were totalled and grossed up in order to account for tax. In the year ended 30th April 1963 Mr. Elvins drew £10,151 0s. 8d. and Mr. Hanly £5,510 1s., and the total of those amounts was shown in the profit and loss account as "directors' salaries." These accounts were signed and approved by Mr. Elvins and Mr. East as directors.

In the following financial year Mr. Elvins drew £9,000, which appeared in the draft profit and loss account, but no final accounts were ever prepared or approved. When Mr. Wood joined the board, Mr. Elvins agreed to accept a lower rate of remuneration of £60 per week. However, from 1st May 1964 to 23rd October 1964 when the company went into voluntary liquidation, Mr. Elvins drew £2,197 15s. 3d. No managing director was ever appointed, and none of the directors had any contract of service.

The liquidator took out a summons claiming from Mr. Elvins the sum of £21,348 15s. 11d.; the total of the amounts paid to him between 30th April 1962 and the liquidation of the company, on the ground that none of these payments had been voted by the company in general meeting. From Mr. Hanly he claimed repayment of the sum of £5,510 1s., and the sum of £4,000 paid to him as compensation for loss of office on the ground that it was excessive, not duly authorised and not *bona fide* for the benefit of the company. He also claimed that Mr. Elvins and Mr Hanly were guilty of misfeasance as directors in permitting a payment to the other, and an order against them jointly and severally to repay the sum of £4,000.

BUCKLEY J.: . . . It is common ground that none of the sums which I have mentioned were authorised by any resolution of the company in general meeting, nor were they authorised by any resolution of any formally constituted board meeting; but it is said on behalf of Mr. Elvins that the payments were made with the full knowledge and consent of all the holders of voting shares in the company at the relevant times, and he contends that in those circumstances the absence of a formal resolution by the company in duly convened meeting of the company is irrelevant. Alternatively, he relies on S.448 of the *Companies Act*, 1948.

. . . The evidence in the present case, I think, establishes that Mr. Elvins and Mr. East both approved the accounts of the company for the year ended April 30th, 1963, and, indeed, they signed a copy of those accounts; and the evidence is that that was done on an occasion when they met together with the auditor of the company. . . . It is not clear from the evidence precisely when that meeting took place, but I think it must be before Mr. Wood joined the board, and at a time when Mr. Elvins and Mr. East were the only two directors of the company, and the only shareholders in the company were Mr. Elvins and Mr. East and the preference shareholder.

. . . Mr. Wright, for the liquidator, has contended that where there has been no formal meeting of the company and reliance is placed upon the informal consent of the shareholders the cases indicate that it is necessary to establish that all shareholders have consented. He argues that as the preference shareholder is not shown to have consented in the present case, that requirement is not satisfied, and that the assent of those shareholders—that is to say, Mr. Elvins and Mr. East—who knew about these matters, and who did approve the figures relating to them in the accounts for the year ending April 30th, 1963, is of no significance. It seems to me that if it had occurred to Mr. Elvins and Mr. East, at the time when they were considering the accounts, to take the formal step of constituting themselves a general meeting of the company and passing a formal resolution approving the payment of directors' salaries, that it would have made the position of the directors who received the remuneration, Mr. Elvins and Mr. Hanly, secure and nobody could thereafter have disputed their right to retain their remuneration. The fact that they did not take that formal step but that they nevertheless did apply their minds to the question of whether the drawings by Mr. Elvins and Mr. Hanly should be approved as being on account of remuneration payable to them as directors, seems to lead to the conclusion that I ought to regard their consent as being tantamount to a resolution of a general meeting of the company. In other words, I proceed upon the basis that where it can be shown that all shareholders who have a right to attend and vote at a general meeting of the company assent to some matter which a general meeting of the company could carry into effect, that assent is as binding as a resolution in general meeting would be. The preference shareholder, having shares which conferred upon him no right to receive notice of or to attend and vote at a general meeting of the company, could be in no worse position if the matter were dealt with informally by agreement between all the shareholders having voting rights than he would be if the shareholders met together in a duly constituted general meeting.

Accordingly, the evidence that I have heard leads to the conclusion that the drawings by Mr. Elvins and Mr. Hanly during the accounting year ending April 30th, 1963 ... cannot now be disturbed.

... As regards the drawings after April 30th, 1964, amounting to £2,197 15s. 3d., it is not disputed that to the extent that they exceed what it was legitimate for Mr. Elvins to draw under the arrangement of £60 a week, Mr. Elvins must repay the excess. ... The evidence, in my judgment, does establish that Mr. East knew of the existence of such an arrangement between Mr. Elvins and Mr. Wood, and that Mr. Weikersheim and Mr. Conisbee also knew. ... So that at a time when the ordinary shares were held exclusively by Mr. Elvins, Mr. East, Mr. Wood, Mr. Weikersheim and Mr. Conisbee, I think it is established that all those shareholders knew of, and agreed to, an arrangement under which Mr. Elvins would henceforth draw not more than £60 a week. At that stage, had a resolution of the company in general meeting been passed to that effect, there would be no question that from May 1st, 1964, to the date of the winding-up resolution, Mr. Elvins would have been entitled to draw at that rate by way of remuneration; and that would be so, I think, notwithstanding that at a later date two other shareholders were added to the list of ordinary shareholders, for those two additional shareholders would be bound by what had been constitutionally done within the company before they became members of it.

The conclusion I reach, therefore, with regard to the drawings after April 30th, 1964, is that Mr. Elvins is liable to repay to the liquidator only such excess as there may be over what he would have been entitled to draw on the basis of the £60-a-week arrangement.

With regard to the compensation for loss of office, the £4,000 paid to Mr. Hanly, the requirements of S.191 of the *Companies Act*, 1948, were not complied with. . . . That section must, I think, require disclosure to all members of the company, and it must require disclosure . . . before the payment is made; and it further requires that the proposal be approved by the company, which must, I think, mean by the company in general meeting.

In the present case it is clear that no particulars of this payment of £4,000 were, before the date that the payment was made, given to all the members of the company, for no such disclosure was at any time made to the preference shareholder. There would, I think, be good reason for making such disclosure to him, notwithstanding that he would have no right to attend at any general meeting convened for the purpose of approving the payment, because although he was not, by virtue of his preference shareholding, entitled to receive notice of general meetings or attend and vote at them, he might nevertheless wish to make his views known to those who would attend and vote at the general meeting. . . . It follows that the payment was an *ultra vires* payment, for it was a payment which the section says it was not lawful for the company to make. The directors responsible for making it are liable in respect of it on the grounds of misapplication of the company's funds unless they ought to be excused under S.448. The section enables the court to grant relief where three circumstances are shown to exist. First of all the position must be such that the person to be excused is shown to have acted honestly; secondly, he must be shown to have acted reasonably; and thirdly, it must be shown that, having regard to all the circumstances of the case, he ought fairly to be excused.

Let me say at once that nobody has impugned Mr. Elvins' honesty in respect of any of these matters. . . . I therefore proceed upon the footing that both in respect of the £4,000 and in respect of his drawings in the year to April 30th, 1964, he acted honestly. Did he act reasonably in those respects, and are the circumstances such that he ought fairly to be excused?

I will deal first with his drawings. Those drawings were made in continuation of the practice adopted in the previous year, which had the approval of his co-director, and it is said on his behalf that he could not be expected to work for the company for nothing and that it was reasonable for him to expect to be remunerated, and that it was reasonable for him to expect that, when the time came, the company would approve his having drawn on account of his remuneration in the way he did. More particularly it is said it was reasonable that he would anticipate that because he was himself the majority shareholder. The mistake arose from the fact that it never occurred to anybody to pass the necessary resolution. On the other hand, the regulations of the company, by reference to Article 76 of Table A, specifically required that the remuneration of a director should be voted by the company in general meeting, from which it follows that in law a director of a company is not entitled to any remuneration at all unless and until it is voted. He is not entitled to say, after a period of service, "I have served the company well and I have earned remuneration and I require the company to vote me a reasonable remuneration for what I have done." He is not entitled to make a claim on a *quantum meruit* basis, and if he chooses to draw on the company in anticipation of a resolution sanctioning those drawings and then, for some reason or another, no such resolution is ever passed, he is not entitled

to say: "It is right that I should be allowed to retain what I
have drawn." In these circumstances can it be said that a
director acts reasonably when he makes drawings on account
of remuneration to which he is not presently entitled but to
which he hopes to become entitled as the result of some resolution to be passed in the future? Whether he acts reasonably
or not must, it seems to me, to some extent depend upon the
way in which matters have been handled in the company in the
past, and I think that it is difficult to say that Mr. Elvins did
not act reasonably in continuing to make his drawings in the
same sort of way in which he had made drawings in the previous
year. . . .

But ought he to be excused from his liability to repay the
amount of those drawings having regard to the legal position
in which he stood? . . . Directors must, I think, take the
trouble to discover just what their rights and obligations are,
and if they draw on account of remuneration to which they
are not entitled in anticipation of its being voted to them in the
future, then normally the director could not be said to be acting
reasonably and ought not to be excused.

However there is, in the present case, I think, this important
circumstance, that at the time he made these drawings Mr.
Elvins was in control of this company. He could have passed,
in general meeting, any resolution he chose. It was an over-
sight that no resolution was ever passed authorising him to
retain the amount of these drawings. He has not held the
company to ransom in any way by what he did. . . . Here the
error was one of substance, but still of a technical nature.

It was just that he did not appreciate that, in order to
retain what he had in all honesty drawn as his remuneration
from the company, he ought to procure the passing of a resolution.

In the special circumstances of this case I think that it is
one in which I can excuse Mr. Elvins in respect of the drawings
during the year ended April 30th, 1964.

As regards the £4,000 paid to Mr. Hanly. He was not in a
strong position to stipulate for any compensation for loss of
office. He had no contract of service, he had no security of

tenure of his seat on the board, his conduct during the twelve months or so preceding his departure from the board appears, from the evidence, to have been such as to merit very little consideration from the point of view of remuneration for his services during that period. He had been constantly in default in the performance of his duties and had been causing his co-directors a great deal of trouble, and his conduct seems to have been likely to have caused the company considerable damage. Nevertheless, in respect of the last twelve months or so of his service as a director of the company he received remuneration of the order of £5,000, and there really was no ground at all on which he could claim any compensation for loss of office as a director of the company. On the other hand, I think it is very probable that Mr. Elvins and Mr. East were justified in their view that he could have made himself a considerable nuisance to the company had he chosen to do so after he had ceased to be a director. It never seems to have occurred to Mr. Elvins or to Mr. East that it would be desirable to obtain any professional advice as to the strength of Mr. Hanly's bargaining position. They obtained no legal advice and no professional advice of any other kind, except so far as they had advice from their accountant and auditor. . . . Neither Mr. Elvins nor Mr. East appear to have taken into account that, under the *Companies Act*, 1948, the company could have removed Mr. Hanly from his office as a director. . . .

. . . The question which I have to ask myself is whether, in acting in the way in which he did, Mr. Elvins acted reasonably. I do not think that he was acting in the way in which a man of affairs dealing with his own affairs with reasonable care and circumspection could reasonably be expected to act in such a case, for I think that any such imaginary character would take pains to find out all the relevant circumstances, many of which in this case depended on some knowledge of the law, and ought to have encouraged Mr. Elvins to seek the assistance of a legal adviser. Moreover, it was Mr. Elvins' failure to seek legal advice that resulted in this payment being made in contravention of S.191 of the Act and constituted it an *ultra vires* payment which the company could not lawfully make. In these circumstances I do not think that the provisions of S.448 avail Mr. Elvins in respect of this sum.

To summarise the result of this judgment, I therefore reach the conclusion that the claim put forward by the liquidator fails as regard all the sums claimed except the £4,000 and so much of the £2,197 15s. 3d. as constitutes an excess over the amount which Mr. Elvins was properly entitled to draw under the £60-a-week arrangement.

. . . I have been directing my mind to Mr. Elvins throughout this judgment. Of course, it does mean that Mr. Hanly is also liable in respect of the £4,000, with interest.

Bushell v. Faith. [1970] A.C. 1099

S.184 Companies Act, 1948, provides that an ordinary resolution will suffice to remove a director, but does not prevent the attachment by the articles of special voting rights to shares even where it has the effect of making the section inoperative.

The facts sufficiently appear from the speech of LORD UPJOHN in the House of Lords.

LORD REID: My Lords, I agree with the majority of your Lordships that this appeal must be dismissed. Article 9 of the articles of association of this company is obviously designed to evade S.184 (1) of the *Companies Act*, 1948. . . . The extra voting power given by that article to a director, whose removal from office is proposed, makes it impossible in the circumstances of this case for any resolution for the removal of any director to be passed if that director votes against it.

. . . [T]he practice of giving special voting rights or special lack of voting rights to a particular class of shares is old and is recognised in article 2 of Table A in the First Schedule to the 1948 Act. . . . [I]t may be that the whole practice will be reviewed when amendments to the *Companies Act* are being proposed. But we must take the law as we find it.

LORD MORRIS: . . . I would allow the appeal.

LORD GUEST: My Lords, I have had the advantage of reading

the opinion of my noble and learned friend, LORD DONOVAN, with which I agree. I would dismiss the appeal.

LORD UPJOHN: My Lords, this appeal raises a question of some importance to those concerned with the niceties of company law, and the relevant facts, which are not in dispute, can be very shortly stated.

The respondent company, Bush Court (Southgate) Ltd., . . . was incorporated on September 19th, 1960, and at all material times had an issued capital of 300 fully paid up shares of £1 each held as to 100 shares each by a brother and his two sisters, namely, the appellant Mrs. Bushell, the respondent Mr. Faith and their sister Dr. Kathleen Bayne.

Mr. Faith was a director but his conduct as such displeased his sisters who requisitioned a general meeting of the company which was held on November 22, 1968, when a resolution was proposed as an ordinary resolution to remove him from his office as director. On a show of hands the resolution was passed, as the sisters voted for the resolution; so the brother demanded a poll and the whole issue is how votes should be counted upon the poll having regard to special article 9 of the company's articles of association.

The company adopted Table A in the First Schedule to the *Companies Act*, 1948, with variations which are immaterial for present purposes. . . .

Special article 9 is as follows:

"In the event of a resolution being proposed at any general meeting of the company for the removal from office of any director, any shares held by that director shall on a poll in respect of such a resolution carry the right to three votes per share and regulation 62 of Part I of Table A shall be construed accordingly."

Article 96 of Table A . . . is excluded by the articles of the company so that the appellant relies on the mandatory terms of S.184 (1) of the *Companies Act*, 1948. . . . It is not in doubt that the requirements of subsection (2) have been satisfied. So the whole question is whether special article 9 is valid and applicable, in which case the resolution was rejected by 300 votes to 200, or whether that article must be treated as over-ridden by S.184 and therefore void, in which case the resolution was passed by 200 votes to 100. So to test this matter the appellant began an action for a declaration that the respondent was removed from office as a director by the resolution of November 22, 1968, and moved the court for an interlocutory injunction restraining him from acting as a director. This motion comes by way of appeal before your Lordships.

The appellant argues that special article 9 is directed to frustrating the whole object and purpose of S.184 so that it can never operate where there is such a special article and the director in fact becomes irremovable. So she argues that, having regard to the clear words "notwithstanding anything in its articles" in S.184, special article 9 must be rejected and treated as void. The learned judge, UNGOED-THOMAS J., so held. He said: "It would make a mockery of the law if the courts were to hold that in such a case a director was to be irremovable." And later he concluded his judgment by saying: "A resolution under article 9 is therefore not in my view an ordinary resolution within S.184. The plaintiff succeeds in the application."

The brother appealed, and the Court of Appeal (HARMAN, RUSSELL and KARMINSKI L.JJ.) allowed the appeal. HARMAN L.J. did so on the simple ground that the Act of 1948 did not prevent certain shares or classes of shares having special voting rights attached to them and on certain occasions. He could find nothing in the Act of 1948 which prohibited the giving of special voting rights to the shares of a director who finds his position attacked. RUSSELL L.J. in his judgment gave substantially the same reasons for allowing the appeal. . . .

My Lords, when construing an Act of Parliament it is a canon of construction that its provisions must be construed in the light of the mischief which the Act was designed to meet. In this case the mischief was well known; it was a common practice, especially in the case of private companies, to provide in the articles that a director should be irremovable or only removable by an extraordinary resolution; in the former case the articles would have to be altered by special resolution before the director could be removed and of course in either case a three-quarters majority would be required. In many cases this would be impossible, so the Act provided that notwithstanding anything in the articles an ordinary resolution would suffice to remove a director. That was the mischief which the section set out to remedy; to make a director removable by virtue of an ordinary resolution instead of an extraordinary resolution or making it necessary to alter the articles.

An ordinary resolution is not defined nor used in the body of the Act of 1948 though the phrase occurs in some of the articles of Table A in the First Schedule to the Act. But its meaning is, in my opinion, clear. An ordinary resolution is in the first place passed by a bare majority on a show of hands by the members entitled to vote who are present personally or by proxy and on such a vote each member has one vote regardless of his shareholding. If a poll is demanded then for an ordinary resolution still only a bare majority of votes is required. But whether a share or class of shares has any vote upon the matter and, if so, what is its voting power upon the resolution in question depends entirely upon the voting rights attached to that share or class of shares by the articles of association.

I venture to think that Ungoed-Thomas J. overlooked the importance of article 2 of Table A which gives to the company a completely unfettered right to attach to any share or class of shares special voting rights upon a poll or to restrict those rights as the company may think fit. Thus, it is commonplace that a company may and frequently does preclude preference shareholders from voting unless their dividends are in arrear or their class rights are directly affected. It is equally commonplace that particular shares may be issued with specially loaded voting rights which ensure that in all resolutions put before the shareholders in general meeting the holder of those particular shares can always be sure of carrying the day, aye or no, as the holder pleases.

Mr. Dillon, for the appellant, felt, quite rightly, constrained to admit that if an article provided that Mr. Faith's shares

should, on every occasion when a resolution was for consideration by a general meeting of the company, carry three votes
such a provision would be valid on all such occasions, including any occasion when the general meeting was considering
a resolution for his removal under S.184.

My Lords, I cannot see any difference between that case and
the present case where special voting rights are conferred only
when there is a resolution for the removal of a director under
S.184. Each case is an exercise of the unfettered right of the
company under article 2. . . . Parliament has never sought
to fetter the right of the company to issue a share with such
rights or restrictions as it may think fit. There is no fetter
which compels the company to make the voting rights or
restrictions of general application and it seems to me clear
that such rights or restrictions can be attached to special
circumstances and to particular types of resolution. This makes
no mockery of S.184; all that Parliament was seeking to do
thereby was to make an ordinary resolution sufficient to remove a director. Had Parliament desired to go further and
enact that every share entitled to vote should be deprived of
its special rights under the articles it should have said so in
plain terms by making the vote on a poll one vote one share.
Then, what about shares which had no voting rights under the
articles? Should not Parliament give them a vote when considering this completely artificial form of ordinary resolution?
Suppose there had here been some preference shares in the
name of Mr. Faith's wife, which under the articles had in the
circumstances no vote; why in justice should her voice be
excluded from consideration in this artificial vote?

I only raise this purely hypothetical case to show the great
difficulty of trying to do justice by legislation in a matter which
has always been left to the corporators themselves to decide.

I agree entirely with the judgment of the Court of Appeal,
and would dismiss this appeal.

LORD DONOVAN: My Lords, the issue here is the true construction of S.184 of the *Companies Act*, 1948: and I approach it
with no conception of what the legislature wanted to achieve

by the section other than such as can reasonably be deduced from its language.

Clearly it was intended to alter the method by which a director of a company could be removed while still in office. It enacts that this can be done by the company by ordinary resolution. Furthermore, it may be achieved notwithstanding anything in the company's articles, or in any agreement between the company and the director.

Accordingly any case (and one knows there were many) where the articles prescribed that a director should be removable during his period of office only by a special resolution or an extraordinary resolution, each of which necessitated *inter alia* a three to one majority of those present and voting at the meeting, is over-ridden by S.184. A simple majority of the votes will now suffice; an ordinary resolution being, in my opinion, a resolution capable of being carried by such a majority. Similarly any agreement, whether evidenced by the articles or otherwise, that a director shall be a director for life or for some fixed period is now also overreached.

The field over which S.184 operates is thus extensive for it includes, admittedly, all companies with a quotation on the Stock Exchange.

It is now contended, however, that it does something more; namely, that it provides in effect that when the ordinary resolution proposing the removal of the director is put to the meeting each shareholder present shall have one vote per share and no more: and that any provision in the articles providing that any shareholder shall, in relation to *this* resolution, have "weighted" votes attached to his shares, is also nullified by S.184. A provision for such "weighting" of votes which applies generally, that is as part of the normal pattern of voting, is accepted by the appellant as unobjectionable: but an article such as the one here under consideration which is special to a resolution seeking the removal of a director falls foul of S.184 and is over-ridden by it.

Why should this be? The section does not say so, as it easily could. And those who drafted it and enacted it certainly would have included among their numbers many who were familiar with the phenomenon of articles of association carrying "weighted votes." It must therefore have been plain at the outset that unless some special provision were made, the mere direction that an ordinary resolution would do in order to remove a director would leave the section at risk of being made inoperative in the way that has been done here. Yet no such provision was made, and in this Parliament followed its practice of leaving to companies and their shareholders liberty to allocate voting rights as they pleased.

When, therefore, it is said that a decision in favour of the respondent in this case would defeat the purpose of the section and make a mockery of it, it is being assumed that Parliament *intended* to cover every possible case and block up every loophole. I see no warrant for any such assumption. A very large part of the relevant field is in fact covered and covered effectively. And there may be good reasons why Parliament should leave some companies with freedom of manoeuvre in this particular matter. There are many small companies which are conducted in practice as though they were little more than partnerships, particularly family companies running a family business; and it is, unfortunately, sometimes necessary to provide some safeguard against family quarrels having their repercussions in the boardroom. I am not, of course, saying that this is such a case: I merely seek to repel the argument that unless the section is construed in the way the appellant wants, it has become "inept" and "frustrated."

I would dismiss the appeal.

XV. FRAUD ON THE MINORITY

North-West Transportation Company, Limited _v._ Beatty. (1887) 12 A.C. 589

A shareholder at a general meeting is entitled to vote on any matter as he pleases, even though he is a director of the company.

This was an appeal to the Judicial Committee of the Privy Council.

The facts are sufficiently stated in the judgment, which was delivered by SIR RICHARD BAGGALLAY.

SIR RICHARD BAGGALLAY: The action, in which this appeal has been brought, was commenced on the 31st of May, 1883, in the Chancery Division of the High Court of Justice of Ontario. The plaintiff, Henry Beatty, is a shareholder in the North-West Transportation Company, Limited, and he sues on behalf of himself and all other shareholders in the company, except those who are defendants. The defendants are the company and five shareholders, who, at the commencement of the action, were the directors of the company. The claim in the action is to set aside a sale made to the company by James Hughes Beatty, one of the directors, of a steamer called the United Empire, of which previously to such sale he was sole owner.

The general principles applicable to cases of this kind are well established. Unless some provision to the contrary is to be found in the charter or other instrument by which the company is incorporated, the resolution of a majority of the shareholders, duly convened, upon any question with which the company is legally competent to deal, is binding upon the minority, and consequently upon the company, and every shareholder has a perfect right to vote upon any such question, although he may have a personal interest in the subject-matter opposed to, or different from, the general or particular interests of the company.

On the other hand, a director of a company is precluded from dealing, on behalf of the company, with himself, and from entering into engagements in which he has a personal interest conflicting, or which possibly may conflict, with the interests of those whom he is bound by fiduciary duty to protect; and this rule is as applicable to the case of one of several directors as to a managing or sole director. Any such dealing or engagement may, however, be affirmed or adopted by the company, provided such affirmance or adoption is not brought about by unfair or improper means, and is not illegal or fraudulent or oppressive towards those shareholders who oppose it.

The material facts of the case are not now in dispute.

The company was incorporated under the provisions of the *Canada Joint Stock Companies Letters Patent Act* of 1869. By its charter, dated the 5th of March, 1877, it was authorised to carry on business in the province of Ontario, and to construct, acquire, and maintain steam, sailing, and other vessels for the conveyance of passengers and goods over the navigable waters within or bordering upon the Dominion of Canada, to and from any foreign ports, with power, amongst other things, to sell, charter or dispose of any of such vessels, and to make contracts with any person or corporation whatever.

By SS.16, 18, and 22 of the Act of 1869, it was provided that the affairs of every company incorporated under its provisions should be managed by a board of directors, the major part of whom should at all times be resident in Canada, and subjects of Her Majesty, and that the directors should have power to make for the company any description of contract into which the company might by law enter, and from time to time to make bye-laws not contrary to law, but every bye-law so made, unless in the meantime confirmed at a general meeting duly called for that purpose, should only have force until the next annual meeting of the company, and, in default of confirmation thereat, should . . . cease to have force; and the powers conferred upon the directors by S.22 were made subject to a proviso that one fourth part in value of the shareholders of the company should at all times have the right to call a special meeting for the transaction of any business specified in such written requisition and notice as they might issue to that effect.

By bye-laws, made in March, 1877, and duly confirmed, it was provided that the affairs of the company should be managed by a board of five directors; that the qualification for a director should be the holding of five shares in the company; that every shareholder should have as many votes as he had shares in the company; that the annual meeting should be held on the first Wednesday in February in each year; and that at such meetings the directors should be annually elected, retiring directors being eligible for re-election.

The company commenced business shortly after its incorporation, and acquired for its purposes a fleet of several steamers. In the autumn of 1882, one of its steamers, the Asia, was lost, and another, the Sovereign, was deemed unsuitable for the company's business. At this time the steamer United Empire was in process of building for the defendant James Hughes Beatty, and was approaching completion; the contract for her construction had been entered into in December, 1880, and she was in fact completed on the 20th of May, 1883, a few days before the commencement of the action. The acquisition of the United Empire by the company had been suggested to the directors and had been the subject of consideration by them and others interested in the company as early as the close of the year 1881; the loss of the Asia led to the matter being further considered, and the sale to the company was brought about in the following manner.

The annual meeting for the year 1883 was held on the 7th of February, and, at such meeting, the defendants were elected directors for the ensuing year; at the same meeting, a discussion took place as to the suggested purchase of the United Empire, and it was resolved that a special meeting of the shareholders should be held on the 16th for the purpose of having submitted to them a bye-law for the purchase of the steamer United Empire, and also to consider the advisability of selling the steamer Sovereign.

At a meeting of the directors held on the 10th of February, 1883, and at which all the directors except the defendant William Beatty were present, it was resolved that a bye-law, which was read to the meeting, for the purchase of the United Empire should pass. . . . [A]fter reciting an agreement between the company and the defendant James Hughes Beatty, that the company should buy and the defendant should sell the steamer United Empire for the sum of $125,000, to be in part paid in cash and in part secured, . . . it was enacted that the company should purchase the steamer from the defendant upon those terms. . . .

The agreement recited in the bye-laws was executed at the same meeting.

At a meeting of shareholders, held, as arranged, on the 16th of February, 1883, the bye-law which had been enacted by the directors was read by the secretary, and, after being modified in its terms, with respect to the price, was adopted by a majority of votes.

The United Empire, on her completion, was delivered to the company, and has ever since been employed in the ordinary business of the company.

It is proved by uncontradicted evidence, and is indeed now substantially admitted, that at the date of the purchase the acquisition of another steamer to supply the place of the Asia was essential to the efficient conduct of the company's business; that it was not within the power of the company to acquire any other steamer equally well adapted for its business; and that the price agreed to be paid for the steamer was not excessive or unreasonable.

Had there been no material facts in the case other than those above stated, there would have been, in the opinion of their Lordships, no reason for setting aside the sale of the steamer; it would have been immaterial to consider whether the contract for the purchase of the United Empire should be regarded as one entered into by the directors and confirmed by the shareholders, or as one entirely emanating from the shareholders; in either view of the case, the transaction was one which, if carried out in a regular way, was within the powers of the company; in the former view, any defect arising from the fiduciary relationship of the defendant James Hughes Beatty to the company would be remedied by the resolution of the shareholders, on the 16th of February, and, in the latter, the fact of the defendant being a director would not deprive him of his right to vote, as a shareholder, in support of any resolution which he might deem favourable to his own interests.

There is, however, a further element for consideration, arising out of the following facts, which have been relied upon in the arguments on behalf of the plaintiff, as evidencing that the resolution of the 16th of February was brought about by unfair and improper means.

It appears that, at the commencement of the year 1883, 595 of the 600 shares in which the capital of the company was divided were held by seven living shareholders, and five belonged to the estate of a deceased shareholder; that, of the seven living shareholders,

The defendant J. H. Beatty held	200	shares.
The plaintiff	120	,,
S. Neelon (then a director)	101	,,
F. S. Hankey	71	,,
The defendant J. D. Beatty	59	,,
J. C. Graham	39	,,
The defendant W. Beatty	5	,,

It further appears that the defendant J. H. Beatty purchased the 101 shares of S. Neelon, and that they were transferred to him on the last day of January, 1883, the number of shares held by the defendant being thus raised to 301, an actual majority of all the shares in the company; that on the morning of the 7th of February, before the annual meeting of that day, the defendant J. H. Beatty transferred five of his shares to the defendant Rose, and the like number to the defendant Laird, whereby they respectively became qualified to be elected directors; and that on the same day they were elected directors.

The defendants Rose and Laird deny, and their denial is unimpeached, that there was any agreement or understanding between them or either of them and the defendant J. H. Beatty that they would support his views in respect of the sale of his steamer to the company; they both, however, admit that, previously to the transfers of the shares to them, they considered that the purchase of the steamer would be beneficial to the company, that they accepted the transfer with the view of becoming directors, and that the defendant was well aware of the opinions and views entertained by them. Indeed, the defendant Rose states that he would not have joined the company but for the intention to purchase the steamer.

By the transfers to the defendants Rose and Laird, the number of shares held by the defendant J. H. Beatty was reduced to 291, but the united voting power of the three last-named defendants was such that they could command a majority at any meeting of the shareholders.

Though there was a discussion, at the annual meeting on the 7th of February, as to the expediency of purchasing the steamer, the resolution directing a bye-law to be prepared appears to have been passed without any division.

At the meeting of the directors of the 10th, the same three defendants were in a position to carry any resolution or to pass any bye-law upon which they were agreed.

At the shareholders meeting of the 16th the voting was as follows:

For the confirmation of the bye-law,—

	Votes.
The defendant J. H. Beatty . . .	291
The defendant J. E. Rose . . .	5
The defendant R. Laird . . .	5
The defendant William Beatty . .	5
Total . .	306

Against the confirmation,—

	Votes.
John C. Graham	39
F. L. Hankey	71
The plaintiff	120
The defendant John D. Beatty . .	59
Total . .	289

It follows that the majority of votes in favour of the confirmation of the bye-law was due to the votes of the defendant J. H. Beatty.

These last-mentioned facts were stated by the plaintiff in his claim in the action, and he not only insisted that the defendant J. H. Beatty was in such a fiduciary relation to the company that it was not competent for him, under any circumstances, to enter into the contract for the sale of his steamer to the company, but he made various charges of fraud and collusion against the defendant directors, other than the defendant J. D. Beatty, who was also the secretary of the company.

These charges of fraud and collusion were abandoned at the trial of the action, but the facts before referred to were pressed upon the judges, before whom, in succession, the action came, and afforded to those judges who were of opinion that the sale should be set aside the substantial grounds for their decisions.

The action first came on to be heard before the Chancellor of Ontario, who, on the 6th of May 1884, ordered the sale to be set aside, with the usual consequential directions. All charges of fraud and collusion being discarded, the Chancellor treated the question as one of "purely equitable law," and held that the threefold character of director, shareholder, and vendor, sustained by the defendant J. H. Beatty, involved a conflict between duty and interest, and that, being so circumstanced, he could not be permitted, in the conduct of the company's affairs, to exercise the balance of power which he possessed, to the possible prejudice of the other shareholders.

The defendants appealed against the order of the Chancellor, and, on the 17th of April, 1885, the Court of Appeal of Ontario allowed the appeal, and ordered that the plaintiff's bill should be dismissed, with costs. In the opinion of the members of that Court, the resolution to purchase the steamer was a pure question of internal management, and the shareholders had a perfect right, either to ratify the act of the directors, or to treat the matter as an original offer to themselves, and to assent to and complete the purchase.

From the order of the Court of Appeal the plaintiff appealed to the Supreme Court of Canada, and on the 9th of April, 1886, the Supreme Court reversed the order of the Court of Appeal, and affirmed that of the Chancellor. It appears to have been the opinion of the judges of the Supreme Court that the case turned entirely on the fiduciary character of the defendant J. H. Beatty as a director; that, if the acts or transactions of an interested director were to be confirmed by the shareholders, it should be by an exercise of the impartial, independent, and intelligent judgment of disinterested shareholders and not by the votes of the interested director, who ought never to have departed from his duty; that the course pursued by the defendant J. H. Beatty was an oppressive proceeding on his part; and that, consequently, the vote of the shareholders, at the meeting of the 16th of February, 1883, was ineffectual to confirm the bye-law which had been enacted by the directors. The nature of the transaction itself does not appear to have been taken into consideration by the judges in their decision of the case.

From this decision of the Supreme Court of Canada the appeal has been brought with which their Lordships have now to deal. The question involved is doubtless novel in its circumstances, and the decision important in its consequences; it would be very undesirable even to appear to relax the rules relating to dealings between trustees and their beneficiaries; on the other hand, great confusion would be introduced into the affairs of joint stock companies if the circumstances of shareholders, voting in that character at general meetings, were to be examined, and their votes practically nullified, if they also stood in some fiduciary relation to the company.

It is clear upon the authorities that the contract entered into by the directors on the 10th of February could not have been enforced against the company at the instance of the defendant J. H. Beatty, but it is equally clear that it was within the competency of the shareholders at the meeting of the 16th to adopt or reject it. In form and in terms they adopted it by a majority of votes, and the vote of the majority must prevail, unless the adoption was brought by unfair or improper means.

The only unfairness or impropriety which, consistently with the admitted and established facts, could be suggested, arises out of the fact that the defendant J. H. Beatty possessed a voting power as a shareholder which enabled him, and those who thought with him, to adopt the bye-law, and thereby either to ratify and adopt a voidable contract, into which he, as a director, and his co-directors had entered, or to make a similar contract, which latter seems to have been what was intended to be done by the resolution passed on the 7th of February.

It may be quite right that in such a case, the opposing minority should be able, in a suit like this, to challenge the transaction, and to show that it is an improper one, and to be freed from the objection that a suit with such an object can only be maintained by the company itself.

But the constitution of the company enabled the defendant J. H. Beatty to acquire this voting power; there was no limit upon the number of shares which a shareholder might hold, and for every share so held he was entitled to a vote; the charter itself recognised the defendant as a holder of 200 shares, one-third of the aggregate number; he had a perfect right to acquire further shares, and to exercise his voting power in such a manner as to secure the election of directors whose views upon policy agreed with his own, and to support those views at any shareholders' meeting; the acquisition of the United Empire was a pure question of policy, as to which it might be expected that there would be differences of opinion, and upon which the voice of the majority ought to prevail; to reject the votes of the defendant upon the question of the adoption of the bye-law would be to give effect to the views of the minority, and to disregard those of the majority.

The judges of the Supreme Court appear to have regarded the exercise by the defendant J. H. Beatty of his voting power as of so oppressive a character as to invalidate the adoption of the bye-law; their Lordships are unable to adopt this view; in their opinion the defendant was acting within his rights in voting as he did, though they agree with the Chief Justice in the views expressed by him in the Court of Appeal, that the matter might have been conducted in a manner less likely to give rise to objection.

Their Lordships will humbly advise Her Majesty to allow the appeal; to discharge the order of the Supreme Court of Canada; and to dismiss the appeal to that Court. . . .

Burland and Others *v.* Earle and Others. [1902] A.C. 83

The Court will not interfere with the internal management of companies acting within their powers.

In order to redress a wrong done to the company, the action should be brought by the company, except where the wrongdoers are themselves the majority shareholders. In that case the complaining shareholders may bring an action in their own names, but will have no greater right to relief than the company itself would have if it were plaintiff. They cannot sue in respect of acts which are valid if done with the approval of the majority or which can be confirmed by the majority, with the result that they may sue only where the acts complained of are fraudulent or ultra vires.

A shareholder may vote as he wishes, even though he has an interest in the subject-matter of the vote.

A company is not compelled to distribute all its profits to the shareholders: this is a matter of internal management. It may lawfully form a reserve fund out of profits and invest it in such securities as the directors may select, subject to the control of the general meeting. It may invest in the name of a sole trustee.

A director who buys property on his own account and later sells it to the company at a profit cannot be made to account for that profit, though the company may rescind the contract for non-disclosure.

The action in this case was brought in the Queen's Bench Division of the High Court of Ontario by the respondents as shareholders in the American Bank Note Company to compel the appellants, as directors, to distribute a reserve fund as dividend. They also sought to obtain a declaration that certain investments of the company's funds by Burland (a director) were illegal, that he had purchased property of the Burland Lithographic Company as a trustee for the American Bank Note Company and ought therefore to account for the profit made by him out of its re-sale to that company, and that certain salaries had been wrongfully paid and should be refunded.

The Chief Justice of the Queen's Bench Division gave judgment for the plaintiffs, and the appellants accordingly appealed to the Court of Appeal of Ontario. This court again gave judgment for the plaintiffs, whereupon the appellants appealed to the Privy Council where the judgment of LORD HOBHOUSE, LORD DAVEY, LORD ROBERTSON and SIR RICHARD COUCH was delivered by LORD DAVEY.

LORD DAVEY: The appellants and respondents . . . are alike shareholders in a joint stock company, called the British American Bank Note Company. . . .

The company was incorporated by letters patent dated June 16, 1866, under the provisions of an Act (27 & 28 Vict. c. 23) of the old Province of Canada. The objects for which the company was formed were "to engrave and print bank notes, debentures, bonds, postage and bill stamps, and bills of exchange, and to carry on all other branches incidental thereto." The capital of the company was originally $100,000, divided into shares of $100 each, but was subsequently increased to $200,000, of which $170,000 only has been issued. . . .

The company was formed by the union of two groups, one represented by the appellant George B. Burland, and the other by a Mr. Smillie and the respondent Earle. Mr. Smillie was the first president, and Burland and the respondent Earle were first directors. Mr. Smillie retired from the company in 1881 and sold his shares. Burland from time to time increased his holding, and at the date of the commencement of the action he held 1,077 shares. He was also the president and manager of the company.

The . . . respondents hold between them 433 shares. The respondent Earle continued on the board of directors until the year 1890, when he resigned. The respondent Mrs. Cunningham sues as the administratrix of James Cunningham, deceased, who was at one time the auditor, and from 1887 until his death in 1892 was a director of the company. The respondent Thomas J. Gillelan was from the year 1892, and at the commencement of the action, a director of the company. . . .

The action was commenced by the respondents on December 7, 1897. . . . Their Lordships will confine their attention to the points which have been discussed on these appeals. These are—(1) the formation of the . . . reserve fund; (2) the investment of it; (3) a claim by the respondents to treat Burland as a trustee of the plant and material of a certain insolvent company called the Burland Lithographic Company, which he purchased at a sale by auction and resold at an enhanced price to this company, and to make him account to the company accordingly for the profit made by the resale; (4) a question as to certain sums drawn as salaries. . . .

It is an elementary principle of the law relating to joint stock companies that the Court will not interfere with the internal management of companies acting within their powers, and in fact has no jurisdiction to do so. Again, it is clear law that in order to redress a wrong done to the company or to recover moneys or damages alleged to be due to the company, the action should prima facie be brought by the company itself. These cardinal principles are laid down in the well-known cases of *Foss* v. *Harbottle* and *Mozley* v. *Alston*. . . . But an exception is made to the second rule, where the persons against whom the relief is sought themselves hold and control the majority of the shares in the company, and will not permit an action to be brought in the name of the company. In that case the Courts allow the shareholders complaining to bring an action in their own names. This, however, is mere matter of procedure in order to give a remedy for a wrong which would otherwise escape redress, and it is obvious that in such an action the plaintiffs cannot have a larger right to relief than the company itself would have if it were plaintiff, and cannot complain of acts which are valid if done with the approval of the majority of the shareholders, or are capable of being confirmed by the majority. The cases in which the minority can maintain such an action are, therefore, confined to those in which the acts complained of are of a fraudulent character or beyond the powers of the company. A familiar example is where the majority are endeavouring directly or indirectly to appropriate to themselves money, property, or advantages which belong to the company, or in which the other shareholders are entitled to participate, as was alleged in the case of *Menier* v. *Hooper's*

Telegraph Works. It should be added that no mere informality or irregularity which can be remedied by the majority will entitle the minority to sue, if the act when done regularly would be within the powers of the company and the intention of the majority of the shareholders is clear. This may be illustrated by the judgment of MELLISH L.J. in *Macdougall* v. *Gardiner*.

There is yet a third principle which is important for the decision of this case. Unless otherwise provided by the regulations of the company, a shareholder is not debarred from voting or using his voting power to carry a resolution by the circumstance of his having a particular interest in the subject-matter of the vote. This is shown by . . . *North-West Transportation Co., Ltd.* v. *Beatty*. . . .

If these elementary considerations are borne in mind, the solution of the principal questions arising in these appeals will not present any real difficulty. . . .

Their Lordships are not aware of any principle which compels a joint stock company while a going concern to divide the whole of its profits amongst its shareholders. Whether the whole or any part should be divided, or what portion should be divided and what portion retained, are entirely questions of internal management which the shareholders must decide for themselves, and the Court has no jurisdiction to control or review their decision. . . . And it makes no difference whether the undivided balance is retained to the credit of profit and loss account, or carried to the credit of a . . . reserve fund, or appropriated to any other use of the company. These are questions for the shareholders to decide subject to any restrictions contained in the articles of association. . . .

If the company may form a reserve fund or retain a balance of undivided profits, it must, it would seem, have power to invest the moneys so retained. The junior counsel for the respondents contended that the company, in the absence of express power to invest, could employ the money only in its own business. This contention has no support either in principle or in authority, and, if it were sound, the objects for which a reserve fund is needed would in many cases be defeated. . . . Upon what securities, then, may the company invest its undivided profits or reserve fund? It is conceded at the bar that the company is not confined to such investments as trustees are authorised to make. The answer, therefore, can only be that the reserve fund may lawfully be invested on such securities as the directors may select subject to the control of a general meeting. . . .

The investments were wholly or for the most part made in the name of Burland alone. This was, for obvious reasons, unwise and imprudent; but it must have been within the knowledge of the respondent Earle, the late Mr. Cunningham, and the respondent Gillelan, and no complaint or remonstrance seems to have been made until the institution of the present suit. Burland is of course bound to account for all the moneys of the company come to his hands. . . . It is not *ultra vires* for the company, if it thinks fit to do so, to invest in the name of a sole trustee, however imprudent or undesirable such a course may be. . . .

The next matter to which the appeal relates is the sale to the company by Burland of the lithographic plant, etc., of the Burland Lithographic Company. It appears that that company had been carrying on business in Montreal, and, having become insolvent, was wound up. . . . Burland was interested in the company as a stockholder and a creditor. At the public sale by the liquidator on May 10, 1892, Burland bid for and purchased all the assets of the company in four lots. The price paid by him for lot 1 was $21,564, and he shortly afterwards sold the property comprised in that lot to the . . . company for $60,000. The property, together with some other plant purchased from another company, was subsequently sold to a company formed for the purpose at an enhanced price payable in shares, which were distributed as a bonus amongst the shareholders of the company.

In these circumstances Burland has been ordered to pay to the company the sum of $38,436, being the amount of the profit realised by him on the resale. Both Courts have held that the resale was by Burland's advice and influence, and was made without disclosing to the company the price at which he had purchased. It was also held in the Court of Appeal that Burland had bought the property with the intention and for the purpose of reselling it to the company. . . . But their Lordships . . . are of opinion that the relief . . . granted in the Courts below is altogether misconceived. There is no evidence whatever of any commission or mandate to Burland to purchase on behalf of the company, or that he was in any sense a trustee for the company of the purchased property. It may be that he had an intention in his own mind to resell it to the company; but it was an intention which he was at liberty to carry out or abandon at his own will. It may be also that a person of a more refined self-respect and a more generous regard for the company of which he was president would have been disposed to give the company the benefit of his purchase. But their Lordships have not to decide questions of that character. The sole question is whether he was under any legal obligation to do so. . . . The case seems to their Lordships to be exactly that put by LORD CAIRNS in *Erlanger* v. *New Sombrero Phosphate Co.* . . .

Reference may also be made to the judgments of PEARSON J. and COTTON and FRY L.JJ. in *In re Cape Breton Co.* To rescind the sale is one thing, but to force on the vendor a contract to sell at another price is a totally different thing.

The question of salaries stands in this wise. Burland's salary as manager was fixed in the year 1879 at $5,000 per annum. This was increased from time to time to $12,000. It was not disputed that he is entitled to draw a salary of that amount, and both Courts have so held. But, in addition to this fixed salary, he has since 1888 drawn a further sum of large amount to which he claims to be entitled under the terms of a resolution of the board of directors of April 24, 1888. . . . The Court of Appeal thought that the question turned on the true construction of the resolution . . . and, holding that Burland was not entitled to the increment under the terms of the resolution, ordered him to repay the amount thereof drawn by him since the date of the resolution. . . . On the whole their Lordships are not prepared to differ from the Court of Appeal on this point. . . .

Cook *v.* G. S. Deeks and Others. [1916] 1 A.C. 554

Where directors appropriate to themselves the benefit of a contract which properly belongs to the company, they are guilty of a breach of duty to the company and cannot retain the benefit of the contract for themselves. It belongs in equity to the company and they cannot use their voting power to make a present of it to themselves, since this would be oppression of the minority.

The action in this case was brought in the High Court Division of the Supreme Court of Ontario by the appellant, suing on behalf of himself and all other shareholders in the Toronto Construction Company, Limited, against the respondents G. S. Deeks, G. M. Deeks, T. R. Hinds and the Dominion Construction Company, Limited, for a declaration that the respondents were trustees for the Toronto Construction Company, Limited (who were joined as defendants), of the benefit of a contract dated 1st April 1912 between the individual respondents and the Canadian Pacific Railway Company.

MIDDLETON J. dismissed the action and his decision was affirmed by the Appellate Division of the Supreme Court of Ontario.

The appellant then appealed to the Privy Council where the judgment of LORD BUCKMASTER L.C., VISCOUNT HALDANE, LORD PARKER OF WADDINGTON and LORD SUMNER was delivered by LORD BUCKMASTER.

LORD BUCKMASTER L.C.: . . . The respondent the Toronto Construction Company was formed some time in 1905. . . . It appears that at the date of its incorporation all the parties were in business in various parts of the Dominion of Canada and the United States of America as contractors. The two defendants G. S. Deeks and G. M. Deeks were in partnership. . . . In 1905 the Canadian Pacific Railway were asking for tenders for the construction of a line . . . known as the Toronto Sudbury line, and the tenders of G. S. Deeks, made, as it would appear, on behalf of the firm of Deeks and Deeks, were accepted by the company. Before tendering arrangements had been made by Messrs. Deeks with a firm of Winters, Parsons & Boomer that they should take an interest in the contract to the extent of one-half if G. S. Deeks were successful in obtaining it. Mr. Winters, however, had assumed certain obligations which rendered him unwilling to accept his full share of responsibility, and the plaintiff and the defendant Hinds were accordingly introduced by him to Mr. Deeks in order to supplement his obligation, with the result that all the parties agreed to share in the contract in the following proportions: G. S. Deeks and G. M. Deeks to take three-eighths, the plaintiff and the defendant Hinds to take three-eighths, and Winters, Parsons & Boomer one quarter. In order to place these relationships upon a fixed foundation . . . the Toronto Construction Company was formed and its share capital distributed in the proportions mentioned, the company taking over and carrying out the work under the contract.

In 1906 Messrs. Winters and Boomer withdrew from the company, and the stock that they held was divided equally among the remaining parties, so that the plaintiff and each of the three defendants G. S. Deeks, G. M. Deeks, and T. R. Hinds held one-fourth of the entire capital of the company, with the exception of four shares held by Mrs. Deeks (the wife of G. S. Deeks), whose introduction as a shareholder was necessary in order to provide the total number of five. These interests have remained unchanged down to the present time.

The board of directors was comprised of Messrs. Deeks, Hinds, and the plaintiff, and, in addition, G. S. Deeks was appointed president of the company, the plaintiff was general manager, and Hinds was secretary and treasurer. . . . The company appears to have carried out the work of laying the Toronto Sudbury line to the entire satisfaction of the Canadian Pacific Railway, and they continued to tender and were fortunate in obtaining a considerable number of other contracts of great value from the Canadian Pacific Railway. Apart, however, from this work they undertook no other contracts. . . . [D]uring part of the time of the operations of the company the plaintiff and the three defendants were associated together in various other enterprises of a similar nature . . . in the west, but no contracts were taken in the east excepting by the Toronto Construction Company. In 1907 disagreement appears to have arisen between the parties, and the different firms which had been constructed between them, and were all partnerships at will, were dissolved, and the parties refused to enter into any further voluntary arrangements between themselves. . . .

The South Shore contract is the one which has given rise to the present dispute. . . . The representative of the Canadian Pacific Railway Company was a Mr. Leonard, and it was he who arranged some . . . of the contracts effected with the Toronto Construction Company on behalf of the railway company. His negotiations were always carried out either with Mr. Deeks or with Mr. Hinds. He never discussed any details with any other person, and he never saw the plaintiff in the office, though he sometimes saw him on the line. The management of Messrs. Deeks and Hinds of the affairs of the construction company was eminently satisfactory; but so far as railway construction was concerned the whole of their reputation for the efficient conduct of their business had been gained by them while acting as directors of the Toronto Construction Company. In 1911, and probably at an earlier date, the three defendants had settled that they would no longer continue business relationships with the plaintiff. . . . While still retaining their position as directors, while still actually acting as managers of the company, and with their duties to the company of which the plaintiff was a shareholder entirely unchanged, they proceeded to negotiate with Mr. Leonard for the new Shore Line contract, in reality on their own behalf, but in exactly the same manner as they had always acted for the company. . . .

During the whole of this discussion . . . it does not appear that at any moment the representatives of the Canadian Pacific Railway Company were told that this contract was in any way different from the others that had been negotiated in the same manner on behalf of the Toronto Construction Company. . . . But after all the necessary preliminaries of the contract had been concluded Mr. Hinds made to Mr. Leonard this statement: "Remember, if we get this contract it is to be Deeks and I, and not the Toronto Construction Company."

On March 12, 1912, the Canadian Pacific Railway Company

made the necessary appropriation for the contract. . . . As from this moment, although the formal contract was not signed until April 1, 1912, the defendants became certain of their position, and knew that they had obtained the contract for themselves. They then for the first time informed the plaintiff of what had happened. He protested without result, and the defendant the Dominion Construction Company was formed by the three defendants G. S. Deeks, G. M. Deeks, and T. R. Hinds to carry out the work. The contract was accordingly taken over by this company, by whom the work was carried out and the profits made.

On March 20, 1912, there was a meeting of directors of the Toronto Construction Company, at which the three defendants were present, and they resolved that a fresh meeting of the shareholders be held to consider the question of the voluntary liquidation of the company. Ultimately . . . on April 26, 1913, resolutions were passed owing to the voting power of the defendants G. S. Deeks, G. M. Deeks, and T. R. Hinds, approving the sale of part of the plant of the company to the Dominion Construction Company, and a declaration was made that the company had no interest in the Shore Line contract, and that the directors were authorised to defend this action, which had in the meantime been instituted.

Two questions of law arise out of this long history of fact. The first is whether, apart altogether from the subsequent resolutions, the company would have been at liberty to claim from the three defendants the benefit of the contract which they had obtained from the Canadian Pacific Railway Company; and the second, which only arises if the first be answered in the affirmative, whether in such event the majority of the shareholders of the company constituted by the three defendants could ratify and approve of what was done and thereby release all claim against the directors.

. . . [T]he real matter for determination is what, in the special circumstances of this case, was the relationship that existed between Messrs. Deeks and Hinds and the company that they controlled. Now it appears plain that the entire management of the company, so far as obtaining and executing contracts in the east was concerned, was in their hands. . . . The way they used this position is perfectly plain. . . . [T]hey intentionally concealed all circumstances relating to their negotiations until a point had been reached when the whole arrangement had been concluded in their own favour and there was no longer any real chance that there could be any interference with their plans. This means that while entrusted with the conduct of the affairs of the company they deliberately designed to exclude, and used their influence and position to exclude, the company whose interest it was their first duty to protect.

. . . [T]hroughout the whole of the judgments, both of the learned judge who tried this case and of the Appellate Division, there is underlying rather the question as to whether the transaction was not one which, by virtue of their preponderating influence in the company, the defendants would be able ultimately to put right than the real question of whether it was one into which, consistently with their duty, they were at liberty to enter.

It is quite right to point out the importance of avoiding the establishment of rules as to directors' duties which would impose upon them burdens so heavy and responsibilities so great that men of good position would hesitate to accept the office. But, on the other hand, men who assume the complete control of a company's business must remember that they are not at liberty to sacrifice the interests which they are bound to protect, and, while ostensibly acting for the company, divert in their own favour business which should properly belong to the company they represent.

Their Lordships think that, in the circumstances, the defendants T. R. Hinds and G. S. and G. M. Deeks were guilty of a distinct breach of duty in the course they took to secure the contract, and that they cannot retain the benefit of such contract for themselves, and must be regarded as holding it on behalf of the company.

There remains the more difficult consideration of whether this position can be made regular by resolutions of the company controlled by the votes of these three defendants. . . .

In their Lordships' opinion the Supreme Court has insufficiently recognised the distinction between two classes of case and has applied the principles applicable to the case of a director selling to his company property which was in equity as well as at law his own, and which he could dispose of as he thought fit, to the case of a director dealing with property which, though his own at law, in equity belonged to his company. The cases of *North-West Transportation Co.* v. *Beatty* and *Burland* v. *Earle* both belonged to the former class. In each, directors had sold to the company property in which the company had no interest in law or in equity. If the company claimed any interest by reason of the transaction. it could only be by affirming the sale, in which case such sale, though initially voidable, would be validated by subsequent ratification. If the company refused to affirm the sale the transaction would be set aside and the parties restored to their former position, the directors getting the property and the company receiving back the purchase price. There would be no middle course. The company could not insist on retaining the property while paying less than the price agreed. This would be for the Court to make a new contract between the parties. It would be quite another thing if the director had originally acquired the property which he sold to his company under circumstances which made it in equity the property of the company. The distinction to which their Lordships have drawn attention is expressly recognised by LORD DAVEY in *Burland* v. *Earle* and is the foundation of the judgment in *North-West Transportation Co.* v. *Beatty*, and is clearly explained in the case of *Jacobus Marler Estates* v. *Marler*. . . .

If, as their Lordships find on the facts, the contract in question was entered into under such circumstances that the directors could not retain the benefit of it for themselves, then it belonged in equity to the company and ought to have been dealt with as an asset of the company. Even supposing it be not *ultra vires* of a company to make a present to its directors, it appears quite certain that directors holding a majority of votes would not be permitted to make a present to themselves. This would be to allow a majority to oppress the minority. To such circumstances the cases of *North-West Transportation Co.* v. *Beatty* and *Burland* v. *Earle* have no application. In the same way, if directors have acquired for themselves property or rights which they must be regarded as holding on behalf of the company, a resolution that the rights of the company should be disregarded in the matter would amount to forfeiting the interest and property of the minority of shareholders in favour of the majority, and that by the votes of those who are interested in securing the property for themselves. Such use of voting power has never been sanctioned by the Courts, and, indeed, was expressly disapproved in the case of *Menier* v. *Hooper's Telegraph Works.*

. . . It follows that the defendants must account to the Toronto Company for the profits which they have made out of the transaction. Their Lordships will therefore humbly advise His Majesty that the judgments of MIDDLETON J. and of the Appellate Division be set aside. . . .

Phillips *v.* Manufacturers' Securities, Ltd. (1917) 86 L.J. Ch. 305

Members of a company voting at a general meeting properly convened have no fiduciary obligation either to the company or to the other shareholders.

The plaintiff Albert Phillips was managing director of Albert Phillips, Ltd., bedstead manufacturers, which, along with many other similar companies, had joined a federation of bedstead makers formed in 1912 to protect trade interests.

Rule 4 of the rules of the federation provided for the formation of a limited company for the investment of all moneys received from members of the federation. In pursuance of this rule the defendant company, Manufacturers' Securities, Ltd., was formed in 1912 with a capital of £60,000 in £1 shares and the plaintiff Phillips became a director of it.

Article 96 of the articles of Manufacturers' Securities, Ltd. read as follows:

"The company in general meeting may, by resolution passed by a majority of not less than three-fourths of the votes of the members of the company . . . entitled to vote as may be present in person or by proxy . . . and who vote on such resolution, determine that the shares of any member shall within 30 days after the passing of such resolution be offered for sale by the company to the other members, and any such resolution may fix the price to be paid for such shares, provided that such price shall not be less than one shilling per share, and in case no such price shall be so fixed the price shall be one shilling per share."

Rule 15 of the rules of the federation provided for the payment by each member of 1 per cent of each month's sales to form a reserve fund which was to be invested by Manufacturers' Securities, Ltd. and the income paid to the federation members. The practice followed was that sums so paid by members were paid to Manufacturers' Securities, Ltd. and shares in that company were then issued to members in respect of their payments.

In the case of Albert Phillips, Ltd., the shares were at first issued to the company; but later they were transferred to Albert Phillips, and all subsequent issues were made to him. By October 1914 he held 1,058 shares in Manufacturers' Securities, Ltd. on trust for Albert Phillips, Ltd.

In October 1914 Albert Phillips, Ltd. withdrew from the federation, which held a meeting in November 1914 at which it was resolved to remove Phillips from the board of Manufacturers' Securities, Ltd. and to have his shares sold under Article 96. In consequence his directorship was ended in February 1915 and a resolution passed in April 1915 for the sale of his shares under Article 96 to the other members at the price of one shilling per share.

It was admitted that at this time the shares were worth at least £1 per share, and the resolution passed with the intention of forfeiting the shares as a penalty on Albert Phillips, Ltd. for leaving the federation.

Albert Phillips, Ltd. and Albert Phillips commenced an action claiming a declaration that the resolution was *ultra vires* the company and an injunction to restrain the company from acting on it. They claimed that the directors were not acting in good faith, but oppressively to cause loss and injury to the plaintiffs, and that the members voting in favour of the resolution did not vote *bona fide* or in the interests of the company as a whole, but oppressively.

PETERSON J. held that, on the true construction of Article 96, it was within the powers of the majority of the shareholders to fix the price at 1*s*. and, this being the bargain between persons becoming shareholders of the company, there was no ground of complaint against the company in respect of the resolution.

From this decision the plaintiffs appealed and the case accordingly came before the Court of Appeal.

LORD COZENS-HARDY M.R.: . . . [T]he real question, and, in my opinion, the only question . . . is this: What is the true construction of article 96? . . . I am clearly of opinion that this article 96 does not impose upon the company any obligation to put article 96 into operation only on the footing that the sale directed is at a fair price. . . . [A]rticle 96 . . . in terms, as it seems to me, negatives any idea of a fair value and leaves it to the general meeting either to fix any price they think fit, not being less than 1*s*. a share, or to fix no price at all, in which case it is under the article to be 1*s*. a share. . . . On the construction of this article I have no hesitation in saying it is reasonably clear, as a matter of construction, that it does authorise a resolution compelling any member to sell his shares at a price which may be as low as 1*s*. a share. Article 96 is a clause which affects all the members of the company. Any member may be exposed to the operation of this clause if so resolved by a majority of three-fourths at a general meeting called expressly for the purpose of passing such a resolution, and in the present case such a resolution was passed unanimously by the nine members who were present at the meeting. *Prima facie* it was within the powers of the general meeting to pass that resolution. We have heard in the argument a good deal about *bona fides* and acting *mala fide*, and attention has been called to partnership, in which it has been held that partners must act *bona fide* in matters affecting another partner, whether there is a provision to that effect in the articles of partnership or not; but I know of no authority, and I do not think any authority can be found, which says that this doctrine applies to shareholders acting in general meeting. Directors stand in a fiduciary position, and may, of course, be subject to obligations that would not affect other shareholders; but members of a company voting at a general meeting properly convened have no fiduciary obligation either to the company or to the other shareholders. I think that doctrine is really made manifest when you consider the distinction which was drawn by VICE-CHANCELLOR WOOD in *East Pant Du United Mining Co.* v. *Merryweather* (1864) 2 H. & M. 254. In that case the action sought to impeach a transaction, under which one of the directors had sold to the company some property in consideration of a sum in cash and £3,000 in shares; so that he was a large shareholder, as well as being a director. There was an express provision in the company's deed of settlement that a director should not vote as a director in respect of any matter in which he was personally interested, and indeed I think the same result would follow on general principle if there had been no such provision. The company sought to set aside the whole transaction, and commenced an action for the purpose. An extraordinary general meeting was then held, at which a member moved that the action be not proceeded with, but that the matter be referred to arbitration. That resolution was carried by the votes of the director in respect of the shares obtained on the contract sought to be set aside. VICE-CHANCELLOR WOOD there drew the distinction between what a man could do as director in respect of a transaction of this kind and what he could do as a shareholder, although he was voting in his own interest, and held that the resolution must be treated as having been carried. That decision can only have proceeded on the footing that a shareholder in general meeting does not owe any duty either to the company or to the other shareholders.

But then it is said that this is a case of fraud. I will assume for the moment, without really deciding it . . . that if a fraud could be proved this doctrine would not apply. I must not be taken as deciding that; but, assuming it to be so, has any fraud been proved? Plainly not. The general meeting are simply doing that which they are told may be done by article

96—that is to say, compelling a sale of shares at less than their true value. . . .

Then it is said by the plaintiffs that there was a malicious intention to punish Mr. Phillips for leaving the federation, and that it is a case of malice. Personally, I do not care whether there is malice or not in view of the decision in *Bradford Corporation* v. *Ferrand* [1902] 2 Ch. 655 where the Bradford Corporation did not succeed in preventing a man from tapping a stream of water on his own land, and so diminishing the spring from which Bradford was partly supplied with water, because he was doing that which he was entitled to do, however malicious his motive. . . .

For these reasons it seems to me that the view taken by the learned Judge in the Court below was perfectly right.

WARRINGTON L.J.: I am of the same opinion . . . [I]t is said that, if it is shewn that the shareholders have been acting not *bona fide* or not in the interests of the company, the transaction may be avoided, although it is within the terms of the articles, and although they are exercising a power inherent in the nature of the property which the plaintiff Phillips holds—namely, shares in the company. For that contention reliance is placed upon a statement contained in the judgment of LORD LINDLEY, then Master of the Rolls, in *Allen* v. *Gold Reefs of West Africa* [1900] 1 Ch. 656. . . . I will assume for the present purpose, without deciding it, that the expressions there used in reference to a different subject-matter, are applicable . . . to the transaction in the present case—I do not say they are; I will assume it; then we come to the question, Have the plaintiffs proved that the power which the company possesses, though exercised in the manner required by law, has not been exercised *bona fide* and for the benefit of the company as a whole, and has it been exceeded? In the first place, the power here certainly has not been exceeded. That follows from the construction which I put upon the articles. Secondly, the mere fact that the price fixed was 1*s.* a share is no evidence that the resolution was arrived at otherwise than *bona fide*, for that the requisite majority might fix such a price was contemplated by the provision which the plaintiffs are impugning. Have the plaintiffs proved that the resolution was not passed for the benefit or in the reasonable belief of those who passed it that it would be for the benefit of the company? In my opinion there is not a particle of evidence to prove any such thing. So far as the evidence goes, it to my mind establishes that the majority of the company believed, and reasonably believed, that the resolution which they passed was in furtherance of the objects of the company, and therefore for its benefit. . . .

It seems to me, therefore, . . . that the resolution in question was within the power contained in article 96, and that the plaintiffs . . . have not established that that power was exercised in any improper way or for any improper purpose; and therefore, in my opinion, the judgment of Mr. Justice PETERSON is correct.

LUSH J.: . . . I think it has become fairly clear that the real question, and indeed the only question, is: What is the true construction of article 96? . . . [T]he correct construction of the article being plainly contrary to the plaintiffs' contention, there is an end of their case, unless they are in a position to establish, first, that . . . the powers under article 96 may be exercised so oppressively or *mala fide* or fraudulently . . . as to entitle them to relief; and secondly, that upon the evidence the proper inference to be drawn was that the power has been so exercised. I will assume for the purpose of argument—I desire to express no opinion about it one way or the other, but I will assume it—that this power may be exercised under such circumstances that the plaintiffs may be entitled to relief. . . .

It is quite true there is evidence to support the inference that the shareholders were minded to impose a penalty upon the plaintiff Phillips because his company had left the federation; but the object of imposing the penalty on this evidence clearly was not with a view to malicious persecution of this plaintiff, but with a view to deterring other persons who belonged to the federation from leaving it. . . . That is not, to my mind, capable of being said to be *mala fides*. On the contrary, having regard to the memorandum of association, and to the fact that the main object of this company was to further the interest of the federation, it seems to me the only proper inference to draw from the evidence was that the shareholders were doing the very thing which . . . the memorandum contemplated being done by the company.

In my opinion the judgement of the learned Judge in the court below was perfectly correct.

Greenhalgh v. Arderne Cinemas, Ltd. and Others. [1951] Ch. 286

When a man comes into a company, he is not entitled to assume that the articles will always remain in a particular form. Nevertheless, a resolution to alter them may be impeached if its effect is to discriminate between majority and minority shareholders, so as to give the former an advantage of which the latter are deprived.

The resolution must be passed bona fide *for the benefit of the company as a whole. This means not two things but one thing, namely, that the shareholder must proceed on what, in his honest opinion, is for the benefit of the company as a whole.*

The phrase "the company as a whole" does not mean the company as a commercial entity: it means the corporators as a general body.

The first defendants, Arderne Cinemas, Ltd. were a private company in which 205,000 ordinary shares of 2s. each had been issued. 155,000 of these shares were fully paid, and of this number the plaintiff, Greenhalgh, held 4,213 while the second defendant, Mallard, who was the managing director of the company, held with his relatives and friends 85,815.

Article 10 of the articles of association provided:

"(a) No shares in the company shall be transferred to a person not a member of the company so long as a member of the company may be willing to purchase such shares at a fair value. . . .

(b) If any member desires to sell or transfer his shares . . . he shall notify his desire to the directors by . . . notice in writing. . . .

(d) If the directors shall be unable within one month . . . to find a purchaser . . . among the members of the company, the selling member may sell such shares . . . to any person though not a member of the company at any price but subject to the right of the directors (without assigning any reason) to refuse registration of the transfer when the proposed transferee is a person of whom they do not approve, or where the shares . . . are shares on which the company has a lien."

In April 1948 Mallard opened negotiations with the third defendant, Sol Sheckman, for the sale of a controlling interest in the company to him. By agreements of 4th June 1948, Mallard agreed to sell or procure the sale to Sheckman of 85,815 fully paid ordinary shares in the Arderne company, at 6s. a share.

In order to give effect to these agreements an extraordinary meeting of the company was held on 30th June 1948 at which the following special resolution was passed:

"That the articles of association of the company be altered by adding at the end of article 10 the following additional clause: 'Notwithstanding the foregoing provisions of this article any member may with the sanction of an ordinary resolution passed at any general meeting . . . transfer his shares . . . to any person named in such resolution as the proposed transferee, and the directors shall be bound to register any transfer which has been so sanctioned.'"

That resolution was followed by an ordinary resolution sanctioning the transfer by Mallard of 500 shares to Sheckman. The remaining shares which Sheckman was acquiring were to be transferred to his nominees.

Immediately afterwards Greenhalgh issued a writ claiming a declaration that the resolutions were void on the ground that the interests of the minority had been sacrificed to those of the majority, and that the transfers of shares under them should be set aside.

ROXBURGH J. held that Mallard had not been guilty of dishonesty and dismissed the action. Greenhalgh appealed and the case accordingly came before the Court of Appeal.

EVERSHED M.R.: The burden of the case is that the resolution was not passed *bona fide* and in the interests of the company as a whole. . . .

Certain principles, I think, can be safely stated as emerging from the authorities. In the first place, I think it is now plain that *"bona fide* for the benefit of the company as a whole" means not two things but one thing. It means that the shareholder must proceed upon what, in his honest opinion, is for the benefit of the company as a whole. The second thing is that the phrase "the company as a whole," does not (at any rate in such a case as the present) mean the company as a commercial entity, distinct from the corporators: it means the corporators as a general body. That is to say, the case may be taken of an individual hypothetical member and it may be asked whether what is proposed is, in the honest opinion of those who voted in its favour, for that person's benefit.

I think that the matter can . . . be more accurately . . . stated by looking at the converse and by saying that a special resolution of this kind would be liable to be impeached if the effect of it were to discriminate between the majority shareholders and the minority shareholders, so as to give to the former an advantage of which the latter were deprived. . . . It is therefore not necessary to require that persons voting for a special resolution should . . . dissociate themselves altogether from their own prospects. . . . If . . . an outside person makes an offer to buy all the shares, *prima facie*, if the corporators think it a fair offer and vote in favour of the resolution, it is no ground for impeaching the resolution that they are considering their own position as individuals.

. . . [T]his is merely a relaxation of the very stringent restrictions on transfer in the existing article, and it is to be borne in mind that the directors, as the articles stood, could always refuse to register a transfer. . . . [W]hen a man comes into a company, he is not entitled to assume that the articles will always remain in a particular form; and . . ., so long as the proposed alteration does not unfairly discriminate in the way which I have indicated, it is not an objection, provided that the resolution is passed *bona fide*, that the right to tender for the majority holding of shares would be lost by the lifting of the restriction. . . .

In my opinion, . . . this was, in substance, an offer by an outside man to buy the shares of this company at 6s. a share from anybody who was willing to sell them. As commonly happens, the defendant Mallard, as the managing director of the company, negotiated and had to proceed on the footing that he had with him sufficient support to make the negotiation a reality. That was the substance of what was suggested. It discriminated between no types of shareholder. Any who wanted to get out at that price could get out, and any who preferred to stay in could stay in.

That being the substance of the thing, and the evidence . . . clearly suggesting that 6*s.* a share (allowing for the privilege of control) was a fair price, I can see no ground for saying that this resolution can be impeached, and I would dismiss the appeal.

ASQUITH L.J.: I entirely agree.

JENKINS L.J.: I also agree.

Edwards and Another *v.* Halliwell and Others. [1950] 2 All E.R. 1064

The rule in Foss v. *Harbottle has no application where the act complained of is* ultra vires *the company, or where the wrong-doers are themselves in control of the company, or where the act is one which could be validly done or sanctioned only by some special majority, or where the wrong is done, not to the company, but to the personal and individual rights of each member.*

Rule 19 of the rules of the National Union of Vehicle Builders provided:

"The regular contributions of employed members shall be as per tables . . . and no alteration to same shall be made until a ballot vote of the members has been taken and a two-thirds majority obtained."

In December 1943 a delegate meeting of the union, without taking any ballot, passed a resolution increasing the amount of the contributions of employed members. The plaintiffs, two members of the union, claimed against two members of the executive committee and the union itself a declaration that this alteration was invalid.

VAISEY J. granted the declaration and the defendants appealed. The case accordingly came before the Court of Appeal.

ASQUITH L.J.: . . . Counsel for the defendants relied on the alleged principle that, when an action is brought by an individual in respect of a mere irregularity in a matter that is *intra vires* a trade union and concerns its internal management, the court will not as a rule intervene. For this purpose he conceded that a "mere irregularity" meant something not involving fraud, oppression or unfairness. I confess I should have thought the action complained of here was strongly tinctured, not, indeed, with fraud, but with "oppression" and "unfairness." Here were men who had a right not to have their contributions increased except after a ballot resulting in a two-thirds majority. This right was clearly violated. An unauthorised increase was sought to be extorted, and when they refused to pay, as they were entitled to do, severe penalties were imposed or threatened. To call this a mere informality or irregularity without any element of oppression or unfairness would be an abuse of language. When in circumstances such as I have described a remedy is sought by an individual, complaining of a particular act in breach of his rights and inflicting particular damage on him, it seems to me the principle of *Foss* v. *Harbottle*, which has been so strongly relied upon by the defendants, does not apply either by way of barring the remedy or supporting the objection that the action is wrongly constituted because the union is not a plaintiff. . . . I think the appeal should be dismissed.

JENKINS L.J.: I will pass to the argument based on the reluctance of the court to interfere with the domestic affairs of a company or association on the ground of mere irregularity in form in the conduct of those affairs, and the argument based on the more general proposition commonly called the rule in *Foss* v. *Harbottle*. As to the contention that . . . the court should not interfere because the omission to hold a ballot and obtain a two-thirds majority . . . was a mere irregularity in point of form, in my judgment, that argument can be shortly dismissed by saying that this was not a matter of form. It was a matter of substance. . . . It seems to me that the executive committee's disregard of that express provision in the rules was a wrong done to each individual member on a point of substance. . . . In my judgment, the case cited on this part of the argument—*Amalgamated Society of Engineers* v. *Jones* (1913) 29 T.L.R. 484—has no bearing on the facts of the present case. In that case a meeting had been held and certain resolutions passed, and it was suggested that the mode of convening the meeting was irregular. The learned judge was able to hold that there had been no wrong done as a matter of substance, but that there had been a mere irregularity in procedure and he took the view that . . . the court should not interfere. . . . I regard the present case as an entirely different one.

The rule in *Foss* v. *Harbottle*, as I understand it, comes to no more than this. First, the proper plaintiff in an action in respect of a wrong alleged to be done to a company or association of persons is *prima facie* the company or the association of persons itself. Secondly, where the alleged wrong is a transaction which might be made binding on the company or association and on all its members by a simple majority of the members, no individual member of the company is allowed to maintain an action in respect of that matter for the simple reason that, if a mere majority of the members of the company or association is in favour of what has been done, then *cadit quaestio*. No wrong had been done to the company or association and there is nothing in respect of which anyone can sue. If, on the other hand, a simple majority of members of the company or association is against what has been done, then there is no valid reason why the company or association itself should not sue. In my judgment, it is implicit in the rule that the matter relied on as constituting the cause of action should be a cause of action properly belonging to the general body of corporators or members of the company or association as opposed to a cause of action which some individual member can assert in his own right.

The cases falling within the general ambit of the rule are subject to certain exceptions. It has been noted in the course of argument that in cases where the act complained of is wholly *ultra vires* the company or association the rule has no application because there is no question of the transaction being confirmed by any majority. It has been further pointed out that where what has been done amounts to what is generally called . . . a fraud on the minority and the wrongdoers are themselves in control of the company, the rule is relaxed in favour of the aggrieved minority who are allowed to bring what is known as a minority shareholders' action on behalf of themselves and all others. The reason for this is that, if they were denied that right, their grievance could never reach the court because the wrongdoers themselves, being in control, would not allow the company to sue. Those exceptions . . . show, especially the last one, that the rule is not an inflexible rule and it will be relaxed where necessary in the interests of justice.

There is a further exception which seems to me to touch this case directly. That is the exception noted by ROMER J. in *Cotter* v. *National Union of Seamen* [1929] 2 Ch. 58. He pointed out that the rule did not prevent an individual member from suing if the matter in respect of which he was suing was one which could validly be done or sanctioned, not by a simple majority of the members of the company or association, but only by some special majority, as, for instance, in the case of a limited company under the *Companies Act*, a special resolution. . . . As ROMER J. pointed out, the reason for that exception is clear, because otherwise, if the rule were applied in its full rigour, a company which, by its directors, had broken its own regulations by doing something without a special resolution which could only be done validly by a special resolution could assert that it alone was the proper plaintiff in any consequent action and the effect would be to allow a company acting in breach of its articles to do *de facto* by ordinary resolution that which according to its own regulations could only be done by special resolution. That exception exactly fits the present case. . . . In my judgment, therefore, the reliance on the rule in *Foss* v. *Harbottle* . . . may be regarded as misconceived on that ground alone.

I would go further. In my judgment, this is a case of a kind which is not even within the general ambit of the rule. It is not a case where what is complained of is a wrong done to the union, a matter in respect of which the cause of action would primarily and properly belong to the union. It is a case in which certain members of a trade union complain that the union . . . has invaded the individual rights of the complainant members. . . . The gist of the case is that the personal and individual rights of membership of each of them have been invaded by a purported, but invalid, alteration of the tables of contribution. In those circumstances, it seems to me the rule in *Foss* v. *Harbottle* has no application at all, for the individual members who are suing sue, not in the right of the union, but in their own right to protect from invasion their own individual rights as members.

I would be content so to hold as a matter of self-evident principle, but the matter is not free from authority. It will, I think, be enough for the present purposes if I refer, briefly, to a passage in the judgment of SIR GEORGE JESSEL, M.R., in *Pender* v. *Lushington* (1877) 6 Ch. D. 70. . . . In my judgment precisely the same conclusions as are there expressed apply in the present case, and the rule in *Foss* v. *Harbottle* affords no answer to the action. It was sought to show that this was not a matter affecting the individual rights of any particular member of the union because all were subject to the same alteration of the tables and, therefore, it was a matter which affected the general body of members as a whole. I do not agree. . . . [I]t seems to me that, although all the members are liable to pay the subscriptions appropriate to their respective categories, the right of each member to maintain himself in membership by paying his subscription . . . is an individual right of his own which he himself is entitled to protect by an action on his own behalf. . . .

Accordingly, I agree that the appeal fails and should be dismissed.

SIR RAYMOND EVERSHED, M.R.: I am entirely of the same opinion.

XVI. THE REMEDY UNDER S.210 AGAINST OPPRESSION

Scottish Co-operative Wholesale Society Ltd. *v.* Meyer and Another. [1959] A.C. 324

Whenever a subsidiary company has an independent minority of shareholders, it is the duty of the holding company, if it is engaged in the same class of business, so to conduct its affairs as to deal fairly with its subsidiary.

The facts sufficiently appear from their Lordships' opinions in the House of Lords.

Viscount Simonds: My Lords, in this appeal from an interlocutor of the First Division of the Court of Session I am in such full agreement with their Lordships both in their findings of fact and in their conclusions of law that I do not think it necessary to trouble the House at such length as I otherwise might. But, inasmuch as your Lordships have for the first time to consider a new and important section of the *Companies Act,* 1948, it is right that I should state my views upon it.

On May 7, 1946, there was incorporated as a private limited company the Scottish Textile and Manufacturing Co. Ltd., which I will call "the company." It had an authorised share capital of £25,000 divided into 25,000 shares of £1 each. Its substantial object was the manufacture and merchanting of rayon fabrics. The respondents, formerly of German but now of British nationality, who had left Germany when the Nazis obtained power in that country, had a large experience and extensive connections in the continent of Europe in the rayon trade, and one of them, Dr. Meyer, had already in 1945 been appointed textile adviser to the appellant society. Into this trade the society wished to enter and, though they would have preferred to carry it on as a branch of their own business, this was for more than one reason not practicable. The respondents were unwilling to act merely as employees of the society and, since at that time licences had to be obtained for the manufacture of rayon, and were granted only to persons who could satisfy the cotton control authorities that they commanded the necessary skill and experience, it was mutually advantageous to the society and the respondents that a subsidiary company should be formed in which they should both be interested. The company was accordingly formed and 7,900 shares were issued, 4,000 to the society, 3,450 to Meyer, 450 to Lucas. Thus the society had such control as a majority shareholding could give. Moreover, of the five directors of the company three were at all material times nominees of the society, the other two being the respondents, who were the managing directors. Nor was there lacking control by the society of a practical sort. For from the outset it was contemplated that, at any rate until a factory could be built or acquired for it, the company should be substantially dependent for its supplies upon the society's mill at Falkland which in 1956 was partially idle. Accordingly, under arrangements with cotton control, the production of a number of looms at Falkland was allocated to the company and the looms were licensed for rayon production. Dr. Meyer made arrangements for the supply of rayon yarn to be used in the manufacture of the finished cloth, the yarn being purchased by the society and invoiced to them at Falkland Mill. There it was woven and the woven cloth sold to the company ready for dyeing and finishing. This was the plan, and from the beginning it flourished greatly.

But, my Lords, it was a plan which demanded the utmost good faith on both sides, and, as your Lordships will see, it was the lack of it on the part of the society which led to this discreditable tale.

I must hark back for a moment to the year 1947. It seems that in March of that year an agreement between the parties was made for what was curiously called a realignment of their shareholding, so that, instead of approximately equal holdings, the society should hold 70% and the respondents 30% of the issued capital. That was in March 1947, but nothing was done to carry the agreement into effect until the year 1951. In November of that year, the company being then apparently very prosperous, the nominee directors, as I will call them, under the instructions of the board of the society raised the question: numerous proposals were put forward, some of which involved the purchase by the society of some of the respondents' shares. It is unnecessary to go into the details of this episode, for in the end nothing was done. The significance of it lay in the fact that the society's representatives adopted the view that they were entitled to acquire at par any shares they might get under the so-called realignment and, upon a refusal of this unjust demand, threatened that the society would liquidate the company if it was not met. This and other threats led to legal advice being sought. The solicitor to the society and the company advised that the shares should be valued and bought at a valuation: they were valued by the company's auditors at no less than £6 0s. 11d. a share and thereafter the society proceeded no further in the matter. It is impossible after reading the voluminous evidence in this case not to see that the society, thus foiled in their attempt to obtain a grossly unfair advantage of the respondents, determined to seize any opportunity of procuring for themselves the benefit of the trade which had been largely built up by their efforts.

It is at this stage convenient to refer to the section of the Act under which the respondents petitioned the court for relief and obtained the order, against which this appeal is brought, that the society should buy their shares in the company at £3 15s. 0d. per share. . . . It is common ground that at the date of presentation of the petition on July 13, 1953, it was just and equitable that the company should be wound up. It could hardly be denied that to wind up the company would unfairly prejudice the respondents. The only question is whether its affairs were being conducted in a manner oppressive to the respondents and, if so, whether the court ordained the appropriate remedy . . .

The last event that I mentioned was the failure of the society to acquire at par shares that were worth a far greater sum. This was at a time of the company's great prosperity which, subject to the ups and downs of the textile trade, might be expected to continue. It was, however, followed by a recession in the rayon trade, of which the dates of beginning and ending were a matter of dispute. Such dates cannot be precisely determined and are of no consequence. It is, however, to be noted that it was in the course of it that rayon control came to an end, so that neither the society nor the company any longer depended on the personality of the respondents to get supplies of yarn. It was also in the course of it that the respondent Meyer was anxious to visit Germany with a view to increasing the company's trade in that country but was prevented by his co-directors from doing so. This was undoubtedly the cause of much ill-feeling. . . . During the same period other incidents occurred which aggravated the hostile relations between Meyer and Schofield, the manager of the society's Falkland Mill.

An important consequence of the removal of cotton control was this. In or about June, 1951, a new department of the society had been formed called the merchant converting department. It was under the control of a Mr. Wand, the manager of the drapery department, and its function was to convert loom state cloth by dyeing, printing and finishing into material for manufacture into garments. It therefore became possible upon the removal of cotton control and upon a revival of the rayon trade for the society to divert to their own converting department the product of their Falkland Mill. It was the fact, as they were well aware, that the company which had throughout been practically tied to them for the greater part of its supplies, would have great difficulty upon a revival of trade in getting them elsewhere. Deliberately they supplied the necessary material to the converting department but, in spite of Meyer's protests, declined to supply the company except at higher and non-competitive prices. An attempt to justify this discrimination was rightly regarded by their Lordships of the First Division as unsatisfactory. I have no doubt that at any rate by the end of 1952 it was the policy of the society by one means or another to destroy the company it had created, knowing that the minority shareholders alone would suffer in that process. But it is, in truth unnecessary to seek to draw inferences from ambiguous facts. For in January, 1953, a Mr. Robert Taylor, a director of the society and then chairman of the company, had an interview with Meyer and Lucas. He cannot be absolved from a share in the lethal policy of the society but is entitled to what credit may be due for the attempt to make the death as merciful as possible. He told them frankly that the society was out to destroy the company, that they had no chance against such a powerful organisation, and that they should make their peace with the society by offering to sell their shares, and he offered to draft, and, two days later, drafted, a letter for them to send to the society. It is not surprising that Meyer wrote, though not in terms suggested by Taylor, offering on behalf of Lucas and himself to sell their shares at a negotiated price. This letter having been referred to a joint meeting of the society's finance sub-committee and the furnishing sub-committee, those sub-committees met and agreed that the company had served its purpose and should be liquidated if possible. At about the same time the finance sub-committee interviewed the respondents, who intimated that in their opinion a fair price for the shares was 96s. per share and also that they were prepared after selling their shares to stay on in the service of the company. The same sub-committee recommended that Dr. Meyer should be informed that the society did not wish to accept the offer to sell "at the present time." These recommendations were approved by the board of the society on February 9, 1953, and a letter was duly sent to Meyer informing him of the decision not to accept the offer to sell "at the present time." He was not told and did not learn, until in these proceedings the minute was produced, that the society had decided that "the company had served its purpose" and should be liquidated if possible.

At this time the three nominee directors of the company were aware (Taylor by his own confession) of the policy of the society. It is undeniable that persons so placed may find themselves in a difficulty. But in all the evidence I have not been able to find the least trace that they regarded themselves as owing any duty to the company of which they were directors. They were the nominees of the society and, if the society doomed the company to destruction, it was not for them to put out a saving hand. Rather, they were to join in that work, and, when a frank and prompt statement to their co-directors might have enabled them to retrieve its fortunes, they played their part by maintaining silence. That is how they conducted the affairs of the company, and it is impossible to suppose that that was not part of the deliberate policy of the society. As I have said, nominees of a parent company upon the board of a subsidiary company may be placed in a difficult and delicate position. It is, then, the more incumbent on the parent company to behave with scrupulous fairness to the minority shareholders and to avoid imposing upon their nominees the alternative of disregarding their instructions or betraying the interests of the minority. In the present case the society pursued a different course. It was ruthless and unscrupulous in design and it was effective in operation, and, as I have said, it was promoted by the action or inaction of the nominee directors. The company, which might have recovered its former prosperity, had "served its purpose." It could conveniently be liquidated. . . . [O]n August 24, 1953 (that is, after the presentation of the petition under S.210) Meyer and Lucas were given three months' notice of termination of their appointments as managing directors, and Mr. Wand, the manager of the society's drapery department, was appointed manager of the company.

My Lords, upon the facts, . . . it appears to me incontrovertible that the society have behaved to the minority shareholders of the company in a manner which can justly be described as "oppressive." They had the majority power and they exercised their authority in a manner "burdensome, harsh and wrongful"—I take the dictionary meaning of the word. But, it is said, let it be assumed that the society acted in an oppressive manner: yet they did not conduct the affairs of the company in an oppressive manner. My Lords, it may be that the acts of the society of which complaint is made could not be regarded as conduct of the affairs of the company if the society and the company were bodies wholly independent of each other, competitors in the rayon market, and using against each other such methods of trade warfare as custom permitted. But this is to pursue a false analogy. It is not possible to separate the transactions of the society from those of the company. Every step

taken by the latter was determined by the policy of the former.
. . . It is just because the society could not only use the ordinary
and legitimate weapons of commercial warfare but could also
control from within the operations of the company that it is
illegitimate to regard the conduct of the company's affairs as a
matter for which they had no responsibility. After much consideration of this question, I do not think that my own views
could be stated better than in the late Lord President Cooper's
words on the first hearing of this case. "In my view," he said,
"the section warrants the court in looking at the business
realities of a situation and does not confine them to a narrow
legalistic view. The truth is that, whenever a subsidiary is
formed as in this case with an independent minority of shareholders, the parent company must, if it is engaged in the same
class of business, accept as a result of having formed such a
subsidiary an obligation so to conduct what are in a sense its
own affairs as to deal fairly with its subsidiary." At the opposite
pole to this standard may be put the conduct of a parent
company which says: "Our subsidiary company has served its
purpose. Therefore let it die," and, having thus pronounced
sentence, is able to enforce it and does enforce it not only by
attack from without but also by support from within. If this
section is inept to cover such a case, it will be a dead letter
indeed. I have expressed myself strongly in this case because,
on the contrary, it appears to me to be a glaring example of
precisely the evil which Parliament intended to remedy. . . .

The appeal should accordingly, in my opinion, be dismissed. . . .

LORD MORTON OF HENRYTON concurred.

LORD KEITH OF AVONHOLM: . . . [T]here was here, in my
opinion, oppression by the society of the minority shareholders
and it was, I consider, oppression in the conduct of the affairs
of the company. Oppression under S.210 may take various
forms. It suggests, to my mind, . . . a lack of probity and fair
dealing in the affairs of a company to the prejudice of some
portion of its members. The section introduces a wide power
to the court to deal with such a situation in an equitable manner

which it did not have in the case of a company prior to the passing of the Act of 1948. The court has here acted, in my opinion, within the powers conferred upon it.

It was said that appeal could not be made to S.210 unless the company had a continuing life ahead of it and here it was clear that the company would have to be wound up. But that means that if oppression is carried to the extent of destruction of the business of the company no recourse can be had to the remedies of the section. This would be to defeat the whole purpose of the section. The present position is due to the oppression and but for the oppression it must be assumed that the company would be an active and presumably flourishing concern. The section is, in my opinion, very apt to meet the situation which has arisen. . . .

I would dismiss the appeal.

LORD DENNING: . . . It must be remembered that we are here concerned with the manner in which the affairs of the textile company were being conducted. That is, with the conduct of those in control of its affairs. They may be some of the directors themselves, or, behind them, a group of shareholders who nominate those directors or whose interests those directors serve. If those persons—the nominee directors or the shareholders behind them—conduct the affairs of the company in a manner oppressive to the other shareholders, the court can intervene to bring an end to the oppression.

What, then, is the position of the nominee directors here? Under the articles of association of the textile company the co-operative society was entitled to nominate three out of the five directors, and it did so. It nominated three of its own directors and they held office, as the articles said, "as nominees" of the co-operative society. These three were therefore at one and the same time directors of the co-operative society—being three out of twelve of that company—and also directors of the textile company—three out of five there. So long as the interests of all concerned were in harmony, there was no difficulty. The nominee directors could do their duty by both companies without embarrassment. But, so soon as the interests of the two companies were in conflict, the nominee directors were placed in an impossible position. Thus, when the realignment of shareholding was under discussion, the duty of the three directors to the textile company was to get the best possible price for any new issue of its shares, . . . whereas their duty to the co-operative society was to obtain the new shares at the lowest possible price—at par, if they could. Again, when the co-operative society determined to set up its own rayon department, competing with the business of the textile company, the duty of the three directors to the textile company was to do their best to promote its business and to act with complete good faith towards it; and in consequence not to disclose their knowledge of its affairs to a competitor, and not even to work for a competitor, when to do so might operate to the disadvantage of the textile company, . . . whereas they were under the self-same duties to the co-operative society. It is plain that, in the circumstances, these three gentlemen could not do their duty by both companies, and they did not do so. They put their duty to the co-operative society above their duty to the textile company in this sense, at least, that they did nothing to defend the interests of the textile company against the conduct of the co-operative society. They probably thought that "as nominees" of the co-operative society their first duty was to the co-operative society. In this they were wrong. By subordinating the interests of the textile company to those of the co-operative society, they conducted the affairs of the textile company in a manner oppressive to the other shareholders.

It is said that these three directors were at most only guilty of inaction—of doing nothing to protect the textile company. But the affairs of the company can, in my opinion, be conducted oppressively by the directors doing nothing to defend its interests when they ought to do something—just as they can conduct its affairs oppressively by doing something injurious to its interests when they ought not to do it.

. . . [Y]our Lordships are giving a liberal interpretation to S.210. But it is a new section designed to suppress an acknowledged mischief. When it comes before this House for the first time it is, I believe, in accordance with long precedent . . . that

your Lordships should give such construction as shall advance
the remedy. And that is what your Lordships do today.

I would dismiss the appeal.

Re H. R. Harmer Ltd. [1959] 1 W.L.R. 62

*The applicant to the court under S.210 must show oppression of
some part of the members (including himself) in their capacity of
members of the company. He must show that oppression as a
continuing process, i.e. as a course of conduct. The motive for
the oppression is immaterial, and it need not be to obtain a
pecuniary benefit.*

Henry Revell Harmer, the chairman of H. R. Harmer Ltd.
and hereinafter referred to as "the father," was born in
1869. He founded the business subsequently acquired by
the company of philatelic auctioneers and valuers, in 1918
according to the evidence of the petitioners, and in 1894
according to his own evidence, and carried it on with the
assistance of his two sons Cyril and Bernard.

Cyril had been employed in the business continuously
since 1921 and Bernard since 1931. By 1935 Cyril had become responsible for the day-to-day management of the
London office, and thereafter the father's participation in
the conduct of the business gradually declined. In 1940 the
father opened a branch in New York. In June 1940 a
United States company called H. R. Harmer Inc. was
incorporated to take over the American business, and all
the shares were then owned by the father. In 1946 Bernard
went to New York to become vice-president of the
American company, of which his father was president and
Cyril a director, although Bernard was in charge of its day-
to-day business.

H. R. Harmer Ltd., the respondent company, was
incorporated on 1st July 1947 with a view to acquiring the
father's business, including the issued share capital of the
American company which belonged to him. By its articles
of association the first directors were the father, Cyril,
Bernard and another son who resigned in 1950. They
were to be life directors not subject to retirement at annual
general meetings. The father was to be chairman of the

board of directors for life with a casting vote, and also governing director, but the articles contained no provision conferring any powers on the governing director or restricting the powers of the other directors. Article 68 of Table A of the *Companies Act*, 1929, which applied to the company, was modified so that a managing director or manager was not liable to have his tenure of office determined by a resolution of the company in general meeting. The quorum of directors was two.

The ordinary shares of the company were held as to a little over 10 per cent by the father, and as to the remainder by Cyril and Bernard approximately equally, but owing to the ordinary share capital consisting partly of "A" shares with no votes and partly of "B" shares carrying the whole of the voting power, the voting control of the company was held approximately as to 49 per cent by the father, as to 21 per cent by Cyril and Bernard and their wives, and as to 29 per cent by the father's wife. Accordingly the father was able to control the company by the use of his own and his wife's votes, since Mrs. Harmer had agreed with her husband to vote as he directed.

In 1957 Cyril and Bernard presented a petition for relief under S.210 of the *Companies Act,* 1948, the respondents to the petition being their father and the company. They alleged that their father had continued to regard the business of the company as his own, and had ignored the interests of the shareholders, the wishes of his co-directors, and resolutions of the board of directors.

They prayed for the following relief: (1) That the regulations of the company might be altered so as to give the holders of ordinary shares the right to one vote per share. (2) Alternatively, that the father should be ordered to sell to them all his ordinary shares, or alternatively, all his "B" ordinary shares at named figures or such price as the court should think proper. (3) That the father should be relieved from his office as a director. (4) That such other order might be made as might be just.

It was common ground that at the date of the petition it was just and equitable that the company should be wound up.

ROXBURGH J. granted relief under S.210 but not in the terms of the prayer of the petition. He ordered, *inter alia*, that the company should contract for the services of the father as philatelic consultant at a named salary, that the father should not interfere in the affairs of the company otherwise than in accordance with the valid decisions of the board of directors, and that he should be appointed president of the company for life but that this office should not impose any duties, rights or powers.

From this decision the father appealed, and the case accordingly came before the Court of Appeal.

JENKINS L.J.: . . . I should next say a word or two as to the scope and effect of S.210 of the Act. . . . It is to be observed, first, that the person permitted to apply to the court under S.210 is "any *member* of the company," and he must show "that the affairs of the company are being conducted in a manner oppressive to some part of the members (including himself)." This indicates that the oppression complained of must be complained of by a member of the company and must be oppression of some part of the members (including himself) in their or his capacity as a member or members of the company as such. Secondly, it is to be noted that the section does not purport to apply to every case in which the facts would justify the making of a winding-up order under the "just and equit-able" rule, but only to those cases of that character which have in them the requisite element of oppression. Thirdly, the phrase "the affairs of the company are being conducted" sug-gests prima facie a continuing process and is wide enough to cover oppression by anyone who is taking part in the conduct of the affairs of the company whether *de facto* or *de jure*. Fourthly, the section gives no guidance as to the meaning of the word "oppressive," although it does, as already mentioned, indicate that the victim or victims of the oppressive conduct must be a member or members of the company as such. Prima facie, therefore, the word "oppressive" must be given its ordinary sense and the question must be whether in that sense the conduct complained of is oppressive to a member or members as such. Inasmuch as in the present case it is not in dispute that the facts would justify a winding-up order under the "just and equitable" rule and it is recognised that such an order would unfairly prejudice the complaining members, this would appear to be in effect the only question in issue.

There is no English case before this one in which an order has been made under the section, but there have been two such cases in Scotland. . . . The first of the Scottish cases is *Elder* v. *Elder & Watson, Ltd.* Inevitably the result of applications under S.210 in different cases must depend on the particular facts of each case, the circumstances in which oppression may arise being so infinitely various that it is impossible to define them with precision. . . . I think what is said in that case as to the scope of S.210 is, if I may respectfully say so, well founded, and the caution administered in regard to it should be borne constantly in mind when any application under S.210 falls to be considered.

The other Scottish case is *Meyer* v. *Scottish Co-operative Wholesale Society Ltd.* . . . I attach importance to Viscount Simonds' adoption of the meaning of "oppression" as "burdensome, harsh and wrongful."

. . . I turn to the particular matters of complaint alleged by the two sons in their petition. It should be remembered that they are to some extent in the nature of illustrations of the general course of conduct complained of. . . . There were in the course of the history of this unfortunate matter a remarkable number of appointments of directors and retirements of directors brought about in one way or another by the father. This is an aspect of the case one must approach with caution. It cannot be denied that the holder of the majority in voting power of the shares in a company may, broadly speaking, appoint any person he thinks fit as director, and the appointment cannot be challenged merely on the ground that he might have found some more suitable person than the person he selected, or that the person he selected was his friend; but I take it that the majority shareholder's power of appointing directors must within broad limits be exercised for the benefit of the company as a whole and not to secure some ulterior advantage. With that caution, I would observe that as part of the history of this matter, and considered in conjunction with the father's whole course of conduct in relation to the company, the changes in the directorate . . . are, to my mind, not without their materiality.

. . . [T]he story of the directorate . . . does seem to me to support the conclusion that the father was guided in making his appointments by the question whether they could be expected with certainty always to vote in accordance with his wishes. But, as I have said, the facts of this case are by no means usual, and I would not have it go forth that every time a majority shareholder appoints directors of his own choosing, he has done something wrong, or something which can be challenged by a dissatisfied minority, but if he goes on, having seen to it that the requisite majority is obtained, to state his motives for having Mr. A rather than Mr. B, and says: "Mr. A will always vote in the way I tell him to," then it seems to me it is impinging on dangerous ground. I pass from this matter of the directorate simply with the observation that it does appear to me to afford some support for the petitioners' case when looked at in conjunction with the whole course of the father's conduct.

. . . The question remains whether . . . the petitioners were rightly granted the relief which ROXBURGH J. thought fit to grant under S.210. Upon this issue Mr. Harold Brown, for the father, made in effect these submissions. . . . First, he said that the sons should not be heard to complain since they acquired their shares through the generosity of their father, who having built up the business, proceeded to turn it into a company and to hand over a major part of the beneficial interest in the form of shares to his sons virtually by way of gift. As to this, the sons did at all events pay for their preference shares, and if they had not paid anything, two of them at all events had long been working in the business. . . . Moreover, the question of consideration appears to me to be irrelevant, a mere matter of prejudice. Suppose the transaction was a mere matter of gift, the gift, if valid (and there is no suggestion it was not) must surely have conferred the same rights as if the transaction had been for full consideration.

Mr. Harold Brown's second point was that the sons knew full well when the company was formed that the father was to retain control by means of his predominant holding of "B" shares so long as he lived. I agree, but I cannot concur with Mr. Brown in adducing from this that the sons must be taken to have assumed that the father would exercise his control irregularly by doing what he thought fit without reference to the board or in defiance of the board's decisions.

Then the third submission of Mr. Harold Brown was that what was done by the father was not oppressive of the rights of the sons as members, but merely oppressive of their rights as directors. I cannot accept this. It appears to me that the sons as members and not merely as directors were oppressed by the singular conduct of the father. The oppression must no doubt be oppression of members as such, but it does not follow that the fact that the oppressed members are also directors is a disqualifying circumstance when the question of relief under S.210 arises. I think there may well be oppression from the point of view of member-directors where a majority shareholder (that is to say, a shareholder with a preponderance of voting power) proceeds, on the strength of his control, to act contrary to the decisions of, or without the authority of, the duly constituted board of directors of the company.

Fourthly, Mr. Harold Brown said that the acts complained of might have been restrained by injunction in so far as they were acts done without the authority of the board. As to this, I do not think a wrongdoer in this field can well complain that the person wronged might have chosen another remedy.

Then fifthly, Mr. Harold Brown said that the acts complained of were not in their result oppressive, because it cannot be demonstrated that the company suffered any loss from any of them. I cannot agree. The acts complained of were, I should say for the most part, calculated to damage the company in one way or the other.

Sixthly, Mr. Harold Brown said that the acts complained of might have been lawfully done by calling a general meeting and passing the requisite resolutions . . . As to this, I think the sons were at least entitled to require that the proper procedure should be applied.

Then seventhly, Mr. Harold Brown said that this is not a case of discrimination between different shareholders or classes of shareholders. I agree, but see no reason for holding that S.210 is necessarily confined to cases of discrimination, though it is to be expected that cases calling for its application would most usually take that form.

Finally, he submitted that the father got no pecuniary benefit out of what he did. That is not literally true, but even if it was, I do not think it is essential to a case of oppression that the alleged oppressor is oppressing in order to obtain pecuniary benefit. If there is oppression, it remains oppression even though the oppression is due simply to the controlling share-holder's overwhelming desire for power and control, and not with a view to his own advantage in the pecuniary sense. It seems to me the result rather than the motive is the material thing.

. . . I would dismiss this appeal.

ROMER L.J.: I agree. At an early stage of Mr. Harold Brown's opening in this case he suggested that even if the father had been shown to have been conducting the affairs of the company in an oppressive way, . . . nevertheless it was not open to the sons to base a petition under S.210 on that footing, because he said the sons had been given the bulk of their shares by the father and owed everything to his bounty, and they could not complain, even though other people in similar circumstances might. But I think that leaves entirely out of account the fact that the father did in fact create the company. He created proprietary interests in this business, and he cannot now disre-gard the legal entity which was brought into being and the shares which were created therein. . . .

Viewing the evidence as a whole, no one could doubt but that the father acted oppressively in the sense in which that word is ordinarily used. He rode roughshod over his sons and everybody else, and dictated the general conduct of the com-pany's affairs and its policy with an intolerant disregard of the wishes of his co-directors, and indeed, in some instances, in disregard of the best interests of the company itself. The question, however, is whether it has been shown within S.210 of the Act that the affairs of the company were being conducted by the father in a manner oppressive to the shareholders, including the petitioners, who are in a voting minority. . . .

In considering whether the way in which he did conduct the company's affairs was oppressive, I agree with the judge that although naturally attention must be paid to the various incidents of which the petitioners complain taken by themselves, the court is concerned really to consider the history of the matter as a whole, and to see whether a course of conduct by the father has been established which constitutes an oppression of the other shareholders. . . . It is true that the mere use of voting power at board meetings or at a general meeting to secure the passing of resolutions, which the other members of the board or shareholders oppose, would not in general constitute oppression for the purpose of the section or for any other purpose. For a petition to succeed it must be shown that there has been oppression in a real sense of members *qua* shareholders, and not merely a subordination of their wishes to the power of a voting majority.

. . . Members are entitled to expect that their board shall perform its functions as a board, and that the proceedings of the directors shall be carried out in a normal and orthodox manner. . . . If the board is browbeaten and either ignored or overruled by one of its number, in this case the father, in reliance on his superior voting power, the proprietary interests of the minority shareholders cannot fail to be affected, and a case of oppression within S.210 is, in my judgment, made out.

. . . I agree that the appeal should be dismissed.

WILLMER L.J.: I agree that this appeal fails. . . .

The only question which in the event has to be decided in the case is whether or not the affairs of H. R. Harmer Ltd. were being conducted in a manner oppressive to some part of the members, including the petitioners. . . . [T]he question . . . is a pure question of fact to be determined in accordance with the circumstances of the particular case, . . . and I venture to make these two comments on the correct way to approach the question of fact which arises in a case such as this. The first is that in my judgment it is quite impossible to lay down *a priori* certain categories of conduct which in all circumstances either are or are not capable in law of amounting to conduct which is oppressive within the meaning of the section; in other words, each case has to be examined in the light of its own particular facts and, I would venture to add, in the light of the personality of the individual persons concerned. The second matter . . . is this, that one must be careful to study the course of conduct complained of as a whole.

. . . Viewing the conduct complained of as a whole, *i.e.* as a course of conduct extending over the years, it appears to me that there was abundant evidence to justify the judge in his conclusion of fact . . . [B]y one means or another the father has sought to impose his will in the conduct of the affairs of the company to the exclusion of the wishes of other people who might be concerned. . . . [T]he various matters complained of fall into different categories, according to the method adopted by the father. One method complained of was his use or abuse of his voting power, primarily to secure the election to the board of people who were his nominees. Another method which he adopted was to use the mere threat of his voting power to impose his wishes on the rest of the board. The third method adopted was simply to go behind the backs of the board and, after a decision had been taken by the board, to take it upon himself to countermand it on his own authority and to give his own instructions. . . . It is not the mere fact that the father in this case sought to get his own friends on to the board; what is objected to, and as I think rightly objected to, was securing the election of the particular people concerned with the avowed object of securing people who would be "certainties," to use the word which the father himself used. But the most dangerous and most oppressive form of conduct is, I think, the habit that the father had of going behind properly constituted decisions of the board and taking it upon himself to countermand them. It seems to me that such conduct cuts at the very root of proper company procedure and makes it virtually impossible for the business of a company to be carried on. . . . I venture to think it is an illuminating comment on the state of affairs which has arisen if it becomes necessary, whenever any meeting is held, to have a recording machine which will take down every word that is said by anybody, and to have solicitors sitting at the elbows of the various parties. . . . I am abundantly satisfied that all this led inevitably to damage to the interests of the company. There was some evidence of actual financial loss. . . . But of far more importance than that, as it seems to me, was . . . that it was becoming increasingly difficult to carry on business at all. . . .

. . . [T]he judge appears to have . . . come to the conclusion that the father did know perfectly well that he was going outside his powers. For myself I doubt very much whether it makes very much difference whether the father did or did not know that he was exceeding his powers, because, in the view which I take, oppressive conduct would not cease to be oppressive merely if it were unconscious, though of course it may be said— if I may be forgiven for once more borrowing a phrase used in connection with a matrimonial cause—that which is done consciously strikes with a sharper edge. It seems to me that the question whether the conduct complained of was conscious or unconscious is more material on the question of what relief ought to be accorded. If, as the judge thought, the father persisted in his conduct well knowing it to be wrong, there can of course be less assurance of the discontinuance of such conduct in future, and therefore possibly all the more need for a stringent order to protect the interests of the shareholders.

. . . I do not think there is any other course open to us but to dismiss the appeal. I am satisfied that this company was suffering damage, and is in danger of suffering further damage from the oppressive manner in which its affairs were conducted by the father; and I am satisfied that the petitioners, as shareholders (and I stress the words "as shareholders") and not merely as directors, were suffering and are in danger of suffering further from the damage inflicted on the company.

XVII. WINDING UP UNDER S.222 (f)

Ebrahimi (A. P.) *v*. Westbourne Galleries Ltd. and Others.
[1973] A.C. 360

The words "just and equitable" in S.222 (f) are not confined to matters eiusdem generis as the preceding clauses of the section, nor to proved cases of mala fides. They are general words which must not be reduced to the sum of particular instances, nor confined to circumstances affecting the petitioner in his capacity of shareholder.

They enable the court to subject the exercise of legal rights to equitable considerations through the force of the words themselves, and not because the company's structure is in any way analogous to a partnership.

The facts sufficiently appear from the speech of LORD WILBERFORCE in the House of Lords.

LORD WILBERFORCE: My Lords, the issue in this appeal is whether the respondent company Westbourne Galleries Ltd. should be wound up by the court on the petition of the appellant who is one of the three shareholders, the personal respondents being the other two. The company is a private company which carries on business as dealers in Persian and other carpets. It was formed in 1958 to take over a business founded by the second respondent (Mr. Nazar). It is a fact of cardinal importance that since about 1945 the business had been carried on by the appellant and Mr. Nazar as partners, equally sharing the management and the profits. When the company was formed, the signatories to its memorandum were the appellant and Mr. Nazar and they were appointed its first directors. Of its issued share capital, 500 £1 shares were issued to each subscriber and it was found by the learned judge . . . that Mr. Ebrahimi paid up his shares out of his own money. Soon after the company's formation the third respondent (Mr. George Nazar) was made a director, and each of the two original shareholders transferred to him 100 shares, so that at all material times Mr. Ebrahimi held 400 shares, Mr. Nazar 400 and Mr. George Nazar 200. The Nazars, father and son, thus had a majority of the votes in general meeting. Until the dispute all three gentlemen remained directors.

The company made good profits, all of which were distributed as directors' remuneration. No dividends have ever been paid. . . .

On August 12, 1969, an ordinary resolution was passed by the company in general meeting, by the votes of Mr. Nazar and Mr. George Nazar, removing Mr. Ebrahimi from the office of director, a resolution which was effective in law by virtue of S.184 of the *Companies Act*, 1948, and article 96 of Part I of Table A. Shortly afterwards the appellant presented his petition to the court.

This petition was based in the first place upon S.210 of the *Companies Act*, 1948, the relief sought under this section being an order that Mr. Nazar and his son be ordered to purchase the appellant's shares in the company. In the alternative it sought an order for the winding up of the company. The petition contained allegations of oppression and misconduct against Mr. Nazar which were fully explored at the hearing before PLOWMAN J. The learned judge found that some were unfounded and others unproved and that such complaint as was made out did not amount to such a course of oppressive conduct as to justify an order under S.210. However, he made an order for the winding up of the company under the "just and equitable" provision. I shall later specify the grounds on which he did so. The appellant did not appeal against the rejection of his case under S.210 and this House is not concerned with it. The company and the individual respondents appealed against the order for winding up and this was set aside by the Court of Appeal. The appellant now seeks to have it restored.

My Lords, the petition was brought under S.222 (f) of the *Companies Act*, 1948, which enables a winding up order to be made if "the court is of opinion that it is just and equitable that the company should be wound up." This power has existed in our company law in unaltered form since the first major Act, the *Companies Act*, 1862. Indeed, it antedates that statute since it existed in the *Joint Stock Companies Winding-up Act*, 1848. For some fifty years . . . the words "just and equitable" were interpreted so as only to include matters *eiusdem generis* as the preceding clauses of the section, but there is now ample authority for discarding this limitation. There are two other restrictive interpretations which I mention to reject. First, there has been a tendency to create categories or headings under which cases must be brought if the clause is to apply. This is wrong. Illustrations may be used, but general words must remain general and not be reduced to the sum of particular instances. Secondly, it has been suggested . . . that (assuming the petitioner is a shareholder and not a creditor) the words must be confined to such circumstances as affect him in his capacity as shareholder. I see no warrant for this either. No doubt, in order to present a petition, he must qualify as a shareholder, but I see no reason for preventing him from relying upon any circumstances of justice or equity which affect him in his relations with the company, or, in a case such as the present, with the other shareholders.

One other signpost is significant. The same words "just and equitable" appear in the *Partnership Act*, 1890, S.35 as a ground for dissolution of a partnership and no doubt the considerations which they reflect formed part of the common law of partnership before its codification. The importance of this is to provide a bridge between cases under S.222 (f) of the Act of 1948 and the principles of equity developed in relation to partnerships.

The winding up order was made following a doctrine which has developed in the courts since the beginning of this century . . . (T)his was that in a case such as this, the members of the company are in substance partners, or quasi-partners, and that a winding up may be ordered if such facts are shown as could justify a dissolution of partnership between them. The common use of the words "just and equitable" in the company and partnership law supports this approach. Your Lordships were invited by the respondents' counsel to restate the principle on which this provision ought to be used; it has not previously been considered by this House. The main line of his submission was to suggest that too great a use of the partnership analogy had been made; that a limited company, however small, essentially differs from a partnership; that in the case of a company, the rights of its members are governed by the articles of association which have contractual force; that the court has no power or at least ought not to dispense parties from observing their contracts; that, in particular, when one member has been excluded from the directorate, or management, under powers expressly conferred by the *Companies Act* and the articles, an order for winding up whether on the partnership analogy or under the just and equitable provision, should not be made. Alternatively, it was argued that before the making of such an order could be considered the petitioner must show and prove that the exclusion was not made *bona fide* in the interests of the company. . . .

My Lords, . . . (t)he foundation of (the law) lies in the words "just and equitable" and, if there is any respect in which some of the cases may be open to criticism, it is that the courts may sometimes have been too timorous in giving them full force. The words are a recognition of the fact that a limited company is more than a mere judicial entity, with a personality in law of its own: that there is room in company law for recognition of the fact that behind it, or amongst it, there are individuals, with rights, expectations and obligations *inter se* which are not necessarily submerged in the company structure. That structure is defined by the *Companies Act* and by the articles of association by which shareholders agree to be bound. In most companies and in most contexts, this definition is sufficient and exhaustive, equally so whether the company is large or small. The "just and equitable" provision does not . . . entitle one party to disregard the obligation he assumes by entering a company, nor the court to dispense him from it. It does, as equity always does, enable the court to subject the exercise of legal rights to equitable considerations; considerations, that is, of a personal character arising between one individual and another, which may make it unjust, or inequitable, to insist on legal rights, or to exercise them in a particular way.

It would be impossible, and wholly undesirable, to define the circumstances in which these considerations may arise. Certainly the fact that a company is a small one, or a private company, is not enough. There are very many of these where the association is a purely commercial one, of which it can safely be said that the basis of association is adequately and exhaustively laid down in the articles. The superimposition of equitable considerations requires something more, which typically may include one, or probably more, of the following elements: (i) an association formed or continued on the basis of a personal relationship, involving mutual confidence—this element will often be found where a pre-existing partnership has been converted into a limited company; (ii) an agreement, or understanding, that all, or some (for there may be "sleeping" members), of the shareholders shall participate in the conduct of the business; (iii) restriction upon the transfer of the member's interest in the company—so that if confidence is lost, or one member is removed from management, he cannot take out his stake and go elsewhere.

It is these, and analogous, factors which may bring into play the just and equitable clause, and they do so directly, through the force of the words themselves. To refer . . . to "quasi-partnerships" or "in substance partnerships" may be convenient but may also be confusing. It may be convenient because it is the law of partnership which has developed the conceptions of probity, good faith and mutual confidence, and the remedies where these are absent, which become relevant once such factors as I have mentioned are found to exist: the words "just and equitable" sum these up in the law of partnership itself. And in many, but not necessarily all, cases there has been a pre-existing partnership the obligations of which it is reasonable to suppose continue to underlie the new company structure. But the expressions may be confusing if they obscure, or deny, the fact that the parties (possibly former partners) are now co-members in a company, who have accepted, in law, new obligations. A company, however small, however domestic, is a company not a partnership or even a quasi-partnership and it is through the just and equitable clause that obligations, common to partnership relations, may come in.

My Lords, this is an expulsion case, and I must briefly justify the application in such cases of the just and equitable clause. The question is, as always, whether it is equitable to allow one (or two) to make use of his legal rights to the prejudice of his associate(s). The law of companies recognises the right, in many ways, to remove a director from the board. S.184 of the *Companies Act*, 1948, confers this right upon the company in general meeting whatever the articles may say. Some articles may prescribe other methods: for example, a governing director may have the power to remove. . . . And quite apart from removal powers, there are normally provisions for retirement of directors by rotation so that their re-election can be opposed and defeated by a majority, or even by a casting vote. In all these ways a particular director-member may find himself no longer a director, through removal, or non-re-election: this situation he must normally accept, unless he undertakes the burden of proving fraud or *mala fides*. The just and equitable provision nevertheless comes to his assistance if he can point to, and prove, some special underlying obligation of his fellow member(s) in good faith, or confidence, that so long as the business continues he shall be entitled to management participation, an obligation so basic that if broken, the conclusion must be that the association must be dissolved. And the principles on which he may do so are those worked out by the courts in partnership cases where there has been exclusion from management . . . even where under the partnership agreement there is a power of expulsion.

I come to the facts of this case. It is apparent enough that a potential basis for a winding-up order under the just and equitable clause existed. The appellant after a long association in partnership, during which he had an equal share in the management, joined in the formation of the company. The inference must be indisputable that he, and Mr. Nazar, did so on the basis that the character of the association would, as a matter of personal relation and good faith, remain the same. He was removed from his directorship under a power valid in law. Did he establish a case which, if he had remained in a partnership with a term providing for expulsion, would have justified an order for dissolution? This was the essential question for the judge. PLOWMAN J. dealt with the issue in a brief paragraph in which he said: ". . . while no doubt the petitioner was lawfully removed, in the sense that he ceased in law to be a director, it does not follow that in removing him the respondents did not do him a wrong. In my judgment, they did do him a wrong, in the sense that it was an abuse of power and a breach of the good faith which partners owe to each other to exclude one of them from all participation in the business upon which they have embarked on the basis that all should participate in its management. The main justification put forward for removing him was that he was perpetually complaining, but the faults were not all on one side and, in my judgment, this is not sufficient justification. For these reasons, in my judgment, the petitioner . . . has made out a case for a winding-up order." Reading this in the context of the judgment as a whole, . . . I take it as a finding that the respondents were not entitled, in justice and equity, to make use of their legal powers of expulsion and that . . . the only just and equitable course was to dissolve the association. To my mind, two factors strongly support this. First, Mr. Nazar made it perfectly clear that he did not regard Mr. Ebrahimi as a partner, but did regard him as an employee. But there was no possible doubt as to Mr. Ebrahimi's status throughout, so that Mr. Nazar's refusal to recognise it amounted, in effect, to a repudiation of the relationship. Secondly, Mr. Ebrahimi, through ceasing to be a director, lost his right to share in the profits through directors' remuneration, retaining only the chance of receiving dividends as a minority shareholder. It is true that an assurance was given . . . that the previous practice (of not paying dividends) would not be continued, but the fact remains that Mr. Ebrahimi was henceforth at the mercy of the Messrs. Nazar as to what he should receive out of the profits and when. He was, moreover, unable to dispose of his interest without the consent of the Nazars. All these matters lead only to the conclusion that the right course was to dissolve the association by winding up.

I must deal with one final point which was much relied on by the Court of Appeal. It was said that the removal was . . . *bona fide* in the interests of the company. . . . This formula, "*bona fide* in the interests of the company" is one that is relevant in certain contexts of company law and I do not doubt that in many cases decisions have to be left to majorities or directors to take which the courts must assume had this basis. It may, on the other hand, become little more than an alibi for a refusal to consider the merits of the case, and in a situation such as this it seems to have little meaning other than "in the interests of the majority". Mr. Nazar may well have persuaded himself . . . that the company would be better off without Mr. Ebrahimi but if Mr. Ebrahimi disputed this, or thought the same with reference to Mr. Nazar, what prevails is simply the majority view. To confine the application of the just and equitable clause to proved cases of *mala fides* would be to negative the generality of the words. It is because I do not accept this that I feel myself obliged to differ from the Court of Appeal.

I would allow the appeal and restore the judgment of PLOWMAN J.

VISCOUNT DILHORNE: My Lords, . . . I agree that the appeal should be allowed.

LORD PEARSON: My Lords, . . . I would allow the appeal and restore the judgment of PLOWMAN J.

LORD CROSS OF CHELSEA: My Lords, . . . I would . . . allow the appeal.

LORD SALMON: My Lords, I concur and would allow the appeal.

XVIII. SCHEMES OF ARRANGEMENT AND TAKE-OVER BIDS

Re Sussex Brick Company Ltd. [1961] Ch. 289

A scheme to which S.209 applies will bind a dissenting share-holder unless he can show it to be affirmatively, patently, obviously and convincingly unfair.

The applicant, Frank Cunningham, the holder of 5,500 shares in the Sussex Brick Co. Ltd., sought a declaration under S.209 of the *Companies Act*, 1948, that the respondent company, Redlands Holdings Ltd., was neither entitled nor bound to acquire his shares in the Sussex Brick Co. Ltd. on the terms of a scheme or contract dated 16th September 1958, notwithstanding that the same had been approved by the holders of nine-tenths in value of the shares whose transfer was involved.

VAISEY J.: This matter arises out of an offer made by the respondent company, Redlands Holdings Ltd., to acquire the preference and ordinary shares of the Sussex Brick Co. Ltd., on certain terms set out in a scheme dated September 16, 1958 sent to the various shareholders, or, at any rate, to the ordinary shareholders, together with an explanatory letter. The offer, in effect, was that for every three shares in the brick company, two shares in the respondent company would be taken in lieu. The applicant was unwilling to accept that offer and he brings this summons under S.209 of the *Companies Act*, 1948, to establish his right to refuse to do so: he is an ordinary shareholder and he says that he does not want to have the shares which he holds in the brick company replaced by shares in Redlands Holdings Ltd. . . .

The matter has been considered in more than one case, and the governing considerations were well stated by MAUGHAM J. in *In re Hoare & Co. Ltd.* Summarising his judgment, it really comes to this: that an applicant, taking advantage of S209, has, in effect, to show that the scheme is to him unfair, and that is the yardstick which is accepted and adopted as the criterion which enables a shareholder to get out of the provisions of the section. I think that it is now admitted that unless this scheme is to the applicant unfair he is not entitled to act as a dissenting shareholder under the section and obtain a declaration that he is not bound to transfer his shares.

Whether one's sympathies are with the man who wants to hold on to his shares and not to have them expropriated, or whether one regards such a person as being rather troublesome and not deserving much sympathy, is a matter having nothing to do with this case. . . . [T]he fact remains that procedure under S.209 is for the acquiring, on terms, of the shares of a man who does not want to part with his shares. . . .

. . . I think that the present scheme and the present offer are undoubtedly open to criticism, and that a clever business man, a man well versed in company law and matters which influence dealings on the Stock Exchange, could find a good many loopholes in it. . . . That the scheme is open to criticism I have no doubt, but can it be said therefore to be unfair? I think it rather difficult to predicate unfairness in any case in which there has been perfect good faith on the side of the person who is alleged to have been unfair. I think that the applicant is faced with the very difficult task of discharging an onus which is undoubtedly the heavy one of showing that he, being the only man in the regiment out of step, is the only man whose views ought to prevail. . . .

A scheme must be obviously unfair, patently unfair, unfair to the meanest intelligence. It cannot be said that no scheme can be effective to bind a dissenting shareholder unless it complies to the extent of 100 per cent. with the highest possible standards of fairness, equity and reason. After all, a man may have an offer made to him and, although he would prefer something better, would be quite prepared to accept it because it was good enough in all the circumstances. It may be that the grounds for criticising the present scheme are not grounds of such a nature as to render the whole thing unfair in the sense in which MAUGHAM J. used the words in the case which I have cited. . . .

So far as the Stock Exchange is concerned I have some information about the present share values. . . . The shares were less than half the value of the shares given in substitution for them, and it is a little hard to see that such a bad bargain has been driven. . . . If I accede to [the applicant's] request I do not see that a very attractive prospect lies before him. If he retains his shares in the company they will not be quoted, and will probably be quite unsaleable. Ninety per cent. of the shareholders think the scheme is all right.

. . . I do not think that unfairness in the sense in which it has been used in the reported cases has been established. It must be affirmatively established that, notwithstanding the view of the majority, the scheme is unfair, and that is a different thing from saying that it must be established that the scheme is not a very fair or not a fair one: a scheme has to be shown affirmatively, patently, obviously and convincingly to be unfair. . . .

I am not satisfied that this scheme is unfair in the sense in which MAUGHAM J. used the words and the application ought not to succeed.

Re Bugle Press Ltd. [1961] Ch. 270

Where as a matter of substance the persons who are making the offer are the same persons whose acceptance of it binds the dissenting shareholder, the burden of proof is reversed and it is for the offeror to show that the scheme is fair.

In 1950 Bugle Press Ltd. was incorporated to carry on the business of booksellers, publishers and other like businesses referred to in its memorandum of association. Its principal business was the publication of a magazine devoted to advertisement for the sales of secondhand cars and to similar advertising. Its authorised and issued share capital was 10,000 shares of £1 each fully paid, all of one class, of which 9,000 were at all material times held in equal moieties by George Douglas Shaw and Henry Robert Jackson, who were the two directors of the company. The

remaining 1,000 shares were at all material times held by
Henry Charles Treby.

On 5th September a company, Jackson and Shaw (Holdings) Ltd., was incorporated. It was promoted by Jackson
and Shaw who were its only members and directors, each
of them holding fifty of its 100 issued shares. It apparently carried on no business, but on 4th July 1959, solicitors
acting for it wrote stating that the company was proposing
to make an offer to purchase the whole of the issued share
capital of Bugle Press Ltd. The letter continued: "To this
end, there have been given facilities for an independent
firm of accountants to value the said shares. This has been
done by Messrs. Price Waterhouse & Co. and their figures
are £100,000. It is a known fact that Messrs. Jackson and
Shaw, the holders of 90 per cent. of the issued capital, will
accept this offer. Your client (Treby) would receive should
he accept £10,000."

Treby did not accept that offer because he considered
that the value of his holding of shares in Bugle Press Ltd.
was considerably more than the amount offered for it.
The offer having been declined, Jackson and Shaw (Holdings) Ltd. gave Treby notice under S.209 of the *Companies
Act*, 1948, that it intended to exercise its statutory rights of
compulsory acquisition under that section.

Treby applied for a declaration under the section that
Jackson and Shaw (Holdings) Ltd. was neither entitled nor
bound to acquire his shares in Bugle Press Ltd. on the terms
of a "scheme and contract" dated 14th July 1959, notwithstanding that it had been approved by the majority of the
shareholders.

BUCKLEY J.: . . . In the ordinary case of an offer under this
section, where the 90 per cent. majority who accept the offer
are unconnected with the persons who are concerned with
making the offer, the court pays the greatest attention to the
views of that majority. In all commercial matters, where
commercial people are much better able to judge of their own
affairs than the court is able to do, the court is accustomed to
pay the greatest attention to what commercial people who are
concerned with the transaction in fact decide. . . . [W]here
there is a large majority (and, of course, a 90 per cent. majority

is necessarily a large majority) of shareholders who are only concerned to see that they get what they consider to be a fair price for their shares, and who are in favour of accepting the offer, the burden is a heavy one on the dissentient shareholder to say that the offer is not one which he ought reasonably to have to accept. . . .

This case, however, seems to me to be quite the reverse of that, because here, although as a matter of law the body making the offer must be regarded as distinct from the persons who hold shares in that body, nevertheless, as a matter of substance the persons who are putting forward this offer are the majority shareholders, the only two shareholders in the transferee company, and they are the holders of the 90 per cent. majority shareholding, whose acceptance of that offer it is suggested binds the dissenting shareholder also to accept the offer. In a case of this kind it seems to me that the onus must clearly be on the other side, and that it must be incumbent on the majority shareholders to satisfy the court that the scheme is one with which the minority shareholder ought reasonably to be compelled to fall in. . . .

In my view, . . . the onus which I consider rests on the transferee company has not been discharged, and having regard to the unusual nature of this case—unusual in the sense that the 90 per cent. majority shareholders are, themselves, in substance the transferee company—I think this is certainly a case in which the court ought to "order otherwise" within the meaning of the section. In my judgment, the applicant ought not to be compelled to sell his shares at the proposed price in these circumstances.

I propose, therefore, to declare: that the transferee company is not entitled to acquire . . . the shares of the applicant in the Bugle Press Ltd., or any of them on the terms of the scheme, notwithstanding that it has been approved by nine-tenths of the shareholders of Bugle Press Ltd.

From this decision of BUCKLEY J. Jackson and Shaw (Holdings) Ltd. appealed, and the case accordingly came before the Court of Appeal.

LORD EVERSHED M.R.: . . . Mr. Instone [*counsel for Jackson and Shaw (Holdings) Ltd.*] freely accepts that the mechanism of the section has here been invoked by means of the incorporation of this holding company, Jackson and Shaw (Holdings) Ltd., especially for the purpose, and in order to enable the two persons, Shaw and Jackson, to expropriate the shares of their minority colleague, Treby. He says that although that is undoubtedly true, nevertheless, in the result, the case does fall within the strict language of the section and falling within it the consequences must follow. If that argument is right, it would enable by a device of this kind the 90 per cent. majority of the shareholders always to get rid of a minority shareholder whom they did not happen to like. And that, as a matter of principle, would appear to be contrary to a fundamental principle of our law that prima facie, if a man has a legal right which is an absolute right, then he can do with it or not do with it what he will.

. . . Even, therefore, though the present case does fall strictly within the terms of S.209, the fact that the offeror, the transferee company, is for all practical purposes entirely equivalent to the nine-tenths of the shareholders who have accepted the offer, makes it in my judgment a case in which, for the purposes of exercising the court's discretion, the circumstances are special. . . . It is no doubt true to say that it is still for the minority shareholder to establish that the discretion should be exercised in the way he seeks. . . . But if the minority shareholder does show, as he shows here, that the offeror and the 90 per cent. of the transferor company's shareholders are the same, then as it seems to me he has, prima facie, shown that the court ought otherwise to order, since if it should not do so the result would be . . . that the section has been used not for the purpose of any scheme or contract properly so called or contemplated by the section but for the quite different purpose of enabling majority shareholders to expropriate or evict the minority; and that, as it seems to me, is something for the purposes of which, prima facie, the court ought not to allow the section to be invoked—unless at any rate it were shown that there was some good reason in the interests of the company for so doing, for example, that the minority shareholder was in some way acting in a manner destructive or highly damaging to the interests of the company from some motives entirely of his own. . . .

For these reasons I think that we could not properly, and should not, interfere with BUCKLEY J.'s exercise of discretion.

HARMAN L.J.: I agree. In my judgment this is a barefaced attempt to evade that fundamental rule of company law which forbids the majority of shareholders, unless the articles so provide, to expropriate a minority. . . . [The minority shareholder], having applied to the court under the section, had, like any other applicant, to prove his case, that is to say, to set up a case which the respondents had to answer. He did that, it seems to me, as it seemed to my Lord, quite simply by showing that the transferee company was nothing but a little hut built round his two co-shareholders, and that the so-called "scheme" was made by themselves as directors of that company with themselves as shareholders and the whole thing, therefore, is seen to be a hollow sham. . . . The minority shareholder has nothing to knock down; he has only to shout and the walls of Jericho fall flat. I am surprised that it was thought that so elementary a device would receive the court's approval.

I would dismiss this appeal.

DONOVAN L.J.: I agree with both judgments.

Re Hellenic & General Trust, Ltd. [1976] 1 W.L.R. 123

Where in a scheme of arrangement under S.206 one of the members is the wholly-owned subsidiary of the company which is to purchase the shares under the scheme, that member forms a separate class for the purpose of the meetings required under the section, since it has different interests from the other members.

The facts sufficiently appear from the judgment.

TEMPLEMAN J.: This is an opposed petition for the sanction by the court under S.206 of the *Companies Act*, 1948 of an arrangement relating to the ordinary shares of the company, Hellenic & General Trust Ltd.

The company carries on business as an investment trust.

The ordinary shares . . . are held as to 53.01 per cent. by Merchandise and Investment Trust Ltd. (known as M.I.T.). All the shares of M.I.T. are held by Hambros Ltd. and therefore M.I.T. is a wholly owned subsidiary of Hambros. The objectors, National Bank of Greece S.A., hold 13.95 per cent. of the ordinary shares of the company proposed to be dealt with by the arrangement. By the arrangement the ordinary shares of the company will be cancelled. New ordinary shares will be issued to Hambros and the company will thus become, like M.I.T., a wholly owned subsidiary of Hambros. The former shareholders of the company will be paid by Hambros 48p per share for the loss of their former shares. The result is equivalent to a purchase by Hambros of the ordinary shares of the company at 48p per share.

. . . [I]n the present case if there was a proper class meeting which agreed to the arrangement by the requisite majorities, and if this court sanctions the arrangement, then the objectors will lose their shares in the company and will receive 48p per share from Hambros instead. The objectors do not wish this to happen.

In the present case the court, on the petition of the company, summoned a meeting of all the ordinary shareholders. A resolution agreeing to the arrangement was carried, some 91 per cent. of the shareholders by value attending and voting. M.I.T., holding 53.01 per cent., voted in favour of the arrangement. The National Bank of Greece, the objectors, holding 13.95 per cent. of the ordinary shares, voted against the arrangement. The arrangement was approved by 86.61 per cent. in number and 84.67 per cent. in value of those who attended and voted. The votes of M.I.T. were vital. If they had not attended and voted the requisite majority could not have been achieved against the opposition of the objectors. The objectors now pursue their opposition to the arrangement in this court. . . .

The first objection put forward is that the necessary agreement by the appropriate class of members has not been obtained. The shareholders who were summoned to the meeting consisted, it is submitted, of two classes. First there were the outside shareholders, that is to say the shareholders other than

M.I.T.; and secondly M.I.T., a subsidiary of Hambros. M.I.T. were a separate class and should have been excluded from the meeting of outside shareholders. Although S.206 provides that the court may order meetings, it is the responsibility of the petitioners to see that the class meetings are properly constituted, and if they fail then the necessary agreement is not obtained and the court has no jurisdiction to sanction the arrangement. Thus in *In re United Provident Assurance Company Ltd.* [1910] 2 Ch. 477 the court held that the holders of partly paid shares formed a different class from holders of fully paid shares. The objection was taken that there should have been separate meetings of the two classes, and SWINFEN EADY J. upheld the objection, saying: ". . . the objection that there have not been proper class meetings is fatal, and I cannot sanction the scheme. . . ."

The question therefore is whether M.I.T., a wholly owned subsidiary of Hambros, formed part of the same class as the other ordinary shareholders. What is an appropriate class must depend upon the circumstances but some general principles are to be found in the authorities. In *Sovereign Life Assurance Co.* v. *Dodd* [1892] 2 Q.B. 573, the Court of Appeal held that for the purposes of an arrangement affecting the policyholders of an assurance company the holders of policies which had matured were creditors and were a different class from policyholders whose policies had not matured. LORD ESHER M.R. said:

". . . they must be divided into different classes . . . because the creditors composing the different classes have different interests; and, therefore, if we find a different state of facts existing among different creditors which may differently affect their minds and their judgment, they must be divided into different classes."

BOWEN L.J. said:

"It seems plain that we must give such a meaning to the term 'class' as will prevent the section being so worked as to result in confiscation and injustice, and that it must be confined to those persons whose rights are not so dissimilar as to make it impossible for them to consult together with a view to their common interest."

Vendors consulting together with a view to their common interest in an offer made by a purchaser would look askance at the presence among them of a wholly owned subsidiary of the purchaser.

In the present case on analysis Hambros are acquiring the outside shares for 48p. So far as the M.I.T. shares are concerned it does not matter very much to Hambros whether they are acquired or not. If the shares are acquired a sum of money moves from parent to wholly owned subsidiary and shares move from the subsidiary to the parent. The overall financial position of the parent and the subsidiary remain the same. . . . From the point of M.I.T., provided M.I.T. is solvent, the directors of M.I.T. do not have to question whether the price is exactly right. Before and after the arrangement the directors of the parent and the subsidiary could have been made the same persons with the same outlook and the same judgment. Mr. Heyman, on behalf of the petitioners, submitted that since the parent and subsidiary were separate corporations with separate directors, and since M.I.T. were ordinary shareholders in the company, it followed that M.I.T. had the same interests as the other shareholders. The directors of M.I.T. were under a duty to consider whether the arrangement was beneficial to the whole class of ordinary shareholders, and they were capable of forming an independent and unbiased judgment, irrespective of the interests of the parent company. This seems to me to be unreal. Hambros are purchasers making an offer. When the vendors meet to discuss and vote whether or not to accept the offer, it is incongruous that the loudest voice in theory and the most significant vote in practice should come from the wholly owned subsidiary of the purchaser. No one can be both a vendor and a purchaser and in my judgment, for the purpose of the class meetings in the present case, M.I.T. were in the camp of the purchaser. Of course this does not mean that M.I.T. should not have considered at a separate class meeting whether to accept the arrangement. But their consideration will be different from the considerations given to the matter by the other shareholders. Only M.I.T. could say, within limits, that what was good for Hambros must be good for M.I.T. . . .

Accordingly I uphold the first objection, which is fatal to the arrangement. But . . . I will consider the other objections which are raised by Mr. Wright [*counsel for the National Bank*] and which are material if the class meeting . . ., contrary to my view, was properly constituted.

The second objection is founded on the analysis of the arrangement as an offer by Hambros to acquire the ordinary shares for 48p. S.209 provides safeguards for minority shareholders in the event of a takeover bid and in a proper case provides machinery for a small minority of shareholders to be obliged to accept a takeover against their wishes. . . . If the present arrangement had been carried out under S.209, M.I.T. as a subsidiary of Hambros would have been expressly forbidden to join in any approval for the purposes of S.209, and in any event the objectors could not have been obliged to sell because they hold 10 per cent. of the ordinary shares of the company.

The fact that an arrangement under S.206 produces a result which is the same as a takeover under S.209 is not necessarily fatal. It is not always so unfair as to preclude the court from exercising its discretion in favour of the scheme. Thus in *In re National Bank Ltd.* [1966] 1 W.L.R. 819, where a similar objection was taken, PLOWMAN J. considered the argument that the scheme in that case ought to be treated as a S.209 case needing a 90 per cent. majority. He said:

". . . I cannot accede to that proposition. . . . [T]he two sections, S.206 and S.209, involve quite different considerations and different approaches. Under S.206 an arrangement can only be sanctioned if the question of its fairness has first of all been submitted to the court. Under S.209, on the other hand, the matter may never come to the court at all. If it does come to the court, then the onus is cast on the dissenting minority to demonstrate the unfairness of the scheme. There are, therefore, good reasons for requiring a

smaller majority in favour of a scheme under S.206 than the
majority which is required under S.209 if the minority is to be
expropriated.''

Accepting that, the present proposals nevertheless seem to me
to place the petitioners in an inescapable dilemma. They cannot succeed under S.209 because of the express provisions of
that section and the size of the shareholding of the objectors.
They can only succeed under S.206 by using the votes of their
own subsidiary company, M.I.T., to secure the necessary
majority. In these circumstances I agree with Mr. Wright that
the court should not in the exercise of its discretion authorise
the acquisition of the shares of the objectors, the National
Bank of Greece, against the wishes of the bank. The petitioners
cannot succeed at all under S.209 and in my judgment they
cannot fairly succeed under S.206.

. . . [T]he decision in *In re Bugle Press, Ltd.* fortifies me in
thinking that where one has what is in effect a S.209 scheme
then, putting it at its lowest, there must be a very high standard
of proof on the part of the petitioner to justify obtaining by
S.206 what could not be obtained by S.209, especially when there
is the added element that S.206 itself only works with the help
of a wholly owned subsidiary of the petitioners.

The third . . . objection raised by Mr. Wright is that the
arrangement is unfair to all the ordinary shareholders. I am
satisfied that it is more than fair. . . . [T]he offer price of
48p . . . is 20 per cent. to 25 per cent. more than the shareholders can now obtain elsewhere. . . .

That leaves the final objection; why if the scheme is beneficial is it not acceptable to the objectors? . . . [S]ubstantially
the objectors' view is coloured by the fact that they will . . .
become liable to a swingeing capital gains tax in Greece. . . .
[I]t seems to me that it is unfair to deprive the objectors of
shares which they were entitled to assume were safe from
compulsory purchase and with the effect of putting on the
objectors a swingeing fiscal impost which, if the matter had
proceeded under S.209, they could have avoided simply . . . by
refusing to join in approving the scheme under that section.

Accordingly . . ., both as a matter of jurisdiction and as a matter of discretion, I am not prepared to make any order approving this scheme.

TABLE OF CASES

A

	Page
Aerators, Ltd. *v.* Tollitt [1902] 2 Ch. 319	27
Allen *v.* Gold Reefs of West Africa, Ltd. [1900] 1 Ch. 656	110
Ashbury Railway Carriage and Iron Company, Ltd. *v.* Riche (1875) L.R. 7 H.L. 653	37

B

Bamford *v.* Bamford [1970] Ch. 212	299
Bell Houses, Ltd. *v.* City Wall Properties, Ltd. [1966] 1 Q.B. 207; [1966] 2 Q.B. 656	56
Bellerby *v.* Rowland and Marwood's Steamship Company, Ltd. [1902] 2 Ch. 14	204
Bloomenthal *v.* Ford [1897] A.C. 156	241
Bradford Banking Company, Ltd. *v.* Henry Briggs, Son and Company, Ltd. (1885) 29 Ch.D. 149; (1886) 12 A.C. 29	235
Bugle Press, Ltd., *Re* [1961] Ch. 270	417
Burland *v.* Earle [1902] A.C. 83.	362
Bushell *v.* Faith [1970] A.C. 1099	346

C

Cape Breton Company, *Re* (1885) 29 Ch.D. 795	285
Charterbridge Corporation, Ltd. *v.* Lloyds Bank, Ltd. [1970] Ch. 62.	106
City Equitable Fire Insurance Company, Ltd., *Re* [1925] 1 Ch. 407.	311
Cook *v.* Deeks [1916] 1 A.C. 554	368
Copal Varnish Company, Ltd., *Re* [1917] 2 Ch. 349	249
Cotman *v.* Brougham [1918] A.C. 514	49
Craven-Ellis *v.* Canons, Ltd. [1936] 2 K.B. 403	262

D

Dean *v.* Prince [1954] Ch. 409	232
Dimbula Valley (Ceylon) Tea Company, Ltd. *v.* Laurie [1961] Ch. 353	224
Duomatic, Ltd., *Re* [1969] 2 Ch. 365	338
Durham Fancy Goods, Ltd. *v.* Michael Jackson, Ltd. [1968] 2 Q.B. 839	32

E

East *v.* Bennett Brothers, Ltd. [1911] 1 Ch. 163	326
Ebrahimi (A. P.) *v.* Westbourne Galleries, Ltd. [1973] A.C. 360	407
Edwards *v.* Halliwell [1950] 2 All E.R. 1064	383
Eley *v.* Positive etc. Life Assurance Company, Ltd. (1876) 1 Ex.D. 20, 88	132
Emma Silver Mining Company, Ltd. *v.* Lewis (1879) 4 C.P.D. 396.	153
Erlanger *v.* New Sombrero Phosphate Company (1878) 3 A.C. 1218.	142

Page

Evans *v.* Brunner, Mond and Company, Ltd. [1921] 1 Ch. 359 . 95
Ewing *v.* Buttercup Margarine Company, Ltd. [1917] 2 Ch. 1 . 30

F

Forest of Dean Coal Mining Company, *Re* (1878) 10 Ch.D. 450 . 278
Foss *v.* Harbottle (1843) 2 Ha. 461 1
Foster *v.* New Trinidad Lake Asphalt Company, Ltd. [1901] 1 Ch.
208 222
Freeman and Lockyer *v.* Buckhurst Park Properties, Ltd. [1964] 2
Q.B. 480 269

G

Galloway *v.* Hallé Concerts Society [1951] 2 Ch. 233 . . 247
German Date Coffee Company, Ltd., *Re* (1882) 20 Ch.D. 169 . 45
Gluckstein *v.* Barnes [1900] A.C. 241. 162
Governments Stock Investment Company, Ltd. *v.* Christopher [1956]
1 W.L.R. 237 177
Greenhalgh *v.* Arderne Cinemas, Ltd. [1951] Ch. 286 . . . 380

H

Harmer (H. R.), Ltd., *Re* [1959] 1 W.L.R. 62 397
Heald *v.* O'Connor [1971] 1 W.L.R. 497 215
Hellenic and General Trust, Ltd., *Re* [1976] 1 W.L.R. 123 . 421
Hutton *v.* West Cork Railway Company (1883) 23 Ch.D. 654 . 86

I

Industrial Development Consultants, Ltd. *v.* Cooley [1972] 1 W.L.R.
443 303
Introductions, Ltd. *v.* National Provincial Bank, Ltd. [1970] Ch. 199 83

K

Kingston Cotton Mill Company (No. 2), *Re* [1896] 2 Ch. 279 . 228

L

Lee, Behrens and Company, Ltd., *Re* [1932] 2 Ch. 46 . . . 98
Leeds and Hanley Theatres of Varieties, Ltd., *Re* [1902] 2 Ch. 809. 168
London Flats, Ltd., *Re* [1969] 1 W.L.R. 711 . . . 337

M

Mahony *v.* East Holyford Mining Company, Ltd. (1875) L.R. 7 H.L.
869 255
Morgan *v.* Gray [1953] Ch. 83 329
Mosely *v.* Koffyfontein Mines, Ltd. [1904] 2 Ch. 108 . . 191
Musselwhite *v.* C. H. Musselwhite and Son, Ltd. [1962] Ch. 964 . 333

N

North-West Transportation Company, Ltd. *v.* Beatty (1887) 12 A.C.
589 353

O

Ooregum Gold Mining Company of India *v.* Roper [1892] A.C. 125 183

P
   Page

Panorama Developments, Ltd. *v.* Fidelis Furnishing Fabrics, Ltd.
[1971] 2 Q.B. 711 321
Parke *v.* Daily News, Ltd. [1962] Ch. 927. . . . 100
Payne (David) and Company, Ltd., *Re* [1904] 2 Ch. 608 . 65
Percival *v.* Wright [1902] 2 Ch. 421 291
Phillips *v.* Manufacturers' Securities, Ltd. (1917) 86 L.J. Ch. 305 . 374

R

Rama Corporation, Ltd. *v.* Proved Tin and General Investments,
Ltd. [1952] 2 Q.B. 147 267
Rayfield *v.* Hands [1960] Ch. 1 137
Regal (Hastings), Ltd. *v.* Gulliver [1967] 2 A.C. 134 . . 294
Richmond Gate Property Company, Ltd.. *Re* [1965] 1 W.L.R. 335 139
Roith (W. and M.), Ltd., *Re* [1967] 1 W.L.R. 432 . . 103
Rowell *v.* John Rowell and Sons, Ltd. [1912] 2 Ch. 609 . 209
Royal British Bank *v.* Turquand (1855) 5 E. & B. 248; (1856) 6 E. &
B. 327 253

S

Salomon *v.* Salomon and Company, Ltd. [1897] A.C. 22 . 8
Scottish Co-operative Wholesale Society, Ltd. *v.* Meyer [1959] A.C.
324 388
Shuttleworth *v.* Cox Brothers and Company, Ltd. [1927] 2 K.B. 9. 125
Sidebottom *v.* Kershaw, Leese and Company, Ltd. [1920] 1 Ch. 154 120
Simpson *v.* Molsons' Bank [1895] A.C. 270. . . . 237
Sinclair *v.* Brougham [1914] A.C. 398 68
Smith (Howard), Ltd. *v.* Ampol Petroleum, Ltd. [1974] A.C. 821 . 306
South of England Natural Gas and Petroleum Company, Ltd., *Re*
[1911] 1 Ch. 573 175
Spargo's Case (1873) L.R. 8 Ch. 407 180
Sussex Brick Company, Ltd., *Re* [1961] Ch. 289 . . . 415
Sutton *v.* English and Colonial Produce Company, Ltd. [1902] 2 Ch.
502 318

T

Trevor *v.* Whitworth (1887) 12 A.C. 409 195

V

Verner *v.* General and Commercial Investment Trust [1894] 2 Ch. 239 218
Victor Battery Company, Ltd. *v.* Curry's, Ltd. [1946] Ch. 242 . 212

W

West Canadian Collieries, Ltd., *Re* [1962] Ch. 370 . . 332
Whaley Bridge Calico Printing Company, Ltd. *v.* Green and Smith
(1879) 5 Q.B.D. 109 158

INDEX

Agent:
  company as, 10, 13–16, 24–5
  director as, 254–5, 258, 268–9, 271–8
Articles of association:
  alteration of, 40, 114–20, 122–5, 129–32
  effect of, 114, 130–1, 134, 136
  function of, 40
Auditors:
  duty of, 229–32

Bill of exchange, 33–6

Capital:
  accretions to, 221, 223–4, 226
  circulating, 221–2
  loss of, 219–22
  reduction of, 197, 199–201, 205–6, 209, 212
  uncalled, 208
Capital redemption reserve fund, 226
Certificate of incorporation, 51–2, 55
Charge:
  floating, 23
Compensation for loss of office:
  disclosure of, 342

Directors:
  appointment of, 258–9, 261, 400–1
  duty of care of, 314
  fiduciary relation of, 167, 278–81, 287–8, 292–3, 295–8, 304–5, 308–11, 354

independent board of, 146, 148, 150, 167, 170, 173
  legal position of, 278–81, 313–14
  removal of, 348–50
  remuneration of, 92, 140, 265
  share qualification of, 319
Dividends:
  funds distributable as, 223–4, 226–7
  payment out of capital of, 219–22, 226–7

Gratuitous payments, 88–94, 96–9, 101–2, 106, 108–9

Laches, 149, 151, 153
Lien of company on shares, 113–20
Limited liability, 17, 185, 188–90, 196, 219

Meeting:
  notice of, 113, 332–3
  powers of, 4, 301–2, 373–4
Memorandum of association:
  construction of, 43, 47–8, 54
  function of, 39–41, 108
  subscribers to, 18, 22
Motive:
  malicious, 122–4, 129–30, 378–9
  relevance of, 12, 15, 108–9, 378

Name:
  publication of, 34–5
  relevance of, 47, 54
  similarity of, 28–32

Objects:
  purpose of statement of, 53–5
Oppression:
  meaning of, 393–4, 399–400, 404–6

Partners:
  duty of, 149
Powers:
  distinguished from objects, 54–5, 85, 96
  specified as objects, 53
Promoters:
  definitions of, 155–6, 160
  disclosure by, 165, 169
  duties of, 156, 172
  fiduciary position of, 147–8, 150–2, 171
  remedies against, 172
  secret profits of, 160–1
Prospectus:
  liability for omissions from, 176–7
  meaning of, 178–9

Resolution:
  ordinary, 349–51

Secretary:
  authority of, 323–5
Share certificate:
  estoppel by, 244–7
Shareholder:
  bankrupt, 330–1
  voting by, 353, 360, 365, 377
Shares:
  forfeiture of, 199–200, 203–4, 206–9, 211
  issued at a discount, 186–9, 192–4, 208
  issued at a premium, 226
  payment for, 186, 191–2
  payment in cash for, 181–2
  payment otherwise than in cash for, 187–8
  unpaid vendor of, 336–7
  voting rights of, 346, 348–52
  surrender of, 199–200, 203–4, 206, 209, 211–12
  transfer of, 251–2

Tracing, 69–82
Trust:
  entry in register of members of, 19
  notice of, 238–41